Cognitive Processes and Pavlovian Conditioning in Humans

Edited by

Graham Davey
The City University, London

JOHN WILEY & SONS
Chichester · New York · Brisbane · Toronto · Singapore

Library of Congress Cataloging-in-Publication Data:

Cognitive processes and Pavlovian conditioning in humans.
1. Classical conditioning. 2. Human information processing. 3. Learning, Psychology of. 4. Human behavior. I. Davey, Graham.
BF319.C576 1987 153 86-19036
ISBN 0 471 90791 X

British Library Cataloguing in Publication Data:

Cognitive processes and Pavlovian conditioning in humans.
1. Conditioned response
I. Davey, Graham
153.1′5 BF319

ISBN 0 471 90791 X

Printed and bound in Great Britain

Contents

List of contributors

GRAHAM C. L. DAVEY	The City University, London
PETER DAVIES	University of Bradford
MICHAEL E. DAWSON	University of Southern California, Los Angeles
H. J. EYSENCK	Institute of Psychiatry, London
JOHN J. FUREDY	University of Toronto
KENNETH HUGDAHL	University of Bergen, Norway
M. J. KELLEY	Institute of Psychiatry, London
A. B. LEVEY	MRC Applied Psychology Unit, Cambridge
IRVING MALTZMAN	University of California, Los Angeles
IRENE MARTIN	Institute of Psychiatry, London
BOB REMINGTON	University of Southampton
DIANE M. RILEY	Addiction Research Foundation, Toronto
ANNE M. SCHELL	Occidental College, Los Angeles
DAVID A. T. SIDDLE	Macquarie University, Australia

Preface

Cognitive Processes and Pavlovian Conditioning in Humans is a book that I hope will help to fill a serious gap in the contemporary psychological literature. At times during the past 20 years or so the study of human conditioning has trodden an awkward and sometimes apparently aimless path through psychological theory and has frequently received what can only be described as a 'bad press'. It has received this 'bad press' largely because psychologists have tacitly realized that a knowledge of fundamental learning processes is a necessary feature of the understanding of many aspects of human behaviour—yet this knowledge did not appear to be available. Hence, there was the temptation to resort to outdated and inadequate accounts of human conditioning which clearly failed to fulfil the needs to which they were being stretched. This failure was to some extent the fault of conditioning theorists. In recent years, our knowledge of the processes of animal conditioning has expanded considerably, to the point where it is no longer the study of simplistic associative learning, but the study of complex information processing capacities which account for how the animal acquires knowledge about its environment, how it cognitively represents this knowledge, and how it translates this knowledge into new behaviour. Sadly, during the 1960s and early 1970s, the study of human conditioning ignored these trends and appeared to travel along a relatively idiosyncratic path steeped in physiology and the dilemmas of conscious experience. Fortunately, in the last few years things have changed thanks to a number of writers and experimentalists. They attempted to tackle the problem of constructing models of human conditioning by moving away from the antiquated processes of Watsonian reflexology into the more fruitful realms of cognitive information processing. Pavlovian conditioning in humans is *not* about the unconscious learning of reflexes. Contemporary human conditioning theory is concerned with processes involved in learning about relationships between events, and, equally importantly, how this learning is translated into the behaviour we observe. The components that combine to make up this theory vary dramatically and radically from the simple tenets of contiguity learning and reflex transfer outlined by Watsonian behaviourism and which are inexplicably utilized by many writers as a means to demonstrate the supposed inadequacy of conditioning theories.

In preparing this volume I attempted to ensure that most contemporary views on Pavlovian conditioning in humans were represented. The contributors were given a fairly free hand to be as theoretically speculative as they felt was necessary. However, there were three rather more specific instructions: (a) to attempt to integrate the knowledge we have recently acquired on human conditioning processes with that which exists in the contemporary non-human animal conditioning literature, (b) to emphasize the practical applications of contemporary human conditioning theory—largely to the areas of psychopathology and psychotherapy, and (c) to impress upon the reader new to conditioning theory that human conditioning is a complex cognitive process rather far removed from the simplistic associative notions presented in many introductory psychology texts. Sadly, one or two currently influential writers were unable to contribute to the volume because of other commitments. However, their views are fully represented throughout this book and I hope they feel that they have been represented clearly and fairly.

Finally, 'conditioning' means many things to many people. It is a means of changing behaviour, it is an adaptive learning process, and it is also a useful tool for studying other psychological processes. I hope all of these views are expressed here. However, my hope is that this volume will provide the impetus towards a comprehensive and integrated account of human Pavlovian conditioning which will prove useful to psychologists of very many persuasions. The information provided in this book should prove stimulating to cognitive psychologists, physiological psychologists, animal learning theorists, and clinical psychologists to name but a few. The psychologist unfamiliar with mechanisms of conditioning may well still 'reflexively' reach for Hilgard and Marquis's historic tome—but I hope they will also thumb through the pages of this one before they finalize their views of what conditioning in humans entails.

GRAHAM DAVEY
London, December 1986

Cognitive Processes and Pavlovian Conditioning in Humans
Edited by G. Davey

Chapter 1

Human Pavlovian autonomic conditioning and the cognitive paradigm

John J. Furedy
University of Toronto

and

Diane M. Riley
Addiction Research Foundation, Toronto

During the last two decades, there has been a change in the pre-theoretical assumptions of experimental psychologists: the mantle of scientific respectability that used to cloak S-R theorizing has gradually come to cover cognitive theorizing instead. Segal and Lachman (1972) called this change of pre-theoretical mood a 'paradigm shift', and one set of arguments has centred around the question of whether this label is appropriate, or whether psychology is still a 'pre-paradigmatic' science. However those arguments are resolved, it is the case that a change in emphasis has occurred in experimental psychology, with the focus now being on the processing of propositional information rather than on the learning of a response.

The overall aim of this chapter is to offer an evaluation of the effect of this change in emphasis on human Pavlovian autonomic conditioning (HPAC). This is an experimental preparation that employs, as dependent variables, autonomically controlled, non-invasively measurable physiological functions like changes in skin resistance (the so-called GSR), peripheral vasomotor changes, and heart-rate changes. However, because human Pavlovian autonomic conditioning is a form of learning, we shall begin our analysis with a historical account of the issue that was the central concern of learning theorists of the 1930s, 1940s and 1950s: the problem of what is learned. Our account of this conflict between S-R and S-S approaches of the Hull–Tolman era will then move to the current cognitive 'paradigm' shift, and the effects of this shift on the prevailing view of Pavlovian conditioning. In our view, this shift represents a form of S-S 'imperialism' (akin to the S-R imperialism of the Hullians), and by way of contrast we shall present a two-process view of Pavlovian conditioning which distinguishes between S-R and S-S factors and assigns an explanatory role to both processes. The third section of this chapter will contend that there are certain serious scientific limitations of the current imperialistic cognitive paradigm for understanding the nature of learning in general, and HPAC in particular. The final section will take up some more general philosophical considerations that seem to us to arise from the preceding discussion, considerations that relate to the role of instrumentalism in both science and technology.

1 The problem of what is learned: The S-R vs. S-S Conflict in the Hull–Tolman era

The historical account we offer is factually based, but like all historical accounts, it is itself only an interpretation. However, so that we can be as clear as possible about what the interpretation is, we begin by considering the crux of the matter: the meaning of the term 'cognitive'.

1.1 Cognitive as propositional

It is widely accepted that the central concern of the Hull–Tolman conflict was whether the cognitive, Tolmanian view was valid, but the acceptance of this view does not contribute to a scientific understanding unless it is clear what the meaning of the term 'cognitive' is in this context. This critical term is often used in such a broad sense that its extension is almost unlimited. So in current usage, when the term is in good repute, one finds it used to qualify all sorts of areas in psychology (e.g. social, developmental), including that of *behaviour* therapy, which may appear to be a contradiction in terms. Similarly, in the heyday of Watsonian S-R behaviourism, the term was used almost as widely as one of opprobrium to qualify areas (and even individuals) which were not thought to be scientific. Such broad usage of critical terms is common in politics, as witnessed, for example, in the application of the term 'democratic' to societies ranging from liberal (e.g. West Germany) to totalitarian (e.g. East Germany—called the 'German Democratic Republic') ones.

This sort of broad usage, however, is not helpful for purposes of analysis, which requires that distinctions be made between related but different concepts. The usage we shall adopt in this chapter is one where the term 'cognitive' is coterminous with the term 'propositional' in its epistemological sense. That sense, specifically, refers to any expression that is statable in the form X is Y, where 'X' and 'Y' are subject and predicate terms which are related by the copula ('is'). All such propositional expressions are ones to which the true/false category can be sensibly applied, without being involved in a 'category mistake' (Ryle, 1949). So a propositional relation is a copular one, in contrast to such non-propositional relations like S-R ones (i.e. those between stimuli and responses, to which it is inappropriate to apply labels of truth or falsity).

These somewhat technical considerations are relevant for the Tolman/Hull conflict, as well as to many of the issues of current concern to students of learning. Tolman's cognitive maps in which signs are related to significates are propositional, because it makes sense to speak to these sign-significate relations as either true (when the map is right) or false (when the map is wrong). In contrast, the Hull–Spense $r_g - s_g$ hypothetical mechanism, designed to perform the same explanatory function as that performed by the Tolmanian cognitive map (cf., for example, Spence, 1956), does not express a propositional relationship, because the true/false category cannot be sensibly applied to it. It is also important to recognize that both sorts of hypothetical mechanisms can be loosely thought of as 'information'[1] inasmuch as they can both change behaviour. However, only the (cognitive) Tolmanian one is *propositional*, being sensibly characterizable in terms of a true/false category.

The usage we are proposing here is widely accepted by philosophers but not by psychologists. Current psychological practice tends to not use the term 'propositional' at all, and assigns a broader (almost all-encompassing) meaning to the term 'cognitive', as it does to the term 'information' (for a more detailed critique of this practice than that given above, cf. Furedy, 1980; Riley and Furedy, 1982, 1985; Searle, 1980). We consider, and shall attempt to show below, that our usage is more desirable both because it stems historically from the Hull–Tolman debates, and because it is consistent with traditional epistemological usage (e.g. Armstrong, 1973; Lacey, 1976). In addition, our usage, which equates 'cognitive' with 'propositional' and which therefore employs the former term more restrictively, seems thereby to avoid the universality of extension, and hence 'incurable vagueness' (Ritchie, 1965), that the term 'cognitive' has come to acquire.

1.2 Background of the Hull–Tolman dispute and the relative scientific status of the two camps

As with any dispute, that between the Hullian and Tolmanian camps was multi-faceted. There was, for example, an overall difference in philosophy of science, with the Hullians favouring formalization more than did the Tolmanians. There were also socio-political differences (to be discussed below) that could well have stemmed from the differing personalities of the respective leaders, in addition to their differing social milieux. However, the nub of the scientific dispute between them was this matter of cognition, as we have defined the term here. Specifically, the Hullians claimed that all learning was response learning, whereas the Tolmanians contended, on the basis of experiments like the 'latent-learning' preparation, that cognitions are also learned. It was this issue that was central in that era of 'grand theories', where it was believed that disputes between theorists could be settled by experiments run on laboratory rats as subjects—experimental psychologists' 'little white test-tubes' (Osgood, 1953).

The period of the 1930s to the 1950s also saw the dominance of the Hull–Spence approach. The members of both the Hullian and Tolmanian camps were behaviourists, but in that period it become quite clear who was winning the battle for the 'hearts and minds' of most experimentalists. The fact that the Hullian S-R behaviourists ran more experiments and had more highly formalized theories persuaded most that their approach was the more truly scientific and predictively powerful one. Hull's (1943) *Principles of Behaviour* was axiomatized along Newtonian lines, and Koch's (1954) detailed unmasking of the lack of genuine predictability in Hull's system did not reach the consciousness of most psychologists until at least the late 1950s. Likewise, Spence's (1956) influential book enjoyed high repute among many psychologists at least partly because it represented the first time that a psychologist had been asked to give the prestigious Silliman lectures.

On the other hand, the Tolman approach appeared much less tight. There were no attempts at formalization to speak of, with even MacCorquodale and Meehl's (1948) paper being only entitled a 'preliminary' set of 'suggestions to a formalization of expectancy theory'. Moreover, the rate of 'production' from the 'data factories' was far less in a laid-back Berkeley than at either Yale or Iowa. It is little wonder that, especially at some Midwestern departments even as late as the mid-1960s, many felt it correct to ask 'What's on your *behaviour*?' even in casual conversation, lest they be thought to be tender-minded, woolly-thinking, mentalistic cognitivists. And neither Hull nor Spence could be characterized as easy-going personalities, in marked contrast to Tolman (though he by no means lacked moral fibre—witness his outspoken opposition to the invidious Loyalty Oath).

This is not to say that the cognitive behaviourists of those days went under without a struggle. However, considered in terms of conversion of the neutrals—the aim of every scientific controversialist, since the opposition is, by definition, impossible to convince—their efforts were mostly in vain. In the next section we provide an illustration of a cognitivist who, although in hindsight, had a clear logical advantage, lost out to his S-R opponent.

1.3 The Kendler vs. Ritchie dispute

Kendler (1952), in an influential paper, argued that the issue of what is learned—the main bone of contention between the S-R and cognitive behaviourists—was not an empirical one, and should be resolved in terms of 'modern methodology', or in terms of which approach was considered to be more fruitful by the majority of experimental psychologists. Because of the current *Zeitgeist*, it was not hard to predict how this criterion of fruitfulness would determine the outcome at that time. Six months later, and in the same journal, a reply appeared by one of Tolman's associates: Ritchie (1953). Unlike Kendler's (1952) paper, Ritchie's reply is not well known (for the extent of its obscurity, see also below), so let us briefly summarize it, although we would also urge readers to check on our accuracy by reading the paper. In essence, Ritchie's paper is a *reductio ad absurdum* of Kendler's position. Kendler has proposed that fruitfulness rather than evidence is applicable for evaluating the S-R claim that 'All learning is response learning'. In a logical extension of Kendler's proposal, Ritchie applies this 'modern methodological' criterion to a proposition taken from the science of geography, namely that 'The earth is flat', and thereby demonstrates the absurdity of Kendler's position.

In terms only of logical considerations, one would expect a reply from Kendler, because Ritchie's critique was so damaging to Kendler's position. However, no reply was ever written, and at least in terms of what happened in the next thirty years, this proved to be adaptive on Kendler's part. Not only was Kendler to become a far more eminent experimental psychologist than Ritchie, but also Kendler's (1952) defence of S-R behaviourism is well known and became frequently cited, whereas Ritchie's (1953) cognitivist counter-claim is almost unknown and hardly ever cited.

There is, indeed, reason to believe that this anti-cognitivist bias was more than passive in form. A book written to educate undergraduates concerning major controversies (Goldstein, Krantz, and Rains, 1965) included the Kendler (1952) paper. However, not only was Ritchie's (1953) reply omitted, but it was not even referenced in these authors' preamble to the issue discussed in Kendler's paper. Moreover, 'the interested reader' was referred to papers by 'Campbell (1954), Rozeboom (1958), and Smedslund (1953)' for 'some of the reactions to, and comments upon' Kendler's article (Goldstein *et al.*, 1965, p. 2), instead of being referred to Ritchie's paper which was the one most clearly opposed to Kendler's position. Cognition appears to have been well and truly 'circumnavigated' (to use Ritchie's terminology) by the S-R behaviourism-dominated literature of that period. The conflict over the role of cognition in behaviour was resolved paradigmatically (or politically), rather than in terms of logic and empirical evidence. It was to be expected that when the pendulum swung in the cognitive direction, the forces responsible would also be more political than evidential.

2 The current cognitive shift, effects on view of Pavlovian conditioning, and an alternative two-process view

2.1 The triumph of neo-Tolmanianism: Emergence of modern cognitive psychology

By the late 1960s, the cognitive 'paradigm shift' (Segal and Lachman, 1972) was already underway, and it is clear that the last score of years has seen the S-R approach fall into disfavour. The neo-Tolmanian score of years may be viewed as beginning in Pavlovian conditioning with the landmark paper of Rescorla (1967) on the 'proper controls' for this seemingly simple learning phenomenon. It is of special interest to consider the impact of the cognitive approach to Pavlovian theorizing, because the phenomenon, considered to be the 'simplest' form of learning, had usually been considered to be at the core of hard-nosed, S-R, Hull–Spence behaviourism. The immediate methodological impact of Rescorla's (1967) paper on the small but control-conscious group of Pavlovian experimentalists was enormous. Almost overnight the conventional 'explicitly unpaired' control acquired a seedy air of methodological inadequacy, and only the 'truly random' control was considered to be appropriate for true scientists. The fact that later work showed that, at least in autonomic conditioning preparations, there was no empirical difference between the two controls (e.g. Furedy, 1974), and the fact that, as noted by Gormezano and Kehoe (1975), Rescorla himself returned to the (more convenient) unpaired control in his later experiments, went generally unnoticed. Even nowadays, the 'truly random' control is considered by most workers to be empirically superior to the unpaired control, and the concept of 'conditioned inhibition' in the sense specified by Rescorla (1969) is considered quite basic to any Pavlovian conditioning phenomenon.

The reason why these sorts of facts proved to be so harmless to the 'contingency' (Rescorla, 1967, 1969) position is that the methodological principle of the 'truly random' control follows from what is essentially a cognitive, Tolmanian view of Pavlovian conditioning: that what is learned is the propositional, contingency relationship between the CS (sign) and the US (significate). Of course, Rescorla's (1967) paper had impact partly because it was so well argued and written, but at least part of the reason for its tremendous influence is that it rode the crest of the new cognitive wave, according to which Pavlovian conditioning *was* simply the association of the CS with the US, i.e. nothing more nor less than S-S, rather than S-R, learning.

Another illustration of how the cognitive shift came to be mirrored in current Pavlovian theorizing is the fate of the interstimulus interval (ISI), which is the temporal interval between the onsets of the CS and US. The next section is devoted to a more detailed analysis of the fate of the ISI than has, to our knowledge, been given before by students of Pavlovian conditioning.

2.2 Fate of the ISI as an illustration of the cognitive shift's impact

Like the account of the Hull–Tolman dispute, our account of the ISI is factually based, but still an interpretation.

2.2.1 The glory years

Until the early 1960s, the ISI was considered to be the most important determinant of Pavlovian conditioning. There were theories of conditioning formulated almost exclusively with the aim of explaining the various ISI-related findings (e.g. Jones, 1962), but, more importantly, there were 'hard data' or facts to support the ISI's vital importance as a parameter. Of these facts, the most relevant set was available from eyelid conditioning—the most common Pavlovian experimental preparation of that era. In that preparation, it was known even to undergraduate students of learning that optimal performance was obtained at slightly less than 0.5 sec ('the short half second' optimal ISI), and, even more importantly, ISIs exceeding 2 sec produced such little conditioning that they were sometimes used as control (i.e. no-conditioning) conditions in eyelid conditioning experiments. Corresponding to this set of ISI-related facts about conditioning is the set of historical facts about writings on conditioning of the period. Arguably the most important and perhaps even the only serious text on conditioning was Kimble's (1961) text. This book, which was often required cover-to-cover reading for North American graduate comprehensive examinations, stressed the absolute importance of the ISI for all forms of Pavlovian conditioning. By the mid-1960s, however, the literature began to evidence the change that would eventually remove the ISI from the consciousness not only of most graduate students, but also most researchers of Pavlovian conditioning.

2.2.2. Kamin and the Conditioned Emotional Response (CER) preparation: Contrary database

Following a conference in 1963, Prokasy (1965a) edited a book on Pavlovian conditioning that was a sort of North American Pavlovian conditioners' Who's Who, and that, in the absence of a formal textbook, became as influential as a textbook. Prokasy's own chapter (Prokasy, 1965b) was in a minority cognitively oriented mode, but it is best discussed in the context of Rescorla's (1967) paper (see 2.2.3), which was a more influential version of a similar view. The other significant cognitively oriented paper in the Prokasy

(1965a) volume was by Kamin (1965). This chapter provided extensive data to show that in one form of Pavlovian conditioning—the CER preparation—increasing the duration of the ISI up to intervals of several minutes had no effect on performance. In interpreting his data, Kamin did not restrict his conclusion about the ISI's lack of importance to the CER preparation, but rather contended that the data were relevant to all forms of Pavlovian conditioning. Nevertheless, it bears emphasis that Kamin did feel it incumbent to provide a large (if not broad, in the sense of spanning several preparations) database for his claims.

2.2.3 The Rescorla–Wagner (1972) model: Paradigmatic dominance

This well-known and highly influential model had its origins in the previously cited Rescorla (1967) paper. Like Kamin (1965), Rescorla applied his methodological espousal of the 'truly random' control to all forms of Pavlovian conditioning. Unlike Kamin, however, Rescorla (1969) provided no extensive data for his contention, but only a single experiment that was based on a version of the CER preparation (Rescorla and LoLoredo, 1965). Nor was there any explicit reference to the ISI in either the methodological (Rescorla, 1967) or empirical (Rescorla, 1969) papers, but it does follow from a thoroughgoing contingency (propositional) account that the ISI should be relatively unimportant. In Tolmanian terms, it is the semantic rather than the temporal relationship between sign and significate that should be important in determining whether the two are associated in the sign-significate expectancy. By the time the currently dominant Rescorla-Wagner (1972) model of Pavlovian conditioning emerged, the neo-Tolmanian, cognitively oriented, contingency[2] shift was sufficiently marked that, to our knowledge, no one remarked on the fact that the ISI was not even a parameter in this purportedly rather complete, and precisely predictive, account of conditioning.

An observer who expects scientific theories to be restricted by the facts must be puzzled. What of eyelid conditioning, where even in the cognitive psychological world of today it remains a fact that ISIs of more than about 2 sec produce no conditioning, and the closer one is to about 450 msec, the more conditioning is produced? The seeds of a logical resolution of this problem were first offered by Gormezano and Kehoe (1975), who distinguished between two sorts of Pavlovian preparations that they called CS-CR and CS-IR. Briefly, the former sort of preparation is one where the effect of the CS on the CR is observed by directly measuring the CR itself; eyelid, GSR, and salivary conditioning are all instances of CS-CR preparations. The latter sort of preparation involves measuring the effect of the CS on the CR indirectly, through observing the CS's effect on some instrumental response (IR) like lever pressing, shuttling, or choice behaviour; the CER and the poison avoidance preparations are instances of these CS-IR preparations.

The Gormezano–Kehoe distinction is an empirical, operational one. The distinction was used by them to argue that, as a measure of conditioning, CS-IR paradigms were inferior, because of certain interactions that could confound the measurement of the critical dependent variable: the CR. Their argument was made against the implicitly stated cognitivist position that, because the CS-IR (e.g. CER) preparations generally produced more lawful data (i.e. fewer subjects required to obtain significant differences), it was these preparations that were the 'proper' (Rescorla, 1967) measures of Pavlovian conditioning. One sign of the current dominance of the cognitive view is that both their comments on Rescorla's later use of the 'explicitly unpaired' control, and their distinction between the two sorts of preparation, have failed to receive even negative commentary in the literature. In particular, current textbooks on learning and conditioning (e.g. Schwartz, 1978) accept completely the cognitive view of Pavlovian conditioning: that it is a process of S-S learning in which the ISI factor plays a negligible role, and where the only critical control is to ensure that there be a condition where the contingency between the CS and US is 'truly random'.

2.2.4 Garcia's work, view, and ascribed view on the ISI

In the mid-1960s Garcia provided research evidence to show that an association could be learned between an event and another, even when the interval between them (i.e. the ISI) was as long as several days. The negative reception that this work received from journal editors is by now as well known as it was unfair, and when the work was finally published (Garcia and Koelling, 1966), the place of publication was not particularly high-profile. Nor was Garcia's own stated view of this work either then or now a position that was at all extraordinary or extreme. That position is that, in some preparations (in terms of the Gormezano-Kehoe distinction, the CS-IR sort), much longer ISIs were tolerable. What led to the legendary status of Garcia's work, and its highly damaging impact on the perceived importance of the ISI, was a view ascribed to him by others, namely that in Pavlovian conditioning, in general, the ISI was irrelevant. Such undifferentiated views are helpful for promoting political movements, but progress in scientific understanding requires that distinctions be made rather than blurred. In the next section we outline a two-process view of Pavlovian conditioning which distinguishes between S-R and S-S factors, and, rather than ignoring either sort or assigning that sort to epiphenomenal status, assigns explanatory roles to both processes.

2.3 A two-process view of Pavlovian conditioning

We begin with a critique of the Gormezano–Kehoe (1975) distinction, and propose an improved version of the distinction by differentiating between response vs. (cognitive) state learning processes. We then illustrate the relevance of this distinction, first by referring to actual, and then to 'thought', experiments. Finally, we contrast the two-process, 'minority' view with the dominant, cognitive view in both Pavlovian and (more briefly) instrumental conditioning.

From the time we have already given it, our high opinion of the Gormezano–Kehoe distinction is obvious. However, in our view, the distinction as stated does have two shortcomings, being too empirical and too judgemental. Regarding the first shortcoming, the problem with purely operational-level distinctions is that it is possible to make an infinite number of them, so that the relative value of each cannot be determined. In fact the distinction is a valuable one, but this can only be recognized if one is prepared to speculate concerning the underlying process responsible for the apparent divergence of results between the CS-CR and CS-IR preparations.

It will not surprise the reader that our particular hypothesis is that the distinction underlying the difference between the two preparations is that between non-cognitive, response-learning processes on the one hand, and cognitive, propositional learning processes on the other hand. So in a CS-CR preparation like eyelid and GSR conditioning, the ISI parameter is important, and the empirical difference between random and unpaired control stimuli negligible. In such preparations, learning occurs mainly through contiguity (and possibly also reinforcement—see, for example, Furedy, 1965; Jones, 1962). On the other hand, in a CS-IR preparation like the CER and taste aversion, the dominant learning process is cognitive (i.e. propositional), which is sensitive to such contingency-based differences as that between a random and unpaired control CS. And, of course, in the acquiring of knowledge about the relation between signs and significates, the physical time interval between the two events (i.e. the ISI) is much less important than such factors as the semantic similarity between the two events. This, of course, accounts for the 'constraints on learning' experiments (e.g. Shettleworth, 1972), where it is whether the connection between CS and US is 'prepared' (Seligman, 1970) that is critical rather than the temporal interval between the two events.

The other shortcoming that the Gormezano–Kehoe distinction has, in our opinion, is that it is judgemental in the sense of characterizing one preparation (the CS-IR) as being superior to the other in the sense that it is a more direct measure of the CR. This judgement is acceptable only to those who believe that the central process in Pavlovian conditioning is necessarily response-like. Our position, rather, is that both response and cognitive processes play an important role, and that the task is to determine, empirically, the extent of the importance of each in different sorts of preparations and under a variety of conditions.

It is important to recognize that such investigations of both sorts of processes are ideally carried out not between different laboratories, each with its own (cognitive vs. non-cognitive) emphasis, but within the same lab, and, preferably, within the same experiment. In human autonomic conditioning, this strategy was advocated by Furedy (1973) for measuring the cognitive awareness of the CS-US contingency continuously throughout the experiment, and with a precision approaching that used for such autonomic variables as the GSR. Experiments that used the 'subjective contingency' (SC) measure concurrently with the autonomic variables found that SC and GSR were by no means in a completely one-to-one relationship (e.g. Furedy and Schiffmann, 1973; Schiffmann and Furedy, 1977). Rather, whereas the cognitive SC dependent variable was sensitive to the difference between 'truly random' and 'explicitly unpaired' control CSs, the GSR was not. This pattern of results, obtained in a large number and variety of GSR conditioning experiments, suggested that the GSR was at least partly controlled by non-cognitive factors, even though it appeared that knowledge of the CS-US contingency was *necessary* for GSR conditioning (Dawson and Furedy, 1976).

On the other hand, those experiments could be interpretable simply as indicating that the GSR was not sufficiently sensitive to produce differential results. A similar argument could be advanced to account for the finding in those experiments that the extent of SC discrimination and GSR differential conditioning was not significantly correlated. What is needed to counter this insensitivity argument is to arrange a situation where cognitive factors predict differential outcomes in one direction, and non-cognitive factors predict differential outcomes in the opposite direction.

It so happens that there is an arrangement in GSR conditioning that provides this situation, where opposing differential outcomes are predicted on the basis of the two sorts of factors. This is the arrangement where US onset precedes CS onset by an interval that is shorter than the onset latency of the unconditional GSR. In such a short-interval (say, about 0.75 sec) US-CS arrangement, an S-R account (e.g. Jones, 1962) predicts excitatory conditioning because, in terms of the relationship between the CS and the UR, the arrangement is a forward rather than backward conditioning one. In line with this prediction, some papers (e.g. Champion and Jones, 1961; Furedy, 1967), though not some others (e.g. Zimny, Stern, and Fjeld, 1966), have reported excitatory GSR conditioning with these short-interval 'backward' US-CS arrangements.

However, these experiments of the 1960s did not measure cognitive contingency awareness as well. The point of such measurement is that SC would be expected to show *inhibitory* rather than excitatory conditioning. Moreover, as detailed in Furedy, Arabian, Thiels, and George (1982), these directionally opposing predictions can be specified relative to an 'explicitly unpaired' CS (euCS) condition. So, according to the S-R position, performance to the 'backward' CS (bCS) should exceed that to the ueCS, the latter being viewed as the proper control for conditioning, i.e. bCS > euCS. On the other hand, it can be shown that on the basis of the Rescorla–Wagner (1972) contingency model, bCS is more inhibitory than euCS, so that the cognitive position predicts bCS < CS. The results of the study run along these lines (Furedy *et al.*, 1982, Exp. III) were that whereas the GSR conformed to the non-cognitive, S-R predictions, the SC conformed to the cognitive, S-S contingency position. It is also of interest to note that in terms of the Gormezano-Kehoe distinction, the GSR may be considered to be an instance of the CS-CR paradigm, whereas the SC measure is analogous to a CS-IR paradigm. The important point, however, is that both 'paradigms' were treated as different dependent variables rather than as different preparations run in competing laboratories.

Nor is this 'double-paradigm' preparation confined to humans. Because the SC measure is obtained by asking subjects to move a rotary *lever* to indicate their beliefs about the CS-US contingency (see, for example, Furedy, 1973), an animal-learning oriented psychologist (Honig, personal communication, 1976) once facetiously suggested to the first author that extension of this strategy to rats would have to wait until they had learned to work a rotary lever. However, animals too can be used to gather both CS-IR (i.e. cognitive) and CS-CR types of dependent-variable information. What is needed is the sort of experiment sketched in previously (Furedy, 1979, footnote 3), wherein both sorts of dependent-variable information are collected in the same study. The experiment proposed was one where differential conditioning with two tones of differing frequencies as CS+ and CS− would be given to rabbits with the nictitating membrane response (NMR) as one dependent variable at a CS-US interval of 30 sec. With such long CS-US intervals, the NMR would show little or no discrimination between CS+ and CS−, suggesting the operation of a non-cognitive factor. However, a CS-IR independent-variable measure could be readily generated by later giving the animals a choice of entering compartments where either CS+ or CS− are sounded. It is very likely that this cognitive, CS-IR measure would show a reliable preference for the CS− compartment, indicating that the subjects had learned the sign-significate, contingency relationship between CS+ and the US (shock), even though they had not learned to make the contiguity-based NMR differentially to CS+.

More sophisticated versions of these animal double-paradigm preparations are also possible. For example, one could pit contingency against CS-UR contiguity by contrasting two conditions. In the Contingency condition, the CS+ would be followed by the US 100 per cent of the time, whereas the CS− would be 'explicitly unpaired' in the sense that it would always signal a US-free period. However, the CS-US interval for the CS+ would be 10 sec (too long for any appreciable NMR conditioning to occur). In the Contiguity condition, the CS+ would be followed by the US only 75 per cent of the time, but then at an interval of 0.4 sec, while the CS− would be 'truly random' rather than 'explicitly unpaired'. For the NMR the prediction is that discrimination would be superior in the Contiguity condition, whereas any test of preference for compartments associated with CS+ and CS− should show greater discrimination in the Contingency condition.

Neither the animal nor the human double-paradigm experiments are difficult to instrument, and they do appear to be of theoretical interest. Yet to our knowledge such experiments have continued to be quite rare. In animals, a CS-CR preparation like that of the NMR in rabbits is used in studies designed to uncover physiological mechanisms (e.g. Berger and Thompson, 1978), but hardly ever in conjunction with CS-IR preparations like the CER or poison-avoidance in order to differentiate cognitive from non-cognitive psychological learning processes. Similarly, in human GSR conditioning, most workers (e.g. Grings, 1977; Prokasy, 1977) view the conditional GSR as simply a way of studying cognitive contingency processes, and so have not employed concurrent SC measures to look for any dissociations between cognitive and non-cognitive processes. Pavlovian conditioning, then, is now seen by most workers as solely in the Tolmanian, S-S, sign-significate, expectancy mode, so that Pavlovian learning is simply considered to be S-S contingency learning.

The view of instrumental conditioning has undergone a similar transformation, which will here be alluded to quite briefly. Just as Rescorla's (1967) paper may be considered to be primary for the shift to the cognitive view in Pavlovian conditioning, so Bolles's (1970) paper may be considered seminal for the cognitive approach to instrumental conditioning. Bolles, a former student of Tolman, talks in terms of R-S connections or contingencies as constituting what is learned in instrumental conditioning. And this notion of learning that a given response leads to a given stimulus situation is, of course, formally equivalent to the Tolmanian cognitive map, inasmuch as it expresses a proposition with the R and S serving, respectively, as the subject and predicate terms. Accordingly, in both Pavlovian and instrumental conditioning, the current cognitive emphasis views propositional learning (about S-S or R-S relationships) as constituting the whole of the learning process.

3 Limitations of the current imperialistic cognitive paradigm

We are aware that the term 'imperialistic' is an evaluative one, but we consider it to be applicable to cognitivism as it has been adopted by most current psychologists. The shift from non-cognitive to cognitive processes has been almost total. From the earlier Hull–Spence equally imperialistic S-R position, where the organism was viewed as being *only* capable of learning responses to stimuli, and totally insensitive to propositional relationships (or information), we now seem to have come to the opposing extreme view—that of an organism that is *purely* cognitive, sensitive only to propositional relationships. It is no accident that the use of the computer analogy is ubiquitous in current writings. That analogy is not influential only when specifically referred to. It is also evident in the use of such terms as information processors, input–output, encoding, and so on. In the following two brief sections, we indicate what this exclusive concentration on propositional relationships or information has produced in Pavlovian-conditioning research, and in applications that are at least partly based on Pavlovian conditioning.

3.1 Forgetting the response in modern Pavlovian theory

It is somewhat ironic that a preparation which was based, originally, on Pavlov's study of the salivary ***reflex***, has now come to be regarded by most workers solely as a tool for exploring how organisms come to learn cognitive sign-significate relations (or contingencies) in their environment. This use of Pavlovian conditioning, as an expectancy index, is particularly attractive in (subhuman) animal learning, where language is not available as a convenient indicator of what knowledge has been learned by the subject. But in this process, it appears that, as in the case of instrumental autonomic conditioning or biofeedback (Furedy, 1979), there is a need to 'remember the response' when one is seeking not only to use Pavlovian conditioning as a tool, but to understand it a phenomenon.

So in a preparation like that of poison avoidance, the learning of responses has almost totally been forgotten. This preparation may be eminently useful as an index of how organisms come to acquire expectancies about safe and unsafe foods, but consider it as a method for studying the conditional response (CR). What is the CR, and is it systematically measured in these arrangements? In fact, not even the unconditional response or UR (illness) is systematically measured, and certainly not its conditionable component (nausea) in the typical poison-avoidance study. The focus is only on the expectancy index, which is some measure of preference or intake.

The CER preparation (another CS-IR one, in terms of the Gormezano–Kehoe distinction) has a similar exclusively cognitive-index use. It might be thought from the original name that what was being studied was the learning of the 'emotional response', but, in fact, no such feelings of fear elicited by the CS are ever measured. Not that the measurement of the CS-elicited fear response was something that had never been attempted. Preparations like the probe-stimulus one of Brown, Kalish, and Farber (1951) were designed to measure just that conditional fear *response*, and provided information about such response properties as latency (suggesting that the onset latency was significantly longer than that of a motor response in a reaction-time task). But that sort of concern, despite its original name, was never evident in the CER. Of course, there is measurement of behaviour, namely the bar press, but that behavioural measure indexes only the cognitive sign-significate learning process, and not any conditional emotional response elicited by the CS. Perhaps in recognition of this fact (that the learning of an emotional conditional response was not of interest), the name of the CER preparation has more recently been changed to that of 'response suppression', which is certainly a more accurate and neutral way of indicating the expectancy-index status of the CER.

However, even in CS-CR preparations like the GSR, the dominance of the cognitive orientation has been evident. As indicated elsewhere (Furedy, 1973) and above, the GSR is considered by most current workers as an expectancy or contingency index, and only S-S factors are viewed as important. This view of autonomic conditioning also has implications for more applied-oriented endeavours. Some years ago, the Toronto laboratory modified the slow positive tilt technique used by physicians into a fast negative tilt to produce large-magnitude (some 35 beats per min), non-habituating heart-rate (HR) decelerative responses with a stimulus that could be repeated readily at least as often as one per minute. In other words, as detailed elsewhere (Furedy and Poulos, 1976, Exp. I), we had developed an ideal US-UR preparation for eliciting a medically relevant and desirable myocardial function: HR deceleration. However, as also detailed elsewhere (Furedy, 1977), when it came to the practical issue of how to transfer a goodly part of this target response to a CS (i.e. how to *teach* subjects to decelerate in the absence of the tilt), we found little help in current cognitive Pavlovian theories to help us. Indeed, as in eyelid conditioning, the most critical parameter appeared to be the one that modern cognitive theorists have ignored—the ISI, with little or no conditioning obtained with a 5-sec ISI, in contrast to some 5 beats per minute (bpm) with a 1-sec ISI (Furedy and Poulos, 1976, Exp. II).

It might be thought that the improvement in CR magnitude (from about 5 to 10 bpm) which was yielded by adopting the 'imaginational' form of the preparation (Furedy and Klajner, 1978), as well as later work which indicated that imagery ability played a role in modulating the CR in this preparation (Arabian, 1982; Arabian and Furedy, 1983), constitute evidence for the relevance of cognitive factors. However, in the propositional sense of cognitive used here, this is not the case. The image of the US (which subjects are instructed to produce at CS onset) is not a propositional expression. Though mental, it is a response and not a cognition. Indeed, the relevant cognitive factor is the awareness that the CS is a sign of the US (which is a proposition that all subjects readily learn), and that factor has played no role at all in the negative tilt preparation. In the next section we consider a broader class of therapies that are viewed as at least partially based on Pavlovian theories.

3.2 Cognitive behaviour therapy and Guthrie's jibe revisited

To put the matter in a rather colloquial nutshell, the result of the cognitive emphasis is that although current theories say much about what organisms think, they say nothing about what they do. More specifically and in terms of applications, modern learning psychologists have become quite unhelpful in teaching people how to respond appropriately, no matter how much those people may know what they ought to be doing.

It is, in our view, no accident that the S-R theorist Guthrie's major jibe at Tolman's cognitive explanations was that they 'left the rat buried in thought'. In 1.3 we sided with Ritchie's assertion that the evidence clearly indicated the falsity of the basic S-R assumption that all learning was response learning. However, to come down on the cognitive side on this issue is not to say that, *in general*, cognitive theory gave a superior account of behaviour than the S-R position. The basic problem with Tolmanian cognitive theory—the problem nicely captured by Guthrie's jibe—was that there was no account of how the behaviour got started once the organism, on the basis of the expectancies that it had learned, had 'decided' to carry the behaviour out.

One probable reason for not even attempting to account for actions was that Tolmanian theory was not only cognitive, but also purposive or teleological. Such positions consider purposes to be sufficient explanations of behaviour, whereas, at best, purposes are no more than summary descriptions. On the other hand, as detailed elsewhere (Furedy and Riley, 1984), the connection between cognitivism and purposivism is merely historical or contingent, rather than logical or necessary (Maze, 1983). Nevertheless, it is a contingent fact that modern cognitive accounts have also tended to neglect actions or responses. In operant autonomic or biofeedback conditioning, most current procedures leave the patient 'mired in information' (Furedy, 1979). That is, the patient is given extremely accurate propositions concerning the target autonomic behaviour to be modified (e.g. heart-rate deceleration), but it is simply *assumed* that this information *per se* will lead to an increase in control over the target response. More colloquially, the patient is shown, in great detail, *what* is going on, but not *how* to do it.

Similarly, as detailed by Furedy, Riley, and Fredrikson (1983), if the cure of phobias is considered to be a problem of extinguishing a Pavlovian fear reaction, then the application of purely 'rational' methods (i.e. cognitive behaviour therapy) will not be effective, because response-learning processes are thereby ignored. It is not, of course, suggested that a clinician with common sense would adopt such a purely cognitive approach, because contact with a real phobia quickly establishes that purely rational methods are ineffective. However, our point is that with the current cognitive imperialism, the clinician has no theoretical underpinning for those of his/her methods that involve response learning, because current Pavlovian theory has largely 'forgotten the response'.

Throughout this chapter, there has been a suggestion that current approaches to problems are unconcerned with the facts, but this suggestion has not been systematically developed. A more systematic treatment is desirable, if only because the suggestion that scientists are unconcerned with facts appears, at first blush, to be a peculiar one. This issue is examined a little more systematically—albeit still briefly—in the last major section of this chapter.

4 A more general look at the problems: Instrumentalism in science and technology

Although not stated in those specific terms, the doctrine that ultimately the facts do not matter has a considerable following both in science (basic research) and technology (applications of that research). In what follows we provide a critical appraisal of the doctrine of instrumentalism in science and technology.

4.1 In science: Cognitive status of theory

In terms of the philosophy of science, the issue that instrumentalism speaks to is the 'cognitive status' of theories (Nagel, 1960). In apparent contradiction to realism, according to which theories (and hypotheses) are to be evaluated in terms of their truth or falsity, instrumentalism suggests that theories are not true or false but are rather more or less useful, fruitful, or heuristically helpful. The instrumentalist alternative has wide currency in psychology. Perhaps the best indication of its sway comes from examining most modern introductory textbooks. The few paragraphs on the role of theory usually indicate that in a less sophisticated period psychologists used to think of their theories as being true or false, but that in these more sophisticated days theories or models (the two terms being used interchangeably) are to be evaluated in terms of their usefulness. Sometimes the text mentions that the reason for the abandonment of the realist conception is that the truth of theories can never be certainly determined.

The impossibility of ever proving the truth of theories in any empirical science is only a convincing refutation of *naïve* realism, and is, therefore, a straw-man argument. The non-naïve realist view of the philosophy of science maintains that epistemological uncertainty is a given, but that ontological issues exist independently of human beliefs about those issues. The realist–instrumentalist debate can be traced back to the differeing approaches of

Socrates and Sophists like Protagoras whose *dictum* that 'man is the measure of all things' is that of instrumentalism (see Furedy and Furedy, 1982). In current philosophy of science the debate is between thinkers like Popper (1959) and Scheffler (1967) on the realist side, and those like Feyerabend (1975) and Kuhn (1970) on the instrumentalist side, although it must be recognized that there are strains of the opposing camp's views in the writings of those on each side of the debate. Because this is a complex and controversial issue in the philosophy of science that has been exhaustively debated by specialists in the area, we do not intend to give a complete analysis. Rather, our intention is simply to comment on the issue from the psychology-of-learning stance of this book, and in those terms only, to suggest that the realist approach is preferable. Accordingly, we shall not state the technical philosophical arguments against instrumentalism, of which the most convincing appears to us to be that the doctrine is fundamentally incoherent (see, for example, Anderson, 1962; Maze, 1983). Instead, we shall simply consider how 'useful' the criterion of usefulness has been in advancing the science of the psychology of learning.

The basic problem with the instrumentalist approach is that although it is clear that theories are abandoned in favour of other theories, it is much less clear whether such changes in theories represent progress in the understanding of the phenomena in question. It is, of course, often said that theories are abandoned only when a 'better' theory is available, but it is not at all clear on what grounds the label 'better' is validly applied. To put it in more objectionable—but not obviously refutable—terms, we may ask whether the changes in psychological theoretical approaches that do occur are any different from the changes in skirt-length approaches that occur in the world of fashion. The reason why the skirt-length analogy appears ridiculous is that dress fashions change for the sake of change, whereas scientific theoretical change is expected to occur because of the evidence, and is expected to lead to progress in understanding the phenomena. However, it is just that evidential relevance that instrumentalism has replaced with man as the measure of truth. So it is not surprising that the skirt-length analogy, while emotively undesirable, cannot readily be dismissed on rational grounds.

The application of the skirt-length analogy to the recent cognitive paradigm shift is also less than completely far-fetched. In support of the analogy, it does appear to be the case that, as detailed above, the shift from S-R to cognitive theorizing occurred not through consideration of the evidence, but through a consensus that the cognitive now constituted a more 'useful' theoretical 'framework'. Moreover, disputes within modern cognitive psychology between competing positions also seem to be settled in terms not of the evidence but of the relative fruitfulness (measured by such aspects as amount of research generated) of differing 'frameworks'. So, for example, Lockhart and Craik (1978) defended the Craik–Lockhart (1972) levels-of-processing position against their critics (e.g. Eysenck, 1978) on the grounds that their position was merely an approach to the mind rather than a hypothesis concerning how the mind actually works, and therefore was not subject to criticism through contrary evidence.

The trouble with adopting the instrumentalist approach to science is that, as in the fashion business, it is hard to see whether change represents any more than simply change for its own sake: there is no real progress in understanding of the phenomena of interest. In particular, if the change in paradigm involves ignoring a set of factors that do, in fact, influence behaviour, then paradigm changes do not represent scientific progress.

In this connection it is relevant to recall that, as detailed above, when the S-R paradigm was dominant the instrumentalist doctrine was used to support it over and above seemingly contradictory evidence that pointed to the influence of cognitive factors. The Kendler–Ritchie debate of the early 1950s can be viewed as one between an instrumentalist and a realist approach to science. At this level of analysis it is not Kendler's (1952) S-R view that is important, but his 'modern methodological' (i.e. instrumentalist) approach by which he proposed to 'circumnavigate' (Ritchie, 1953) the fact that cognitive factors influence behaviour. Though still not using the term instrumentalism, Ritchie continued his critique of this approach a decade later, when he complained of the 'incurable vagueness' in psychological (learning) theories (Ritchie, 1965), and gave extensive quotations to indicate that the leading theorists seemed to glory in their positions' vagueness or untestability. The lack of emphasis on 'strong inference' (Platt, 1964) is a direct result of the adoption of the instrumentalist approach by most of the psychological scientific community.

4.2 In technology: The apparently pragmatic attitude

Workers who regard themselves as more practical and pragmatic than 'ivory-tower' basic researchers, and who have to deal with real-life problems, are also mostly instrumentalist in their outlook. This instrumentalist strain is evident in such slogans as, 'As long as it works, I don't care how'. It is also expressed in the view that placebo effects are useful in the long-term technological sense, it being unnecessary either to understand the principles of operation or to determine whether the treatment has the specific effects that are attributed to it by its proponents. Yet another expression of instrumentalism is the notion of 'clinical evidence' as something that is epistemologically superior to 'mere' research evidence. In particular, this view asserts (most often implicitly) that a particular technique's efficacy may be adequately supported in the absence of well-controlled research studies, as long as there is 'clinical evidence' that it works. When the term 'clinical evidence' is unwrapped, it turns out to refer to clinicial *experience*, with in turn is an elaborate way of stating that, in the *opinion* of the clinician, the technique is efficacious. Of course, what this view ignores is the fact that the history of medicine is replete with instances where the practitioners were convinced that their own particular technique was efficacious, despite the availability of convincing observational evidence to the contrary. Just as scientific theorists will tend to protect their own theory against unfavourable evidence, so practitioners have too strong a vested interest in their favoured techniques to serve as an adequate testing ground of those techniques.

More generally, our counter-view (which is a realist one) to instrumentalism in technology is that the approach suffers from the same shortcomings as it does in science. Specifically, it does not allow improvement in methods, but rather ensures only that methods will change with changing fashions. A technology that relies on placebo effects and evidence based on inadequately controlled observations is one that, in the long run, will prove to be ineffective. To take an example from modern physical medicine, no matter how technically sophisticated coronary by-pass operations may become, if their performance is decided on the basis of clinical intuition rather than in terms of evidence based on controlled observations, the technology of treatment of myocardial dysfunction will remain at a snake-oil level of medicine. This is not to say that there will not be powerful and beneficial placebo effects. A particular surgeon with certain patients may work 'magic' through a placebo factor, but magic is no substitute for effective technology.

The same applies, in our view, to current biofeedback treatments. As long as there is no interest in establishing whether biofeedback has any specific effects over and above placebo ones, the notion that we are pragmatic is an illusory one. A true pragmatist determines whether a particular treatment works on the basis of evidence, and that determination cannot be *efficiently* made if the evidence is based on uncontrolled observation. Moreover, such observation is uncontrolled if the thing that is supposed to work is left unspecified, i.e. if biofeedback is conceived of in such broad terms that it includes all that happens between the therapist and patient. The witch-doctor medicine of primitive societies was often extremely powerful, but the power lay solely in placebo effects which are conditional on local culture. Modern scientifically based medicine is effective (where it is so, as in immunology) because it is evidence—rather than doctrine-based in its approaches, i.e. it is genuinely pragmatic. Instrumentalism in technology, then, is undesirable because, in the long run, the approach yields instruments that do not really work, being dependent on doctrine rather than the facts.

Notes

1 The term 'information', as originally used in information and systems theory, referred to the transmission of messages in a system (Shannon and Weaver, 1949).

According to this definition, 'information' is a term which is used when speaking of *meaning* being conveyed from one part of a system to another. When speaking of meaning, some form of understanding is assumed. So the term 'information' implies that some message is being understood. This original sense of the term is clarified when it is remembered that information theory originally dealt with the relaying of human messages in a telephone system. The use of 'information' in areas such as systems theory is therefore quite appropriate to the extent that the system can be properly said to *understand*, i.e. to be able to relate the information to other information. In systems theory terminology, systems that are not built with the capacity to understand are said to receive signals rather than to process information. In this case no assumptions are being made regarding the capability of the system to process information.

Despite the fact that the term 'information' does imply meaning and understanding (i.e. it implies that there is a particular kind of psychological process in operation), the term is now widely used in psychology and physiology to refer to events ranging from neural impulses in response to environmental signals to complex instructions. Clearly, such broad usage can only lead to confusion as to the capabilities of the systems involved in each instance. While it may be popular to refer to synapses as 'processing information', to describe them as doing so assumes that meaning is being conveyed and that understanding is taking place. It would, however, seem somewhat premature to ascribe these psychological properties to single neurons. If it were the case that synapses could indeed carry out such processes, then the implications would be extremely important. But implying that they do so obscures the need to determine which parts of the nervous system can and do process information, and what kind of information is processed by different systems. To use terms so loosely only tends to make us lose sight of the very important differences between different systems. If every part of the nervous system is said to process information and therefore to understand, what sense can be made of the differences between psychological and non-psychological events, or of differences between different types of psychological processes?

2 Although the Rescorla–Wagner model is frequently referred to as a *contiguity* account of Pavlovian conditioning, it is, strictly speaking, a contingency model. The Rescorla–Wagner model is characterized by themselves and other theorists (e.g. Gray, 1975; Mackintosh, 1973) as a contiguity model because it is said to avoid explicit reference to expectancies and mentalism, and presents the Pavlovian conditioning process as one of gradual incrementation as opposed to 'insight'. The Rescorla–Wagner model is, in fact, a contingency account because it requires that the organism process propositional information about the *relationships* between events rather than simply requiring that the organism react to events. That is, it is a model based on the learning of S-S relationships, a process requiring representation. The Rescorla–Wagner organism learns that the CS is a sign of the US—a proposition, and therefore a contingency relationship. A contiguity, or S-R account, on the other hand, can only be based upon the learning of responses to stimuli, a process requiring no representation or processing of propositions. Thus, despite a popular characterization as a contiguity model, the Rescorla–Wagner model is a contingency account. It differs from a model explicitly labelled 'contingency' such as that of Mackintosh, only in the precision of the propositions learned by the organism. For example, as reviewed by Gray (1975), Mackintosh (1973) performed an experiment that appears to refute the Rescorla–Wagner position. In that experiment rats showed greater inhibition in a transfer (to excitatory conditioning) test to a CS that had been random with respect to the US than to a CS that had simply been presented alone. According to the Rescorla–Wagner model, the

conditional probability value of both CSs is equal. We agree with Gray (1975) that this constitutes a refutation of the Rescorla–Wagner position, not because it is a contiguity position, but rather because the contingencies it specifies do not make as precise distinctions between known sign-significate relationship propositions as are, in fact, made by the organism. Specifically, with the random CS the organism learns the proposition that 'This sign is a signal of the US being completely unpredictable' (1), whereas with the CS alone the proposition learned is that 'This sign is not a signal for anything' (2). Now during the test (excitatory conditioning) stage, both groups learn the proposition that 'This sign is a signal for the US' (3). To the extent that propositions (1) and (2) are distinguishable to the organism, the degree of contradiction between (1) and (3) is greater than between (2) and (3). Hence, the results emerge that are contrary to the over-simplistic Rescorla–Wagner model, which, however, is still a propositional, representational, sign-significate, *contingency* model.

References

Anderson, J. (1962). *Studies in Empirical Philosophy*, Angus & Robertson, Sydney.

Arabian, J. M. (1982). Imagery and Pavlovian HR decelerative conditioning. *Psychophysiology*, **19**, 286–93.

Arabian, J. M., and Furedy, J. J. (1983). Individual differences in imagery ability and Pavlovian HR decelerative conditioning. *Psychophysiology*, **20**, 325–31.

Armstrong, D. M. (1973). *Belief, Truth and Knowledge*, Cambridge University Press, Cambridge.

Berger, T. W., and Thompson, R. F. (1978). Neronal plasticity in the limbic system during classical conditioning of the rabbit nictitating membrane response. I The hippocampus. *Brain Research*, **145**, 323–46.

Bolles, R. C. (1970). Species-specific defense reactions in avoidance learning. *Psychological Review*, **71**, 32–48.

Brown, J.S., Kalish, H. I., and Farber, I. E. (1951). Conditioned few as revealed by magnitude of startle response to an auditory stimulus. *Journal of Experimental Psychology*, **41**, 317–28.

Champion, R. A., and Jones, J. E. (1961). Forward, backward, and pseudoconditioning of the GSR. *Journal of Experimental Psychology*, **62**, 58–61.

Craik, F. I. M., and Lockhart, R. S. (1972). Levels of processing: a framework for memory research. *Journal of Verbal Learning: Verbal Behavior*, **11**, 671–784.

Dawson, M. E., and Furedy, J. J. (1976). The role of awareness in human differential autonomic classical conditioning: The necessary-gate hypothesis. *Psychophysiology*, **13**, 50–3.

Eysenck, M. W. (1978). Levels of processing: A critique. *British Journal of Psychology*, **69**, 157–69.

Feyerabend, P. K. (1975). *Against Method*, New Left Books, London.

Furedy, J. J. (1965). Reinforcement through UCS offset in classical aversive conditioning. *Australian Journal of Psychology*, **17**, 205–12.

Furedy, J. J. (1967). Aspects of reinforcement through UCS offset in classical aversive conditioning. *Australian Journal of Psychology*, **19**, 159–68.

Furedy, J. J. (1973). Some limits of the cognitive control of conditioned autonomic behavior. *Psychophysiology*, **10**, 108–11.

Furedy, J. J. (1974). Experimental assessments of the importance of controlling for contingency factors in human classical differential electrodermal and plethysmographic conditioning. *Psychophysiology*, **11**, 308–14.

Furedy, J. J. (1977). Pavlovian and operant-biofeedback procedures combined produce large-magnitude, conditional heart rate decelerations, in *Biofeedback and Behavior*, (eds. J. Beatty and H. Legewie), Plenum, New York.

Furedy, J. J. (1979). Teaching self-regulation of cardiac function through imaginational Pavlovian and biofeedback conditioning: Remember the response, in *Biofeedback and Self-regulation*, (eds. N. Birnbaumer and H. D. Kimmel), Erlbaum, Hillsdale, N.J.

Furedy, J. J. (1980). Cognition is bodily: But cognition is what? Review of F. J. McGuigan's *Cognitive Psychophysiology: Contemp. Psychology*, **25**, 10–11.

Furedy, J. J., Arabian, J. M., Thiels, E., and George, L. (1982). Direct and continuous measurement of relational learning in human Pavlovian conditioning. *Pavlovian Journal of Biological Science*, **17**, 69–79.

Furedy, J. J., and Furedy, C. P. (1982). Socratic and sophistic strains in the teaching of undergraduate psychology: Some implicit conflicts made explicit. *Teaching of Psychology*, **9**, 14–20. (Special issue devoted to 'The Challenges facing undergraduate Psychology Education in the Next Decade'. C. Morris (ed.).)

Furedy, J. J., and Klajner, F. (1978). Imaginational Pavlovian conditioning of large-magnitude cardiac decelerations with tilt as US. *Psychophysiology*, **15**, 538–43.

Furedy, J. J., and Poulos, C. X. (1976). Heart rate decelerative Pavlovian conditioning with tilts as US: Towards behavioral control of cardiac dysfunction. *Biological Psychology*, **4**, 93–106.

Furedy, J. J., and Riley, D. M. (1984). Undifferentiated and 'moat–beam' percepts in Watsonian–Skinnerian behaviorism. *Behavioral and Brain Sciences*, **7**, 625–6.

Furedy, J. J., Riley, D. M., and Fredrikson, M. (1983). Pavlovian extinction, phobias, and the limits of the cognitive paradigm. *Pavlovian Journal of Biological Science*, **18**, 126–35.

Furedy, J. J., and Schiffmann, K. (1973). Concurrent measurement of autonomic and cognitive processes in a test of the traditional discriminative control procedure for Pavlovian electrodermal conditioning. *Journal of Experimental Psychology*, **100**, 210–17.

Garcia, J., and Koelling, R. (1966). Relation of cue to consequences in avoidance learning. *Psychonomic Science*, **4**, 123–4.

Goldstein, H., Krantz, D. L., and Rains, J. D. (1965). *Controversial Issues in Learning*, Appleton-Century-Crofts, New York.

Gormezano, I., and Kehoe, E. J. (1975). Classical conditioning: Some methodological–conceptual issues, in *Handbook of Learning and Cognitive Processes* (vol. 2) (eds. W. K. Estes), Lawrence Erlbaum, Hillsdale, N.J.

Gray, J. A. (1975). *Elements of a Two-process Theory of Learning*, Academic Press, London.

Grings, W. W. (1977). Orientation, conditioning and learning. *Psychophysiology*, **14**, 343–9.

Hull, C. L. (1943). *Principles of Behaviour*, Appleton-Century-Crofts, New York.

Jones, J. E. (1962). Contiguity and reinforcement in relation to CS-UCS intervals in classical aversive conditioning. *Psychological Review*, **69**, 176–86.

Kamin, L. (1965). Temporal and intensity characteristics of the conditioned stimulus, in *Classical Conditioning: A Symposium* (ed. W. F. Prokasy), Appleton-Century-Crofts, New York.

Kendler, H. H. (1952). 'What is learned?' A theoretical blind alley. *Psychological Review*, **59**, 269–77.

Kimble, G. A. (1961). *Hilgard and Marquis' conditioning and learning*, Appleton-Century-Crofts, New York.

Koch, S. (1954). Clark L. Hull. in W. K. Estes *et al.*, *Modern Learning Theory*, Appleton-Century-Crofts, New York.

Kuhn, T. (1970). *The Structure of Scientific Revolutions*, 2nd edn. Chicago University Press, Chicago.

Lacey, A. (1976). A *Dictionary of Philosophy*, Routledge & Kegan Paul, London.

Lockhart, R., and Craik, F. I. M. (1978). Levels of processing: A reply to Eysenck. *British Journal of Psychology*, **69**, 171–5.

MacCorquodale, K., and Meehl, P. E. (1948). On a distinction between hypothetical constructs and intervening variables. *Psychological Review*, **55**, 95–107.

Mackintosh, N. J. (1973). Stimulus-selection: learning to ignore stimuli that predict no change in reinforcement, in *Constraints on Learning* (eds. R. A. Hinde and J. T. Stevenson-Hinde), Academic Press, London.

Maze, J. R. (1983). *The Meaning of Behaviour*, Allen & Unwin, London.

Nagel, E. (1960). *The Structure of Science*, Harcourt, Brace, & World, New York.

Osgood, C. E. (1953). *Method and Theory in Experimental Psychology*, Oxford University Press, New York.

Platt, J. R. (1964). Strong inference. *Science*, **146**, 347–352.

Popper, K. R. (1959). *The Logic of Scientific Discovery*, Hutchinson, London.

Prokasy, W. F. (1965a). Classical eyelid conditioning: Experimenter operations, task demands, and response shaping, in *Classical Conditioning: A Symposium* (ed. W. F. Prokasy), Appleton-Century-Crofts, New York.

Prokasy, W. F. (1965b). Classical eyelid conditioning: Experimenter operations, task demands, and response shaping, in *Classical Conditioning* (ed. W. F. Prokasy), Appleton-Century-Crofts, New York.

Prokasy, W. F. (1977). First interval skin conductance responses: Conditioned or orienting responses? *Psychophysiology*, **14**, 360–7.

Rescorla, R. A. (1967). Pavlovian conditioning and its proper control procedures. *Psychological Review*, **74**, 71–80.

Rescorla, R. A. (1969). Pavlovian conditioned inhibition. *Psychological Bulletin*, **72**, 77–94.

Rescorla, R. A., and LoLoreto, V. M. (1965). Inhibition of avoidance behavior. *Journal of Comparative and Physiological Psychology*, **59**, 406–12.

Rescorla, R. A., and Wagner, A. R. (1972). A theory of Pavlovian conditioning: Variations in the effectiveness of reinforcement and non-reinforcement, in *Classical Conditioning* (vol. 2) (eds. A. H. Black and W. F. Prokasy), Appleton-Century-Crofts, New York.

Riley, D. M., and Furedy, J. J. (1982). Reply to Mulholland, in *Clinical Biofeedback: Efficacy and Mechanisms* (eds. L. White and B. Tursky, Guilford, New York.

Riley, D. M., and Furedy, J. J. (1985). Psychological and physiological systems: Modes of operation and interaction, in *Stress: Psychological and Physiological Interaction* (ed. S. Burchfield), Hemisphere, New York.

Ritchie, B. H. (1953). The circumnavigation of cognition. *Psychological Review*, **60**, 216–21.

Ritchie, B. H. (1965). Concerning an incurable vagueness in psychological theories, in *Scientific Psychology: Principles and Approaches* (eds. B. B. Wolman and E. Nagle), Basic Books, New York.

Ryle, G. (1949). *The Concept of Mind*, Penguin, Harmondsworth.

Scheffler, I. (1967). *Science and Subjectivity*, Bobbs-Merrill, New York.

Schiffmann, K., and Furedy, J. J. (1977). The effect of CS-US contingency variation on GSR and on subjective CS-US relational awareness. *Memory and Cognition*, **5**, 273–7.

Schwartz, B. (1978). *Psychology of Learning and Behavior*, McCleod, Toronto.

Searle, J. R. (1980). Minds, brains and programs. *Behavioral and Brain Sciences*, **3**, 417–58.

Segal, E. M., and Lachman, R. (1972). Complex behavior or higher mental process: Is there a paradigm shift? *American Psychologist*, **27**, 45–55.

Seligman, M. E. P. (1970). On the generality of the laws of learning. *Psychological Review*, **77**, 406–18.

Shannon, C. E., and Weaver, W. (1949). *The Mathematical Theory of Communication*, University of Illinois Press, Urbana.

Shettleworth, S. (1972). Constraints on learning, in *Advances in the Study of Behavior* (vol. 4) (eds. D. S. Lehrman, R. A. Hinde, and E. Shaw), Academic Press, New York.

Spence, K. W. (1956). *Behavior Theory and Conditioning*, Yale University Press, New Haven, Conn.

Zimny, G. H., Stern, J. A., and Fjeld, S. P. (1966). Effects of CS and UCS relationship on electrodermal response and heart rate. *Journal of Experimental Psychology*, **72**, 177–81.

Cognitive Processes and Pavlovian Conditioning in Humans
Edited by G. Davey

Chapter 2

Human autonomic and skeletal classical conditioning: The role of conscious cognitive factors

Michael E. Dawson
University of Southern California, Los Angeles

and

Anne M. Schell
Occidental College, Los Angeles

Classical conditioning can be defined by a set of experimental operations—which involves establishing a contingency between a relatively neutral conditioned stimulus (CS) and a significant response-eliciting unconditioned stimulus (UCS) (Prokasy, 1965). The contingency is such that the probability of the UCS is higher during or shortly following presentation of the CS than at other times in the experimental situation (Rescorla, 1967). The term 'classical conditioning' can be defined strictly operationally as the response modifications that follow upon establishing the CS-UCS contingency, or more theoretically in terms of the processes which underlie the response modifications. Strict adherence to the stimulus contingency definition of classical conditioning leads one to consider a conditioned response (CR) any behaviour which can be shown to be due to exposure to the CS-UCS contingency. Some investigators (e.g. Gormezano and Kehoe, 1975) would require that the CR resemble or at least appear in the same effector system as the unconditioned response (UCR) elicited by the UCS. However, we believe that this requirement is unnecessarily restrictive and it is best at the present time to define classical conditioning broadly as any response modification which can be attributable solely to exposure to the CS-UCS contingency (see also Öhman, 1983). The term 'classical conditioning' is used at times in this chapter to refer to the operational stimulus contingency, and at other times as a shorthand term to refer to the underlying theoretical processes; the sense in which it is used should be clear from the context.

The present chapter is concerned with the role of conscious cognitive factors in determining the effects of CS-UCS contingencies on human autonomic behaviour. The specific experimental situation in which the autonomic effects have been most often measured is the aversive discrimination classical conditioning paradigm. In this paradigm, subjects are presented two different CSs on separate trials with occurrence of an aversive UCS contingent upon only one of the CSs. For example, subjects may be presented tones of two different pitches with an uncomfortable electric shock or loud noise presented following one pitch tone and never following the other pitch tone. The stimulus upon which presentation of the UCS is made contingent is called CS+ whereas the remaining stimulus is referred to as CS−. It is customary to first demonstrate that CS+ and CS− do not originally differ in elicitation of autonomic responses and then measure any autonomic response differences between CS+ and CS− which emerge upon exposure to the differential CS-UCS contingency as evidence of discrimination classical conditioning.

If the time interval between CS onset and UCS onset (the interstimulus interval, ISI) is relatively long, e.g. in the order of 5–10 seconds, multiple autonomic CRs often can be observed. Figure 2.1 shows an example of multiple skin conductance responses (SCRs) which may occur following CS+ in an aversive discrimination classical conditioning paradigm. The first SCR begins shortly following CS+ onset, the second SCR usually begins shortly before the UCS is due, and the third SCR begins shortly following the omission of the UCS on a non-reinforced test trial. With an 8 sec CS-UCS interval, the latency intervals during which each of the three SCRs begin are generally as follows: (a) 1.0–4.0 sec following CS onset, (b) 4.0–9.0 sec following CS onset, and (c) 1.0–4.0 sec following the point at which the UCS was due but omitted. Discrimination classical conditioning is inferred typically on the basis of larger and/or more frequent responses to CS+ than CS− within any of these intervals. Multiple CRs also have been documented with other autonomic response systems, e.g. the conditioned heart rate response often consists of a triphasic decelerative-accelerative-decelerative series of changes (e.g. Headrick and Graham, 1969), but the multiple response phenomenon has been studied most thoroughly with the electrodermal response system.

Several different methods of labelling the multiple electrodermal responses have been suggested (see Prokasy and Kumpfer, 1973, for a review). Some

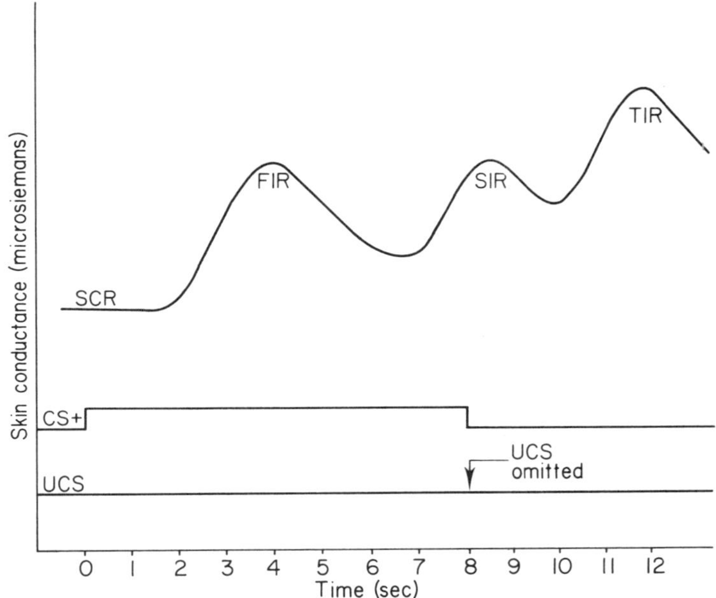

Figure 2.1 Three distinct skin conductance responses (SCRs) which can occur on non-reinforced test trials of CS+ with an 8 sec ISI. FIR refers to first interval response, SIR refers to second interval response, and TIR refers to third interval response

labelling methods have implied theoretical mechanisms underlying the responses, whereas other have relied upon a more descriptive atheoretical approach. In the theoretical vein, Stewart, Winokur, Stern, Guze, Pfeiffer, and Hornung (1959) referred to the first response as a sensitized 'orienting response', the second as a conditioned 'anticipatory response', and the third as a 'UCS-omission response'. More atheoretical and descriptive terms have been suggested by Grings, Lockhart, and Dameron (1962), Lockhart (1966), Prokasy and Ebel (1967), and Prokasy and Kumpfer (1973). In this chapter, we will use the descriptive terminology of 'first interval response' (FIR), 'second interval response' (SIR), and 'third interval response' (TIR). In terms of latency defined responses, the FIR corresponds to the orienting response, the SIR corresponds to the anticipatory response, and the TIR corresponds to the UCS-omission response. Theoretical interpretations of these responses will be presented later in this chapter.

Certainly one of the 'big questions' that one can ask about human autonomic classical conditioning concerns the relationship between such conditioning and higher mental processes. Humans have evolved higher cortical structures and cognitive functions. For example, humans have evolved the ability to speak to others and to themselves in richly complex symbols. What do these evolutionary developments imply about human classical conditioning? How does human conditioning differ from that of lower animals? Can humans be conditioned in the same sense as lower animals? Can humans be conditioned without their conscious awareness? Are certain types or levels of consciousness necessary for human classical conditioning? The present chapter will address questions such as these. In many cases, final answers are not yet available; however, considerable information regarding these issues has been acquired over the past decade or two and important advances on these fundamental issues have been made.

The first section of this chapter will review a programme of research dealing with the role of conscious cognitive factors in human autonomic classical conditioning which has been ongoing in our laboratory for nearly 20 years. In the second section, we will compare human classical conditioning results with those reported in lower animals. This phylogenetic comparison will suggest a multi-stage hypothesis regarding fundamentally different roles of conscious cognitive factors in autonomic and skeletal classical conditioning. In the third section, this multi-stage hypothesis of human conditioning will be presented, along with supporting evidence. In the fourth section, we will conclude with a brief overview of the implications of this multi-stage approach to conditioning.

1 Conscious cognitive factors in human autonomic conditioning

Most early investigators of the phenomena of classical conditioning adopted the viewpoint that conscious processes were largely irrelevant to conditioning. However, it gradually became apparent that cognitive manipulations such as instructing human subjects about CS-UCS relationships prior to the presentation of actual pairings, or instructing them that the UCS would no longer be presented, had marked effects on the strength of the CR (e.g. Cook and Harris, 1937; Mowrer, 1938).

In order to accommodate such findings with traditional conditioning notions, several theorists, most prominently Razran (1955, 1965, 1971), adopted a 'levels of learning' theory. This theory holds that a hierarchy of levels of learning exists in humans, ranging from simple non-associative learning, through simple associative learning such as classical conditioning, to complex levels of symbolic verbally mediated learning unique to mankind. Each higher level is seen as evolved from the lower level. Processes which operate at different levels are thought to obey different laws, but the higher cognitive processes are seen as being able to influence lower conditioning processes. Thus, according to the levels of learning theory, CS-UCS pairings are capable of producing at least two interactive processes in human subjects:

(a) formation of classically conditioned CRs due to simple associative learning, and (b) conscious perception of the relationship of the CS to the UCS, referred to as relational learning or contingency learning. Verbal instructions or other essentially cognitive manipulations can affect contingency learning and through it the more primitive conditioning process. According to this theory, 'true' classical conditioning can only be observed in its purest form if the conscious, cognitive processes are eliminated.

According to a levels of learning theory, pure classical conditioning uncomplicated by the higher cognitive processes should be observable under at least two experimental conditions. First, pure classical conditioning should occur best in human subjects when they are prevented from becoming aware of the stimulus and response contingencies. Second, pure classical conditioning should occur best in animals relatively low on the phyletic scale. In the remainder of this section we will review the first line of evidence, conditioning among human subjects kept unaware of the critical contingency. The reader interested in a more detailed review of this first line of evidence should consult Dawson and Schell (1985). The second section of the present chapter reviews the second line of evidence, conditioning among lower animals.

1.1 Acquisition of autonomic CRs

Studies of conditioning in the absence of awareness of the CS-UCS contingency have generally employed some sort of masking task to engage and distract the subject, so that the CS-UCS pairings could be embedded within the task without contingency learning occurring. After a series of conditioning trials has been presented, awareness of the CS-UCS contingency must then be assessed to detect those subjects who became aware in spite of the masking task. Conclusions about the possibility of conditioning occurring in the absence of awareness have tended to change over time as methods of assessing awareness have become more precise (Dawson and Schell, 1985).

Early investigators such as Diven (1937) and Haggard (1943) used a free-association masking task with shock paired with some of the words to which subjects associated, and reported that subjects who were not aware of the CS-UCS relation none the less showed electrodermal CRs to the CS words. However, neither investigator included a true pseudo-conditioning control group, and methods of assessing awareness were either unreported or insensitive.

Lacey and Smith (1954) pointed out the inadequacies of the earlier studies, and used a discrimination conditioning paradigm, presenting both CS+ and CS− words to each subject within the masking task to control for pseudo-conditioning. They also interviewed subjects more extensively, following the conditioning session, about their awareness of when the shock UCS would come. Subjects who could not quickly and correctly verbalize the CS-UCS relationship were considered unaware. They found greater anticipatory heart rate responses to CS+ than to CS− among unaware subjects, although the effect was not strong.

Chatterjee and Eriksen (1960) repeated Lacey and Smith's procedures, but measured the SCR rather than heart rate and more intensively assessed awareness. After the conditioning trials, subjects were presented with each CS+ and CS− word and were asked to indicate the probability that each had been followed by shock, in addition to being generally questioned about their expectancy of shock. Like Lacey and Smith, Chatterjee and Eriksen found that subjects who could not clearly verbalize the CS-UCS relation showed differential conditioning, again of a weak and erratic nature. However, SCRs did not differ between actual CS+ words and other words rated by the subjects as possibly or probably followed by shock. Thus, Chatterjee and Eriksen concluded that they had found that autonomic conditioning was no more specific than the subjects' verbalizations.

Dawson (1973) and Grings and Dawson (1973) pointed out that most investigators who reported conditioning without awareness had employed *recall* questionnaires to assess awareness, which consist of questions such as 'Did you know when you were going to receive the shock?' and other open-ended questions (Haggard, 1943; Lacey and Smith, 1954; Fuhrer and Baer, 1969; Wilson, Fuhrer, and Baer, 1974). Conversely, most investigators who found conditioning only among aware subjects employed *recognition* questionnaires, which specifically present each CS to the subjects and require them to state whether or not that CS was followed by the UCS (Dawson, 1970; Dawson and Grings, 1968). Dawson and Reardon (1973) compared the sensitivity of recall and recognition post-conditioning questionnaires in detecting awareness in a study in which the probability of awareness occurring was experimentally manipulated. They found a short recognition questionnaire to be clearly the most valid, and concluded that conditioning in the absence of awareness could be wrongly inferred if the insensitive recall questionnaires were used.

In order to further pursue this issue, Dawson (1970) designed a masking task presented to subjects as an auditory perception test. On each conditioning trial, subjects were presented with an initial tone and then with five comparison tones, one of which matched the initial tone in frequency. They were told to determine on each trial which of the five comparison tones had matched the initial tone, which of the five had been highest in pitch (always 1200 Hz), and which had been lowest (always 800 Hz). Unbeknown to the subjects, the highest and lowest tones served as CS+ and CS− and an electric shock served as the UCS. (The shock was explained to subjects as being used to alter their physiological state, to determine whether or not that would affect auditory perception.) This task ensures that the CS+ and CS− are perceived, but none the less masks the CS-UCS relationship from the majority of subjects when sensitive recognition questionnaires are used to assess awareness.

Dawson and his colleagues have carried out seven studies using this basic procedure (Dawson, 1970, Experiment I and Experiment II; Dawson and Reardon, 1973, Experiment I and Experiment II; Dawson and Biferno, 1973; Biferno and Dawson, 1977; Dawson, Catania, Schell, and Grings, 1979). The consistent result was that classical conditioning of autonomic responses occurred *only* among those subjects who were aware of the CS-UCS contingency as assessed by the more sensitive recognition questionnaire.

In order to more precisely assess the temporal relationship between the development of autonomic CRs and the development of contingency learning, Dawson and Biferno (1973) employed a trial-by-trial measure of the subject's expectancy of the shcok UCS, rather than relying solely on the subject's memory during a post-conditioning questionnaire. Using the auditory masking task, subjects indicated their expectancies of the shock continuously during each tone (8.0 sec in duration) by pressing a series of buttons. Awareness of the CS-UCS relation was inferred if a subject consistently expressed greater expectancy of the UCS during CS+ than during CS−. Dawson and Biferno found SCR differential conditioning only among subjects whe became aware, and only at and after the trial on which awareness first occurred. No conditioning was observed among unaware subjects, or in aware subjects before the point in time at which differential expectation of the shock was first expressed. These results have been replicated by Öhman, Ellstrom, and Bjorkstand (1976), Biferno and Dawson (1977), and most recently by Dawson, Schell, and Banis (in press).

These results, taken together, suggest that awareness of the CS-UCS relationship is a necessary condition for classical autonomic conditioning in humans (Dawson and Furedy, 1976), and that the acquisition of autonomic CRs is not an automatic process, but rather requires conscious cognitive processing of the stimulus contingency.

The concept of conscious cognitive processes has been integrated into contemporary cognitive psychology by relating it to the concept of a limited capacity central processing system (e.g. Posner, 1978; Posner and Snyder, 1975). The limited capacity notion provides behavioural operational criteria for distinguishing between conscious and unconscious cognitive processes. For example, conscious cognitive processes are those which interfere with performance on a secondary task. This is so because the two conscious cognitive processes must compete for the same limited pool of processing resources. Unconscious or automatic cognitive processes do not interfere with secondary task performance because such processes do not require allocation of processing resources from this pool of limited capacity.

Thus, if classical conditioning is an unconscious automatic cognitive process, then the acquisition of autonomic CRs should proceed without interfering with other concurrent secondary tasks. If, on the other hand, conditioning necessarily involves conscious processes, the presentation of a CS+ should result in greater allocation of cognitive processing capacity than CS− and hence greater interference with other ongoing activity, because of the more significant information carried by the CS+. Dawson, Schell, Beers, and Kelly (1982), adapting the secondary reaction time technique employed by Posner and his colleagues, required subjects to react as quickly as possible to the presentation of a brief tone by pressing a key switch during a discrimination classical conditioning paradigm. After a series of reaction time (RT) practice trials, classical discrimination conditioning was begun with a visual CS+ and CS− (different coloured lights 7.0 sec in duration) and a shock UCS. During the conditioning trial series the reaction time tone continued to be presented, both at various points during CS+ and CS− (300, 500, 3500, or 6500 msec after CS onset) and during the intertrial interval. Discrimination conditioning of the SCR was successfully obtained. More relevant to the present issue, RTs were found to be significantly slower to tones presented during CS+ than to those presented during CS−, particularly at the 300 msec point. Subjects who gave the largest SCRs to the CS+ exhibited the greatest lengthening of RT during CS+. These results suggest that greater cognitive processing capacity was allocated to the CS+ than to CS−, and indicate that the conditioning process is not automatic, but rather is associated with conscious cognitive processing of information by the subject.

In summary, evidence from two different lines of research, one regarding the possibility of CR acquisition without awareness of the CS-UCS relationship and the other regarding processing capacity allocation during conditioning, indicates that classical autonomic conditioning critically involves conscious cognitive processes.

1.2 Performance of previously acquired CRs

The distinction between the acquisition of new responses and the performance of already learned responses is of importance in all theories of learning. A learned response may require conscious processing during acquisition but not during later performance. This is certainly the case with many well-learned motor skills, which require the full focus of conscious attention during original learning, but with practice can be carried out automatically, without interfering with other cognitive activity. In theory, this also could be true of the performance of well-learned classically conditioned autonomic responses. We will now briefly examine the research evidence concerning whether or not this sort of dissociation between conscious expectancy of the UCS after the CS and performance of a CR does in fact occur. We will first consider evidence of an anecdotal or clinical character which is suggestive but not conclusive. We will then examine laboratory evidence which more clearly suggests that autonomic CRs can be performed after conscious expectancy of the UCS has extinguished. Finally, the question of whether a CR can be performed when the CS is not consciously perceived will be considered.

Clinical phobias are often considered examples of the performance of strong learned emotional responses, with marked autonomic components, in spite of conscious beliefs that the fear is irrational. The fear, which may be based on a one-trial association between a previously neutral CS and a highly traumatic UCS, may exist even though the individual cannot consciously recall the original association (Marks, 1969; Nemiah, 1980). Dissociations between cognitive expectancies of a UCS and performance of a CR may be pronounced.

Such dissociations of a milder degree appear to be fairly common in normal, everyday experience. Many people report experiencing strong emotional responses to various simple or complex stimuli which seem to be based on memory of past experience, but for which the original experience or association cannot be recalled. Thus, the odour of a perfume may elicit an emotional response even though one cannot remember why. A mail questionnaire survey of 400 of our faculty and staff colleagues revealed that 69 per cent of those responding, and 23 per cent of the total contacted, had had such experiences. These emotional responses, although evidently requiring conscious processing for original learning, appear to have become automatic (Dawson and Schell, 1985).

Recent evidence from the realm of neuropathology also supports the possibility of automaticity of well-learned autonomic responses. Bauer (1984) and Tranel and Damasio (1985) studied a total of three patients with prosopagnosia, the inability to visually recognize or to experience as familiar faces which should be familiar, a condition caused by bilateral damage to the medial occipitotemporal cortex. These patients were unable to consciously recognize pictures of family members, close friends, famous persons, or in fact their own faces when presented among pictures of unfamiliar faces. However, they produced larger SCRs to the faces which should have been familiar. Thus there appear to be several lines of anecdotal and clinical evidence that the performance of autonomic CRs may not require supporting conscious cognitions.

Turning to the realm of controlled laboratory studies, there are again numerous findings which suggest performance of autonomic CRs in the absence of supporting conscious processes. The first set of studies to be discussed are those which investigated the possibility of CR persistence after the point at which conscious expectancy of the UCS had been extinguished, either by specific extinction instructions or by presentation of an extinction trial series.

Biferno and Dawson (1977), in an experiment mentioned previously, monitored subjects' expectancies of the UCS and conditioned SCRs during an extinction trial series. Extinction of the conditioned SCR was found only among subjects whose expectancy of the UCS extinguished; however, close temporal synchrony between SCR extinction and expectancy extinction was not observed. Differential SCRs to CS+ and CS− were still present after expectancy extinction had occurred.

Dawson, Schell, and Banis (in press) also monitored UCS expectancy on a trial-by-trial basis during an extinction session. The CSs were potentially phobic stimuli (pictures of snakes and spiders) or neutral stimuli (pictures of flowers and mushrooms). These potentially phobic stimuli were those reported by Öhman and his colleagues (e.g. Öhman, Fredrickson, Hugdahl, and Rimmö, 1976) to acquire autonomic CRs particularly resistant to extinction. Dawson *et al*. identified a subgroup of subjects who exhibited expectancy extinction during the extinction series, expressing consistent certainty that the UCS would no longer follow CS+. Expectancy extinction was associated with a sudden and sharp reduction in differential SCR responding to CS+ and CS−; however, there was still significant although diminished differential electrodermal responding even following the point of expectancy extinction. The overall resistance to extinction was greater among subjects who had received potentially phobic stimuli as CSs; however, differential responding following the point of expectancy extinction was no greater with potentially phobic CSs than with neutral CSs. The Dawson, Schell, and Banis (in press) and the Biferno and Dawson (1977) studies suggest that, although the arrival of expectancy extinction may be associated with the weakening of autonomic CRs, this conscious cognitive event does not wholly abolish the autonomic CR. An interesting possibility for further research in this area would be to use the secondary task technique to determine whether or not differential cognitive processing of the CS+ and CS− terminates at the point of expectancy extinction.

Other investigators have sought to create rapid expectancy extinction by informing subjects at the beginning of the extinction series that the UCS would no longer be presented. In some cases, these instructions were reinforced by removal of the shock electrodes. The data of subjects who expressed doubts post-experimentally about the truthfulness of these instructions were discarded. Mandel and Bridger (1967, 1973), Wickens, Allen, and Hill (1963), Grings and Lockhart (1963), Hugdahl and Öhman (1977) with potentially phobic CSs, and Fuhrer and Baer (1980) all found some degree of persistence of the electrodermal CR following instructions which were apparently successful in producing expectancy extinction. The general finding has been that, although extinction instructions significantly weaken the autonomic CR, they do not completely and immediately abolish it (see reviews by Dawson and Schell, 1985; Grings and Dawson, 1973).

One additional line of evidence also suggests that established autonomic CRs may be retained and performed independently of supporting conscious cognitive mediation. In an intriguing series of studies, Corteen and Wood (1972) and Corteen and Dunn (1974) conditioned SCRs to semantic categories of words (e.g. city names) by associating these words with a shock

UCS. Subjects then performed a dichotic listening task in which they verbally shadowed (echoed) a prose passage presented to their right ear while a series of unrelated words was presented to their left ear. The to-be-ignored words included the CS+ and semantically related words. SCRs were elicited more frequently by CS+ and semantically related words than by non-shocked words although the subjects were unable to report having heard the critical words in the non-attended ear.

The Corteen *et al.* results must be interpreted cautiously, however, since prose material is shadowed in phrases interspersed with pauses, rather than word by word. These pauses may have been associated with attention shifts to the non-attended message, allowing CS+ to be consciously processed. Such brief shifts might have gone unreported by the subjects, particularly since the importance of avoiding attention shifts was emphasized to the subjects.

In order to rule out this possibility, Dawson and Schell (1982) required subjects to shadow a series of unrelated words presented in rapid sequence to one ear, rather than a prose passage, while a synchronized list of to-be-ignored words was presented to the other ear. Half the subjects shadowed the right ear message while the other half shadowed the left ear message. During initial acquisition, CS+ words were presented to the attended ear and followed immediately by shock UCS. During a subsequent test phase, the CS+ words and semantically related words were presented in the non-attended ear without the UCS.

Differential SCR conditioning to CS+ and CS− words was established in the initial acquisition phase. During the test phase, trials on which shadowing errors occurred were eliminated from the data analysis because attention shifts may have occurred on these trials. Trials which included CS+ words and semantically related words which subjects reported hearing in the non-attended message were also eliminated. When only trials on which there were no indications of attention shifts were included, differential conditioned SCR performance was still found, but only among subjects who had the non-attended CSs presented to their left ear (as had been the case for Corteen *et al.*'s subjects). Dawson and Schell (1982) interpreted these results in terms of cerebral hemisphere specialization for speech production. In any event, these experiments suggest that an established autonomic CR may be performed without interfering with other ongoing cognitive activity (verbal shadowing) and in the apparent absence of conscious awareness of the CS.

2 Comparison of autonomic and skeletal conditioning in humans and animals

The evidence reviewed in the preceding section rather clearly indicates that conscious awareness of the CS-UCS contingency is necessary for acquisition of human autonomic discrimination classical conditioning, whereas this requirement may not exist for performance of previously established conditioned autonomic responses. The acquisition findings are contrary to the predictions made by the levels of learning theory. No evidence of a pure, reflexive, automatic, classical conditioning process was found in the absence of conscious awareness of the CS-UCS relation. Given the apparently central role of conscious cognitive factors in the acquisition of human autonomic CRs, one may seriously question whether classical conditioning in humans and lower animals is really the same process. Perhaps the evolution of higher mental processes in humans has qualitatively altered the fundamental conditioning process. For this reason, and because the levels of learning theory predicts pure classical conditioning in animals relatively low on the phyletic scale, we now turn our attention to conditioning in lower animals.

A classical conditioning preparation used quite extensively in lower animals during the past quarter of a century involves conditioning of the rabbit nictitating membrane response (NMR). The nictitating membrane consists of a fold of conjuctiva which moves from the inner canthus of the eye laterally across the cornea (Gormezano, 1966). In the typical rabbit NMR conditioning preparation, the CS is a tone, the UCS is a shock delivered to the paraorbital region of the eye, the ISI is 400 msec, and occurrence of NMRs measured during the ISI is the index of conditioning. Note that this preparation usually involves conditioning to one CS rather than discrimination conditioning, although discrimination conditioning has been demonstrated in this preparation (Moore, 1972). A summary of the results obtained with this productive animal conditioning preparation can be found in Gormezano, Kehoe, and Marshall (1983).

Comparison of conditioning results obtained with the rabbit NMR and with human autonomic responses rather quickly reveals several large differences, three of which will be enumerated here. First and perhaps most obviously, acquisition of the rabbit NMR CR occurs at an extremely slow rate compared to human autonomic CRs. The rabbit NMR CR usually requires at least 50 CS-UCS pairings before it begins to occur reliably; then it gradually increases in frequency until reaching a stable asymptote after approximately 300 stimulus pairings (Gormezano, Kehoe, and Marshall, 1983, p. 205). In contrast, the human autonomic CR, especially the FIR SCR, usually occurs rather suddenly after only one or two CS-UCS pairings; it then often decreases in magnitude after between five and ten trials (e.g. Pendery and Maltzman, 1977). A second difference concerns the effects of the ISI on acquisition. The rabbit NMR CR is acquired best with ISIs in the 200–400 msec range, and occurs poorly if at all with ISIs greater than 2000 msec (Gormezano, Kehoe, and Marshall, 1983, p. 215). Human autonomic CRs, on the other hand, can be acquired easily with relatively long ISIs, as well as with short ISIs (Lockhart and Grings, 1963). Whether the underlying conditioning process is the same at short and long ISIs is an important and unsettled issue, but the fact that autonomic conditioning can be established with long ISIs certainly distinguishes it from the rabbit NMR conditioning. The third difference concerns the topography of the CRs. In the rabbit NMR preparation, there is a single response which is initiated on relatively early trials just before the UCS occurs. With repeated CS-UCS pairings, initiation of the CR moves to the mid-point of the ISI and the peak of the NMR CR occurs at about the time of the UCS (Gormezano, Kehoe, and Marshall, 1983, p. 216). In human electrodermal classical conditioning with sufficiently long ISIs, the topography of the CR is as shown in Figure 2.1. That is, there are multiple CRs, with the FIR occurring shortly after CS onset and the SIR occurring shortly before UCS onset. In the sense of its temporal relationship to the UCS, the rabbit NMR CR resembles the electrodermal SIR but in terms of its acquisition function, ISI function, and change in latency across trials, the two responses are not similar.

The differences between the rabbit NMR CR and the human autonomic CR documented above may reflect important species differences in conditioning, but just as likely may be due to differences in response systems. In fact, there is considerable evidence that the differences in CR performance noted above have more to do with differences between skeletal and autonomic responses than with differences between rabbits and humans. Schneiderman (1972) and his colleagues have simultaneously measured NMR CRs and heart rate CRs in the rabbit classical conditioning paradigm and found important differences between these response systems with species held constant. Yehle (1968), for example, found that discrimination conditioning of heart rate responses occurred after only a few CS-UCS trials, whereas NMR discrimination conditioning required nearly 100 trials for reliable CRs to occur and several hundred trials for asymptotic performance to be reached (see Schneiderman, 1972, pp. 344–6). Vandercar and Schneiderman (1967) varied the ISI across four groups of rabbits at 0.25, 0.75, 2.25, and 6.75 sec and found that HR conditioning occurred at the 6.75 interval but NMR conditioning did not (see Schneiderman, 1972, pp. 355–9). Optimal ISIs for NMR conditioning were 0.25 sec and 0.75 sec in that order, whereas the optimal ISIs for HR conditioning were 2.25 sec and 6.75 sec in that order.

As for CR topography differences, Vandercar and Schneiderman did not perform a detailed second × second or beat × beat analysis of the rabbit HR CR. All that was mentioned in this regard is that the HR CR consisted of bradycardia and the maximum HR deceleration had a longer latency with the long ISI than the shorter ISIs. Lockhart and Steinbrecher (1970), however, did analyse second × second changes in a differential HR conditioning paradigm with rabbits. With a 5 sec ISI, the HR CR consisted of a rapid onset and generally sustained bradycardia. The deceleration response began 1 second after CS onset and became more deceleratory until near the time the UCS was due. Thus, the topography of the rabbit HR CR appears to differ somewhat from both the NMR CR and the human HR CR topographies. Unlike the NMR CR, the rabbit HR CR begins shortly after CS onset. Unlike the human HR CR, the rabbit HR CR is not a triphasic deceleration-acceleration-deceleration and does not seem to have distinctive multiple components.

All in all, the evidence shows marked differences in the rate of acquisition, ISI function, and CR topography between the rabbit NMR CR and HR CR. More recent evidence also suggests important differences in the neuroanatomical substrates of rabbit skeletal and autonomic conditioning. Powell, Hernandez, and Buchanan (1985), for example, reported differential effects of intraseptal injections of scopolamine on heart rate and eyeblink classical conditioning in the rabbit. Although injections of scopolamine into the medial septum impaired acquisition of the eyeblink CR, these injections enhanced the magnitude of the conditioned HR decelerations. These results as well as others indicate that the central nervous system substrates of skeletal and autonomic classical conditioning are at least partially different.

An additional source of information regarding autonomic conditioning in lower animals comes from the study of electrodermal classical conditioning in cats. Van Twyver and King (1969) presented 40 tone–shock pairings with a 5 sec ISI to a group of five cats, and presented the same stimuli unpaired to a control group of five cats. The group exposed to the stimulus contingency exhibited larger electrodermal responses than the control group within five trials, thus demonstrating rapid electrodermal conditioning with a relatively long ISI. Moreover, graphical tracings show the existence of FIRs, SIRs, and TIRs, and the investigators noted that TIRs occurred on non-reinforced extinction trials only in the paired group. Thus, electrodermal classical conditioning in the cat much more closely resembles human electrodermal classical conditioning than it does rabbit NMR conditioning. This constitutes additional evidence that the differences between rabbit NMR conditioning and human autonomic conditioning are due to differences between skeletal and autonomic response systems and not principally to differences between rabbit and human conditioning.

If there are fundamental differences between skeletal and autonomic CRs as suggested above, then human skeletal and autonomic classical conditioning should exhibit differences which parallel those found by Schneiderman and his colleagues with rabbits. In fact, comparisons of the human skeletal conditioning literature (primarily eyeblink conditioning) with the human autonomic conditioning literature reveal precisely those expected differences. Human eyeblink conditioning usually requires between ten and twenty CS-UCS pairings to occur reliably and between forty and fifty trials to gradually reach asymptote (Spence, 1956). Hence, human eyeblink CRs are acquired considerably more slowly than human autonomic CRs, although they are acquired faster than the rabbit NMR CR. Human eyeblink conditioning, unlike human autonomic conditioning, occurs best at short ISIs (generally in the neighbourhood of 500 msec) and occurs poorly if at all with ISIs greater than 2000 msec (Kimble, 1961). The topography of the human eyeblink CR is similar to the rabbit NMR and dissimilar to human autonomic CRs. That is, the typical eyeblink CR consists of a single response which begins immediately prior to and overlaps the UCS (the reader is referred to Martin and Levey, 1969, for a thorough discussion of the topography of the eyeblink and autonomic CRs).

The comparisons of human skeletal conditioning with human autonomic conditioning made above are based on generalizations drawn from different literatures by different investigators testing different subjects under different conditions. There is, unfortunately, a paucity of studies which have measured human skeletal responses and autonomic responses simultaneously from the same subjects under identical classical conditioning situations. However, one such study was reported by Putman, Ross, and Graham (1974). The procedures in that study consisted of employing different frequency tones as CS+ and CS−, an air puff to the eye as the UCS, and an ISI of 800 msec. Subjects were divided into good and poor differential eyeblink conditioners. Both groups exhibited a triphasic heart rate change to CS+ and CS−, consisting of an early deceleration lasting 2 sec, followed by an acceleration also lasting 2 sec, and finally a slower recovery phase. The good and poor eyeblink conditioners differed in terms of the heart rate deceleration response. Good conditioners exhibited heart rate deceleration on the early conditioning trials which habituated on the later trials, whereas poor conditioners exhibited a large heart rate deceleration response which did not habituate. Assuming that the heart rate decelerative response reflects an orienting response (Graham, 1979), these results suggest that the orienting response to the CS is intensified during the early phase of acquisition and then habituates as CRs become established. This view of orienting responses as autonomic and conditioned responses as skeletal will be discussed in some detail in the following section.

3 A multi-stage hypothesis of human classical conditioning

Evidence reviewed in the preceding two sections has demonstrated that (a) conscious contingency learning is essential for acquisition of human autonomic CRs and (b) there are substantial parametric differences between the acquisition of autonomic CRs and skeletal CRs. The purpose of this section is to integrate this evidence within a multi-stage hypothesis of human classical conditioning.

It is becoming a generally accepted truism in contemporary learning theory that classical conditioning involves the acquisition of knowledge about relations between environmental events and that the CR is merely an index of this knowledge (e.g. Mackintosh, 1983; Rescorla, 1978). We heartily agree with this view as far as it goes, but we believe it is only a part of the whole story. The hypothesis to be presented here is that human classical conditioning is a complex, multi-component, multi-stage process, and that conscious contingency learning is a critical early stage, and that certain autonomic responses are especially sensitive to the early stage, whereas certain skeletal responses are more direct indicators of later stages. This basic hypothesis is certainly not totally new to us; indeed, hypotheses of varying degrees of similarity and development have been put forth by Maltzman, Weissbluth, and Wolff (1978), Martin and Levey (1969), Öhman (1983), Powell, Milligan, and Mull (1982), Prokasy (1984), and Schneiderman (1972). Although there are several important differences among these hypotheses, as well as between these hypotheses and the present one, the unifying theme is that conditioning occurs in stages and that autonomic and skeletal responses are differentially sensitive to different stages.

The initial stage of importance for the present hypothesis is learning of the CS-UCS contingency. We believe that the evidence strongly suggests that this early 'contingency learning' stage is associated with conscious awareness of the CS-UCS relation, at least in normal adult humans, and that this stage is necessary but not sufficient for acquisition of classically conditioned CRs. Thus, repetitive CS-UCS pairings do not produce autonomic CRs when awareness of the CS-UCS relation is prevented by distracting masking tasks (e.g. Dawson, 1970; Dawson and Reardon, 1973; Dawson, Catania, Schell, and Grings, 1979). Only at or after the point in time that subjects become aware of the CS-UCS contingency do differential autonomic CRs emerge (e.g. Biferno and Dawson, 1977; Dawson and Biferno, 1973; Dawson, Schell, and Banis, 1986; Öhman, Ellstrom and Bjorkstrand, 1976).

Although it is not as well studied nor as widely recognized, there is evidence that the acquisition of human skeletal CRs also is dependent upon contingency learning. Baer and Fuhrer (1982), for example, reported an interesting study in which subjects were administered eighty discrimination classical conditioning trials while eyeblinks and SCRs were recorded, the latter on non-reinforced test trials. Subjects were asked to report their observations, thoughts, and feelings about the study after each block of ten trials. These reports were rated for awareness of the CS-UCS relation by judges who were blind to the subjects' conditioning performance. Differential eyeblink and SCR conditioning was found only for subjects rated as aware of the CS-UCS relation, consistent with earlier findings reported by Perry, Grant, and Schwartz (1977) and Nelson and Ross (1974). There also was evidence that eyeblink and SCR conditioning, when it occurred, developed only after the subjects detected the stimulus contingency. More recently, Perruchet (1985) obtained similar results by monitoring motor reaction time to the UCS as an index of expectancy of the UCS. Based on this behavioural measure, Perruchet found that eyeblink conditioning never occurred in the absence of expectancy, occurred later than the development of expectancy, and was significantly correlated with the degree of expectancy.

When subjects first become aware of the differential CS-UCS contingency, the CS+ becomes an informative signal of the impending UCS. Subjects then show differential orienting to CS+ and CS−. The FIR-SCR, therefore, is an orienting response (OR) to the learned signal significance of CS+ and, as such, the FIR-SCR is an extremely sensitive and useful index of the initial contingency learning stage. Thus, if an investigator wants an objective index of the initial association of the CS with the UCS he would best measure autonomic responses, particularly the FIR-SCR. Other autonomic indices of conditioning, e.g. secondary heart rate deceleration, and skeletal CRs are hypothesized to be dependent upon contingency learning but are also more immediately affected by learning of the ISI and response shaping processes.

The association of the FIR-SCR with an orienting response raises an issue which has haunted the electrodermal literature for nearly a quarter of a century. Is the FIR-SCR a CR or is it an OR? As mentioned earlier, Stewart *et al*. (1959, 1961) argued that the FIR-SCR was only a 'sensitized OR' and not a 'true CR'. This argument led to replies from Lockhart and Grings (1963) and Kimmel (1964), as well as a more recent symposium on the topic published in *Psychophysiology* (Furedy and Poulos, 1977; Grings, 1977; Prokasy, 1977; and Stern and Walrath, 1977).

Our conclusion, one which we believe is consistent with the consensus of investigators in the field, is that the FIR-SCR is a classically conditioned OR. The FIR-SCR qualifies as a classically conditioned response because it is sensitive to the presence of the CS-UCS contingency, particularly in a differential classical conditioning paradigm (Prokasy, 1977). However, the response does not act like a traditional CR; it occurs rather suddenly on the early trials and then habituates. These properties qualify the FIR-SCR as an OR, along with other aspects which have been nicely reviewed by Öhman (1983, p. 333). In sum, the FIR-SCR is an OR to a stimulus whose significance has been learned, and as such is an exquisitely sensitive index of the early contingency learning stage of classical conditioning.

Classical conditioning, however, involves much more than contingency learning and orienting to signal-significant stimuli. Even at the early stage, it involves learning the properties of the individual CSs and UCSs, the probabilities of CSs and UCS, the intervals between the CSs, and especially the interval between the CS and UCS (ISI). Depending on the experimental situation, these types of learning can occur before, during, or after the process of contingency learning. In masking task situations, for example, subjects often learn about the properties and probabilities of the individual stimuli, as well as about the intervals between CSs and CS-UCSs, before learning the differential CS-UCS contingency. Of course, in the usual unmasked classical conditioning paradigm, learning of the CS-UCS contingency and the ISI occurs very rapidly, within a very few trials, although refinements on this learning may continue over later trials.

Learning of the ISI can be indexed by several different autonomic responses, most notably the secondary heart rate deceleration. Bohlin and Kjellberg (1979) have reviewed the evidence which rather clearly shows that the latency of the nadir of the secondary heart rate deceleration closely approximates the ISI, at least with ISIs of 10 sec or less. Within the electrodermal response system, it has been generally assumed that the SIR occurring near the end of the ISI, and the TIR occurring shortly after the point at which the UCS normally would have been presented, can be taken as evidence of ISI learning. Although these are reasonable hypotheses, there is very little research aimed at clearly documenting the sensitivity of the SIR-SCR and the TIR-SCR as indicators of ISI learning. This may be fertile ground for future research.

The primary evidence of ISI learning in the skeletal response system is derived from the study of CR onset and peak latencies. Gormezano, Kehoe, and Marshall (1983) have reviewed extensive evidence that the onset of the rabbit NMR CR shifts over trials from a point almost coincident with UCS onset to a point earlier in the ISI in such a way that the peak of the response finally overlaps the UCS. Within-subject shifts of the ISI also demonstrate that both the rabbit NMR CR (Coleman and Gormezano, 1971) and the human eyelid CR (e.g. Boneau, 1958) change to closely approximate the experimenter-defined ISI. These changes in skeletal CR latency require many trials to be accomplished. Prokasy (1965, 1984) has discussed several aspects of skeletal response learning following the earlier detection of the CS-UCS contingency.

As subjects become aware of the CS-UCS contingency and the length of the ISI, adaptive preparatory processes may occur during the ISI which give an instrumental aspect to the CR. Kimble and Dufort (1956) and Kimble and Ost (1961), working with an eyelid classical conditioning paradigm with human subjects, reported that the UCR amplitude diminished during conditioning trials and increased again when the UCS was presented alone. This reduction in UCR amplitude when the UCS was preceded by a CS occurred even on trials when no CR, which might have physically interfered with the UCR, was present. Kimble and Ost concluded that this UCR reduction reflected the action of a conditioned inhibitory process under the control of the CS.

Reduction of the SCR UCR in a conditioning paradigm with a shock UCS was first reported by Lykken (1959, 1962), who suggested that, during the CS, anticipatory sensory inhibition occurred in the UCS afferent modality, resulting in a lowered sensory impact of a noxious UCS. He termed this process 'preception'. Kimmel and Pennypacker (1962) also reported that the SCR UCR to a shock UCS was reduced during conditioning trials as opposed to following UCS-alone recovery trials, and that the difference in amplitude was related to the number of conditioning trials. As the number of trials increased from four to eight to sixteen, the difference in UCR amplitude increased. Kimmel and Pennypacker used the term 'UCR diminution' to refer to this reduction in the UCR, which they also saw as indicating the presence of a highly adaptive conditioned inhibitory process which reduced unnecessary emotional responding to the UCS.

In a series of experiments, Grings and his co-workers assumed, with Lykken, that UCR diminution was due to a preparatory set adopted by the subject during the CS, due to the expectation that the UCS would follow the CS at a specific point in time. Peeke and Grings (1968) reasoned that the ability of the subject to predict the exact time of UCS onset, and hence to adopt the most efficient preparatory set, would be impaired by varying the ISI during conditioning, and that this would impair the development of UCR diminution relative to a condition in which the ISI remained constant. This prediction was confirmed when they compared UCR magnitude in groups of subjects receiving either unpaired presentations of the CS and UCS, paired presentations of the CS and UCS with a constant ISI of 5.5 sec., or paired presentations with ISIs varying from 0.6 to 11.0 sec, including 5.5 sec trials whose data were used for comparisons with the other two groups. Both conditioning groups showed smaller UCR magnitudes than the control group, and the constant ISI group produced smaller UCRs than the variable ISI group. Instructions given before conditioning to a subgroup of subjects about the CS-UCS contingency and ISI duration produced UCR reduction on the first conditioning trial in the constant ISI group, indicating the importance of this cognitive variable in producing UCR diminution. These results were largely replicated by Grings and Schell (1971).

Schell and Grings (1971), using a loud white noise UCS, had subjects in both a conditioning group and a pseudo-conditioning control group (CS and UCS unpaired) rate the loudness of the UCS on each trial by matching the intensity of a variable loudness tone to the remembered loudness of the UCS. They reasoned that if an adaptive sensory inhibition were involved in UCR diminution, subjects in the conditioning group would rate the UCS as less loud. This prediction was confirmed; in the conditioning group, degree of diminution over trials was correlated with degree of reduction in perceived loudness. Thus, there is evidence of preparatory processes developing as part of the CR.

Thus far, we have argued for a multi-stage approach to classical conditioning, in which conscious contingency learning is an essential early stage. Learning of the exact length of the ISI and accurate prediction of UCS onset would generally follow rapidly. An information processing model for orienting and classical conditioning that is consistent with these formulations has been developed by Öhman (1979). He proposed, in common with other information processing theorists (e.g. Posner and Boies, 1971; Kahneman, 1973; Shiffrin and Schneider, 1977), that focal attention involves the activity of a central channel with limited capacity or resources which carries out voluntarily controlled information processing. Results of central-channel processing are assumed in this model to be available in awareness. Large-capacity pre-attentive mechanisms automatically detect, recognize, and evaluate incoming stimuli without requiring attention, awareness, or allocation of capacity from the central processing channel. When the pre-attentive mechanisms, which interact with the short-term memory store, identify a stimulus which is either novel (does not have a match in the short-term store) or is significant (matches a stimulus primed as significant in the short-term store), a call for central processing capacity occurs and the stimulus will be admitted into the central processing channel—it becomes a focus of attention (unless the central channel is already too occupied with performing other tasks to respond to the call). An orienting response (OR) is elicited whenever a call for central-channel processing is made, whether or not the call is answered. The hypothesis that elicitation of an OR is dependent on the call, rather than upon the actual allocation of processing capacity, is a provocative notion which is yet to be adequately tested. This, then, is another fertile area for future research.

Returning to Öhman's model, central-channel processing and the orienting responses are prerequisites for learning. Only if central-channel processing, involving focused attention, occurs will new associations be stored in short- and long-term memory. Thus, the model is consistent with the large body of data indicating that conscious awareness of the CS-UCS contingency, which would be associated with focused attention and hence central-channel processing, is necessary in order for conditioning to occur. It is also consistent with studies directly indicating the allocation of cognitive processing capacity during conditioning (Dawson, Schell, Beers, and Kelly, 1982).

During classical conditioning following a habituation session, the first presentation of the CS would not elicit a call for processing capacity, since the CS would be a familiar but non-significant stimulus. However, the UCS, arriving immediately after the CS, would be identified as significant and a call for central processing would be initiated, accompanied by autonomic responses. Since the processing of the UCS involves examination of the contents of short-term memory, which would include a representation of the recently presented CS, the CS-UCS contingency would soon be detected. Once the CS-UCS contingency has been stored in short-term and long-term memory, subsequently presented CSs will be identified as significant by the pre-attentive mechanisms and will elicit a call for central processing and an OR. The resulting processing of the CS and the CS-UCS relationship elicits further autonomic responses. Thus, the FIR-SCR in classical conditioning would be a component of the OR elicited by the call for processing of the

CS+, and the longer SIR-SCR components would reflect the effort expended by the central channel in processing the CS, the CS-UCS contingency, information about the exact length of the ISI, and so forth. The SIR-SCR is thus an anticipatory response due to expectancy of the UCS at a certain point in time.

As Öhman (1979) points out, because his model associates an OR with a call for processing capacity whether or not the call is answered, it can account for the findings of Corteen *et al*. (and at least the left ear results of Dawson and Schell, 1982). A CS already tagged as significant would elicit an OR, even it it were not admitted to central processing (and awareness) due to the occupation of the central-channel processor with the dichotic listening shadowing task. Öhman (1979) did not discuss the consistency of his model with the data indicating that an already well-learned CR can be elicited by the CS even if the conscious expectancy of the UCS after the CS has been extinguished. However, we have elsewhere (Dawson and Schell, 1985) suggested a few straightforward extensions of Öhman's model which would account for this phenomenon. We have hypothesized that during extinction, learning that the UCS will no longer follow the CS+ adds a new element to long-term memory, but it does not eliminate the already established memory of the former CS+-UCS contingency. When the CS+ is presented, the pre-attentive mechanisms may be influenced by both memory elements, and will call for processing capacity to be allocated if the CS+-UCS relationship element is more influential than the CS+-no UCS relationship element. The call will result in the production of an OR even if it goes unanswered by the central processor, which may be more influenced by the more recent CS+-no UCS memory element.

4 Implications of the multi-stage approach

The hypothesis that human classical conditioning is a multi-stage process, with conscious contingency learning an essential early stage, has implications for theoretical interpretations of conditioning, for applied uses of conditioning principles and techniques, and for more general philosophical issues.

As for theoretical implications, the present approach clearly indicates that any complete theory of human conditioning must include a theory of how organisms learn about stimulus relationships in their environment. If contingency learning is to be a central focus in the study of classical conditioning then there will be fundamental changes in the techniques, paradigms, and conceptual framework used by investigators in this area. In fact, one can rather clearly see such fundamental changes already occurring, for example, in the emphasis on second-order conditioning as a tool to study the nature of the associations underlying contingency learning (e.g. Rescorla, 1980). We believe that information processing models in general offer promising beginnings towards further understanding of contingency learning, and that Öhman's (1979) model in particular is relevant to integrating contingency learning with autonomic orienting and conditioning. However, much more work is clearly needed in order to understand the nature and controlling variables of contingency learning. If the multi-stage hypothesis is correct, then the effects of contingency learning should be most immediately obvious with autonomic rather than skeletal measures. Therefore, it is no coincidence that the investigators who have focused on the importance of contingency learning in conditioning have been those who measured autonomic rather than skeletal responses.

Our position is that contingency learning is only part of the classical conditioning story. Specifically, contingency learning is considered necessary but not sufficient for acquisition of human CRs, whereas it may not be necessary for later performance of previously established CRs. This formulation allows other variables, e.g. UCS intensity, to affect CR performance independent of conscious cognitive factors after contingency learning has occurred. These explicit distinctions and qualifications distinguish the present position from that of other cognitive interpretations of human conditioning (e.g. Brewer, 1974). Moreover, the present multi-stage approach makes explicit that contingency learning is translated into overt behaviour, and the principles of this translation need to be further explicated. While the dichotomy between contingency learning and response learning is appealing and heuristic, it is likely that many of the same variables affect both stages. For instance, the length of the ISI is a probable determiner of whether subjects will become aware of the CS-UCS contingency as well as a determiner of the topography of the resulting autonomic and skeletal CRs. According to the position outlined in this chapter, there is no reason to expect the CR to resemble the UCR. The CR is conceptualized as reflecting the subject's detection of the CS-UCS contingency (e.g. FIR-SCR) and his-her anticipation and preparation for the UCS (e.g. secondary heart rate deceleration). As mentioned above, there is some evidence based on UCR diminution studies that autonomic and skeletal CRs may be indices of an instrumental coping process dealing with the anticipated UCS. We believe that the possible instrumental properties of human CRs is an important question for future research.

Another potentially fruitful area of research might involve investigation of the differences between the sorts of skeletal CRs we have discussed (eyelid and NMR), which have been referred to by Prokasy (1984) as 'molecular responses', and responses such as crouching and freezing, referred to by Prokasy as a 'molar response'. The latter type of skeletal CR behaves in many ways like an autonomic CR, such as in its rapidity of acquisition.

Another issue in need of further research concerns learning of ISI. How does such learning occur, how does it affect behaviour, what are the most sensitive indices of such learning? One potentially profitable line of future research might be to directly investigate the sensitivity of SCR SIR and TIR latencies to ISI duration. If the timing of these responses does indeed reflect learning of exact ISI length, then systematically changing the ISI in a within-subjects trace conditioning paradigm should systematically alter the timing of the SIR and TIR as the new ISIs are learned. (If these components are sensitive to CS termination *per se* rather than to the ending of the ISI, varying ISI in a trace paradigm should not produce changes in their timing.)

The present multi-stage approach also may have useful implications regarding the application of conditioning principles and techniques to clinical disorders (e.g. behaviour therapy for phobias). First, it was pointed out earlier that phobias may be examples of the performance of previously established CRs without the presence of supporting cognitive mediation. The purpose of behaviour therapy is to extinguish the phobic CR or substitute a new learned response for the phobic CR. Hence, behaviour therapists should ensure that their clients fully understand the new stimulus contingencies being manipulated in the therapeutic process. Without such understanding, the present position asserts that behaviour therapy cannot work. However, it must be remembered that conscious contingency learning, while necessary for human conditioning, is not sufficient for conditioning and hence does not guarantee therapeutic success.

Interpretation of conditioning deficits found in different psychopathological groups also may be aided by the present approach. The multi-stage approach suggests that the deficits in conditioning may be due to dysfunctions at different stages of the conditioning process and that it is important to determine which stage is dysfunctional. For example, Baer and Fuhrer (1969) reported that a group of schizophrenic patients failed to acquire differential SCR CRs. The authors also noted that the majority of patients failed to become aware of the CS-UCS contingency. Therefore, in a subsequent study, Fuhrer and Baer (1970) instructed a subgroup of schizophrenic patients of the correct CS-UCS relation in order to ensure awareness. The instructed aware subgroup of patients exhibited highly reliable SCR conditioning, unlike a subgroup of non-instructed patients. Thus, in this case, the dysfunction being indexed by the deficit in conditioning was a dysfunction in contingency learning. Similar deficits in conditioning found among other psychopathological groups may be due to other dysfunctitons. For example, poor electrodermal classical conditioning in sociopaths is apparently not due to dysfunctions in contingency learning (Ziskind, Syndulko, and Maltzman, 1977).

Finally, the presently hypothesized necessity of conscious contingency learning for conditioning raises certain general philosophical issues about the phylogenetic generality of conscious awareness. For example, the withdrawal reflex of the invertebrate *Aplysia* can be differentially classically conditioned in a single trial (Carew, Hawkins, and Kandel, 1983). Does this mean that the

Aplysia is capable of sudden conscious insight into the CS-UCS contingency? Obviously, we think not. One possible integration of the present hypothesis with the finding that conditioning can occur in lower animals was suggested by Hebb (1958, p. 453): 'Because a simple task could, theoretically, be handled by a simple mechanism does not mean in fact that the brain handles it that way. In an uncomplicated nervous system, yes: but in the complex brain of a higher animal other mechanisms may insist on getting into the act and turn the simple task into a complex one.' Our hypothesis is that human classical conditioning is a 'complex task' in Hebb's sense. The growing realization of that fact is for ever altering the landscape of conditioning experimentation, theory, and practice.

Acknowledgements

Preparation of this chapter was supported by a grant from the National Institute of Mental Health (MH40496). We wish to thank William C. Williams and Diane Filion for many helpful comments and suggestions.

References

Baer, P. E., and Fuhrer, M. J. (1969). Cognitive factors in differential conditioning of the GSR: Use of a reaction time task as the UCS with normals and schizophrenics, *Journal of Abnormal Psychology*, **74**, 544–52.

Baer, P. E. and Fuhrer, M. J. (1982). Cognitive factors in the concurrent differential conditioning of eyelid and skin conductance responses, *Memory and Cognition*, **10**, 135–40.

Bauer, R. M. (1984). Automatic recognition of names and faces in prosopagnosia: A neuropsychological application of the guilty knowledge test, *Neuropsychologia*, **22**, 457–69.

Biferno, M. A., and Dawson, M. E. (1977). The onset of contingency awareness and electrodermal classical conditioning: An analysis of temporal relationships during acquisition and extinction, *Psychophysiology*, **14**, 164–71.

Bohlin, G., and Kjellberg, A. (1979). Orienting activity in two-stimulus paradigms as reflected in heart rate, in *The Orienting Reflex in Humans* (eds. H. D. Kimmel, E. H. Van Olst, and J. F. Orlebeke), pp. 169–97, Erlbaum, Hillsdale, N.J.

Boneau, C. A. (1958). The interstimulus interval and the latency of the conditioned eyelid response, *Journal of Experimental Psychology*, **56**, 464–71.

Brewer, W. F. (1974). There is no convincing evidence for operant or classical conditioning in adult humans, in *Cognition and the Symbolic Processes* (eds. W. Weimer and D. Palermo), pp. 1–42, Erlbaum, Hillsdale, N.J.

Carew, T. J., Hawkins, R. D. and Kandel, E. R. (1983). Differential classical conditioning of a defensive withdrawal reflex in *Aplysia Californica, Science*, **219**, 397–400.

Chatterjee, B. B. and Eriksen, C. W. (1960). Conditioning and generalization of GSR as a function of awareness, *Journal of Abnormal and Social Psychology*, **60**, 396–403.

Coleman, S. R., and Gormezano, I. (1971). Classical conditioning of the rabbit's (*Oryctolagus coniculus*) nictitating membrane response under symmetrical CS-UCS interval shifts, *Journal of Comparative and Physiological Psychology*, **77**, 447–55.

Cook, S. W., and Harris, R. E. (1937). The verbal conditioning of the galvanic skin reflex, *Journal of Experimental Psychology*, **21**, 202–10.

Corteen, R. J., and Dunn, D. (1974). Shock-associated words in a non-attended message: A test for momentary awareness, *Journal of Experimental Psychology*, **102**, 1143–4.

Corteen, R. J., and Wood, B. (1972). Automatic responses to shock-associated words in an unattended channel, *Journal of Experimental Psychology*, **94**, 308–13.

Dawson, M. E. (1970). Cognition and conditioning: Effects of masking the CS-UCS contingency on human GSR classical conditioning, *Journal of Experimental Psychology*, **85**, 389–96.

Dawson, M. E. (1973). Can classical conditioning occur without contingency learning? A review and evaluation of the evidence, *Psychophysiology*, **10**, 82–6.

Dawson, M. E., and Biferno, M. A. (1973). Concurrent measurement of awareness and electrodermal classical conditioning, *Journal of Experimental Psychology*, **101**, 82–6.

Dawson, M. E., Catania, J. J., Schell, A. M., and Grings, W. W. (1979). Autonomic classical conditioning as a function of awareness of stimulus contingencies, *Biological Psychology*, **9**, 23–40.

Dawson, M. E., and Furedy, J. J. (1976). The role of awareness in human differential autonomic classical conditioning: The necessary gate hypothesis, *Psychophysiology*, **13**, 50–3.

Dawson, M. E., and Grings, W. W. (1968). Comparison of classical conditioning and relational learning, *Journal of Experimental Psychology*, **76**, 227–31.

Dawson, M. E., and Reardon, D. P. (1973). Construct validity of recall and recognition postconditioning measures of awareness, *Journal of Experimental Psychology*, **98**, 308–15.

Dawson, M. E., and Schell, A. M. (1982). Electrodermal responses to attended and nonattended significant stimuli during dichotic listening, *Journal of Experimental Psychology: Human Perception and Performance*, **8**, 315–24.

Dawson, M. E., and Schell, A. M. (1985). Information processing and human autonomic classical conditioning, in *Advances in Psychophysiology*, vol. 1 (eds. P. K. Ackles, J. R. Jennings, and M. G. H. Coles), pp. 89–165, JAI Press, Greenwich, Conn.

Dawson, M. E., Schell, A. M., and Banis, H. T. (1986). Greater resistance to extinction of electrodermal responses conditioned to potentially phobic CSs: A noncognitive process? *Psychophysiology*, **23**, 552–61.

Dawson, M. E., Schell, A. M., Beers, J. R., and Kelly, A. (1982). Allocation of cognitive processing capacity during human autonomic classical conditioning, *Journal of Experimental Psychology: General*, **111**, 273–95.

Diven, K. (1937). Certain determiners of the conditioning of anxiety reactions, *Journal of Psychology*, **3**, 291–308.

Fuhrer, M. J., and Baer, P. E. (1969). Cognitive processes in differential GSR conditioning: Effects of a masking task, *American Journal of Psychology*, **82**, 168–80.

Fuhrer, M. J., and Baer, P. E. (1970). Preparatory instructions in differential conditioning of the galvanic skin response of schizophrenics and normals, *Journal of Abnormal Psychology*, **76**, 482–4.

Fuhrer, M. J., and Baer, P. E. (1980). Cognitive factors and CS-UCS interval effects in the differential conditioning and extinction of skin conductance responses, *Biological Psychology*, **10**, 283–98.

Furedy, J. J., and Poulos, C. X. (1977). Short-interval classical SCR conditioning and the stimulus-sequence-change-elicited OR: The case of the empirical red herring, *Psychophysiology*, **14**, 351–9.

Gormezano, I. (1966). Classical conditioning, in *Experimental Methods and Instrumentation in Psychology*, (ed. J. B. Sidowski), pp. 385–420, McGraw-Hill, New York.
Gormezano, I., and Kehoe, E. J. (1975). Classical conditioning: Some methodological-conceptual issues, in *Handbook of Learning and Cognitive Processes*: vol. 2. *Conditioning and Behavior Theory* (ed. W. K. Estes), pp. 143–80, Erlbaum, Hillsdale, N.J.
Gormezano, I., Kehoe, E. J., and Marshall, B. S. (1983). Twenty years of classical conditioning research with the rabbit, in *Progress in Psychobiology and Physiological Psychology* vol. 10 (eds. J. M. Sprague and A. N. Epstein), pp. 197–275, Academic Press, New York.
Graham, F. K. (1979). Distinguishing among orienting, defense, and startle reflexes, in *The Orienting Reflex in Humans* (eds. H. D. Kimmel, E. H. Van Olst, and J. F. Orlebeke), pp. 137–68, Erlbaum, Hillsdale, N.J.
Grings, W. W. (1977). Orientation, conditioning, and learning, *Psychophysiology*, **14**, 343–50.
Grings, W. W., and Dawson, M. E. (1973). Complex conditioning, in *Electrodermal Activity in Psychological Research* (eds. W. F. Prokasy and D. C. Raskin), pp. 203–54, Academic Press, New York.
Grings, W. W., and Lockhart, R. A. (1963). Effects of 'anxiety lessening' instructions and differential set development on the extinction of the GSR, *Journal of Experimental Psychology*, **66**, 292–9.
Grings, W. W., Lockhart, R. A., and Dameron, L. E. (1962). Conditioning autonomic responses of mentally subnormal individuals, *Psychological Monographs*, **76**, (39, whole no. 58).
Grings, W. W., and Schell, A. M. (1971). Effects of trace vs. delay conditioning, interstimulus interval variability, and instructions on UCR diminution, *Journal of Experimental Psychology*, **90**, 136–40.
Haggard, E. A. (1943). Experimental studies in affective processes: I. Some effects of cognitive structure and active participation on certain autonomic reactions during and following experimentally induced stress, *Journal of Experimental Psychology*, **33**, 257–84.
Headrick, M. W., and Graham, F. K. (1969). Multiple component heart rate responses conditioned under paced respiration, *Journal of Experimental Psychology*, **79**, 486–94.
Hebb, D. O. (1958). Alice in wonderland or psychology among the biological sciences, in *Biological and Biochemical Bases of Behavior* (eds. H. F. Harlow and C. N. Woolsey), pp. 451–67, University of Wisconsin Press, Madison.
Hugdahl, K., and Öhman, A. (1977). Effects of instruction on acquisition and extinction of electrodermal responses to fear-relevant stimuli, *Journal of Experimental Psychology: Human Learning and Memory*, **3**, 608–18.
Kahneman, D. (1973). *Attention and Effort*, Prentice-Hall, Englewood Cliffs, N.J.
Kimble, G. A. (1961). *Hilgard and Marquis' Conditioning and Learning*, Appleton-Century-Crofts, New York.
Kimble, G. A., and Dufort, R. H. (1956). The associative factor in eyelid conditioning, *Journal of Experimental Psychology*, **52**, 386–91.
Kimble, G. A., and Ost, J. W. P. (1961). A conditioned inhibitory process in eyelid conditioning, *Journal of Experimental Psychology*, **61**, 150–6.
Kimmel, H. D. (1964). Further analysis of GSR conditioning: A reply to Stewart, Stern, Winokur, and Fredman, *Psychological Review*, **71**, 160–6.
Kimmel, H. D., and Pennypacker, H. S. (1962). Conditioned diminution of the

unconditioned response as a function of the number of reinforcements, *Journal of Experimental Psychology*, **64**, 20–3.

Lacey, J. I., and Smith, R. L. (1954). Conditioning and generalization of unconscious anxiety, *Science*, **120**, 1045–52.

Lockhart, R. A. (1966). Comments regarding multiple response phenomena in long interstimulus interval conditioning, *Psychophysiology*, **3**, 108–14.

Lockhart, R. A., and Grings, W. W. (1963). Comments on 'An analysis of GSR conditioning', *Journal of Experimental Psychology*, **67**, 209–14.

Lockhart, R. A., and Steinbrecher, D. C. (1970). Differential heart-rate conditioning in the rabbit: Failure to find a specific pre-US response, *Psychonomic Science*, **19**, 175–7.

Lykken, D. T. (1962). Preception in the rat: Autonomic response to shock as a function of length of warning interval, *Science*, **137**, 665–6.

Mackintosh, N. J. (1983). *Conditioning and Associative Learning*, Oxford University Press, New York.

Maltzman, I., Weissbluth, S., and Wolff, C. (1978). Habituation of orienting reflexes in repeated GSR semantic conditioning sessions, *Journal of Experimental Psychology: General*, **107**, 309–33.

Mandel, I. J., and Bridger, W. H. (1967). Interaction between instructions and ISI in conditioning and extinction of the GSR, *Journal of Experimental Psychology*, **74**, 36–43.

Mandel, I. J., and Bridger, W. H. (1973). Is there classical conditioning without cognitive expectancy? *Psychophysiology*, **10**, 87–90.

Marks, I. (1969). *Fears and Phobias*, Academic Press, New York.

Martin, I., and Levey, A. B. (1969). *The Genesis of the Classical Conditioned Response*, Permagon Press, Oxford.

Moore, J. W. (1972). Stimulus control: Studies of auditory generalization in rabbits, in *Classical Conditioning II: Current Theory and Research* (eds. A. H. Black and W. F. Prokasy), pp. 206–30, Appleton-Century-Crofts, New York.

Mowrer, O. H. (1938). Preparatory set (expectancy)—A determinant in motivation and learning, *Psychological Review*, **45**, 62–91.

Nelson, M. N., and Ross, L. E. (1974). Effects of masking tasks on differential eyelid conditioning: A distinction between knowledge of stimulus contingencies and attentional or cognitive activities involving them, *Journal of Experimental Psychology*, **10**, 1–9.

Nemiah, J. C. (1980). Phobic disorder, in *Comprehensive Textbook of Psychiatry*, 3rd edn (eds. H. Kaplan, A. Freedman and B. Sadcock), Williams & Wilkins, Baltimore.

Öhman, A. (1979). The orienting response, attention, and learning: An information processing perspective, in *The Orienting Reflex in Humans* (eds. H. D. Kimmel, E. H. Von Olst, and J. F. Orlebeke), Erlbaum, Hillsdale, N.J.

Öhman, A. (1983). The orienting response during Pavlovian conditioning, in *Orienting and Habituation: Perspectives in Human Research* (ed. D. Siddle), John Wiley & Sons, New York.

Öhman, A., Ellstrom, P. E., and Bjorkstrand, P. A. (1976). Electrodermal responses and subjective estimates of UCS probability in a long interstimulus interval conditioning paradigm, *Psychophysiology*, **13**, 121–7.

Öhman, A., Fredrickson, M., Hugdahl, K., and Rimmö, P. A. (1976). The premise of equipotentiality in human classical conditioning: Conditioned electrodermal responses to potentially phobic stimuli, *Journal of Experimental Psychology: General*, **105**, 313–37.

Peeke, S. C., and Grings, W. W. (1968). Magnitude of the UCR as a function of variability in the CS-UCS relationship, *Journal of Experimental Psychology*, **77**, 64–9.

Pendery, M., and Maltzman, I. (1977). Instructions and the orienting reflex in 'semantic conditioning' of the galvanic skin response in an innocuous situation, *Journal of Experimental Psychology: General*, **106**, 120–40.

Perruchet, P. (1985). Expectancy for airpuff and conditioned eyeblinks in humans, *Acta Psychologica*, **58**, 31–44.

Perry, L. C., Grant, D. A., and Schwartz, M. (1977). Effects of noun imagery and awareness of the discriminative cue upon differential eyelid conditioning to grammatical and ungrammatical phrases, *Memory and Cognition*, **5**, 423–9.

Posner, M. I. (1978). *Chronometric Explorations of Mind*, Erlbaum, Hillsdale, N.J.

Posner, M. I., and Boies, S. J. (1971). Components of attention, *Psychological Review*, **78**, 391–408.

Posner, M. I., and Snyder, R. R. (1975). Attention and cognitive control, in *Information Processing and Cognition: The Loyola Symposium* (ed. R. Solso), Erlbaum, Hillsdale, N.J.

Powell, D. A., Hernandez, L., and Buchanan, S. L. (1985). Intraseptal scopolamine has differential effects on Pavlovian eye blink and heart rate conditioning, *Behavioural Neuroscience*, **99**, 75–87.

Powell, D. A., Milligan, W. L., and Mull, P. (1982). Lateral septal lesions enhance bradycardia in the rabbit, *Journal of Comparative and Physiological Psychology*, **96**, 742–54.

Prokasy, W. F. (1965). Classical eyelid conditioning: Experimenter operations, task demands, and response shaping, in *Classical Conditioning: A Symposium* (ed. W. F. Prokasy), pp. 208–25, Appleton-Century-Crofts, New York.

Prokasy, W. F. (1977). First interval skin conductance response. Conditioned or orienting responses? *Psychophysiology*, **14**, 360–7.

Prokasy, W. F. (1984). Acquisition of skeletal conditioned responses in Pavlovian conditioning, *Psychophysiology*, **21**, 1–13.

Prokasy, W. F., and Ebel, H. C. (1967). Three components of the classically conditioned GSR in humans, *Journal of Experimental Psychology*, **73**, 247–56.

Prokasy, W. F., and Kumpfer, K. L. (1973). Classical conditioning, in *Electrodermal Activity in Psychological Research* (eds. W. F. Prokasy and D. C. Raskin), pp. 157–202, Academic Press, New York.

Putman, L. E., Ross, L. E., and Graham, F. K. (1974). Cardiac orienting during 'good' and 'poor' differential eyelid conditioning, *Journal of Experimental Psychology*, **102**, 563–73.

Razran, G. (1955). Conditioning and perception, *Psychological Review*, **62**, 83–95.

Razran, G. (1965). Evolutionary psychology: Levels of learning and perception and thinking, in *Scientific Psychology: Principles and Approaches* (ed. B. Wolman), pp. 207–53, Basic Books, New York.

Razran, G. (1971). *Mind in Evolution*, Houghton Mifflin, New York.

Rescorla, R. A. (1967). Pavlovian conditioning and its proper control procedures, *Psychological Review*, **74**, 71–80.

Rescorla, R. A. (1978). Some implications of a cognitive perspective on Pavlovian conditioning, in *Cognitive Processes in Animal Behavior* (eds. S. H. Hulse, H. Fowler, and W. K. Honig), pp. 15–50, Erlbaum, Hillsdale, N.J.

Rescorla, R. A. (1980). *Pavlovian Secondary-Order Conditioning: Studies of Associative Learning*, Erlbaum, Hillsdale, N.J.

Schell, A. M., and Grings, W. W. (1971). Judgements of UCS intensity and diminution of the unconditioned GSR, *Psychophysiology*, **8**, 427–32.

Schneiderman, N. (1972). Response system divergencies in aversive classical conditioning, in *Classical Conditioning II: Current Research and Theory* (eds. A. H. Black and W. F. Prokasy), pp. 341–76, Appleton-Century-Crofts, New York.

Shiffrin, R. M., and Schneider, W. (1977). Controlled and automatic human information processing II: Perceptual learning, automatic attending, and a general theory, *Psychological Review*, **84**, 127–90.

Spence, K. W. (1956). *Behavior Theory and Conditioning*, Yale University Press, New Haven, Conn.

Stern, J. A., and Walrath, L. C. (1977). Orienting responses and conditioning of electrodermal responses, *Psychophysiology*, **14**, 334–42.

Stewart, M. A., Stern, J. A., Winokur, G., and Fredman, S. (1961). An analysis of GSR conditioning, *Psychological Review*, **68**, 60–7.

Stewart, M. A., Winokur, G., Stern, J., Guze, S., Pfeiffer, E., and Hornung, F. (1959). Adaptation and conditioning GSR in psychiatric patients, *Journal of Mental Science*, **105**, 1102–11.

Tranel, D., and Damasio, A. R. (1985). Knowledge without awareness: An autonomic index of facial recognition by prosopagnosics, *Science*, **228**, 1453–4.

Vandercar, D. H., and Schneiderman, N. (1967). Interstimulus interval functions in different response systems during classical discrimination conditioning in rabbits, *Psychonomic Science*, **9**, 9–10.

Van Twyver, H. B., and King, R. L. (1969). Classical conditioning of the galvanic skin response in immobilized cats, *Psychophysiology*, **5**, 530–5.

Wickens, D. D., Allen, C. K., and Hill, F. A. (1963). Effect of instructions and UCS strength on extinction of the conditioned GSR, *Journal of Experimental Psychology*, **66**, 235–40.

Wilson, R. A., Fuhrer, M. J., and Baer, P. E. (1974). Differential conditioning of electrodermal responses: Effects of performing a masking task during the interstimulus and intertrial intervals, *Biological Psychology*, **2**, 33–46.

Yehle, A. L. (1968). Divergences among rabbit response systems during three-tone classical discrimination conditioning, *Journal of Experimental Psychology*, **77**, 468–73.

Ziskind, E., Syndulko, K., and Maltzman, I. (1977). Evidence for a neurologic disorder in the sociopath syndrome: Aversive conditioning and recidivism, in *Psychopathology and Brain Dysfunction* (eds. C. Shagass, S. Gershon, and A. J. Friedhoff), pp. 255–65, Raven Press, New York.

Cognitive Processes and Pavlovian Conditioning in Humans
Edited by G. Davey

Chapter 3

Learning what will happen next: Conditioning, evaluation, and cognitive processes

Irene Martin
Institute of Psychiatry, London

and

A. B. Levey
MRC Applied Psychology Unit, Cambridge

It is proposed that classical conditioning, evaluations, and certain cognitive processes can be integrated within a biological framework which examines how living beings adapt to the temporal structure of the world to provide an answer to the question: What is going to happen next? By taking this approach, human classical conditioning research can be integrated with the sophisticated body of existing animal research and can also clarify the contribution of conditioning theory to behaviour therapy, a form of therapy based on the assumption that emotional disorders are acquired and can be extinguished by means of learning principles and procedures. An integrated approach is particularly needed at this point in time when animal, human, and applied conditioning theories coexist as non-interacting parts of a total framework.

Learning to anticipate sequential and recurring events in the external world is a major component of adaptive (and hence maladaptive) behaviour. Viewed in the context of registering sequences of indifferent and significant events so that the individual can anticipate and predict what will happen next, learning involves both conditioning and cognitive processes. In this chapter, different types of conditioning and cognitive processes involving anticipation and prediction will be considered.

Probably the simplest type of learning is illustrated in classical conditioning, in which a neutral event is closely followed by a highly salient event. Learning about imperatives and emergencies can occur immediately, in one trial. When event pairs are repeated, individuals can learn the pattern of such pairings, the correlations and contingencies between events, the rules which govern reinforcement. When event sequences occur over a very long time scale, other approaches to learning and memory are required to examine how rules or representations are formulated to summarize and organize the sequential information.

A biological framework is appropriate in that it can comfortably incorporate the orectic and motivational dimensions of behaviour which have been neglected in purely cognitive theories. It acknowledges that evaluation of positive and negative valencies in the world is an imperative and innate feature of all forms of life. Classical conditioning can be regarded as a procedure which leads organisms to assign a positive or negative value to previously neutral stimuli, and our own human conditioning research along these lines will be discussed in detail. The biological approach also recognizes the role of development in current behaviour, and opposes that kind of thinking which examines the here and now structure without asking how it is acquired. This opens up the possibility that problems of human adaptive and maladaptive responding can be not only treated but prevented or anticipated by means of learning formulations.

Such an approach can also encompass cognitive factors. In the human conditioning literature the term 'cognitive' typically refers to such factors as subjects' awareness of stimulus relations, as reflected in their verbalizations. There are, however, more interesting usages of the term in the conditioning context. Another sense, evident in both the animal and the human literature, is the representation of stimuli and stimulus sequences in the nervous system, as in Sokolov's notion of neuronal networks and Konorski's gnostic units. Yet another interpretation of cognitive processing refers to the handling of stimulus input, considering conditioning to refer to the storage of stimulus characteristics of CS and UCS. These various usages can all be considered within the domain of the 'cognitive' and offer a different approach to conditioning than that provided by traditional views of conditioning as a linear associative phenomenon.

Central to our view of the conditioning process is the demonstration that subjective evaluative responses can be conditioned. This research will be discussed, together with a model of conditioning which draws from evaluative conditioning and from our human classical eyelid conditioning studies. These studies began in an era in which theories of conditioning were dominated by the linear and serial processes implied in classical S-R theory and the mathematical models which reflected them. The focus of our early work was on interactive processes in the development of response topography (Levey and Martin, 1968) in conformity with adaptive (anticipatory and predictive) mechanisms which lead to efficient response shaping. These mechanisms could not be accounted for in terms of linear operators and we adopted such terms as 'global', 'holistic', and 'redintegrative' to describe our findings. Throughout the discussion we will retain this terminology and will use the term 'associative' to refer only to encapsulated non-interactive models. That this distinction is now inaccurate will be acknowledged in a final section. Meanwhile it allows us to describe our point of view in the terms in which it was developed.

First, we will elaborate on the biological perspective of this chapter.

1 Biological framework

There is explicit emphasis, in the writings of Pavlov and Anohkin, on the theme of the future, and allied to this is the philosophical reference to the 'reflection of reality'. Pavlov frequently used the term 'signalization' as the most characteristic feature of the conditioned reflex, meaning by that the 'anticipatory reflection of reality'.

For Anohkin (1974), sequence is a universal law of the inorganic and organic world. The most primitive adaptations of developing matter were to sequences of events in the organic world produced by changes of light, temperature, oxygen, enabling organisms to prepare for signals of impending links of sequentially recurring events. These sequences are the basic temporal parameters in response to which conditioning mechanisms evolved for the 'anticipatory reflection of reality'.

Anohkin takes this sequence of recurring events to propose a theory of chemical unification, i.e. that a primitive form of stabilization of chemical chain reactors appeared early in the phylogeny of organisms. According to this view, a molecular chain of chemical reactions is developed in primary organisms, such that in a sequence of external factors, A, B, C, D, the occurrence of A can trigger the whole sequential chain of chemical reactions originally produced by A to D. The conditioned reflex and its basic biological and neurophysiological mechanism is considered to be a specialized case of the universal law of sequence.

There are obvious epistemological issues underlying these views on the perception of time and the reflection of reality. Anohkin attributes to Pavlov a mechanism for anticipating the future. Before Pavlov, he argues, the physiology of animals dealt with two categories of time: the past and the present. Everything concerning the third category of time, the future, was 'relegated to the purposeful behaviour of man and was almost exclusively the domain of idealistic psychology'. Now, adaptation to future events and the anticipation of the future which had been the prerogative of man, could be extended to animals. Thereafter the 'future' in the life of organisms became the object of the same scientific investigation as the other two categories of time.

This sample of Russian thinking illustrates some of its well-known features: a materialist philosophy, a biological perspective, an emphasis on evolution and the interactive nature of the organic and inorganic world, and specific reference to adaptation within a space–time structure. Such an outlook contrasts with a cognitive perspective which gives primacy to the individual knower and to subjective determinants of behaviour. More formally, cognitivism's dominant interest is in structures and processes within the mind: it is the order of human thinking and reasoning that grants an order and meaning to the world of reality. Contemporary cognitive psychology is, however, questioning its subjective bias and examining the argument put forward by Gibson (1966) and others, that the objective world provides the critical elements that determine human perception and that emphasis on subjective determinants is not essential (Costall, 1984; Sampson, 1981). Neisser (1976) urges a more real-wordly outlook: 'We may have been lavishing too much effort on hypothetical models of the mind and not enough on analysing the environment that the mind has been shaped to meet.' One important implication which follows from the cognitivist emphasis is the extent to which mental events and mental operations can themselves be changed to enable the individual to respond more adaptively in the world. Thus the distinction between a cognitive and a biologically oriented world view is beginning to fade. The time is ripe to consider within a single framework how organisms cope with kinds of learning which encompass both the biological imperatives, the need for survival and emergency action (the domain of conditioning, motivation, and emotion), and the longer-term learning of event sequences which make up so much of adaptive learning and which are not comfortably covered by conditioning theory.

2 Learning the rules of the external environment

In recent articles we have examined how a distinction can be made between the conditioning and cognitive contributions to the learning of adaptive or maladaptive behaviour (Levey and Martin, 1983; Martin and Levey, 1985a, 1985b). We proposed that both forms of learning, though distinguishable from one another, be considered together within a unified biological perspective. They both represent adaptations to the problem of learning about event regularities in the environment, the 'rules' of the environment. There should be no conflict between cognitive and conditioning models; rather, we argue, they should be integrated within a single framework.

Perhaps the most primitive form of this learning is the classical conditioning process. At its simplest, this process need only involve a single CS-UCS pairing when the UCS is a strongly evaluated event with significant consequences for individual well-being. It occurs over a brief span of two contiguous events.

We can consider that information about a CS-UCS pair is summarized as a simple statement of this contiguity. Another kind of summary is needed to span events occurring over longer sequences beyond the range of conditioning phenomena. This other type of summary requires more extensive sampling of the environment to obtain a reliable estimate of its invariant features. The information can be stored in some form of ordinal structure, e.g. an alphabet or a map, such that the individual can anticipate the beginning and predict the subsequent development of regularities in the environment. Such summaries are very often in the form of verbal statements. They can be faulty, and fail to correspond to the rules of the environment.

It must be emphasized that the rules are *environmental* rules: they originate in the world and refer to the invariant structure of the physical world. Living creatures learn about the regularities in their environment through active engagement with it, and the reward is greater efficiency in dealing with the organized parts of the world. If we assume that adaptation to the environment essentially involves prediction of about-to-occur events, then ways of obtaining this information become an important focus for study. Classical conditioning is one process, cognitive inference and extrapolation another. They represent different types of learning about the future.

We are suggesting that in the course of evolutionary adaptation to their environments, organisms had to evolve mechanisms for registering some features of event invariance, and that some of these mechanisms come within the realm of conditioning, but others lie outside it. Not all events in the world occur with detectable regularity: some occur at random and others recur so rarely that learning is not possible within a single lifetime. But some events do occur regularly; they may occur in pairs in close succession (to which individuals condition) or in regular and recurring forms (which can be summarized) to provide a basis for the development of adaptive behaviour. Within any sequence, it is the salient, significant or, in the terminology to be developed here, the evaluated event which ensures the individual's attention, and the next section discussed responses of this sort.

3 Evaluative conditioning

The evaluative response has been proposed as a fundamental biological mechanism: all forms of life evaluate their surroundings in terms of what is beneficial and what is harmful. As it begins life, the organism, whether primitive or complex, is equipped ('hard wired') with the essential likes and dislikes which are appropriate to its *probable* environment—probable in the sense that any specific ecological niche will contain certain properties of invariance. Through the mechanism of evaluative conditioning, it early and rapidly acquires new likes and dislikes which serve to adapt it more accurately to its *actual* environment. In simple organisms these likes and dislikes are behaviourally synonymous with approach and avoidance. In more complex life forms this stereotype has been replaced by a more varied response repertoire, but the underlying mechanism is still that of evaluative conditioning.

The evaluative response is postulated as a characteristic internal reaction to environmental stimuli in terms of the evaluation of good/bad, liked/disliked, pleasant/unpleasant. It is subjective in the sense that it is unique to the individual and refers to the individual's own internal state; non-specific in that it is not attributable to a particular sensory modality. It is seen as a mechanism which provides the necessary link between immediate and final (unknowable) consequences with the requirement that immediate consequences must anticipate eventual consequences more often than not to ensure survival.

In our experimental work we have attempted to analyse the nature of human subjective evaluations and have presented evidence that they can be conditioned. It is apparent that the response which is usually observed and measured in any conditioning experiment is not the only response which is conditioned—it is one of many concurrent motor, autonomic, and subjective responses. Our view is that conditioning occurs only if an evaluative response is first elicited, and that what is conditioned is the evaluative response itself. The *behaviours* consequent on occurrence of the conditioned evaluative response will be determined by parameters of the situation in which the response is evoked, and these may include state variables such as hunger or anxiety, or cognitive factors such as perception of outcome. In other words, the primary mechanism of conditioning is the transfer of a positive or negative evaluation to a stimulus which was previously neutral, and this leaves open the behavioural outcomes of conditioning.

A series of experiments has tested various parameters of the evaluative conditioning paradigm. The basic experiment can be described as follows. Stimulus materials are 50 picture postcards of unfamiliar paintings, selected to provide a wide range of subjective preference. Subjects are first asked to sort the pictures into three categories—liked, neutral, or disliked—and then to choose from the appropriate categories the two most liked and the two most disliked. These stimuli serve as UCSs and are paired with pictures from the neutral category. Two further neutral pictures are chosen as a control pair, to make five pairs in all: neutral–liked, neutral–disliked, neutral–neutral, disliked–neutral, and liked–neutral. These pairs are presented tachistoscopically, each pair for a number of trials. The next pair is then substituted, the order being determined by a Latin square design. Following this acquisition phase, subjects are asked to sort the ten pictures into two equal categories, liked and disliked. They are then asked to arrange the pictures in order of preference and assign to each a rating from +100 (maximum liking) to −100 (maximum disliking). The criterion of conditioning in this paradigm is a change in the evaluation of the previously neutral stimulus in the direction of the evaluation of the stimulus with which it has been paired. The essential control is that no change should be observed in the neutral stimulus that has been paired only with another stimulus that is neutral. Results have repeatedly shown that although the experimental stimuli evoke no overt physical responses, the evaluation of like or dislike is acquired by the neutral stimuli. The within-subject design in which contingencies are varied includes both forward and backward as well as the neutral–neutral control which make it difficult for subjects to become aware of stimulus relationships, and the question of demand characteristics or contingency awareness has not arisen (Levey and Martin, 1975; Martin and Levey, 1978).

The formulation offered here is that an unmediated, non-cognitive evaluative response is elicited by evaluatively salient stimuli and transferred to contiguous neutral stimuli by the mechanism of classical conditioning. This view contains several implications. One of these is that the organism need not 'know' in the cognitive sense the significance of its evaluations. Another is that it allows for many levels of responding, from the fully predetermined to the open ended.

The emphasis, then, is on the evaluation of the CS, rather than on its signalling properties. These evaluative processes take place without effort, without awareness, and without interfering with other cognitive processes—thus we have called them 'automatic' non-cognitive processes. A close analogy to this view is to be found in the taste aversion literature, where conditioning to noxious substances is very rapid, frequently occurring in one trial. Garcia *et al.* (1977) comment that 'what is really happening is that you're changing the hedonic tone of a stimulus . . . the organism doesn't learn an if–then relationship . . . if I take this stuff I'm going to get sick at the time *t* in place *p*. All he learns is that he doesn't like this stuff any more'.

The possibility has to be entertained that individuals do learn both the signalling and the evaluative transfer, especially with repeated trials. But the point is, as already mentioned, that propositional 'knowledge' is not essential to this kind of conditioning mechanism. Survival in a world where danger may appear suddenly and where no second chances may be provided requires one-trial learning to ensure immediate and appropriate action on any future occasion when the crucial event pair recurs.

4 The nature of the evaluative response

A major point of the experimental strategy has been to establish a paradigm which can demonstrate that the evaluative characteristics of a stimulus can be conditioned in the absence of overt acts and emotional responses. Most UCSs are strongly aversive or appetitive, have multiple sensory and affective properties, and elicit a range of physiological and motor responses which accompany and overlay the 'pure' evaluative components of the response. We have therefore adopted a second-order paradigm, using as UCSs mild stimulus materials such as art reproductions and photographs, stimuli which have meaning for human subjects and which they can rate along a dimension of like/dislike.

This approach has served to examine classical conditioning at its simplest, by stripping the conditioning paradigm of the usual motor, emotional, and motivating components of the UCS, and considering the evaluative response in 'pure' form. The logic of the approach is that if positive and negative evaluations can be conditioned in the absence of all but evaluative components, then these must be regarded as the sufficient components of classical conditioning. In conditioning paradigms employing highly unpleasant or pleasant stimuli it seems evident that affective reactions of a complex nature can be transferred from UCS to CS. These affects, and associated motor activity, obscure the evaluative process, which can only be assessed within the type of methodology adopted here.

In our previous discussions of these issues we have emphasized the view that evaluative conditioning is 'non-cognitive' and unmediated (e.g. Levey and Martin, 1983; Martin and Levey, 1978, 1985a). The intention was to emphasize the immediacy of the evaluative response, the minimal degree of processing which need take place before the individual evaluates a stimulus as liked/disliked, safe/dangerous, and that if a reflective (cognitive) judgement does occur it is likely to be secondary.

In recent years the unmediated–mediated controversy has been enlivened by Zajonc's discussion of the primacy of 'affect' and his distinction between preferenda and discriminanda. Zajonc (1980) describes an immediate reaction of like/dislike which is basic, inescapable, difficult to verbalize, and non-cognitive. It is often the very first reaction of the individual, can occur without extensive perceptual and cognitive encoding, and is made with greater confidence than cognitive judgements.

The point relevant to the present issue is his assertion that reactions to salient, highly evaluated stimuli take place on the basis of minimal processing.

> A rabbit confronted by a snake has no time to consider all the perceivable attributes of the snake in the hope that he might be able to infer from them the likelihood of the snake's attack, the timing of the attack, or its direction. The rabbit cannot stop to contemplate the length of the snake's fangs or the geometry of its markings. If the rabbit is to escape, the action must be undertaken long before the completion of even a simple cognitive process . . .

Zajonc's thesis is that affect should not be treated as postcognitive, his purpose to assert the evolutionary origins of affective reactions, their freedom from attentive control, their speed, their inescapability. The use of the term 'affect' is problematical in so far as it evokes connotations of emotion, and some more neutral term may be more appropriate. However, the issue centres on how much processing need take place in order for the individual to like or dislike an event.

He reviews evidence which indicates that affective reactions are independent of any particular sensory modality and argues against the assumption that affect or values are attached to the very same features that the subject attends to in a typical detection, recognition, discrimination, or categorization task. Stimulus features which serve well in the cognitive analysis of objects may not be at all relevant to evaluating them. If this is indeed the case, then there must be a class of features that allow us to experience these immediate like/dislike reactions quite early on after the onset of the sensory input. These features might be quite gross, vague, and global. 'Thus they might be insufficient as a basis for most cognitive judgements—judgements even as primitive as recognition, for example. In order to distinguish this class of features from simple discriminanda, I call them *preferenda*' (Zajonc, 1980, p. 159).

There are many aspects of Zajonc's argument which have aroused controversy, particularly his suggestion that affect and cognition are under the control of separate and partially independent systems. This is not of immediate concern here, but two factors of his argument are relevant. One is his description of a reaction of like/dislike which is close if not identical to the evaluative response described here. The second is his use of an information processing model in which the reaction of like/dislike and evaluation occurs at a very early stage, and prior to detailed identification of discriminant features. His view suggests that certain attributes of salient stimuli are given priority processing by the organism and we would conclude that these are the evaluative components which can produce conditioning before the stimulus is completely analysed.

In this connection the recent formulations of Marcel (1983) carry important and radical implications. He proposes that non-conscious, automatic components of stimulus processing do occur immediately and without perceptual mediation. This preliminary sensory analysis 'codes all aspects of what impinges at every level and in every code with which the organism is equipped' (p. 234). While the experimental evidence on which these proposals are based is solely derived from graphic and semantic coding, the principles apply to all forms of stimuli. If 'every code' includes a code for immediate evaluation, the concept of preferenda remains relevant as a subset of discriminanda, but the temporal distinction between cognitive and emotional processing disappears. This formulation is not inimical to the concept of evaluative conditioning in principle, but it would force a redefinition of the evaluative response if it were to be empirically validated for preference materials.

4.1 Evaluative conditioning and stimulus selection

To summarize the argument so far, it is postulated that all organisms are equipped with the ability to detect (with some probabilistic margin of error) those aspects of their environment which are conducive to, and those which are threatening to, survival. The ability to do this is effected by a response mechanism—termed here the evaluative response—which need not operate at a conscious level and may involve only minimal processing. One question which arises is this: Is it only the evaluative dimension, or others alone or in combination, which contributes to the conditioning process? We have carried out some experiments which ask whether only the evaluative features of the UCS are transferred to the CS, or whether stimulus characteristics of other dimensions might also be transferred. In examining this issue we have chosen to work with Osgood's well-known affective dimensions. Osgood's analysis of meaning produced three semantic differential dimensions, labelled evaluation, activity, and potency, of which the evaluative dimension emerged consistently as the strongest factor followed by the activity factor. Osgood considers that these dimensions, although measured primarily at the semantic level, can equally well apply to the most primitive organism when confronted with a novel stimulus: it has to 'decide' how pleasant/unpleasant, how active, and how powerful the stimulus is in order to adjust its motor output in terms of approach or avoidance (Osgood, 1969).

Our recent experiments have examined the role of the activity dimension, asking whether the evaluative dimension alone, activity alone, or both in combination, can be transferred to the CS. Subjects in one group were first asked to divide the stimulus materials (50 unfamiliar postcard reproductions) into three piles: like, neutral, and disliked. They were then asked to divide each of these three piles into a further three categories—active, neutral, and inactive—making nine categories in all. UCSs were selected from the extreme piles to comprise one of each of the following: liked-active; liked-inactive; disliked-active; disliked-inactive. CSs were pictures rated as neutral for both liking and activity, and the usual neutral-neutral control pair was included. Subjects in a second group followed a comparable procedure but in reverse order such that rating on activity was carried out first and evaluation second. Subjects in each group then underwent the acquisition procedure already described. Following this they were asked to rate the ten stimuli both for activity and liking, counterbalancing order within groups.

Significant conditioning effects for evaluation were obtained in the group which rated liking first. That is to say, the neutral stimuli preceding the liked-active and the liked-inactive UCS were rated significantly more positively than the neutral stimuli preceding the disliked-active and the disliked-inactive. No significant effect was found for the activity dimension: that is, activity ratings of the neutral stimuli were the same for those preceding the active-liked and active-disliked and for those preceding inactive-liked and inactive-disliked. There were no significant results when evaluation was rated second (Group 2) for either activity or for evaluation.

The evidence from this experiment suggests that while evaluation can be modified by the classical conditioning procedure, judgements of activity cannot. The effect is easily demonstrated when evaluation is rated first, but is abolished when the rating occurs second. We believe that this reflects the severe attenuation of the evaluative choice when it is limited to stimuli preselected for activity. There was no support for the hypothesis that the two dimensions, evaluation and activity, summate, nor that they cancel one another.

The same arguments apply, however, to the non-significant results for Activity in that they could arise from the complexity of the rating tasks which subjects were asked to carry out. All stimuli were examined by all subjects for both evaluation and activity, and some interference from one to the other rating might have occurred. Although the positive results in Group 1 confirmed the hypothesis that only the evaluative dimension was transferred, the methodological difficulties associated with subjects having to carry out both types of ratings suggested a follow-up experiment in which only the Activity dimension was considered. A further experiment therefore adopted the standard procedure of the evaluative conditioning experiment but ratings were confined to the activity dimension.

Results of this experiment were non-significant. Following the paired presentations, mean values of neutral stimuli preceding active stimuli were similar to the values of neutral stimuli preceding inactive stimuli. There was no evidence of a conditioning effect for the activity dimension. The results therefore support the view that it is only the evaluative dimension which is transferred in conditioning. Not only is the occurrence of the evaluative response *sufficient* to ensure conditioning, it is also *necessary*.

4.2 A model of classical conditioning

The evaluative conditioning paradigm was designed not to study evaluations *per se*, but to test inferences drawn from our model of the genesis of the classically conditioned response (Levey and Martin, 1968, 1974; Martin and Levey, 1969). This model was derived from research on eyelid conditioning; it dealt with CR topography and was intended to explain CR formation and its development. It stated that whenever an organism encounters a salient stimulus or situation in the environment it stores the contents of immediate memory in a comparator store. The term 'immediate memory' simply refers to a state of stimulus registration defined by the temporal contiguity of the salient event (UCS) with the immediately preceding event (CS). The CS-UCS temporal window ensures that the contents of the comparator will contain both stimuli, and we proposed that these are stored as a stimulus (CS/UCS) complex in which the separate stimulus events are undifferentiated.

The proposal has several attractive features relevant to the present discussion. It allows the CS to act as a weak UCS when it is subsequently presented since its presentation activates the whole of the CS/UCS complex. This in turn offers a mechanism for the genesis of the first overt CR. It also provides a matrix against which the elements of a CR/UCR complex can be integrated to produce optimum response efficiency through its topographic development.

According to this view, the external separateness of the two events is not established initially and the resulting stimulus model is integrated in a holistic fashion. The sense in which we intend this term and the reasons for using it have already been described. Although verbally the human subject can identify and label the CS and UCS, the stimuli are represented within a neuronal model as a unit with no separate identity. We suppose that the CS/UCS complex contains the salient stimulus characteristics of all other stimuli which are 'captured' within the temporal window of immediate memory.

The original formulation also defined a CR/UCR response complex and proposed that its topographical development over trials is gradually matched to the characteristics of the neuronal stimulus model. The representation of the stimulus complex was regarded as interacting with the representation of the response complex. This viewpoint, proposed on the basis of detailed quantitative analysis of CR/UCR response characteristics in human eyelid conditioning, has been illuminated by research on the rabbit nictitating membrane (Thompson, 1976) demonstrating that models of the overt response are evident in hippocampal neurones. It may be that both stimulus and response characteristics are closely integrated within a single, complex representational model in this particular response system. For present purposes, however, we want to consider stimulus analysis separately from subsequent responding and response strategies, and have argued this case in detail in discussions of evaluative conditioning (Levey and Martin, 1983).

Such a separation is fairly typical in contemporary thinking, in which declarative learning, i.e. learning to know, is differentiated from procedural knowledge, i.e. knowing what to do. It is probable that more complex theoretical formulations are required to account for how knowledge is translated into behaviour, and the present discussion will be confined to the acquisition of knowledge about event relationships. The focus is on the input side, and we consider what stimulus elements are processed and stored when a significant event occurs.

The original model simply stated that when a salient event sequence occurs, the shared characteristics of the stimuli are stored. The evaluative conditioning experiments have subsequently sought to analyse the definition of 'salience' and to examine the problem of what is stored.

In the context of evaluative conditioning, we have argued that visual materials which are strongly liked or disliked will serve as salient stimuli, and that the stimulus characteristics which lead to a subject's like or dislike of the pictures will transfer to similar materials towards which the subject's attitude was previously neutral. This implies that salience can be defined for classical conditioning in general terms of like/dislike. Opponents of this view could argue that salience can refer to other dimensions of meaning, such as size, power, or activity. Salience might also be defined by a number of ethologically significant stimulus dimensions of which evaluation is only one; possible candidates might include stimuli which evoke disgust, fear, sexual arousal, etc. It would then follow that the exact contents of the CS/UCS complex could be determined by the specific dimension which precipitated the recognition of salience, e.g. if a salience flag is triggered by a sexual stimulus then the CS/UCS complex would store only the sexually relevant stimulus components and their characteristics.

The previous discussion of our analysis of the Osgood dimensions strongly implies the answer to this argument. The dimensions postulated by Osgood were identified in the framework of factor analysis and have been repeatedly confirmed. The advantage of using this framework is that the resulting dimensions are supraordinate to the more specific aspects of fear-evoking or attack-evoking triggers: they are themselves derived from a range of qualities which include the fearful, the disgusting, the annoying. In addition, the three dimensions—of evaluation, potency, and activity—are orthogonal, so that each can be considered independently of the others, as well as interactively. When this is done it is found that only the evaluative dimension is relevant to conditioning. Whether this implies that information storage is limited to the subset of evaluated stimulus elements is a more difficult question.

It becomes apparent that whereas we initially stressed the 'unmediated' and 'non-cognitive' aspects of evaluations and their conditioning, we are now discussing the model within an information processing perspective. The reasons for the earlier emphasis have been outlined above. We next consider some of the implications of this perspective.

4.3 An evaluative conditioning model

A more analytic evaluative conditioning model is outlined in Figure 3.1. It starts by considering two questions: What is stored? What does salient mean? The figure shows that a number of answers are possible, and their combinations give rise to quite different substantive models with differing properties. We had supposed originally that all components of stimuli are stored in the CS/UCS complex, but in more recent research we have examined the possibility that only stimuli which are evaluated lead to registration and storage and hence to conditioning. Inspection of the analytic model shows, however, that if conditioning occurs as a result of the elicitation of an evaluative response no

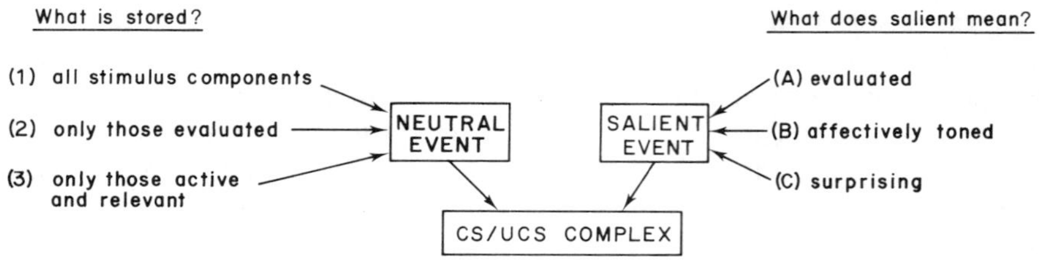

Figure 3.1

necessary constraints are imposed on the storage process. The decision as to which is the definitive model must be referred to experimental evidence. The phenomenon of sensory preconditioning, for example, suggests that storage probably includes all stimulus components rather than the subset which has been the basis of evaluation. This was the position which seemed to serve best the evidence of response topography in our eyelid conditioning studies and it represents the 'holistic' notion which we advocate.

This approach brings our theorizing more in line with contemporary cognitive views, although our emphasis is on primitive processes of evaluation. It is probable that stimulus registration and selection are more refined in complex nervous systems, such that the subsets of relevant stimuli and their characteristics are analysed in greater detail. An immediate primitive CS/UCS complex may be laid down initially, while later cognitive analysis selectively processes those elements which are used in subsequent phases of learning.

Our evaluative conditioning model, with its emphasis on instantaneous evaluative processes, carries with it the implication that conditioning is accomplished rapidly, possibly within a single or very few trials. Conditioning, viewed in this way, is unmediated in the sense that only minimal processing of stimuli need take place, and it seems to involve a holistic type of representation. Evidence suggests that when stimuli are traumatic conditioning is very difficult to extinguish, and it has been argued that instead of extinction, a process of incubation can take place whereby the CS, though unreinforced, produces an increment in conditioned responding which persists over very many trials. Eysenck (1968) has used this phenomenon to account for the growth and maintenance of neurotic fears.

Not all learning is as immediate as one-trial conditioning. Our position, with its emphasis on the early phase of conditioning, acknowledges that some other learning mechanism is required to explain the changes which take place in stimulus processing and in response development over a repeated series of exposures either in the laboratory or real life. We consider this to be an essentially cognitive mechanism, and that conditioning (in the restricted sense in which we use the term) has been accomplished once the shift in evaluation has taken place.

What happens on repetition of event sequences is considered in the next section.

5 Learning about recurring events

Learning about long-term sequences involves cognitive processing of a much more complex order than that postulated in the evaluative conditioning model. We have discussed elsewhere how regular and recurring event sequences are detected and summarized, and how they might develop into the schemata, hypotheses, and scripts which interest cognitive psychologists (Levey and Martin, 1983; Martin and Levey, 1985a). We regard this form of learning as much more general than the conditioning situation.

The term 'sequence' can refer broadly to any summary of order, whether temporal or spatial. Spatial sequences in the form of cognitive or actual maps summarize what will happen next in the sense of telling us what is round the next corner or over the next hill. The same reasoning can be applied to hierarchies, to systems of classification, to social rituals, for example. Civilized rituals invariably follow fixed sequences: weddings, funerals, dinner parties, games, all illustrate elaborate rules of sequence which are learned by members of the group who are quick to detect deviations from the rule. They enable the individual to code information about the order of events in the world for subsequent use. They give rise to expectancies and predictions.

Such information forms the basis on which the individual can develop plans and actions. This is the familiar distinction between knowing and doing, between the structuring of the external world and the processes which lead to action.

Language is intimately involved with the process of summarizing, and in a single 'trial' can provide the individual with a 'rule' predicting events in the environment. In human laboratory experiments this has generated an interesting body of research which examines the relationship between verbally formulated rules (e.g. instructions about event sequences) and the individual's observed responding. It is this issue we consider next.

To recapitulate, the evaluative conditioning model refers to an immediate type of learning in which the evaluative valence of the CS is altered. Another type of learning accounts for ways in which individuals organize and structure what happens over long-term event sequences. The evaluation and the learning of summaries and expectancies are postulated as separate determinants of behaviour, for a variety of reasons. We have suggested that they refer to different learning mechanisms, and that they may be separately implicated in behaviour therapy, where they are referred to broadly in terms of deconditioning and cognitive techniques.

In practice, the two will most likely be interrelated and contribute interactively to behaviour. We can suppose that in certain significant situations a single event which is positively or negatively evaluated will lead to immediate approach/avoidance behaviour. However, evaluations and actions become increasingly uncoupled in more complex situations. Similarly, the evaluations which individuals make of specific events must affect the cognitive summaries derived from these events when they recur over time. When people learn about the relationship between event sequences, this more cognitive learning will inevitably be influenced and possibly biased by the positive and negative evaluations attaching to the events, giving rise to familiar distortion effects.

In the typical conditioning situation, a noxious UCS will initiate a train of responses—not only the negative evaluations but, in the case of 'hard-wired' responses, an observable UCR. Upon repetition of the CS/UCS pair, learning of contingencies and the pattern of reinforcement is likely to take place, but information on reinforcement expectancy should not affect the evaluation of the CS though it could inhibit the overt conditioned response.

In the series of experiments to be described in this section we are interested in the competition between evaluative and cognitive effects on performance. The paradigm employed is that of classical eyelid conditioning, using a corneal airpuff UCS. At some level, the individual presumably evaluates the UCS negatively, and, given that this is a simple reflex system, the eyelid response is a reliable outcome. At another level, the individual learns about the sequence of reinforcement, which trials will and which will not be reinforced.

We can therefore ask: If a set of experimental instructions provides subjects with the rules which enable them to predict the reinforcement pattern in acquisition, will overt behaviour be controlled or governed by this knowledge or by the evaluative component of the UCR? We have carried out a series of experiments considering the relationships between knowledge which subjects can verbalize concerning the pattern (rules) or sequence within the acquisition schedule, and subjects' use of this information in conditioning performance. The question is whether expectancy, manipulated in a conditioning series from trial to trial by the use of summary rules, transfers to performance. In this way it is possible to observe the influence of verbally codified knowledge (rules) on a relatively simple behaviour, that is to say, in the presence or absence of CRs.

The present eyelid conditioning experiments manipulated the degree of subjects' knowledge of the rules governing CS-UCS pairings by means of pre-experimental instructions. We were interested in the extent to which subjects' knowledge of this pattern determines the occurrence or non-occurrence of CRs on reinforced (R) and unreinforced (U) trials. Each experiment employed three groups who received differing levels of information about the stimulus schedule, one being given full information, one being asked to attend to and guess the schedule, and one being given no information (Martin and Levey, in press).

The first experiment employed a simple schedule involving a repeated pattern of RRU, RRU, RRU trials. The schedule of the second experiment was more complex, and followed a rule which could be stated in two propositions: (a) two consecutive trials with CS and UCS are always followed by a trial with CS alone, and (b) a trial with CS alone is always followed by a trial with both CS and UCS.

Results showed that receiving instructions about the pattern of reinforcement in either a simple or a complex schedule does not enable subjects to control their responding accordingly. No significant differences were obtained between responding to reinforced and unreinforced trials within the groups. CR frequency and amplitude are only marginally less on U than on R trials, suggesting that information gained on the reinforced trials is transferred to the unreinforced trials.

Interestingly, results similar to these have been reported before, by Grant and his colleagues. An early experiment examined single and double alternation schedules and found that ability to describe the schedule was unrelated to response patterns (Grant *et al.*, 1950). Subsequently, it was shown that subjects could learn to respond differentially to reinforced trials provided that they had some periodic feedback (Hartman and Grant, 1960, 1962; Hickok and Grant, 1964). Individual differences were noted in that some people appeared unable or unwilling to use the information available.

Prokasy *et al.* (1967) made a similar point in a study designed to examine the effect of partial reinforcement on trial-by-trial increments of associative strength, in order to test his linear operator model. The ability to report the reinforcement pattern was not significantly related to differential performance. The authors noted other features of this aspect of learning: (a) there are marked individual differences in the tendency to use information; (b) to do so the information must be gained or 'earned' by a period of exposure to the stimulus sequence; (c) elements of feedback are important for subjects to be able to utilize stimulus information. Intervention on a periodic or trial-by-trial basis can also facilitate the use of information, although this procedure has rarely been carried out in eyelid conditioning, Baer and Fuhrer (1982) being one of the exceptions. These authors are among the few who have demonstrated a relationship between conditioning performance and contingency awareness although their study again raises the methodological problems of reliance on verbal report as an index of what the subject knows. The significance of these conditioning studies is that they confirm the overriding primacy of a simple emergency mechanism dealing with salient stimuli.

5.1 Cognitive processing

At this point we can summarize our position on learning about recurring events and examine it in relation to cognitive processing.

We have argued that the simplest, most fundamental learning about an event sequence can be accomplished by a single CS-UCS pairing. On the basis, originally, of eyelid conditioning research, subsequently refined in evaluative conditioning studies we opted for a model of conditioning which states that when a salient event (UCS) is first encountered the stimulus characteristics of CS and UCS are laid down in a stimulus complex which fails to discriminate, at least initially, between the stimuli as separate CSs and UCSs. Thus the model was described as holistic and non-associative in the sense defined earlier.

Subsequently, evaluative conditioning studies were carried out which demonstrated that the liking or disliking of a UCS could be transferred to the CS. Evaluative conditioning studies were then designed to consider the nature of the CS/UCS complex, in particular to analyse what features of the stimuli are salient and what role they play in the mechanisms of conditioning. We suggested an interpretation of 'salient' in terms of positively or negatively evaluated stimuli, meaning that when the individual encounters a salient event it is the evaluated characteristics of that stimulus which are transferred from UCS to CS. Alternatively, the stimulus is salient only if it elicits an evaluative response, and this results in storage of all stimulus features, rather than only the evaluated subset. Experiments to date have shown that other dimensions of stimulus appraisal, e.g. activity, do not lead to stimulus salience in either of these senses.

The immediate learning of an event pair and the analysis of those features of the CS and UCS which are salient and which are stored involve automatic mechanisms of a more primitive sort than the parsing and decision making which are usually thought of as cognitive processing. Like Zajonc, we believe that an emergency strategy is available to deal with stimuli requiring immediate action. However, in the context of learning what will come next other forms of processing are obviously available.

Discussing human classical conditioning within a behaviour therapy context, at a time when conditioning and cognitive approaches were believed to be in direct opposition to each other, led us to describe the conditioning of a salient event pair as non-cognitive, as has been discussed, and to apply the label 'cognitive' to a type of learning which considered how people register long-term event sequences and make synopses and summaries of their life experience. We suggested a weak explanation in terms of a cognitive structure which retains the order of the sequence but which can also immediately 'unpack' all the information contained in the structure. We are thus sympathetic to unitized assembly type models (Hayes-Roth, 1977) which illustrate a logical structure such that a single discrete memory can activate the larger information structure of which it is a component; to holographic models, as a physical instance of redintegration in which a cue can reinstate the total image and to distributed memory models of the type discussed by

Murdock (1985) in which two items are fused or blended such that there is no 'link' or 'connection' at all.

In both the human conditioning literature and in the behaviour therapy literature there has been a long debate which contrasts and opposes the 'conditioning' versus the 'cognitive' approaches (see the summary in Levey and Martin, 1983). The traditional hypothesis that the CS will elicit the CR in an 'unconscious, automatic' fashion has been contrasted with the 'radical' position that in the standard human paradigm subjects are developing conscious hypotheses and expectations about the experiment and that these produce the resultant conditioning. The cognitive-awareness hypothesis states that an individual can only be conditioned if he is aware of the CS, the UCS, and the relationship between them. The most widely quoted source is Brewer's (1974) paper, provocatively titled 'there is no convincing evidence for operant or classical conditioning in adult humans'. The argument offered in his paper is that conditioning in human subjects is produced entirely through the operation of higher mental processes.

Such a view misrepresents the evidence. Even in the autonomic conditioning literature, where correlations between level of autonomic responding and degree of awareness have been reported, there are many unresolved issues about the interpretation of such correlations (see, for example, Dulany, 1974). It has also been shown that there is a substantial dissociation between awareness and autonomic responding when awareness is measured on the basis of trial-by-trial expectancy (Furedy, 1980; Furedy *et al.*, 1983). In the human classical eyelid paradigm there is little evidence that cognitive factors are primary determinants of responding (Grant, 1973). Careful examination of alternative forms of awareness—i.e. knowledge of the experimenter's expectations (demand awareness), knowledge of stimulus relations (contingency awareness), or knowledge by the subject of his/her own responses (response awareness)—has failed to relate performance to knowledge in our eyelid conditioning research (Frcka *et al.*, 1983). Post-experimental questionnaires and interviews obtained from subjects in all the evaluative conditioning experiments (which have mainly been conducted on volunteer samples from the general public who are unfamiliar with conditioning concepts) show that awareness of demand characteristics and CS-UCS contingencies occurs rarely and does not relate to conditioning performance.

One thing seems reasonably clear. The thesis in human classical conditioning that 'awareness' determines conditioned responding has diverted human conditioning theory from a proper integration with animal conditioning theory. It has also confused the issue of human conditioning in behaviour therapy by overemphasizing the role of conscious thinking and subjects' verbalization in conditioning. They are probably minor rather than major determinants. The model we have proposed does not include reference to subjects' conscious description of events—indeed, rather the opposite:

whereas introspection may lead one to label 'a CS' and 'a UCS' we have opted for integration of the two events within the representation.

Recent research in autonomic conditioning has studied in more detail the role of subjects' knowledge about stimulus relationships and CS-UCS contingencies, and has adopted a more thoughtful analytic approach than earlier, more exaggerated claims. Thus, this particular issue is falling into its proper perspective.

This discussion indicates the increasingly complex interaction which is developing between the cognitive perspective and conditioning, and how far it has extended beyond the 'awareness' issue. Contemporary cognitive approaches in conditioning theory consider the nature of stimulus processing and storage, and how stimuli and stimulus sequences form representational models of the world. As indicated at the outset of this chapter, representational models of different kinds have been suggested by Anohkin, Konorski, and Sokolov, and they are widely discussed in the contemporary literature. Indeed, when contemporary theorists say that the organism learns about relationships between events in the environment, that assertion is elliptical for the more precise statement that it associates the internal representation of these events (Dickinson, 1980; Mackintosh and Dickinson, 1979; Rescorla, 1980).

6 What comes next?

As human conditioners, we face a most interesting set of paradigmatic and theoretical options. Much of the work on human conditioning in the past has been motivated by the study of individual differences, e.g. in anxiety or cortical arousal. It is to be hoped that this work will be continued and extended, e.g. to mood states, and that the theoretical issues underlying these studies will not be neglected. However, this emphasis has led to a neglect of more paradigmatic aspects of conditioning, such as the well-known blocking experiment with its equally interesting theoretical implications. In this area a working basis is provided by the well-developed framework of contemporary animal conditioning theory with its tightly argued experimental directives, and it is our feeling that animal and human conditioning should not continue to follow divergent paths.

The practical applications of conditioning techniques, which showed considerable promise in the early days of behaviour therapy, have recently been neglected. There are questions raised by behaviour therapists which need to be answered. These stem from their uncertain relationship on the one hand with conditioning theory, perceived as mechanistic, and on the other hand with a type of cognitive approach which emphasizes the subjective, conscious determinants of responding, the role of ideas, thoughts, and strategies. We have attempted to suggest that these two approaches can be integrated in a single framework which is biological in the sense that it recognizes the adaptive function of the learning mechanisms, both cognitive and conditioned, which use the rules of the environment to anticipate what will happen next and to deal with it appropriately.

Most significantly, there is the development in contemporary cognitive theory of a new generation of mathematical models which appear to be capable of dealing with a wide variety of conditioning phenomena. In discussing issues from any of these areas one is immediately faced with differing uses of the common stock of terms such as 'association', 'conditioning', 'cognition' which are difficult to define and quite evidently are shifting in meaning. This makes it no easy task to determine whether the available options represent distinctive positions, or whether they integrate approaches which once would have seemed incompatible.

The term 'association' has a central role in most contemporary theories of learning and memory, but its various meanings indicate a quite marked shift in emphasis from earlier eras. In conditioning history the term referred to linear and serial processes, to a sequence of discrete stimulus–response steps wherein one item is the stimulus for the next as a response, and so on. Associations were posited between the adjacent members of a sequence of items in a chain and these hypothetical bonds between S-R elements were strengthened with repetition of reinforcement. This kind of thinking motivated a decade or more of conditioning research and gave rise to the major controversies of the 1940s and 1950s, e.g. place vs. response learning, continuity vs. discontinuity. The unit of this classical S-R theory was the reflex arc, and the theorizing which stemmed from this model eventually fell from grace. Its important contribution, however, was to establish firmly the notion of excitation or activation of target units thus opening the possibility of quantitative, as distinct from intuitive, descriptions of behaviour.

The linear models of learning which dominated S-R theorizing exemplified this in the concept of 'growth' of a unitary associative strength, usually by the additive combination of a set of operations whose selection determined the characteristics of the particular theory (e.g. Prokasy *et al*., 1967). Models of this sort were unable to deal with interactive aspects of responding which tended to be attributed to innumerate mechanisms such as 'templates' or 'neuronal models' or to vaguely specified processes such as the descriptive notion of redintegration which we invoked to account for interactive aspects of the phenomena of response shaping (Martin and Levey, 1969).

During a similar period of time, cognitive psychologists were concerned with a parallel set of problems arising from the concept of association in verbal learning and memory. Although it had long been acknowledged that memory is organized in chunks, is structured, and is not a passive record of a chain of experience, the field of verbal learning and memory was dominated by a serial form of associationism. Bahrick (1985), in a discussion of the

Ebbinghause legacy and associationism outlines the break with traditional associationist views which occurred in the 1950s with the work of Chomsky in language and with cyberneticists' specification of information retrieval systems, leading to contemporary cognitive psychology's emphasis on interpretative and constructive factors in memory.

One of the principal achievements of contemporary cognitive theory has been to override many of the distinctions between these older patterns of theory construction, together with the antagonisms they engendered. A new family of mathematical models, derived from studies of memory and motor skills, is being developed which allow for distributed processing in complex associative systems. These models all have in common the idea that the association between two items is the fusing or blending of two items. There is no link or connection between them; instead two separate items are combined to form a larger unit that has no necessary resemblances to either item alone (Murdock, 1985). They thus bear little resemblance to the S-R bond familiar for so long to conditioning theorists. They are able to integrate the differing perspectives of organismic (*Gestalt*) field theory, 'purposive' behaviour and nomothetic (Hull–Spence linear chaining) positions and they obviate the distinction between parallel and sequential processing by being able to function in either mode. These models allow for selective retrieval of information by criteria of relevance in memory systems (Murdock, 1983, 1985; Pike, 1984), for selective recognition in perceptual systems (McClelland and Rumelhart, 1981), and they can potentially encompass concepts such as intention (Norman, 1981). In short, they are highly relevant to the analysis of human conditioning, especially in its dynamic aspects.

In addition to these dynamic, interactive characteristics, such models exhibit generalization, can handle degraded information input, and most importantly they can learn these functions without an explicit external program. Applied specifically to classical conditioning (e.g. Sutton and Barto, 1981) they have been shown to model effects of context (blocking, overshadowing, etc.) and to include the most important and adaptive aspect of CR behaviour, namely the anticipation of the UCR. In the light of these developments the notion of a holistic CS/UCS complex can be regarded as shorthand for an interactive processing system whose characteristics we have earlier attempted to specify.

Does this mean a genuine paradigm shift towards new information processing models which can comfortably accommodate conditioning phenomena? More importantly, is there a set of distinctive conditioning phenomena requiring to be accommodated within the new paradigms? We hope to have shown that there is. We have presented the view that conditioning in humans is an essential part of adaptive behaviour, based on immediate anticipation of what is beneficial or harmful, what is liked or disliked in the environment. We believe that this type of information processing occurs largely outside of awareness and that it contributes significantly to human development. It seems very likely that a new paradigm of human behaviour is indeed developing within cognitive psychology. Human conditioning will now need to be studied within the framework of a much wider investigation of all the mechanisms by which the rules of the environment are recognized and acted upon.

Acknowledgements

The research described in this chapter was supported by a Maudsley-Bethlem Joint Hospitals Research Grant. The authors wish to acknowledge the contribution of Irene Daum and Maja Turcan-Parfitt to the execution of the research, and to L. Law for technical assistance.

References

Anohkin, P. (1974). *Biology and Neurophysiology of the Conditioned Reflex and its Role in Adaptive Behaviour*. Pergamon Press, Oxford.

Baer, P. E., and Fuhrer, M. J. (1982). Cognitive factors in the concurrent differential conditioning of eyelid and skin conductance responses. *Memory and Cognition*, **10**, 135–40.

Bahrick, H. P. (1985). Associationism and the Ebbinghaus legacy. *Journal of Experimental Psychology: Learning, Memory and Cognition*, **11**, 439–43.

Brewer, W. F. (1974). There is no convincing evidence for operant or classical conditioning in adult humans. In: W. Weimer and D. Palermo (eds.), *Cognition and the Symbolic Processes*. Lawrence Erlbaum, Hillsdale, N.J.

Costall, A. P. (1984). Are theories of perception necessary? A review of Gibson's The Ecological Approach to Visual Perception. *Journal of the Experimental Analysis of Behaviour*, **41**, 109–15.

Dickinson, A. (1980). *Contemporary Animal Learning Theory*. Cambridge University Press, Cambridge.

Dulany, D. E. (1974). On the support of cognitive theory in opposition to behaviour theory: A methodological problem. In W. Weimer and D. Palermo (eds.), *Cognition and the Symbolic Processes*. Lawrence Erlbaum, Hillsdale, N.J.

Eysenck, H. J. (1968). A theory of the incubation of anxiety/fear responses. *Behaviour Research and Therapy*, **6**, 309–21.

Frcka, G., Beyts, J., Levey, A. B., and Martin I. (1983). The role of awareness in human conditioning. *Pavlovian Journal of Biological Science*, **18**, 69–76.

Furedy, J. (1980). Cognitive and response processes in psychophysiology: Definitions and illustrations from Pavlovian conditioning. In: *Cognitive Psychophysiology: Approaches, Problems and Definitions*. Symposium conducted at the meeting of the Society for Psychophysiological Research, Vancouver.

Furedy, J. J., Riley, D. M., and Fredrikson, M. (1983). Pavlovian extinction, phobias, and the limits of the cognitive paradigm. *Pavlovian Journal of Biological Science*, **18**, 126–35.

Garcia, J., Rusiniak, K. W., and Brett, L. P. (1977). Conditioning food-illness aversions in wild animals: Caveant Canonici. In: Davis, H., and Hurwitz, H. M. B. (eds.), *Operant-Pavlovian Interactions*. Lawrence Erlbaum, Hillsdale, N.J.

Gibson, J. J. (1966). *The Senses Considered as Perceptual Systems*. Houghton Mifflin, Boston.

Grant, D. A. (1973). Cognitive factors in eyelid conditioning. *Psychophysiology*, **10**, 75–81.

Grant, D. A., Riopelle, A. J., and Hake, H. W. (1950). Resistance to extinction and the pattern of reinforcement. 1. Alternation of reinforcement and the conditioned eyelid response. *Journal of Experimental Psychology*, **40**, 53–60.

Hartman, T. F., and Grant, D. A. (1960). Effect of intermittent reinforcement on acquisition, extinction and spontaneous recovery of the conditioned eyelid response. *Journal of Experimental Psychology*, **60**, 89–96.

Hartman, T. F., and Grant, D. A. (1962). Effects of pattern of reinforcement and verbal information on acquisition, extinction and spontaneous recovery of the eyelid CR. *Journal of Experimental Psychology*, **63**, 217–26.

Hayes-Roth, B. (1977). Evolution of cognitive structures and processes. *Psychological Review*, **3**, 260–78.

Hickok, C. W., and Grant, D. A. (1964). Effects of pattern of reinforcement and verbal information on acquisition and extinction of the eyelid CR. *Journal of General Psychology*, **71**, 279–89.

Levey, A. B., and Martin, I. (1968). Shape of the conditioned eyelid response. *Psychological Review*, **75**, 398–408.

Levey, A. B., and Martin, I. (1974). Sequence of response development in human eyelid conditioning. *Journal of Experimental Psychology*, **102**, 678–86.

Levey, A. B., and Martin, I. (1975). Classical conditioning of human 'evaluative' responses. *Behaviour Research and Therapy*, **13**, 221–6.

Levey, A. B., and Martin, I. (1983). Cognitions, evaluations and conditioning. Rules of sequence and rules of consequence. *Advances in Behaviour Research and Therapy*, **4**, 181–223.

McClelland, J. L., and Rumelhart, D. E. (1981). An interactive activation model of the effect of context in perception. Part I. An account of basic findings. *Psychological Review*, **88**, 375–407.

Mackintosh, N. J., and Dickinson, A. (1979). Instrumental (Type II) conditioning. In: A. Dickinson and R. A. Boakes (eds.), *Mechanisms of Learning and Motivation*, pp. 143–69. Lawrence Erlbaum, Hillsdale, N.J.

Marcel, A. J. (1983). Conscious and unconscious perception: Experiments on visual masking and word recognition. *Cognitive Psychology*, **15**, 197–237.

Martin, I., and Levey, A. B. (1969). *Genesis of the Classical Conditioned Response*. Pergamon Press, Oxford.

Martin, I., and Levey, A. B. (1978). Evaluative conditioning. *Advances in Behaviour Research and Therapy*, **1**, 57–101.

Martin, I., and Levey, A. B. (1985a). Conditioning, evaluations and cognitions: an axis of integration. *Behaviour Research and Therapy*, **23**, 167–75.

Martin, I., and Levey, A. B. (1985b). Behaviour therapy needs good behaviour theory. *Cognitive Behaviourist*, **7**, 13–15.

Martin, I. and Levey, A. B. (in press). Knowledge action and control. In: H. J. Eysenck and I. Martin (eds.) *Theoretical Foundations of Behaviour Therapy*. New York: Plenum.

Murdock, B. M., Jr (1983). A distributed memory model for serial-order information. *Psychological Review*, **90**, 316–38.

Murdock, B. M., Jr (1985). The contributions of Hermann Ebbinghaus. *Journal of Experimental Psychology: Learning, Memory and Cognition*, **11**, 469–71.

Neisser, U. (1976). *Cognition and Reality*. San Francisco, Freeman.

Norman, D. (1981). Categorisation of action slips. *Psychological Review*, **88**, 1–15.
Osgood, C. E. (1969). On the whys and wherefores of E, P and A. *Journal of Personality and Social Psychology*, **12**, 194–9.
Pike, R. (1984). Comparison of convolution and matrix distributed memory systems for associative recall and recognition. *Psychological Review*, **91**, 281–94.
Prokasy, W. F., Carlton, R. A., and Higgins, J. D. (1967). Effects of nonrandom intermittent reinforcement schedules in human eyelid conditioning. *Journal of Experimental Psychology*, **74**, 282–8.
Rescorla, R. A. (1980). Pavlovian second-order conditioning. *Studies in Associative Learning*. Lawrence Erlbaum, Hillsdale, N.J.
Sampson, E. E. (1981). Cognitive psychology as ideology. *American Psychologist*, **36**, 730–43.
Sutton, R. S., and Barto, A. G. (1981). Toward a modern theory of adaptive networks: Expectation and prediction. *Psychological Review*, **88**, 135–70.
Thompson, R. F. (1976). The search for the engram. *American Psychologist*, **31**, 201–27.
Zajonc, R. B. (1980). Feeling and thinking. Preferences need no inferences. *American Psychologist*, **35**, 151–75.

Cognitive Processes and Pavlovian Conditioning in Humans
Edited by G. Davey

Chapter 4

An integration of human and animal models of Pavlovian conditioning: Associations, cognitions, and attributions

Graham C. L. Davey
The City University, London

In the course of studying non-human animal learning there has been little disagreement between workers on the broad approach required to understand the mechanisms which underlie simple conditioning. In general, theorists have agreed that animal conditioning can best be comprehended by studying those factors which contribute to *learning* on the one hand, and those which contribute to *performance* on the other. An understanding of the mechanisms which contribute to learning include asking such questions as (a) What associations are learned? (b) What factors affect the rate of formation and the subsequent strength of these associations? and (c) What learned cognitive represenations of external events mediate the appearance of the conditioned response (CR)? However, a study of performance mechanisms involves asking questions about how what is learned is translated into the behaviour we observe in the conditioning situation: i.e. Pavlov's dog may have learnt that the metronome predicts iminent food delivery, but that, in and of itself, does not tell us why the dog salivates during the metronome.

Anyone reading the recent literature on animal learning will see that significant advances have been made over the last fifteen years in the understanding of the mechanisms which mediate associative learning. We now have fairly elaborate models for predicting the associative strength of conditioned stimuli (CSs) (e.g. Rescorla and Wagner, 1972; Mackintosh, 1974; Pearce and Hall, 1980); we have useful inferential techniques for discovering the kinds of associations learnt during conditioning (e.g. Holland and Rescorla, 1975; Rescorla, 1977); and these techniques also give us some knowledge of the cognitive representations that mediate conditioned responding (e.g. Rescorla, 1980; Dickinson, 1980).

As impressive as these recent advances may seem in the light of the rather barren theoretical years of the 1960s, few of them seem to have been either acknowledged or assimilated by those concerned with theoretical issues in human conditioning. The reasons for this apparent lack of cross-fertilization of ideas are not difficult to discover if one examines the rather unique factors that appear to operate in and influence human conditioning. On the face of it, much of the behaviour that is studied in human conditioning experiments appears to violate the laws and principles developed to explain conditioned responding in non-human animals. For instance, (a) rather than obeying the rules of incremental–decremental models of response strength, conditioned responding in humans can be spontaneously acquired or extinguished simply by informing the subject of changes in the CS-UCS relationship (e.g. Dawson and Grings, 1968; Katz *et al.*, 1971; McComb, 1969; Wilson, 1968; Colgan, 1970; Koenig and Castillo, 1969); (b) providing subjects with false information of the CS-UCS contingency will generate responding appropriate to the false information rather than the contingencies actually programmed and experienced by the subject (Deane, 1969; Epstein and Clarke, 1970; Spence and Goldstein, 1961); and (c) the laws of incremental–decremental models of CR strength also appear to be violated by the fact that conditioned responding only appears to be acquired under conditions where the subject is consciously aware of, and able to verbalize, the CS-UCS contingencies (e.g. Baer and Fuhrer, 1968, 1970; Dawson and Biferno, 1973; Biferno and Dawson, 1977; Fuhrer and Baer, 1980; Dawson, 1973; Grings and Dawson, 1973; Ross *et al.*, 1974; Dawson *et al.*, 1979).

If all of this evidence is selectively reviewed—which I do not intend to do in the short space provided here (but see Brewer, 1974; Davey, 1983)—then the factors which influence CR strength most significantly in human conditioning include the subject's ability to verbalize the contingencies involved, the verbal transmission of information about the learning situation to the subject (notably in the form of instructions), and the subject's subsequent interpretation of that information.

At first sight this is clearly difficult to integrate with contemporary models of non-human animal conditioning, since the responding of animals is largely influenced by the experienced CS-UCS relationship and not obviously influenced by either instructions or conscious awareness of contingencies. This discrepancy between human and animal conditioning fostered a number of relatively *ad hoc* models of human conditioning which had little in common heuristically with contemporary models of animal learning (e.g. 'the necessary-gate hypothesis'—Dawson and Furedy, 1976; 'dual process theories'—Baer and Fuhrer, 1973; Grings, 1965; Razran, 1971).

The aim of this chapter is to propose an approach to associative learning in humans which can assimilate theoretical knowledge acquired from animal conditioning and, most importantly, can encompass those facets of human conditioning which appear to be uniquely human. To understand how this might be attempted, it is first necessary to describe some of the basic procedures used in animal studies and their theoretical implications.

1 The study of associative conditioning in animals

If we take the example of Pavlov's prototypical salivating dog we might ask what the animal has learnt when it eventually salivates consistently during the metronome CS. There are at least two obvious possibilities: (a) it may have learnt that the metronome predicts food, and it is the internal representation or 'memory' of the food evoked by the metronome which induces salivation; or (b) it may simply have learnt a relatively mechanistic S-R reflex in which presentation of the metronome CS excites associations directly linked to the salivation reflex. In the latter case, cognitions or memories associated with the food UCS play no role in mediating the CR.

During the 1970s, Rescorla and his colleagues developed inferential techniques designed to distinguish between these possibilities (Holland and Rescorla, 1975; Rescorla, 1973, 1977, 1980; Colby and Smith 1977; Holland and Straub, 1979; Rizley and Rescorla, 1972; Cleland and Davey, 1982). These postconditioning revaluation techniques, as they have come to be known, attempt to discover if conditioned responding is mediated by cognitions related to the UCS by selectively changing the animal's evaluation of the UCS after conditioning has been completed. For instance, Holland and Rescorla (1975) investigated conditioned activity in rats using a food UCS. First, they paired a CS with a food UCS, and then, when conditioned activity to the CS had been established, they reduced the palatability of the food UCS by pairing it with illness (taste aversion learning). After this 'devaluation' of the food for the rat, subsequent presentations of the CS elicited reduced activity. Rescorla (1973, 1977, 1980) has interpreted these results as suggesting that first-order Pavlovian conditioned responding is mediated by the internal representation of the UCS developed by conditioning and hence conditioned responding can be manipulated by manipulating the animal's current evaluation of that UCS. In most cases, reducing the palatability of an appetitive UCS used to promote conditioning reduces conditioned responding to the CS, and in aversive conditioning, habituating the subject to an aversive electric shock UCS subsequently reduces the amplitude of the defensive CR to the previously conditioned CS (cf. Rescorla, 1980; Dickinson, 1980). The picture is somewhat different in second-order Pavlovian conditioning where there is some evidence of reflexive S-R associative learning which is not mediated by cognitive evaluation of the UCS (e.g. Rescorla, 1973; Holland and Rescorla, 1975; Rizley and Rescorla, 1972; cf. Davey, 1983).

Nevertheless, rather than attempt a comprehensive review of this literature, the foregoing discussion is designed to familiarize the reader with the inferential methods used to tease out the kinds of processes operating in simple Pavlovian conditioning procedures. What is interesting about these procedures from the point of view of this present chapter is that while postcondition revaluation techniques provide us with information about the kinds of associations learnt during Pavlovian conditioning, they also imply that the subject's evaluation of the cognitive event mediating the CR is important in determining the strength of that CR. That is, processes which act to cause the revaluation of the UCS can also dramatically influence CR strength, particularly when cognitions relating to that UCS are mediating conditioned responding. This is important from the point of view of human conditioning since conditioned responding in humans seems to be significantly influenced by the evaluation and revaluation of cognitions brought about through instructions. Much of the effect of instructions on conditioned responding in humans might be due to the same processes by which experimental UCS revaluations have their effect on CR strength in animal conditioning studies. That is, under conditions in which the CR is mediated by UCS cognitions, instructions represent a restructuring of knowledge either about the possible occurrence of the UCS (in terms of altering knowledge about contingency relations between the UCS and other stimuli) or about the nature or value of the UCS, and these cognitive changes exert an immediate effect on CR strength. With this in mind, it seems that in the case of human conditioning a useful approach might be to ask:

(a) What associations are formed during conditioning and, as a consequence, determine what cognitive representations (if any) will mediate the CR?
(b) What are the processes that can influence the evaluation of these cognitive representations, and as a result influence the CR?

The first question is similar to the one which has been asked consistently in animal learning theory over the past fifteen years, although it has not been significantly addressed in the case of human conditioning. The second question is one which has been relatively neglected in animal conditioning but would seem to be of utmost importance to those wishing to understand the processes determining CR strength in human subjects. If the majority of conditioned responding in humans turns out to be mediated by cognitions related to the UCS, then processes which might act to restructure the subject's knowledge of the UCS will also have an indirect but substantial effect on the CR.

2 Cognitions mediating the conditioned response in human conditioning

There has been a great deal of speculation in the past about the kinds of associations learnt by human subjects in Pavlovian conditioning situations, with only very little empirical support to justify that speculation. It is quite clear from the animal literature that subjects do not always learn associations which are isomorphic with the stimulus contingencies arranged by the experimenter (cf. Rescorla, 1980), and to suggest that human subjects would do so would appear to be highly speculative. Indeed, even a much cited model of human autonomic conditioning such as the the dual-level model (cf. Davey, 1983) assumes that, first, because the majority of laboratory based human conditioning is influenced by instructions and conscious awareness of contingencies, then it must represent relational or CS-UCS associative learning. Yet there is no independent evidence which identifies that these CS-UCS associations have been formed.

In a couple of early studies in our laboratory, we decided to adapt the postconditioning revaluation techniques used with animals in an attempt to identify the associative substructure mediating certain aspects of human autonomic conditioned responding (Davey and Arulampalam, 1981, 1982; Davey and McKenna, 1983). The paradigm used was a Pavlovian second-order electrodermal conditioning preparation. This was used largely because it had been found that animal studies suggested that second-order classical aversive conditioning generated S-R links between CS_2 and CR_1 (Rescorla, 1973, 1977, 1980; Rizley and Rescorla, 1972). That is, revaluation of both CS_1 and the original UCS had no effect on responding to CS_2. This raised the question of whether human second-order responding would display the same reflexive or 'non-cognitive' aspects as non-human animal second-order responding.

The study by Davey and McKenna (1983) had four procedural stages: (a) pairing of CS_1 (triangle) with UCS (115 dB loud noise), (b) pairing of CS_2 (outline figure) with CS_1 (triangle), (c) revaluation of either CS_1 or UCS, and (d) test presentation of CS_2 to discover if second-order conditioned responding had been retained. There were three types of postconditioning revaluation in stage (c): Group E experienced extinction of responding to CS_1, Group $\bar{T}$ received instructions informing them that there would be no more UCS presentations in the experiment, and Group H received a pseudo-habituation procedure in which they were led to believe that the loud tone UCS was becoming less aversive to them. Thus, Group E received a favourable revaluation of the stimulus (CS_1) used to reinforce second-order responding,

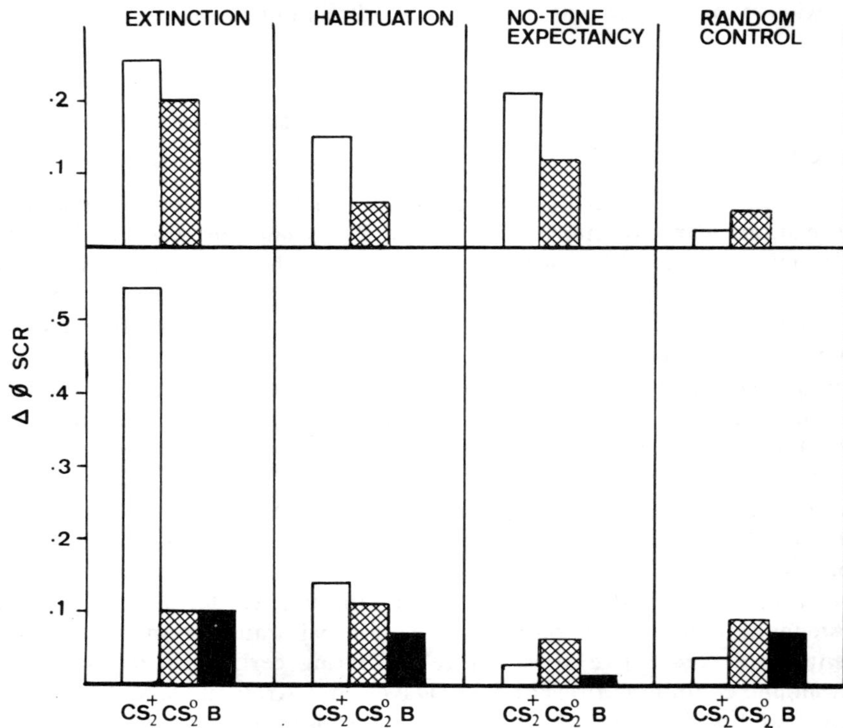

Figure 4.1 Mean ϕSCR values for CS_2^+ and CS_2^0 during second-order conditioning (top panel) and during the final test phase of the experiment. ($\Delta\phi$SCR = change in SCR (range corrected μmho).) (*From Davey and McKenna, 1983; reprinted by permission*)

and Groups $\bar{T}$ and H underwent restructuring of their cognitions related to the UCS—Group $\bar{T}$ through verbal instructions and Group H through experience with the tone UCS. The results (see Figure 4.1) indicated that the second-order CR_2 survived post-conditioning extinction of the response to CS_1 (Group E) ($p > 0.05$), but was abolished when the postconditioning habituation procedure resulted in a favourable revaluation of the tone UCS (Group H) or when subjects were given instructions informing them of no more UCS presentations (Group $\bar{T}$) ($ps < 0.05$). One of the clear implications of these findings is that the second-order CR_2 is being mediated by the subject's cognitions related to the UCS: restructuring knowledge about UCS cognitions using either experimental or instructional manipulations had the same effect. To interpret this rather loosely, while the subject was still fearful of the UCS and still expecting its possible occurrence, then the conditioned electrodermal response to CS_2 remained. The structural scenario for this is of the kind: (a) the CS_2, through direct or indirect associative links, evokes representations of the UCS; (b) the UCS is evaluated as fear producing; (c) this evaluation triggers defensive reactions such as electrodermal changes.

Clearly, this kind of approach can be extended by arguing that if conditioned responses are mediated by cognitive evaluations of the UCS, then any way in which the subjects' evaluation of the UCS can be manipulated will have an effect on the conditioned response. A study by Cracknell and Davey (1985) indicates one way in which this can be achieved. In this study, subjects were given false auditory feedback of their skin conductance levels (SCLs) for a 10 sec period following UCS presentation in a simple first-order electrodermal conditioning procedure. The false feedback given to some subjects indicated they were exhibiting a very strong UCR (Group Hi); the feedback given to other subjects indicated they were exhibiting little or no UCR (Group Lo) (in fact, there was no difference in actual UCR strength between groups). If responding to the CS is being mediated by the subject's evaluation of the UCS then subjects in Group Hi should exhibit a stronger CR than subjects in Group Lo. This is exactly what occurred (see Table 4.1). In fact, the nature of the false UCR feedback not only influenced CR magnitude during conditioning, it also influenced the subsequent rate of extinction of the CR—the CRs of subjects in Group Hi took significantly longer to extinguish than those in Group Lo (Figure 4.2). While it is commonly known that in both animal and human conditioning the intensity of the UCS increases both CR strength and trials to extinction (Annan and Kamin, 1961; Kamin and Brimer, 1963; Maltzman, Langdon, Pendery and Wolft, 1977; Öhman, Björkstrand and Ellström, 1973), the evidence from the Cracknell and Davey study suggests that these effects can be obtained in humans by manipulating *perceived* UCS intensity without affecting actual UCS intensity or UCR magnitude. The evidence here is again consistent with the conclusion that, in this kind of procedure at least, conditioned responding is mediated by UCS cognitions, and the subject's individual evaluation of those cognitions.

Table 4.1 Mean CR and UCR magnitude for all five groups over the six trials of conditioning (range-corrected micromho)

Group	Hi-I	Lo-I	Hi-$\bar{I}$	$\overline{Hi}$-I	$\overline{Lo}$-I
Mean CR magnitude (0SCR)	0.34	0.17	0.30	0.24	0.24
± SEM	0.04	0.02	0.03	0.02	0.02
Mean UCR magnitude (0SCR)	0.40	0.47	0.54	0.46	0.47
± SEM	0.04	0.05	0.04	0.04	0.04

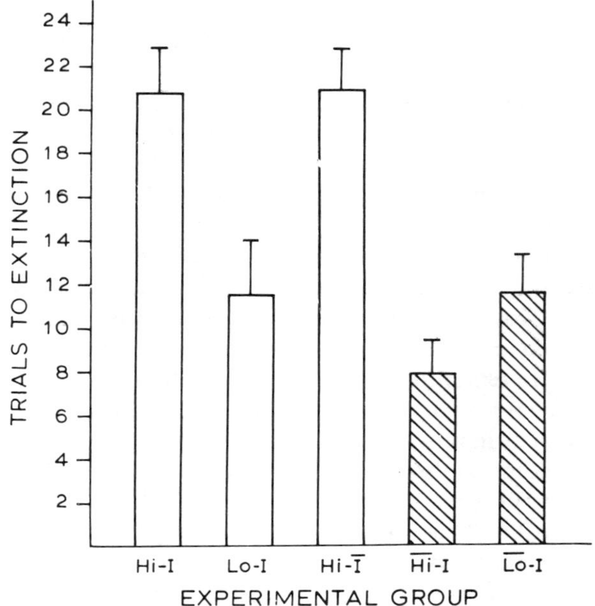

Figure 4.2 Mean number of trials to the extinction criterion. Hi = groups receiving false feedback indicating a high magnitude UCR, Lo = groups receiving false feedback indicating a low magnitude UCR. See text for further detail. (*From Cracknell and Davey, 1985*)

However, this raises the question of whether all Pavlovian responding in humans is mediated via UCS cognitions. This would seem to be unlikely for a number of reasons. First, and most obviously, just because we have not yet found any inferential evidence for S-R associations does not mean that they play no role in human conditioning. One thing is becoming increasingly clear from the animal literature: Pavlovian conditioning—especially of certain defensive reactions—may not be mediated by a single centralized associative system. Learning rapidly about threatening situations and reacting quickly to them would seem to be an attribute that evolutionary processes would select for, and may be mediated subcortically or peripherally by direct associative links with the reflex arc associated with the UCS (cf. Moore, 1979; Pavlov, 1927, pp. 36–8; Hawkins and Kandel, 1984). There is reason to suppose that non-cognitively mediated responding of this kind might be found in certain preparations with human subjects (the eyeblink CR might be one possible candidate—e.g. Frcka, Beyts, Levey and Martin, 1981). Secondly, it is clear from the animal literature that the kinds of associations formed during conditioning can be affected by the nature of the procedure used and the relative saliency of the events in the conditioning situation (cf. Nairne and Rescorla, 1981; Rashotte, Griffin, and Sisk, 1977; Davey 1983). Indeed, during the early stages of conditioning, instrumental responding in rats appears to be mediated by UCS representations, whereas, following extensive training, UCS revaluation appears to have less effect on responding (Adams, 1980; Adams and Dickinson, 1981; but see Colwill and Rescorla, 1985). That is, extended training transfers responding from the control of UCS representations to the control of more reflexive S-R 'habits' which are not controlled by UCS cognitions. Since most human conditioning studies involve single-session training it would seem that the transfer of responding from S-S to S-R control (if it exists in humans) could rarely be observed.

Finally, conditioning without awareness does appear to exist in some limited circumstances (Fuhrer and Baer, 1969; Wilson *et al.*, 1973; Staats and Staats, 1957; but see chapter 2, this volume), and this might lead one to suspect that there are certain procedures which might lend themselves to the generation of conditioned responding which is not mediated by conscious evaluation of the UCS (the prototypical 'conditioning of meaning' paradigm of Staats and Staats is one possibility, another is the adaptation of the subliminal perception paradigm into a conditioning procedure). Indeed, there is even evidence from the clinical sector that responding not mediated by UCS cognitions may exist. Many phobics are acutely aware of their fear reactions to their phobic stimulus or situation, yet they are also aware that information about the non-aversive consequences of that fear will not influence this reaction (Öhman, 1979b; Leitenberg, 1976; Marks, 1969). One of the possibilities that this implies is that if such phobic reactions were acquired through associative learning, it seems clear that these reactions are not primarily mediated by the cognitions related to any possible aversive consequences of the phobic stimulus, i.e. they are not UCS mediated.

3 Cognitions influencing non-associative factors in human conditioning

One of the important considerations when studying the effects of cognitions on human conditioning is not just whether the subjects can discriminate the occurrence of and contingency between CS and UCS, but also whether they can discriminate their own responses to the CS and UCS and how they interpret these reactions. Clearly the electrodermal response (EDR) paradigm is not a particularly good one to use in these circumstances, since the SCR is usually a weak reaction which is poorly discriminated by the individual. Since the Cracknell and Davey (1985) study cited earlier demonstrated that discrimination and interpretation of the UCR by the subject can affect conditioning, then it is quite reasonable to suppose that a subject's discrimination of and interpretation of their own CR will also affect conditioning. While the EDR paradigm is widely used in the study of human Pavlovian conditioning, the fact that SCRs are poorly discriminated suggests that cognitive processes which might influence response strength as a result of response discrimination would rarely be implicated in laboratory studies. This fact is also important when attempting to construct valid analogues of clinical phobias since many phobics are acutely aware of their fear reaction to the phobic stimulus and are also aware that this reaction is irrational and will not respond to information about the non-aversive consequences of their fear. In a series of experiments, we attempted to investigate the effects of increasing the discriminability of the SCR during conditioning and extinction procedures with a view to understanding how cognitions related to the CR might affect conditioning.

The simplest way to provide continuous SCR feedback is with a tone which varies in pitch with changes in skin conductance level (SCL). In two simple experiments[1] we investigated the effects of continuous SCR feedback on CR magnitude during acquisition and on response persistance during extinction. The first experiment suggested that the greater response discriminability provided by SCR feedback resulted in significantly higher levels of conditioned responding (see Figure 4.3) than when no feedback was provided. This superior response amplitude was not apparent at the outset of conditioning but developed with subsequent pairings of the CS and UCS.

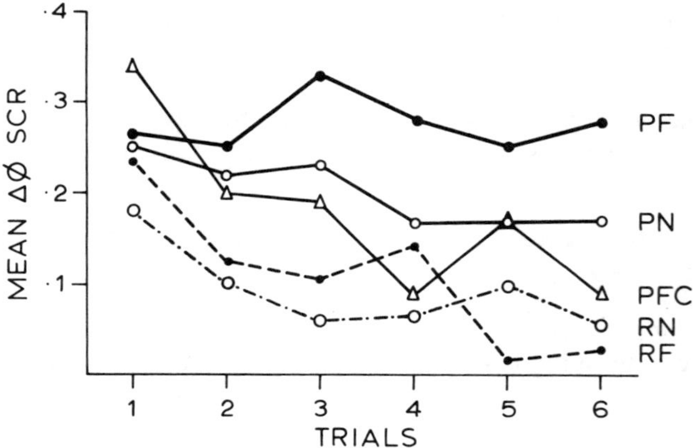

Figure 4.3 Mean CR strength (ΔϕSCR) for all five groups for each of the six acquisition trials. Solid lines represent paired groups and broken lines represent randomly paired control groups. Filled circles represent groups given SCR feedback, open circles represent groups given no SCR feedback

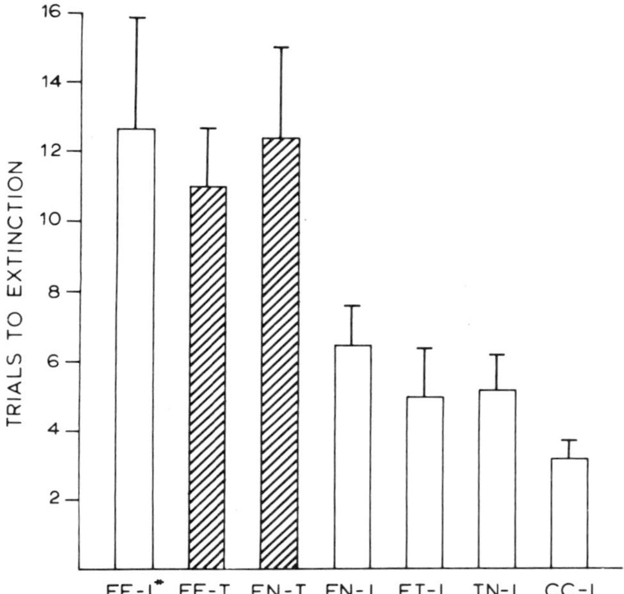

Figure 4.4 Mean (±SEM) of the number of trials to extinction. Hatched bars represent groups given *no* extinction instructions, open bars represent groups told that there would be no UCS presentation in extinction (instructed extinction groups). Groups prefixed FF received SCL feedback during both acquisition and extinction

Furthermore, this greater CR magnitude was not generated simply by feedback producing a greater reactivity to stimulus presentation in general, since groups which received CS and UCS unpaired (Groups RF and RN, Figure 4.3) did not differ in the level of CR at the end of training but were both significantly inferior to the paired feedback group (Group PF). Similarly, this greater response magnitude in Group PF was not simply a result of orienting responses being generated by the pitch changes produced by the feedback tone during CS presentations, since a group which received these pitch changes unrelated to SCL (Group PFC) showed significantly inferior CR levels to Group PF. The higher amplitude CR produced by SCL feedback during conditioning appears to reflect a joint effect of both conditioning and the subjects' interpretation of the SCL feedback.

Figure 4.4 shows the effects of response feedback during extinction. The most interesting result here is that the group which received SCL feedback during instructed extinction (i.e. they were forewarned of the extinction phase and that there were to be no more UCS presentations) took the same mean number of trials to extinguish as subjects who had not been forewarned of extinction. Under most standard conditions, instructed extinction results in the CR extinguishing rapidly and in many fewer trials than for non-instructed subjects (e.g. Colgan, 1970; Koenig and Castillo, 1969). However, in some studies a 'resistance to instructed extinction' has been observed, especially when a particularly noxious UCS has been used during conditioning (e.g. Bridger and Mandel, 1965; Mandel and Bridger, 1973). In the Bridger and Mandel (1965) study, residual responding was observed following instructed extinction when a 'very painful' UCS had been untilized during conditioning.

Clearly, a lot of implications derive from subjects being able to discriminate their own reactions to the stimuli presented in a conditioning procedure, most notably about how they interpret the occurrence and magnitude of their own responses. If subjects do observe themselves making what they consider to be defensive responses to an aversive CS then, amongst others, they might either interpret this as 'I am still frightened of that stimulus' or, more generally, as 'I am still frightened'. Either interpretation could affect the magnitude or persistance of the CR but for subtly different reasons. The former of the two interpretations provides an evaluation of the status of a specific stimulus, the CS. Just as we discussed evaluation of the UCS affecting CR strength via the CS-UCS association in the previous section of this chapter, it is reasonable to suppose that evaluation of, and cognitions relating to, the CS itself can directly influence CR strength. Observation of and interpretation of one's own reaction to a CS provides some evidence for evaluating that stimulus. However, the second interpretation, that 'I am still frightened', would seem to have a more general effect, producing greater response amplitude and persistance by maintaining autonomic arousal, reducing the threshold for defensive CRs and subsequently retarding the habituation of defensive CRs. This could be non-associative in nature and would lead to increased reaction to a wider range of stimuli than the CS itself.

While these interpretations are speculative they are also intuitively sensible and I will address them in more detail in the following section. However, one further experiment[2] we have conducted does shed some light on the way in which response discrimination might be having its response enhancing effects. In this experiment subjects received continuous auditory SCL feedback and were presented with a brief tone followed by fifteen unpaired presentations of a triangle which we have used as a CS in other studies. Two groups of subjects were told that the auditory feedback reflected their arousal levels and two were falsely told that it should be attended to but was merely background stimulation. For some subjects the brief tone which commenced the experiment was of 115 dB intensity (similar to that used as an aversive UCS in our conditioning experiments) and for others it was an innocuous 67 dB tone. Thus the subjects received a string of neutral stimulus presentations (the triangle) but differed according to whether the experiment commenced with an aversive or arousing event, or whether they interpreted the auditory feedback as reflecting arousal levels or merely as irrelevant auditory stimulation. Figure 4.5 illustrates the number of trials to habituation of the SCR to the triangle presentations for the four groups in this experiment. The group which had both SCL feedback and the aversive tone commencing the experiment (Group FT) took significantly longer to habituate to the triangle presentations than the other three groups. The group which had SCL feedback but an innocuous tone starting the experiment (Group $F\bar{T}$) took no longer to habituate than groups which believed the feedback to be irrelevant. This suggests that SCL feedback does not have intrinsic response enhancing effects but that these effects occur in the wake of the presentation of an aversive stimulus. Furthermore, this result implies that the effect of SCL feedback on response strength during conditioning and extinction can be

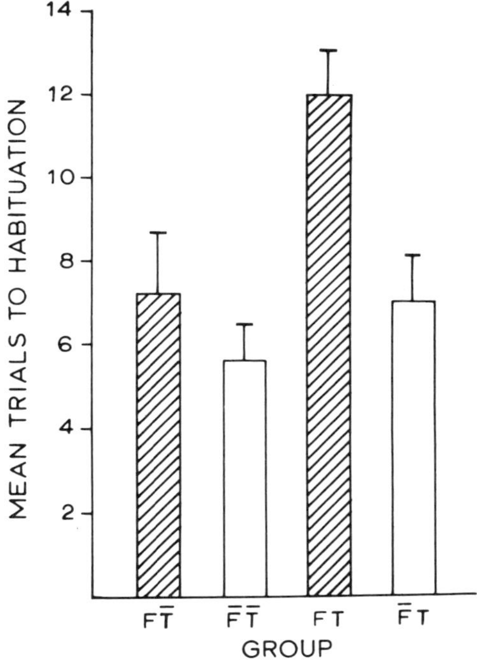

Figure 4.5 Mean number of trials to the habituation criterion (±SEM) for all four groups. Hatched bars represent groups receiving SCL feedback. Groups suffixed T received the aversive tone at the outset of the experiment, those suffixed $\bar{T}$ received the innocuous tone

explained in non-associative terms. When subjects have received an aversive UCS, as during the acquisition phase of Pavlovian conditioning, SCL feedback subsequently retards habituation of the CR during extinction. However, the most important fact is that this retarded habituation is a result of the subjects' *interpretation* of the SCL feedback, since subjects who are given SCL feedback but told it is not related to arousal levels do not show this effect.

How the interpretation of response feedback acts to retard response habituation is not immediately obvious although it is quite clear that it could easily give rise to cognitions which exacerbate the heightened arousal or anxiety precipitated by prior aversive events. If these cognitions are fostered by procedures which utilize response feedback then it still remains for them to be experimentally identified. One possible source of such cognitions is the process of attribution. Whenever individuals observe their own behaviour—and particularly their own autonomic behaviour—they seek to attribute it to some cause (Kelley and Michela, 1980). Subsequently this attribution itself influences the behaviour. The studies described in the following section sought to investigate the involvement of attribution effects in human autonomic conditioning.

4 Attribution effects in human autonomic conditioning

One implication of the phenomenon known as 'resistance to instructed extinction' is that in some circumstances subjects appear to be impervious to information concerning the extinction condition (see Figure 4.4): such subjects take as many trials to extinguish as subjects who have not been forewarned of extinction. This means either that the conditioned response is in some way insulated from these instructions, possibly by being reflexive in nature and not mediated by cognitions related to the UCS, or that subjects are simply ignoring the instructions. The former of these two explanations is quite feasible if the CR is controlled by S-R associations which have been established during conditioning. Such associations have been detected in animals during second-order Pavlovian conditioning (e.g. Rescorla, 1973; Holland and Rescorla, 1975; Rizley and Rescorla, 1972), and following overtraining on instrumental tasks (Rescorla, 1977; Adams, 1980), and it implies that the CR is impervious to manipulation or revaluations of the UCS. Extending this implication to human subjects supposes that, if conditioned responding is maintained by S-R associations, then the CR should be independent of revaluation of and knowledge concerning the UCS. Informing the subject that there will be no more UCS presentations during conditioning is in effect a manipulation which restructures the subjects' knowledge of the UCS, and should thus have no effect if S-R associations govern responding.

The apparently less theoretically exciting alternative explanation of resistance to instructed extinction is that subjects either ignore or disbelieve the extinction instructions. It is, of course, quite plausible that subjects might disbelieve the instructions given to them in an aversive conditioning procedure—a subject might reasonably believe that if experimenters are willing to deliver electric shocks or loud noises to individuals might they not also lie to them? Indeed, it is quite common for experimenters to disregard the data of subjects who claim in post-experimental interviews to doubt the instructions given to them during the experiment. However, if subjects' disbelief is responsible for resistance to instructed extinction we have to explain why it occurs under some conditions and not others. Why, for instance might it occur when subjects are provided with SCL feedback but not occur when no feedback is given? One possibility that we have investigated recently is that response feedback might be giving rise to a cognitive evaluation process which leads subjects to question the validity of the extinction instructions. That is, although instructed extinction subjects are told not to expect any further UCS presentations, and hence should not be fearful, the clear perception of their own reaction to CS presentations provided by the feedback on early extinction trials may lead them to question the validity of the instructions. This might be verbalized as 'I am still responding so I guess I don't really believe those instructions'. This belief would then lead them to take as long to discover the reality of the extinction procedure as uninformed subjects. Under this scenario, doubts about the validity of the extinction instructions would be the direct cause of resistance to instructed extinction.

Alternatively, perceiving their own responses on early extinction trials may lead subjects to believe that they are still fearful: 'I'm still responding so I must still be afraid.' While this belief might itself facilitate continued responding during extinction, attribution theory would suggest that subjects should also look around for the cause of this supposed continued fearfulness. Disbelief in the extinction instructions is one possibility. This scenario would suggest that while resistance to instructed extinction was caused by the belief that they are still fearful, in an attempt to attribute this fearfulness the subjects might report that they disbelieved the extinction instructions.

In both of the above scenarios it would not be disbelief in instructions that caused continued responding, but continued responding that caused a disbelief in instructions, and this is something that can be explored experimentally. If continued responding does influence belief in instructions rather than *vice versa* then we might expect to find an inverse relationship between trials to extinction and subjects' assessment of their confidence in the extinction instructions only when this confidence assessment is made at the end of extinction. Similarly, if the level of confidence in the extinction instructions is determined primarily by the subjects' perception of their responding during extinction, we would *not* expect to find a relationship between confidence estimates and trials to extinction if the confidence evaluation is made prior to extinction.

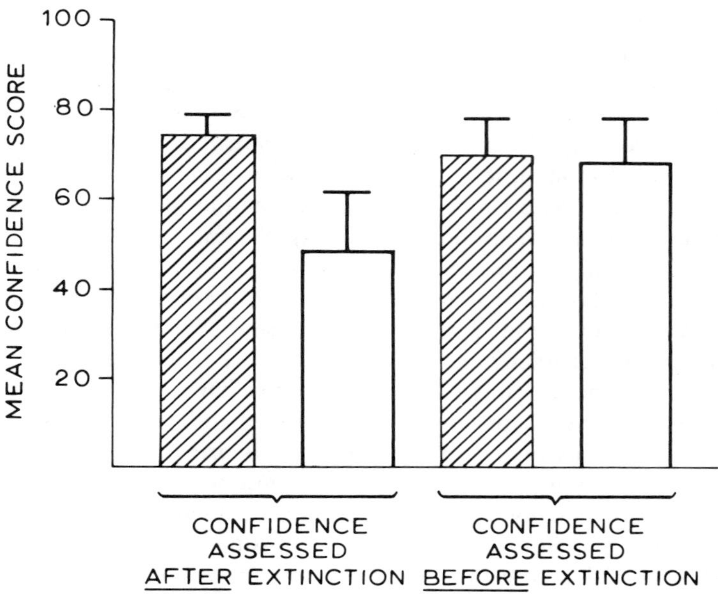

Figure 4.6 Mean 'confidence in instructions' scores (±SEM) for the four groups of subjects. Hatched bars represent 'fast' extinguishers, open bars represent 'slow' extinguishers

In a simple conditioning plus extinction procedure we investigated the above possibility.[3] Subjects were given six pairings of a CS and aversive UCS followed by instructions informing subjects of extinction; following this all subjects had 25 extinction trials where the CS was presented alone. All subjects received immediate auditory feedback of their SCLs throughout extinction. Subjects were also asked to assess their confidence in the extinction instructions on a 100 point scale where 0 = no confidence whatsoever, 50 = neither confident nor unconfident, and 100 = total confidence in the instructions. Half of the subjects were given this questionnaire immediately after the extinction instructions but *before* any extinction trials were presented. The remaining half of the subjects were given the questionnaire *after* the last trial of extinction. Subjects in both the 'before' and 'after' groups were then divided into 'slow' extinguishers or 'fast' extinguishers depending on the number of trials taken for the CR to extinguish ('slow' = >5 trials to extinguish, 'fast' = ≤ 5 trials to extinguish).

Figure 4.6 shows the mean confidence scores for slow and fast extinguishers depending on whether they were given the confidence questionnaire before or after extinction. These results showed no significant difference in confidence scores between 'fast' and 'slow' extinguishers when the questionnaire was presented *before* extinction, but when the questionnaire was presented *after* extinction, slow extinguishers reported a significantly lower confidence score than fast extinguishers. This implies that responding in extinction, is not determined by the subjects' assessment of the validity of the instructions at the outset of extinction, but that the relationship between responding and confidence in instructions develops during extinction itself.

Figure 4.7 illustrates a number of possible ways in which this relationship between responding and confidence in extinction instructions might develop. All of these explanations rest on the fact that subjects observe their own reactions during extinction and make interpretations which lead to either adjustments in response persistence or confidence in instructions.

A more controlled way to investigate these relationships is by intervening to manipulate directly the subjects' perception of their own responding during extinction. Using the response feedback procedure this can be done quite simply by providing subjects with false response feedback which indicates that they have either extinguished very rapidly or are persisting in responding during extinction. In this study,[4] subjects received six conditioning trials and then were given SCL feedback only during subsequent extinction. This feedback was false and indicated that some subjects were persisting in responding throughout extinction (Hi feedback) and that others extinguished

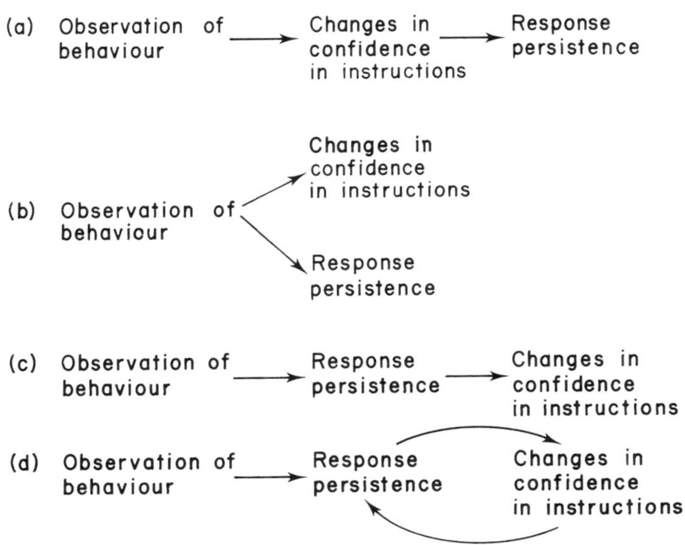

Figure 4.7 Four possible ways in which the relationship between responding and confidence in instructions might develop following the subjects' observation of their own behaviour. See text for further details

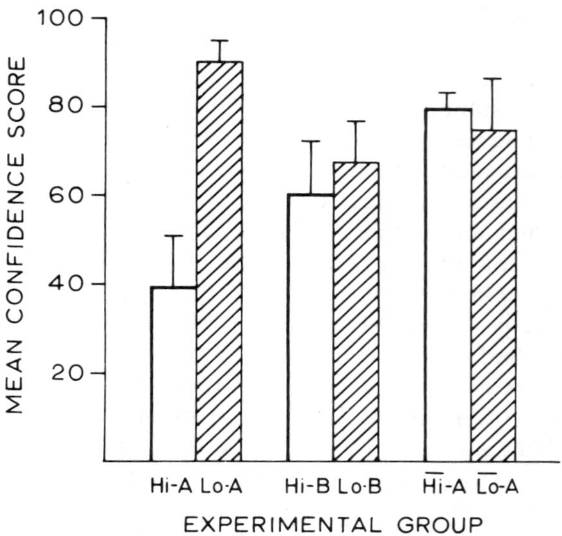

Figure 4.8 Mean 'confidence in instructions' scores (±SEM) for subjects receiving Hi false feedback (open bars) and Lo false feedback (hatched bars). Groups suffixed A had the 'confidence in instructions' questionnaire *after* extinction, those suffixed B had this questionnaire *before* extinction

almost immediately (Lo feedback). Two control groups (H̄i and L̄o) had similar feedback but were informed that the feedback was false. As in the previous experiment some subjects were given the confidence in extinction instructions before extinction (B) and others were given the questionnaire after extinction (A).

Figure 4.8 illustrates the mean confidence scores for the groups in this experiment. Those subjects who received the Hi feedback conditions showed a significantly lower confidence rating than those who received the Lo feedback condition—but only when the questionnaire was presented *after* extinction. There was no difference in confidence ratings when the questionnaire was given prior to extinction (Hi-B vs. Lo-B) nor when the questionnaire was presented after extinction but subjects were forewarned that the feedback was false (H̄i-A vs. L̄o-A). What is also interesting from this study is that subjects who believed they were still responding into extinction (the Hi feedback groups) did actually take significantly longer to extinguish than the Lo feedback subjects (Figure 4.9).

What these results imply is that (a) what subjects believe about the strength of their responding during extinction will in turn influence their confidence in extinction instructions, and (b) if subjects believe they are still responding

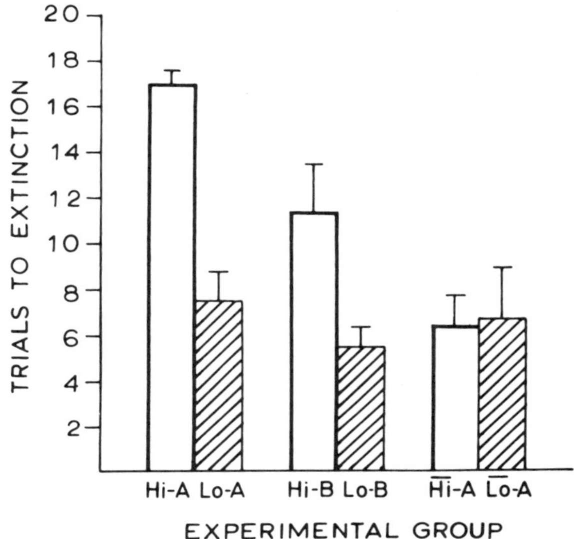

Figure 4.9 Mean number of trials to extinction (±SEM) for subjects receiving Hi false feedback (open bars) and Lo false feedback (hatched bars). Groups suffixed A had the 'confidence in instructions' questionnaire *after* extinction, those suffixed B had this questionnaire *before* extinction

strongly during extinction this will facilitate *actual* response persistence during extinction. The exact causal relationships here are still unclear, but what does matter is that how the subjects perceive and interpret their own reactions is an important contributor to response strength and persistence, not only during extinction but also during acquisition (see the Cracknell and Davey study in section 2 of this chapter).

One possible criticism of these conclusions is that the SCR is a response which does not just reflect components of the defensive systems implicated during aversive conditioning, but also is an indicator of generalized orienting reactions (Siddle, 1983) and centralized information processing (Öhman, 1979a, 1983). For instance, Öhman (1983) has suggested that the SCR during conditioning reflects either the processing of information about the CS-UCS contingency or it reflects a call for central processing: that is, the CS primes the relevant information processing systems ready to process the forthcoming UCS, and the conditioned SCR reflects this priming and subsequent information processing. Clearly, if this is the case, then in the feedback studies I have just reviewed, giving immediate SCL feedback during CS presentation represents extra information that requires processing during

CS presentations. This might imply larger amplitude CRs or, because the SCL feedback provides different information on each new trial, a retardation in habituation of the SCR during conditioning. That is, subjects given immediate SCL feedback may take longer to extinguish because they have more information to process during CS presentations than subjects who receive no response feedback.

However, this possibility seems unlikely for a number of reasons. First, feedback contains intrinsic information and not extrinsic information—it is not a signal calling for processing space and the vast majority of studies have reported no effect of intrinsic information on SCR strength (e.g. Becker and Shapiro, 1980; Pendergrass and Kimmel, 1968). Secondly, if feedback does produce larger and more persistent SCRs because it reflects aspects of central channel processing, it still does not explain why subjects given false feedback suggesting they are continuing to respond during extinction should continue to respond more than subjects given false feedback suggesting they are responding only weakly during extinction. Presumably, the information processing demands in the two conditions should be relatively similar; it is only in the qualitative way that they are interpreted that they differ. Finally, to clarify this issue we decided to conduct a false feedback study[5] where information about responding to the CS during extinction was delayed until some time after CS offset.

In this study subjects received six acquisition trials followed by instructed extinction. During extinction subjects were told that midway through each intertrial interval they would be given a score out of 100 which reflected the strength of their SCR on the previous trial. These scores were to be interpreted as: 0–20, little or no reaction; 20–50, a moderate-average sized reaction; 50–80, a strong reaction; 80–100, an abnormally strong reaction. However, this feedback was false and some subjects received scores during extinction between 60 and 90, indicating continued responding (Hi feedback), and others received scores between 0 and 30, indicating little or no responding (Lo feedback). Two other groups received similar procedures to those of the Hi and Lo groups but were told that the feedback figures were false. Figure 4.10 shows that even when CR feedback is delayed and presented at times other then during the CS, subjects who are led to believe that they are still responding during extinction do actually take significantly longer to extinguish. This result suggests that response persistence in extinction in Hi feedback groups is not necessarily due to the extra information processing requirements imposed when feedback is given during CS presentation.

What conclusions can be drawn from these studies? First, it is clear that when subjects *believe* they are continuing to respond during extinction they *do* actually persist in responding. Secondly, in the situations in which we have studied it, the way in which subjects interpret their behaviour during extinction also influences their confidence in the extinction instructions. The one

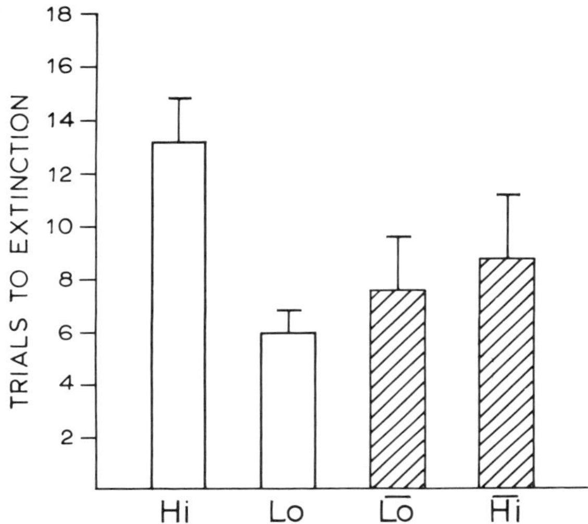

Figure 4.10 Mean number of trials to extinction (± SEM) in the delayed false feedback experiment

inescapable conclusion is that a subject's observation of and interpretation of their responding will itself affect response strength, although the exact mechanism which mediates this effect still needs to be clarified. One possible mechanism is the direct effect of causal attributions. There may, for instance, be a direct causal feedback loop existing between the level of confidence in extinction instructions generated by subjects' perception of their own responding and their subsequent extinction performance. There is evidence in the clinical literature which suggests that the way in which individuals interpret their own autonomic and emotional behaviour does itself influence that behaviour, even when false autonomic feedback is provided (Borkovec and Glasgow, 1973; Valins, 1966; Valins and Ray, 1967). However, the attributions generated in the present studies may be much more general in nature. Observing oneself responding may lead to the attribution that 'I am still afraid', which may simply lower the threshold for defensive reactions to occur to a whole range of stimuli beyond the original CS. This could clearly be better studied in a differential conditioning paradigm employing both CS + s and CS − s. Furthermore, there is no obvious reason why response discrimination should particularly lead either to specific or to generalized attributions each of which might influence behaviour in different ways—the type of attributions generated would intuitively seem to depend on the subjects' previous experience and also on how they are told to interpret response feedback during the experiment. The latter has attractive possibilities experimentally, and implications not only for a theory of human conditioning in general but therapeutically in the treatment of autonomic and emotional disorders. Finally, these effects imply that whenever a CR discriminable to the subject is used in a conditioning study, then attributional effects might be expected. If this is the case, then at the very least, any model of response strength in human conditioning has to include variables which account for the influence on response strength of cognitions concerning the subjects' belief about the nature, implications, and consequences of their responding.

5 The rudiments of a comprehensive model of human conditioning

Much earlier in this chapter I suggested that the contemporary literature on animal conditioning theory implied we should follow two particular directions if we are to understand the mechanisms underlying human conditioning. The first was to come to an understanding of what associations are formed during conditioning and how these associations activate particular cognitive representations. The second was to discover what kinds of processes influence the evaluation of those cognitive representations which mediate conditioned responding. At this stage in the chapter I think these two objectives need putting into perspective.

5.1 The study of associations

In this chapter and elsewhere (Davey, 1983; Davey and McKenna, 1983) I have suggested ways in which we can infer the kinds of associative connections formed during conditioning. The techniques have been adapted from animal conditioning but provide solid inferential evidence about association formation rather than the mere speculation that has been rife in theorizing in human conditioning in the past. Nevertheless, a great deal of empirical work needs to be carried out here and many questions need answering. For instance,

(a) Do different conditioning preparations give rise to different associative links? If they do, this may reflect the evolution of different learning mechanisms designed to cope with differing evolutionary processes, i.e. certain defensive responses may need to be learnt rapidly without central mediation, giving rise to simple S-R learning.

(b) Do variations in the saliency of the events (CSs and UCSs) in the conditioning situation produce variations in the kinds of associative connections learnt? This appears to be the case in animal conditioning (cf. Rescorla, 1980; Nairne and Rescorla, 1981; Rashotte, Griffin, and Sisk, 1977) and may well reflect characteristics of the attention and information processing mechanisms which are necessarily implicated during conditioning (cf. Öhman, 1979a; Dawson and Schell, 1982).

(c) Differing associations may come to control responding at different stages in the conditioning process. While initial learning may be centrally mediated via CS-UCS associations, as might be implied by the fact that autonomic conditioned responding rarely occurs in the absence of conscious awareness or verbalization of the CS-UCS contingencies involved (Baer and Fuhrer, 1968, 1970; Dawson and Biferno, 1973; Biferno and Dawson, 1977; Dawson and Furedy, 1976), overtraining might lead to some transfer of CR control from CS-UCS to more reflexive S-R associations. This has been observed in instrumental animal conditioning (Adams, 1980; Adams and Dickinson, 1981; Colwill and Rescorla, 1985). Very rarely are human subjects given more than a single session of training during Pavlovian conditioning studies. Extended training may well reveal that which is quite intuitively plausible: that the CR eventually becomes a 'habit' which is not centrally mediated (i.e. is no longer mediated by UCS representations or affected by manipulations of that representation) but 'reflexive' in its nature. In such cases the response becomes dissociated from its original consequences and is controlled almost entirely by its antecedent stimuli. A simple example from our everyday lives is when the alarm clock rings early in the morning and we quickly get out of bed and dress for work only to find that it is a Sunday or a holiday.

(d) Asymptotic levels of conditioned responding in humans can be induced very rapidly, and often without a single CS-UCS pairing, if the subjects are informed beforehand of the CS-UCS contingency (Dawson and Grings, 1968; Katz *et al*., 1971; McComb, 1969; Wilson, 1968). What does this imply about the formation of associations? It might suggest that associative links between CS and UCS are formed more rapidly than, but in the same manner as they would be during eventual experience with the CS-UCS contingencies. That is, the CR is mediated by the UCS representation evoked by presentation of the CS. Alternatively, informing subjects of the CS-UCS contingency may simply give rise to an evaluation of the CS without implicating UCS evaluation. That is, it might give rise to a verbalization of the kind 'I'm going to be frightened of that CS' which in and of itself gives rise to a defensive CR. The difference between the associative and evaluative explanations can be investigated fairly easily using the postconditioning revaluation methods described in an early section of this chapter. In the case of either type of explanation, it seems that the incremental–decremental type models of response strength developed to explain animal conditioning (e.g. Rescorla and Wagner, 1972; Pearce and Hall, 1980) would tend to reflect attributes of the information processing systems implicated during progressive *experience* with CS-UCS contingencies and would clearly *not* be applicable to situations which involve sources of information about the CS-UCS contingency other than simple experience of the CS-UCS pairings.

Many of the above issues are speculative, but are nevertheless worthy of serious investigation if a general theory of conditioning is to be evolved, that is, if we are ever to seriously consider integrating models of human and animal conditioning. What is more, both the experimental and inferential techniques are available to study these problems objectively, and in a way which makes the results readily comparable with similar data from the animal literature.

5.2 Cognitive evaluations mediating conditioned responding

Two facts are quite evident from the understanding we have acquired of Pavlovian conditioning. First, conditioning regularly entails the formation of CS-UCS associations, and secondly, conditioned response strength can be manipulated by directly manipulating the organism's evaluation of the UCS through such procedures as taste aversion learning (following appetitive conditioning) or UCS habituation (following aversive conditioning). This second fact has many greater implications for human conditioning than it does for animal conditioning, since the media of human language and social interaction provide many diverse ways in which knowledge about events in the conditioning paradigm might be revalued. The information provided by instructions is one, attributions about an individual's own behaviour is another. These have been touched on in detail in an earlier section. What is important to recognize here is that, just bcause such processes alter evaluations of stimulus events independently of conditioning does not mean that they should be excluded from a theory of conditioning. A thorough model of conditioning is one which takes full account of all those factors which affect the strength of the conditioned response, and to exclude these factors would be tantamount to saying either that we could never develop an adequate model of human conditioning or, more radically, as some have done in the past, there is no such thing as conditioning in humans (e.g. Brewer, 1974). The latter case is a radical and curious view in the extreme, but its validity does depend on what you call 'conditioning'. I have argued in this chapter that a full understanding of conditioning involves understanding (a) what associations are formed, (b) what factors influence the evaluation of cognitions mediating the CR, and (c) what performance rules govern what actual CRs will be emitted. I think this more general view of conditioning has a number of advantages over the minimalist conception held by such people as Brewer (1974) and by the more traditional associationists or neobehaviourists.

First, in the last analysis we must always be concerned with behaviour, and while some might adopt a restricted view of learning such that it concerns primarily the aquisition of associations (e.g. Mackintosh, 1974), we cannot derive a complete predictive picture about the strength or nature of the eventual CR from this restricted view. Just because an organism has learnt a CS-UCS association does not tell us what the nature of the eventual CR will be, nor do incremental–decremental models of associative strength provide clear indications about the effects of postconditioning UCS revaluations. Clearly, if instructions and attributions affect CR strength in humans, then they should be integrated into a model of human conditioning.

Secondly, conditioning theory, when utilized in applied human psychology, has been getting a particularly bad press. This is nowhere more apparent than in theoretical discussions of the aetiology and maintenance of neuroses, clinical phobias, and specific fears. Conditioning theory as an account of these clinical phenomena is usually discussed and summarily rejected (e.g. Marks, 1976; Emmelkamp, 1981; Mathews, Gelder, and Johnston, 1983). However, in these cases, what appears to be being criticized is a very traditional, restricted, and outdated view of conditioning which relies heavily on the tenets of contiguity and simple incremental–decremental accounts of conditioning, and is almost Watsonian in its conception. If we take this traditional view of what conditioning is, then it is quite clear that the basic principles derived from early animal conditioning studies do not even apply to humans in general let alone to a specific category of humans who possess psychopathological problems. What I suggest is required is a more general model of human conditioning of the kind I have outlined in this chapter. If information concerning the CS and UCS, attitudes, beliefs, and response attributions affect CR strength in simple laboratory conditioning studies then they are a necessary part of any model of human conditioning. It is a subsequently constructed model of this kind which would then be the most appropriate for application to psychopathological phenomena.

5.3 Cognitions and stimulus revaluations

So what should this more general model of human conditioning look like? At the very least (a) it has to define how the cognitions which influence stimulus or response evaluations are generated, and (b) it has to specify exactly how these cognitions have their effect in modulating response strength. The first question is one I do not particularly wish to address here, since many of the answers may already exist in the social psychology literature, especially in the literature on attribution theory and cognitive social psychology. The second problem is one to which a few speculative answers might be made on the basis of the results of some of the studies I have described in this chapter.

Figure 4.11 illustrates a very simple model of vow cognitions and evaluations generated during conditioning might affect the strength of the CR in an aversive conditioning paradigm in which it has been identified that conditioned responding is being mediated by CS-UCS associations. In this model the nature of the CR is determined by the nature of the aversive UCS; if the UCS is a loud, sharp noise then the CR will be similar to those responses elicited by the loud, sharp noise itself (orienting responses, heart-rate

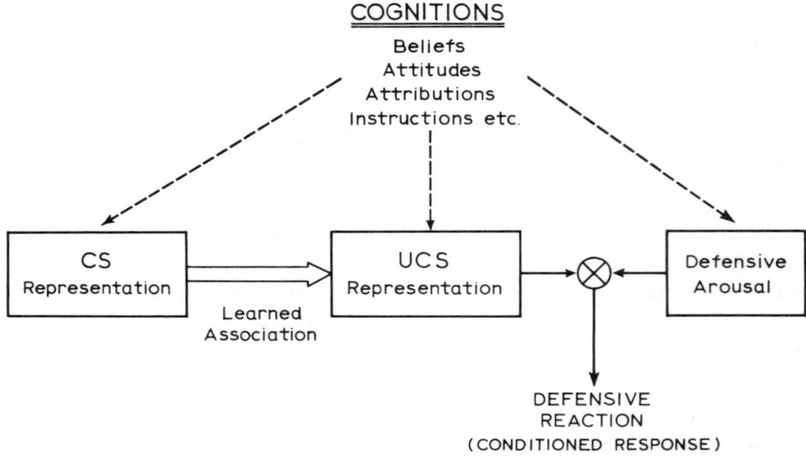

Figure 4.11 A schematic representation of the possible interaction between cognitions, evaluations, and CR strength during conditioning

changes, etc). Furthermore, evocation of the internal representation of this UCS can also elicit these reactions, such that the strength of the CR is a direct result of the strength and salience of the UCS representation and the strength of the individual's defensive arousal, the latter of which determines the threshold for elicitation of the response. Following conditioning, the learned association between CS and UCS results in the CS activating the UCS representation which produces the CR during CS presentation. It is quite plausible from the studies I have reviewed that the cognitions and evaluations generated during conditioning could, according to their nature, have their effect on CR strength by affecting the strength of any one of the three major determinants of CR strength: the CS representation, the UCS representation, or defensive arousal itself.

The most clear example is how these cognitions can affect the strength of the UCS representation and the body of knowledge associated with it. In the Davey and McKenna (1983) study this was achieved by giving subjects the information that the UCS would no longer be presented, or by giving subjects a pseudo-habituation procedure which results in them reporting the UCS as being less aversive; both procedures would result in a revaluation of the UCS as being either less aversive or less threatening, thus weakening the UCS representation's input into the eventual defensive reaction.

A second example is how cognitions generated during conditioning might influence the strength of general defensive arousal or readiness. Providing subjects with real or false SCL feedback gives them an opportunity to evaluate their own reactions. They may attribute continued responding in a general way, generating a cognition of the kind 'I am still frightened' or 'I am still afraid or unsure in this situation'. This kind of cognition would influence the strength of the CR by affecting the level of defensive arousal and lowering the threshold for elicitation of defensive reactions. This type of attribution would be consistent with the effects of response feedback on both CR strength during acquisition and CR persistence during extinction (see section 4).

A third possible example is of the effects of cognitions generated during conditioning on the evaluation of the CS itself. Providing subjects with response feedback that suggests they are continuing to respond might generate a cognition of the kind 'I am still afraid or frightened of the CS'. This would tend to have the effect of exacerbating the CR by a direct revaluation of the CS rather than through the CS's effect on the UCS representation. That is, the CS ceases to be a 'cognitively' neutral stimulus having its effects via the UCS representation it evokes, but acquires intrinsic aversive properties itself.

All of the possibilities generated by this model remain to be thoroughly experimentally identified and tested. The effects of UCS revaluation seem fairly clear and are well documented in our early studies (Davey and Arulampalam, 1981, 1982; Davey and McKenna, 1983; Davey, 1983; Cracknell and Davey, 1985), the effects of response evaluation on defensive arousal are strongly implied in the response feedback and false feedback studies reported earlier in this chapter, and the possibility of CS revaluation is a reasonable extrapolation from these other effects. What clearly needs much more attention is the way in which specific attributions might be identified, and under what conditions different attributions and cognitive evaluations are generated.

Finally, this kind of model—whereby response strength can be influenced by cognitions and response attributions generated during conditioning—is one which is applicable primarily in situations which have generated UCS-mediated responding. In situations where the CR is generated by S-R associations there is clearly less scope for cognitions and attributions to exert an effect, although they might obviously influence defensive arousal and even affect CR strength via their effect on the strength of the CS representation—but presumably only if the S-R association is processed centrally. If conditioning establishes associations peripherally, such that the CS activates directly the reflex arc associated with the UCS, then it would seem that cognitive revaluations of CS and UCS, and response attributions would have little or no influence on CR strength.

6 Conclusions

The aim of this chapter has been to suggest ways in which human and animal models of conditioning might be integrated. The main purpose of this integration is to establish a model of human conditioning which takes account both of the knowledge we have recently acquired about associative learning in animals and of those factors which we know uniquely affect human conditioning. Some of the factors which do uniquely affect human conditioning include the influence of information conveyed through instructions and the effects of response attributions which are developed during conditioning. Clearly, we can adapt the inferential techniques developed in animal conditioning studies to investigate the associative substructure underlying conditioned responding in humans. This will provide a more objective assessment of the associations formed during conditioning and indicate the kinds of cognitive factors mediating conditioned responding. Once we have been able to identify the cognitive structures (such as knowledge about and evaluation of the UCS) which do mediate conditioned responding in a particular preparation, we then have the foundations on which to suggest how information and attributions might affect responding via these mediating cognitions. This chapter has provided some empirical evidence concerning these aims and attempted a speculative model which it is hoped might guide further research. Such an integrated model of human Pavlovian conditioning should have greater predictive value than existing models and provide a more valid basis for assessing the role of conditioning in various human behavioural phenomena.

Notes

1 This experiment was conducted with Imelda McKenna and Sue Cracknell.
2 This experiment was conducted with Andrea Melia.
3 This experiment was conducted with Jeff Gordon.
4 This experiment was conducted with Helen Smith.
5 This experiment was conducted with Andrea Melia.

Acknowledgement

The author is indebted to Bob Boakes for valuable comments on an earlier draft of this chapter.

References

Adams, C. D. (1980). Post-conditioning devaluation of an instrumental reinforcer has no effect on extinction. *Q. Journ. Exp. Psychol.*, **32**, 447–58.

Adams, C. D., and Dickinson, A. (1981). Actions and habits: Variations in associative representations during instrumental learning, in *Memory Mechanisms in Animal Behaviour* (eds. R. Miller and N. E. Spear), Erlbaum, Hillsdale, N.J.

Annan, Z., and Kamin, L. J. (1961). The conditioned emotional response as a function of intensity of the US. *J. Comp. Physiol. Psychol.*, **54**, 428–32.

Baer, P. E., and Fuhrer, M. J. (1968). Cognitive processes during differential trace and delayed conditioning of the GSR. *J. Exp. Psychol.*, **78**, 81–8.

Baer, P. E., and Fuhrer, M. J. (1970). Cognitive processes in the differential trace conditioning of electrodermal and vasomotor activity. *J. Exp. Psychol.*, **84**, 176–8.

Baer, P. E., and Fuhrer, M. J. (1973). Unexpected effects of masking: Differential EDR conditioning without relational learning. *Psychophysiol.*, **10**, 95–9.

Becker, D. E., and Shapiro, D. (1980). Directing attention towards stimuli affects the P300 but not the orienting response. *Psychophysiol.*, **17**, 385–9.

Biferno, M. A., and Dawson, M. E. (1977). The onset of contingency awareness and electrodermal classical conditioning: An analysis of temporal relationships during acquisition and extinction. *Psychophysiol.*, **14**, 164–71.

Borkovec, T. D., and Glasgow, R. E. (1973). Boundary conditions of false heart-rate feedback effects on avoidance behavior: A resolution of discrepant results. *Behav. Res. Therapy*, **11**, 171–7.

Brewer, W. F. (1974). There is no convincing evidence for operant and classical conditioning in humans, in *Cognition and the Symbolic Processes* (eds. W. B. Weimer and D. J. Palermo), Lawrence Erlbaum Assoc., Hillsdale, N.J.

Bridger, W. H., and Mandel, I. J. (1965). Abolition of the PRE by instructions in GSR conditioning. *J. Exp. Psychol.*, **69**, 476–82.

Cleland, G. G., and Davey, G. C. L. (1982). The effects of satiation and reinforcer devaluation on signal-centered behavior in the rat. *Learn. Motiv.*, **13**, 343–60.

Colby, J. J., and Smith, N. F. (1977). The effect of three procedures for eliminating a conditioned taste aversion in the rat. *Learn. Motiv.*, **8**, 404–13.

Colgan, D. A. (1970). Effect of instructions on the skin resistance response. *J. Exp. Psychol.*, **86**, 108–12.

Colwill, R. M., and Rescorla, R. A. (1985). Instrumental responding remains sensitive to reinforcer devaluation after extensive training. *J. Exp. Psychol. Anim. Behav. Processes*, **11**, 520–36.

Cracknell, S., and Davey, G. C. L. (1985). The effect of perceived unconditioned response strength on conditioned responding in humans. Unpublished manuscript.

Davey, G. C. L. (1983). An associative view of human classical conditioning, in *Animal Models of Human Behavior* (ed. G. C. L. Davey), John Wiley & Sons, Chichester.

Davey, G. C. L., and Arulampalam, T. (1981). Second-order electrodermal conditioning in humans. *IRCS Med. Sci.*, **9**, 567–8.

Davey, G. C. L., and Arulampalam, T. (1982). Second-order 'fear' conditioning in humans: Persistance of CR_2 following extinction of CR_1. *Behav. Res. Therapy*, **20**, 391–6.

Davey, G. C. L., and McKenna, I. (1983). The effect of post-conditioning revaluation of CS and UCS following Pavlovian second-order electrodermal conditioning in humans. *Q. Journ. Exp. Psychol.*, **35B**, 125–33.

Dawson, M. E. (1973). Can classical conditioning occur without contingency learning? A review and evaluation of the evidence. *Psychophysiol.*, **10**, 82–6.

Dawson, M. E., and Biferno, M. A. Concurrent measurements of awareness and electrodermal classical conditioning. *J. Exp. Psychol.*, **101**, 55–62.

Dawson, M. E., Catania, J. J., Schell, A. M., and Grings, W. W. (1979). Autonomic classical conditioning as a function of awareness of stimulus contingencies. *Biol. Psychol.*, **9**, 23–40.

Dawson, M. E., and Furedy, J. J. (1976). The role of awareness in human differential autonomic classical conditioning. The necessary-gate hypothesis. *Psychophysiol.*, **13**, 50–3.

Dawson, M. E., and Grings, W. W. (1968). Comparison of classical conditioning and relational learning. *J. Exp. Psychol.*, **76**, 227–31.

Dawson, M. E., and Schell, A. M. (1982). Electrodermal responses to attended and nonattended significant stimuli during dichotic listening. *J. Exp. Psychol.: Hum. Percept. Perform.*, **8**, 315–24.

Deane, G. E. (1969). Cardiac activity during experimentally induced anxiety. *Psychophysiol.*, **6**, 17–30.

Dickinson, A. (1980). *Contemporary Animal Learning Theory*, Cambridge University Press, Cambridge.

Emmelkamp, P. M. G. (1981). *Phobic and Obsessive Compulsive Disorders: Theory, Research and Practise*, New York, Plenum.

Epstein, S., and Clarke, S. (1970). Heart rate and skin conductance during experimentally induced anxiety: Effects of anticipated intensity of noxious stimulation and experience. *J. Exp. Psychol.*, **84**, 105–12.

Frcka, G., Beyts, J., Levey, A. B., and Martin I. (1981). The role of awareness in human conditioning. *Pav. J. Biol. Psychol.*, **18**, 69–76.

Fuhrer, M. J., and Baer, P. E. (1969). Cognitive processes in differential GSR conditioning: Effects of a masking task. *Amer. J. Psychol.*, **82**, 168–80.

Fuhrer, M. J., and Baer, P. E. (1980). Cognitive factors and CS-UCS interval effects in the differential conditioning and extinction of skin conductance responses. *Biol. Psychol.*, **10**, 283–98.

Grings, W. W. (1965). Verbal-perceptual factors in the conditioning of autonomic responses, in *Classical Conditioning: A Symposium* (ed. W. F. Prokasy), Appleton-Century-Crofts, New York.

Grings, W. W., and Dawson, M. E. (1973). Complex conditioning, in *Electrodermal Activity in Psychological Research* (eds. W. F. Prokasy and D. C. Raskin), Academic Press, New York.

Hawkins, R. D., and Kandel, E. R. (1984). Is there a cell-biological alphabet for simple forms of learning? *Psychol. Rev.*, **91**, 375–91.

Holland, P. C., and Rescorla, R. A. (1975). The effect of two ways of devaluing the unconditioned stimulus after first- and second-order appetitive conditioning. *J. Exp. Psychol: Anim. Behav. Proc.*, **1**, 355–63.

Holland, P. C., and Straub, J. J. (1979). Differential effects of two ways of devaluing the unconditioned stimulus after Pavlovian appetitive conditioning. *J. Exp. Psychol: Anim. Behav. Proc.*, **5**, 65–78.

Kamin, L. J., and Brimer, C. J. (1963). The effects of intensity of conditioned and unconditioned stimuli on a conditioned emotional response. *Canad. J. Psychol.*, **17**, 194–8.

Katz, A., Webb, L., and Stotland, E. (1971). Cognitive influences on the rate of GSR extinction. *J. Exp. Research Personality*, **5**, 208–15.

Kelley, H. H., and Michela, J. L. (1980). Attribution theory and research. *Ann. Rev. Psychol.*, **31**, 457–501.

Koenig, K. P., and Castillo, D. D. (1969). False feedback and longevity of the conditioned GSR during extinction: Some implications for aversion therapy. *J. Exp. Psychol.*, **74**, 505–10.

Leitenberg, H. (1976). Behavioral approaches to treatment of neurosis, in *Handbook of Behavior Modification and Behavior Therapy* (ed. H. Leitenberg), Prentice-Hall, Englewood Cliffs, N.J.

McComb, D. (1969). Cognitive and learning effects in the production of GSR conditioning data. *Psychon. Sci.*, **16**, 96–7.

Mackintosh, N. J. (1974). *The Psychology of Animal Learning*, Academic Press, London.

Maltzman, I., Langdon, B., Pendery, M., and Wolft, C. (1977). Galvanic response-orienting reflex and semantic conditioning and generalization with different unconditioned stimuli. *J. Exp. Psychol: Gen.*, **106**, 141–71.

Mandel, I. J., and Bridger, W. H. (1973). Is there classical conditioning without cognitive expectancy? *Psychophysiol.*, **10**, 87–90.

Marks, I. (1969). *Fears and Phobias*, Academic Press, New York.

Marks, I. (1976). Clinical phenomena in search of laboratory models, in *Psychopathology: Experimental Models* (eds. J. D. Maser and M. E. P. Seligman), W. H. Freeman & Co., San Francisco.

Mathews, A. M., Gelder, M. G., and Johnston, D. W. (1983). *Agoraphobia: Nature and Treatment*, Tavistock Publications, London.

Moore, J. W. (1979). Brain processes and conditioning, in *Mechanisms of Learning and Motivation* (eds. A. Dickinson and R. A. Boakes), Lawrence Erlbaum Assoc., Hillsdale, N.J.

Nairne, J. S., and Rescorla, R. A. (1981). Second-order conditioning with diffuse auditory reinforcers in the pigeon. *Learn. Motiv.*, **12**, 65–91.

Öhman, A. (1979a). The orienting response, attention, and learning: An information-processing perspective, in *The Orienting Reflex in Humans* (eds. H. D. Kimmel, E. H. Van Olst, and J. F. Orlebecke), Lawrence Erlbaum Assoc., Hillsdale, N.J.

Öhman, A. (1979b). Instructional control of autonomic respondents: Fear relevance as a critical factor, in *Biofeedback and Self-Regulation* (eds. N. Birbaumer and H. D. Kimmel), Lawrence Erlbaum Assoc., New York.

Öhman, A. (1983). The orienting response during Pavlovian conditioning, in *Orienting and Habituation: Perspectives in Human Research* (ed. D. Siddle), John Wiley & Sons, Chichester.

Öhman, A., Björkstrand, P.-Å., and Ellström, P.-E. (1973). Effect of explicit trial-by-trial information about shock probability in long interstimulus interval GSR conditioning. *J. Exp. Psychol.*, **98**, 145–51.

Pavlov, I. P. (1927). *Conditioned Reflexes*, Oxford University Press, Oxford.

Pearce, J. M., and Hall, G. (1980). A model for Pavlovian learning: Variations in the effectiveness of conditioned but not of unconditioned stimuli. *Psychol. Rev.*, **87**, 532–53.

Pendergrass, V. E., and Kimmel, H. D. (1968). UCR diminution in temporal conditioning and habituation. *J. Exp. Psychol.*, **77**, 1–6.

Rashotte, M. E., Griffin, R. W., and Sisk, C. L. (1977). Second-order conditioning of the pigeon's key peck. *Anim. Learn. & Behav.*, **5**, 25–38.

Razran, G. (1971). *Mind in Evolution*, Houghton Mifflin, New York.

Rescorla, R. A. (1973). Second-order conditioning: Implications for theories of learning, in *Contemporary Approaches to Learning and Conditioning* (eds. F. J. McGuigan and D. Lumsden), Winston, New York.

Rescorla, R. A. (1977). Pavlovian second-order conditioning: Some implications for instrumental behavior, in *Operant-Pavlovian Interactions* (eds. H. Davis and H. M. B. Hurwitz), Lawrence Erlbaum Assoc., Hillsdale, N.J.

Rescorla, R. A. (1980). *Pavlovian Second-order Conditioning: Studies in Associative Learning*, Lawrence Erlbaum Assoc., Hillsdale, N.J.

Rescorla, R. A., and Wagner, A. R. (1972). A theory of Pavlovian conditioning: Variations in the effectiveness of reinforcement and nonreinforcement, in *Classical Conditioning II: Current Research and Theory* (eds. A. H. Black and W. F. Prokasy), Appleton-Century-Crofts, New York.

Rizley, R. C., and Rescorla, R. A. (1972). Associations in second-order conditioning and sensory preconditioning. *J. Comp. Physiol. Psychol.*, **81**, 1–11.

Ross, L. E., Ferreira, M. C., and Ross, S. M. (1974). Backward masking of conditioned stimuli: Effects on differential and single-cue classical conditioning performance. *J. Exp. Psychol.*, **103**, 603–13.

Siddle, D. (1983). *Orienting and Habituation: Perspectives in Human Research*, John Wiley & Sons, Chichester.

Spence, K. W., and Goldstein, H. (1961). Eyelid conditioning performance as a function of emotion-producing instructions. *J. Exp. Psychol.*, **62**, 291–4.

Staats, C. K., and Staats, A. W. (1957). Meaning established by classical conditioning. *J. Exp. Psychol.*, **54**, 84–90.

Valins, S. (1966). Cognitive effects of false heart-rate feedback. *J. Person. Soc. Psychol.*, **4**, 400–8.

Valins, S., and Ray, A. A. (1967). Effects of cognitive desensitization on avoidance behavior. *J. Person. Soc. Psychol.*, **7**, 345–50.

Wilson, G. D. (1968). Reversal of differential GSR conditioning by instructions. *J. Exp. Psychol.*, **76**, 491–3.

Wilson, R. A., Fuhrer, M. J., and Baer, P. E. (1973). Differential conditioning of electrodermal responses: Effects of performing a masking task during the interstimulus and intertrial intervals. *Biol. Psychol.*, **2**, 33–46.

Cognitive Processes and Pavlovian Conditioning in Humans
Edited by G. Davey

Chapter 5

Latent inhibition and human Pavlovian conditioning: Research and relevance

David A. T. Siddle
Macquarie University

and

Bob Remington
University of Southampton

Research and theorizing about Pavlovian conditioning have undergone some quite dramatic changes during the past 20 years. The conceptual framework for the study of associative learning in animals has moved from the idea that conditioning involves the formation of new stimulus–response connections to the view that it involves the learning of relationships between environmental events (Mackintosh, 1983; Rescorla and Holland, 1976). In these terms, the 'conditioned response' (CR) is no longer viewed simply as an acquired reflex, but rather as an index of the fact that the animal has acquired new knowledge. Conditioning work with humans has also shifted—perhaps more slowly—away from a commitment to reflexology and towards a position in which cognitive and conscious processes are accorded considerable status in determining the outcome of conditioning (see Furedy, Riley, and Fredrickson, 1983, Chapter 4).

Despite some apparent similarities, human and animal research have differed in important ways. The animal literature has been characterized by vigorous theorizing in which the aims have been to specify the relationships that are learned in conditioning experiments, the manner in which conditioned stimulus (CS) and unconditioned stimulus (UCS) events are presented, the nature of the associations formed, and the rules that govern the formation of associations (Frey and Sears, 1978; Mackintosh, 1975; Pearce and Hall, 1980; Rescorla and Wagner, 1972; Wagner, 1978). In contrast to the remarkably rapid development of sophisticated information processing based accounts of animal learning, comparable theorising derived from human conditioning data has been slow to emerge. Moreover, specifically human-based theories of conditioning have tended to address rather different questions. In particular, the need to analyse the role of 'awareness' of CS-UCS relationships in determining conditioning outcome (e.g. Dawson and Furedy, 1976) has, until recently, been of central importance. However, human-based theories which are cognitive in the sense of adopting an information processing model have begun to emerge (e.g. Dawson and Schell, 1985, Chapter 2; Öhman, 1979). At the empirical level, human and animal work has also concentrated on different phenomena. Human work has often been concerned with solving the methodological problems inherent in the use of a psychophysiological paradigm with historical roots in reflexology. For example, much attention has been given to the problem of defining 'the CR' and to that of disentangling orienting and conditioned responses (see Öhman, 1983, for a review). In contrast, animal research has been able to utilize more easily interpreted indices of learning. With this methodological advantage, and without the complications raised by questions concerning the role of 'awareness', animal researchers have been able to explore in detail such phenomena as blocking, overshadowing, and latent inhibition—all of which must be explained by any adequate theory of conditioning. This difference in scope is seen clearly in the subject matter of the present chapter, latent inhibition. Whereas latent inhibition has been studied extensively in the animal laboratory in the course of theory development, it has received little systematic investigation with humans.

One purpose of this chapter is to review what is known about latent inhibition in humans. A second aim is to discuss the theoretical significance of latent inhibition and to point to its possible relevance with respect to psychopathology. Because much of the theorizing about latent inhibition has emanated from animal work, we will first provide a brief overview of what is known about the phenomenon in animals.

1 Latent inhibition in animals

Latent inhibition is usually defined as a retardation in conditioning as a result of exposure to the to-be-CS prior to CS-UCS pairings. The term 'latent inhibition' is used for convenience only, in that a preexposed CS does not necessarily acquire conditioned inhibitory properties in the sense in which, for example, Rescorla (1969) has discussed them. Preexposure to a CS retards subsequent inhibitory as well as excitatory conditioning to that stimulus (Reiss and Wagner, 1972; Rescorla, 1971). Thus, a preexposed CS is less likely to enter into *any* new associations than is a novel stimulus. Latent inhibition has been demonstrated across a wide range of species with indices of conditioning such as eyeblink, leg flexion, food aversion, and conditioned suppression (Mackintosh, 1983; Lubow, 1973a). Although there is evidence that latent inhibition is specific to the preexposed stimulus (Carlton and Vogel, 1967; Schnur, 1971), Siegel (1969a) has demonstrated generalization of the effect when the frequency of a tone CS was varied from preexposure to conditioning.

There is some evidence that latent inhibition increases as a function of the number of CS preexposures (Domjan and Siegel, 1971; Lantz, 1973; Siegel, 1969b) and Lubow (e.g. Lubow, 1973a; Lubow, Weiner, and Schnur, 1981) has argued that approximately 20 presentations of CS-alone are required to produce the effect. However, studies of flavour aversion (Best and Gemberling, 1977; Bond and DiGuisto, 1975; Kalat and Rozin, 1973; Westbrook, Provost, and Homewood, 1982) and odour aversion (Rudy and Cheatle, 1978; Westbrook, Bond, and Feyer, 1981) indicate that one CS preexposure is sufficient to produce a retardation of toxicosis conditioning.

Studies that have manipulated the interval between CS preexposure and the CS-UCS pairing phase have indicated that the effects of CS preexposure persist for some considerable time. Preexposure–pairing intervals of 1 hour (James, 1971), 24 hours (Siegel, 1970), 48 hours (Carlton and Vogel, 1967) and 1 week (Crowell and Anderson, 1972) have led to latent inhibition in rabbit eyelid conditioning and in rat conditioned suppression. Moreover, with white noise and tone CSs, latent inhibition does not decrease as the preexposure–pairing interval is increased from a few minutes to 24 hours (Siegel, 1970) or to 1 week (Crowell and Anderson, 1972). In flavour and odour conditioning, on the other hand, latent inhibition declines as a function of the preexposure–pairing interval (Best and Gemberling, 1977; Westbrook *et al.*, 1981). However, this effect is modulated by the duration of preexposure. With a relatively long CS preexposure of 18 minutes, latent inhibition has been observed with preexposure–pairing intervals up to 24 hours. With a relatively short CS preexposure of 2 minutes, latent inhibition has been observed after intervals of 3–4 hours, but not after an interval of 24 hours (Westbrook *et al.*, 1981; Westbrook *et al.*, 1982).

The effects of CS intensity on latent inhibition have been studied exclusively with auditory stimuli. Using a lick suppression measure, Crowell and Anderson (1972) reported more latent inhibition on the first test trial in rats preexposed to a 100 dB white noise CS than in those preexposed to a 70 dB CS. Similarly, Schnur and Lubow (1976) reported that a CS intensity of

91 dB during both preexposure and acquisition produced more latent inhibition than did a CS of 71 dB. On the other hand, Lubow, Markman, and Allen (1968) found no effect of a narrow range (68–77 dB) of CS intensities on latent inhibition of the pinna response in rabbits, and Solomon, Brennan, and Moore (1974) reported a similar amount of latent inhibition of the nictitating membrane response with 75 dB and 95 dB CSs. Hernandez, Buchanan, and Powell (1981) employed CS intensities of 60, 75, and 90 dB during both preexposure and acquisition, but observed latent inhibition of conditioned eyeblink at only 75 dB. Conditioned cardiac deceleration, however, was attenuated by preexposure at all CS intensities, and latent inhibition was more pronounced with a CS of 90 dB than with CSs of either 60 or 75 dB. In summary, the effect of auditory stimulus intensity on latent inhibition remains unclear, and there are no data on the effects of the intensity manipulation with stimuli in other modalities.

The effects of interstimulus interval (ISI) employed during preexposure and of the interpolated presentation of a distractor event between preexposure and acquisition are of considerable theoretical relevance. Unfortunately, the data are again inconclusive. Whereas Lantz (1973) reported that latent inhibition increased as preexposure ISI increased from 2 seconds to 150 seconds, Crowell and Anderson (1972) found no difference with ISIs of 45 seconds and 24 hours. With regard to distractor events, Lantz (1973) found that one presentation of a novel visual stimulus following preexposure to a series of tone CSs attenuated latent inhibition as measured by lick suppression, and Hall and Pearce (1982) showed that latent inhibition can be attenuated by a surprising event prior to the CS-UCS pairing phase. These authors used CS-weak shock during preexposure followed by CS-strong shock during conditioning. Latent inhibition to the CS developed even as the CS acquired associative strength as a result of weak shock in the preexposure phase. However, the latent inhibition effect was attenuated when the acquisition phase was preceded by the interpolation of two CS-alone trials. In the taste aversion literature, the modality of the surprising event seems to be important. Rudy, Rosenberg, and Sandell (1977) found that latent inhibition with a preexposed taste CS could be attenuated by presentation of novel exteroceptive cues prior to the conditioning phase. In contrast, Westbrook *et al.* (1982) found no evidence of attenuation of latent inhibition in flavour conditioning when the distractor event presented between preexposure and conditioning was another flavour (but see Best, Gemberling, and Johnson, 1979).

There is also some evidence that latent inhibition can be attenuated when the CS is paired with another stimulus during preexposure. For example, Lubow, Schnur, and Rifkin (1976) reported that latent inhibition was reduced when the tone CS was regularly followed during preexposure by a light stimulus, and Dickinson (1976) found that latent inhibition of conditioned suppression was greater when the CS was presented alone during preexposure than when it signalled food delivery. Hall and Pearce (1979) reported that when conditioning involved tone–strong shock pairings, preexposure to tone–weak shock pairings produced better conditioning (less latent inhibition) than did preexposure to CS-alone. On the other hand, Szakmary (1977), using an aversive conditioning procedure, observed that preexposure to explicitly unpaired presentations of noise and light resulted in more latent inhibition to the noise CS than did preexposure to noise–light pairings (Experiment 1), but that conditioning in a noise–light preexposure group was not different from that in a no-preexposure control group (Experiment 2).

Of particular theoretical relevance are studies that have examined whether or not latent inhibition is context-specific. That is to say, is latent inhibition reduced when preexposure and acquisition occur in different experimental contexts? Although some data suggest that a change in context from preexposure to acquisition has little effect on latent inhibition (Anderson, O'Farrell, Formica, and Caponigri, 1969; Anderson, Wolf, and Sullivan, 1969), other evidence points to the importance of contextual factors. For example, Channell and Hall (1983) found that latent inhibition of a conditioned appetitive response was attenuated when preexposure and acquisition occurred in different, contexts, and Lubow, Rifkin, and Alek (1976) reported that preexposure actually facilitated learning when the acquisition context was different from that used during preexposure. These studies, however, confounded contextual change with contextual novelty. Nevertheless, there is other evidence that latent inhibition is context-specific even when the acquisition context, although different from the preexposure context, is familiar (Hall and Channell, 1985; Hall and Minor, 1984; Lovibond, Preston, and Mackintosh, 1984). In addition to contextual changes, some studies have examined the effects of further exposure to the context alone between the CS preexposure and acquisition phases. Although some authors have reported that further context exposure reduced latent inhibition (Baker and Mercier, 1982; Wagner, 1979; Westbrook *et al.*, 1981), others have not (Hall and Minor, 1984).

In summary, there has been a considerable amount of parametric work on latent inhibition in animals. In flavour and odour aversion, latent inhibition can occur following only one CS preexposure, whereas with exteroceptive CSs, 15–20 preexposures seem to be necessary. The effects of CS preexposure persist for a considerable period of time, and retardation of conditioning seems to be greater when relatively long ISIs are used during CS preexposure. Latent inhibition appears to be specific to the context employed during preexposure and can sometimes be attenuated by further exposure to the experimental context prior to the CS-UCS pairing phase. Finally, latent inhibition is attenuated when the to-be-CS is followed by another stimulus during the preexposure phase.

2 Latent inhibition in humans

In contrast to the burgeoning animal literature, research on latent inhibition in human subjects has been meagre and somewhat inadequate in methodological terms. In particular, the control procedures necessary to establish an associative deficit which is stimulus-specific have often been lacking. For the most part, research has not been designed to answer theoretical questions of the kind examined in the animal literature, but rather to establish that the latent inhibition phenomenon can be observed in human Pavlovian conditioning paradigms. Of these, eyeblink and electrodermal conditioning have been used extensively. Although early work (Grant, Hake, Riopelle, and Kostlan, 1951; Grant, Hake, and Schneider, 1948) failed to obtain latent inhibition with conditioned eyeblink, the number of CS preexposures (10 and 5 respectively) was possibly too small. Schnur and Ksir (1969) employed 20 preexposures of the CS and demonstrated a subsequent retardation of acquisition in comparison with groups who received either no preexposure or 20 presentations of a stimulus distinct from the CS (tone vs. bell). On the other hand, Perlmuter (1966) obtained only a marginally reliable latent inhibition effect with relatively long ISIs during CS preexposure. Moreover, the effect occurred only late in the acquisition phase when it might have been expected to be at its weakest. However, these data may have been confounded by the fact that each CS was preceded by the spoken work 'ready'. In a further experiment using a within-subjects manipulation of CS preexposure, Perlmuter found no evidence for retarded acquisition following CS preexposure; moreover, CS preexposure had no significant effect on extinction.

Hulstijn (1978) recorded electrodermal activity during eyeblink conditioning. There was no difference in acquisition between preexposed and non-preexposed groups, i.e. no evidence of latent inhibition of an eyeblink CR (cf. Schnur and Ksir, 1969). Analysis of the electrodermal data revealed that although habituation occurred during the CS preexposure phase, presentation of the UCS on the first acquisition trial resulted in skin conductance responding to the CS on the second acquisition trial. Similarly, omission of the UCS on the first extinction trial resulted in an increased electrodermal response to the CS on the second extinction trial. Although the magnitude of skin conductance responses was not a function of preexposure, the absence of a stimulus-specific control for latent inhibition makes interpretation of the data difficult. In a second experiment, Hulstijn measured both electrodermal activity and EEG alpha activity during eyeblink conditioning. All subjects received CS preexposure, but the conditioning phase was accompanied by a masking task for half the subjects. The task and no-task groups did not differ in terms of acquisition, and the absence of a no-preexposure control group prevents an assessment of latent inhibition. The no-task group displayed more electrodermal and EEG alpha blocking responses during acquisition than did the task group.

Using electrodermal conditioning, Zeiner (1970) found no evidence of latent inhibition in human subjects. A differential trace conditioning procedure was employed with electric shock as the UCS. However, subjects were preexposed to only eight presentations each of CS+ and CS−. Rather than demonstrating latent inhibition, Silver (1973) found superior electrodermal conditioning following 16 presentations of the to-be-CS than following 1 or 4 preexposures. However, subjects received three presentations of the UCS (shock) prior to the preexposure presentations, and because the acquisition phase began immediately following 1, 4, or 16 CS presentations, the conditioning data may have been confounded by state differences.

A preexposure effect was demonstrated by Surwit and Poser (1974) who crossed two levels of CS preexposure (50 or 100 trials) with three levels of delay between preexposure and conditioning (no delay, 1 hour, or 24 hours). Probability of electrodermal responding to CS onset during acquisition was lower in the preexposure conditions than in the control conditions in which subjects were preexposed to another stimulus. Electrodermal responding just prior to UCS delivery was lower in the preexposure condition than in the control during the first block of five acquisition trials, but the effect was attenuated by a 1-hour or a 24-hour delay between preexposure and acquisition phases. Unfortunately, there were no controls for Pavlovian conditioning, and the reported abrasion of electrode sites may well have affected the measurement of electrodermal activity.

Maltzman, Raskin, and Wolff (1979) employed a somewhat more sophisticated differential conditioning procedure in an attempt to control for non-associative effects. They used word stimuli as CS+ and CS−, white noise as the UCS and electrodermal activity as the dependent variable. Subjects were exposed to 0, 20, or 40 word stimuli during preexposure, but the CS+ word was not presented at this stage. In this sense, the experiment must be viewed as an investigation of generalization of latent inhibition, although the stimulus-specific controls necessary for a thorough examination of this question were lacking. Evidence for latent inhibition was adduced in three ways. The zero preexposure condition produced larger UCS-omission responses during extinction and larger peak CRs during acquisition. In addition, the zero preexposure condition produced peak CR amplitudes earlier in the acquisition phase than did either of the other conditions. However, neither the peak CR amplitude measure nor the number of acquisition trials prior to peak CR address directly the question of associative conditioning. Rather, this requires an analysis of the effects of CS preexposure on differential responding to CS+ and CS−. In fact, the analysis appropriate to this question revealed no evidence of latent inhibition. Nevertheless, the fact that UCS omission responses were smaller in preexposed groups seems indicative of latent inhibition if we assume that omission responding reflects the strength of conditioning (Siddle, Remington, Kuiack, and Haines, 1983).

Like Maltzman *et al*. (1979), Siddle, Remington, and Churchill (1985) used a differential conditioning procedure to control for non-associative effects of preexposure. In addition, they employed a procedure to control for any non-specific effects of stimulus preexposure. To date, this is the only investigation of latent inhibition in human subjects to utilize both of these control procedures simultaneously. In one experiment, the UCS was a tone that signalled a reaction time requirement, and in another, it was a white noise burst of 105 dB. Prior to conditioning, subjects received either 20 presentations each of the to-be-CS+ and the to-be-CS− (preexposure condition), or 20 presentations each of two control stimuli (non-specific control condition). CS duration was 8 sec and first interval anticipatory responses (FAR) were defined as changes in skin conductance that occurred between 1.0 and 4.5 sec following CS onset. Second interval anticipatory responses (SAR) were scored as changes that occurred between 4.5 and 8.0 sec following CS onset, and, where appropriate, third interval omission responses (TOR) were scored as changes that occurred 1.0–4.5 sec following the time at which the UCS had previously occurred. With the reaction time tone as the UCS, differential FAR responding to CS+ and CS− during acquisition was greater in the control condition than in the preexposure condition, indicating latent inhibition (Figure 5.1, left panel). Moreover, differential FAR responding was maintained during extinction in the control condition, but not in the preexposure condition (Figure 5.1, right panel). Because the procedure included a UCS omission trial that was followed by a further CS-UCS pairing, the effects of preexposure on omission responding and on responding to the representation of the UCS could also be examined. Although CS preexposure had no effect on omission responding, there was marginally reliable evidence that whereas no-preexposure groups displayed larger UCS responses following omission than before, preexposure groups did not. In contrast to the data reported by Maltzman *et al.* (1979), preexposure had no effect on TOR magnitude during extinction, and neither the maximum CS+ response nor the trial on which it occurred was influenced by preexposure. Some of these results were replicated using the white noise UCS. Again, differential FAR responding was greater in control groups than in preexposure groups (Figure 5.2, left panel) and, in addition, differential SAR responding during the first six acquisition trials tended to be smaller in the preexposure conditions (Figure 5.2, right panel). However, CS preexposure had no effect on either UCS omission responding or on UCS responses when the UCS was represented following the omission trial. Moreover, differential FAR, SAR, and TOR responding during extinction was not influenced by preexposure.

In summary, evidence for latent inhibition in human Pavlovian conditioning

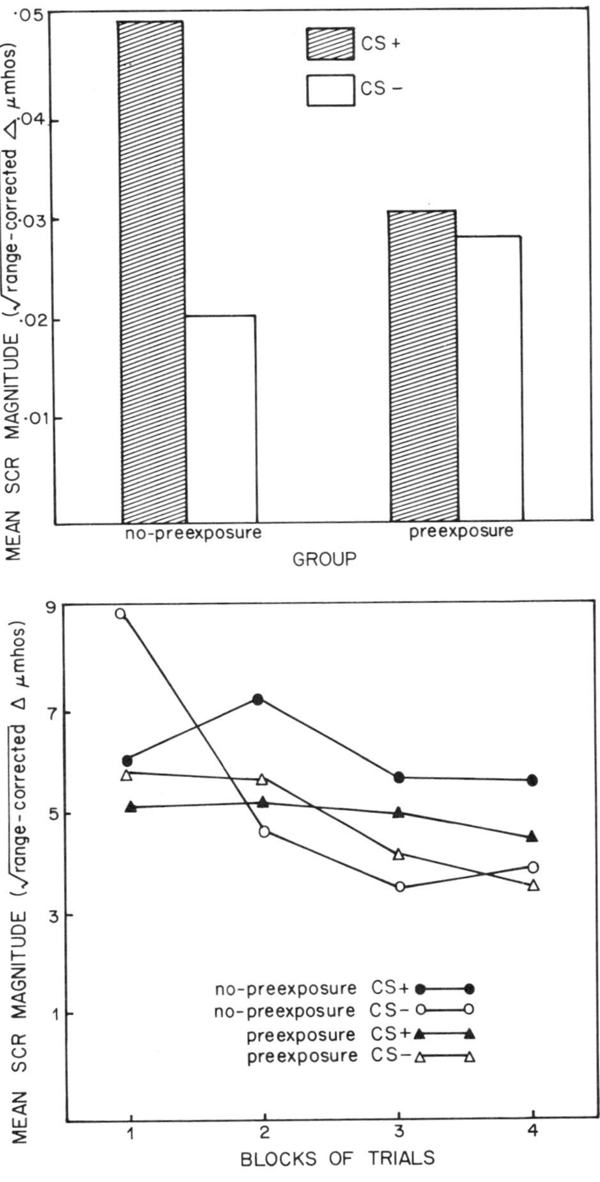

Figure 5.1 Mean FAR responding to CS+ and CS− across blocks of acquisition trials (bottom panel) and mean FAR responding to CS+ and CS− during extinction (upper panel). (*From Siddle, Remington, and Churchill, 1985; reprinted by permission*)

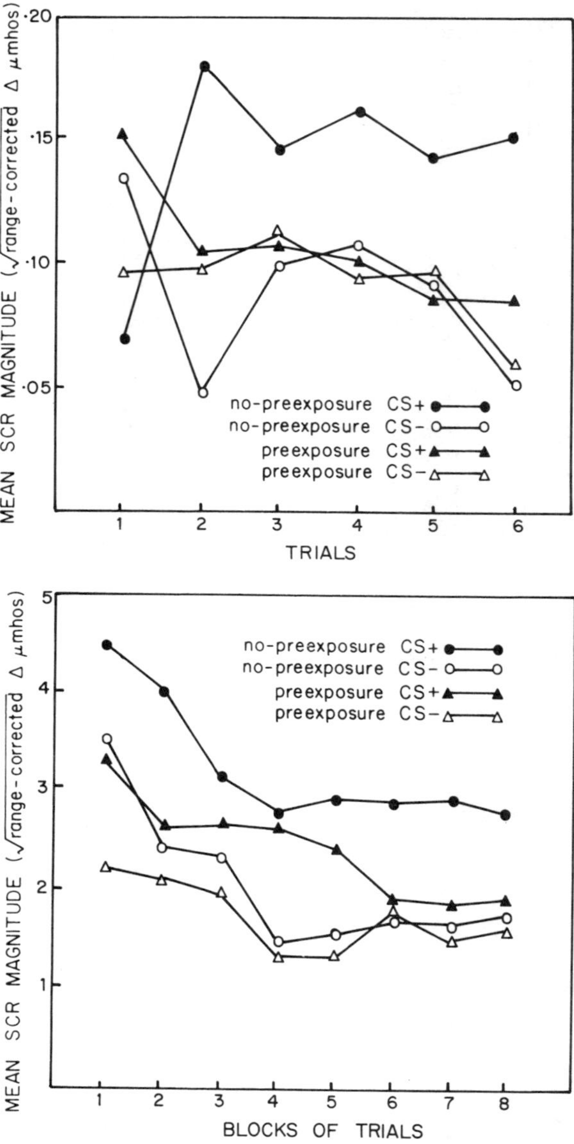

Figure 5.2 Mean FAR responding to CS+ and CS− across blocks of acquisition trials (bottom panel) and mean SAR responding to CS+ and CS− across the first six acquisition trials (upper panel). (*From Siddle, Remington, and Churchill, 1985; reprinted by permission*)

is somewhat weak. Not only are the data equivocal, but many of the studies have not included the appropriate controls. An adequate demonstration of latent inhibition must show that latent inhibition is *specific* to CS preexposure. That is, the effect must be demonstrated by reference to a group that receives the same number of preexposure trials with a stimulus distinct from the CS. In addition, there must be an adequate control for CS-UCS pairings. Without such a control, it cannot be concluded that CS preexposure influences the development of an *associative* process. Finally, theory-driven research is conspicuous by its absence. This is perhaps not too surprising in view of the methodological problems inherent in providing an adequate demonstration of the phenomenon. A reliable experimental paradigm would presumably provide an opportunity for a more systematic parametric exploration of the conditions under which latent inhibition can be observed in humans. As yet, such a paradigm does not seem to be available.

3 Theoretical relevance of latent inhibition

3.1 Animal-based theorizing

As noted earlier, latent inhibition is one of several phenomena for which any adequate theory of Pavlovian conditioning must account. In this section, we will discuss how current theories account for the effects of CS preexposure. Although a detailed examination of theories of Pavlovian conditioning is beyond the scope of this chapter, we must of necessity provide sufficient background to illustrate the manner in which latent inhibition is handled by different theories.

The experimental operations used in the first phase of a latent inhibition experiment (CS preexposure) are procedurally identical to those involved in producing habituation. In view of this, attempts to explain latent inhibition by recourse to the concept of habituation are only to be expected. Indeed, there are data which encourage such an approach. For example, both latent inhibition (Schnur and Lubow, 1976) and habituation (Davis and Wagner, 1968) have sometimes been shown to increase as a function of stimulus intensity, and long ISIs have been shown to produce more habituation (Davis, 1970) and more latent inhibition (Lantz, 1973). However, to say that latent inhibition is produced by habituation is to say little of theoretical interest unless it is possible to specify what *processes* underlie habituation and latent inhibition and to specify the way in which these processes interact. This is precisely the approach adopted by some recent theories.

Wagner (1978) has attempted to account for latent inhibition within a more general theory of Pavlovian conditioning and habituation. The key assumptions of this approach are that surprising or unexpected stimuli are more elaborately processed in short-term memory than are expected stimuli and this is said to result in the transfer of more fully consolidated episodic information to long-term memory, i.e. to more learning. The degree to which a stimulus is expected depends upon the extent to which it is prerepresented or primed in short-term memory. Priming may be self-generated by presentation of the stimulus itself or associatively-generated by retrieval cues. The retrieval cues may be CSs, as in the case of Pavlovian UCSs, or may simply be contextual cues. For associatively generated priming, there is retrieval from long-term memory of relevant episodic information.

Wagner's (1978) treatment of latent inhibition in particular and conditioning in general derives from the Rescorla–Wagner theory of Pavlovian conditioning (Rescorla and Wagner, 1972). Wagner's approach can be expressed most clearly by reference to the way it developed from the original theoretical statements. Rescorla and Wagner have presented a mathematical model which may be used to deduce the associative strength of a stimulus during Pavlovian conditioning operations. Associative strength (V) is an intervening variable determined by CS-UCS contingency, and it, in turn, determines the magnitude of the CR. According to the Rescorla–Wagner theory, change in associative strength, on a trial i, is given by Equation 1:

$$\Delta V_i = \alpha\beta(\lambda - \bar{V}) \tag{1}$$

where α and β are learning rate parameters associated with CS and UCS respectively, λ is the maximum conditioning supportable by the UCS, and $\bar{V}$ is current associative strength. Within the Rescorla and Wagner (1972) theory, α was generally taken to refer to the salience of the CS. Because α was assumed to be a fixed learning rate parameter, probably reflecting the physical properties of the CS, the theory had no ready way of handling the fact that the effectiveness of a CS can apparently be changed by simple exposure.

Wagner's (1978) elaboration of the original theory was in part an attempt to account for variations in the associability of a preexposed stimulus by extending the concept of priming to the CS. The theory can be expressed first as in Equation 2:

$$\Delta V_i = \alpha\beta[\lambda - (\bar{V} + K)] \tag{2}$$

where $\bar{V} + K$ stands for the total UCS representation in short-term memory at the time of UCS presentation, $\bar{V}$ stands for UCS representation due to associatively-generated priming by CS, and K stands for UCS representation due to self-generated priming from prior presentations. Because CS representation can be dealt with in a manner parallel to that for the UCS, the statement can be expanded as in Equation 3:

$$\Delta V_i = \delta[l - (\bar{v} + k)]\beta[\lambda - (\bar{V} + K)] \tag{3}$$

Where l is the maximum conditioning supportable by the CS, $\bar{v}$ is CS representation in short-term memory due to associatively-generated priming by contextual cues, and k is CS representation due to self-generated priming.[1]

The symmetry of Equation 3 reflects Wagner's (1978) intention to integrate habituation and conditioning at a process level. With regard to conditioning, unexpected UCSs (on, for example, the first conditioning trial) are more elaborately processed and result in a relatively large increment in associative strength. As the UCS becomes less unexpected through self-generated and associatively-generated priming, the increased in associative strength that accrues from each conditioning trial becomes less and less. Similarly, in the case of habituation, stimulus repetition results in progressively better priming, less elaborate processing, and progressively smaller responses. Latent inhibition is simply accounted for: latent inhibition is said to result from the priming of the CS representation that occurs during preexposure—the same processing decrement that is said to underlie response habituation. The processing decrement is said to be carried over into the acquisition phase as a result of associatively-generated priming by contextual cues. Because a preexposed CS, unlike a novel CS, is already represented in short-term memory, it is less elaborately processed and this reduces its capacity to enter easily into associations. It follows from Wagner's theory that variables which have attenuating or augmenting effects on habituation during the preexposure phase should also have predictable attenuating or augmenting effects on latent inhibition during acquisition. It also follows that latent inhibition will be attenuated by contextual change and by further exposure to the context alone following the CS preexposure phase. In the case of contextual change, the new context will not be expected to prime a representation of the CS into short-term memory so that despite preexposure, the CS will be processed in a relatively elaborate fashion and will enter quite easily into an association with the UCS. In the case of context exposure, extended experience of the context without further CS presentations is expected to lead to extinction of the context-CS association so that little context-generated priming of the CS remains by the beginning of the acquisition phase. Thus, the CS will be processed elaborately and will enter easily into an association with the UCS.

Hall and his colleagues (e.g. Hall and Pearce, 1979; Pearce and Hall, 1980) have also proposed a general theory of Pavlovian conditioning that contains an account of latent inhibition. However, their approach is fundamentally different from that of Wagner (1978). In order to outline the approach taken by Pearce and Hall (1980), we must first consider, at least in general terms, Mackintosh's (1975) theory of conditioning. We have already seen that Rescorla and Wagner (1972) placed the burden of learning entirely upon decrements in the processing of the UCS, whereas Wagner's (1978) theory allows the possibility of decrements in the processing of both UCS and CS.

Wagner has argued that the effectiveness of any stimulus is decreased to the extent that the organism anticipates it on the basis of antecedent events. When an event, either a CS (in the case of latent inhibition) or a UCS (in the case of Pavlovian conditioning) is fully primed, it fails to be processed by a limited-capacity learning mechanism. However, it could be argued with equal plausibility that the processing a stimulus receives increases to the extent that an organism may use it to predict other important events (Dickinson, 1980). This is the central notion of Mackintosh's (1975) theory of conditioning. With respect to associative learning, Mackintosh has proposed that the occurrence of a UCS leads to a retrospective evaluation of the predictive efficacy of all CSs present at the time of UCS delivery. The evaluation is then used to control CS processing on the next trial, in that the CS that was the best predictor on trial n will receive more processing on trial $n + 1$; CSs with less predictive power on trial n will receive less processing on trial $n + 1$. Essentially, the organism always processes predictors of important events, while learning to ignore irrelevant stimuli. Thus, a major difference between Wagner's and Mackintosh's views of Pavlovian conditioning relates to the question of which stimuli are processed: Wagner believes that the UCS suffers a processing decrement as a result of CS-UCS pairings, whereas Mackintosh asserts that training produces an increment in the processing of a CS, that has reliably predicted the UCS.

Like Mackintosh (1975), Pearce and Hall (1980) have argued that variation in CS processing determines the course of conditioning. However, recall that Hall and Pearce (1979) found that preexposure to CS–weak shock pairings retarded subsequent acquisition with CS–strong shock. Thus, a stimulus can lose associability even as it gains associative strength. Mackintosh's (1975) theory cannot account for these data, because it requires that as a stimulus gains associative strength, it will command more processing, and thus become more associable than other stimuli present during acquisition. To handle their data, Pearce and Hall (1980) have proposed a model of conditioning which asserts that a CS gains access to the processing mechanism if it *fails* to predict its past consequences. That is, CSs that are good predictors of their consequences are *less* elaborately processed (or processed in a different manner), and capacity is devoted to events that are poor predictors. In fact, Pearce and Hall have utilized the distinction between automatic and controlled processing (Shiffrin and Schneider, 1977) to propose that a CS which is a good predictor of the UCS is processed in an *automatic* mode. Thus, although events that are good predictors of their consequences are still able to control behaviour, they cannot easily enter into new associations. New learning is said to require *controlled* processing (see also Dawson and Schell, 1985, Chapter 2; Öhman, 1979).

Like Mackintosh, Pearce and Hall's theory asserts that the predictive power of all CSs present on a trial is evaluated following that trial. Pearce and Hall's

(1980) idea that the associability of a CS on conditioning trial $n(\alpha_A{}^n)$ depends upon how well it has predicted a UCS is expressed in Equation 4:

$$\alpha_A{}^n = |\lambda^{n-1} - V_A{}^{n-1}| \tag{4}$$

Associability on trial n is thus a function of the absolute difference between the intensity of the UCS on the previous trial (λ^{n-1}) and the associative strength of the CS on that trial ($V_A{}^{n-1}$). In essence, the associability of a CS is increased to the extent that there is a discrepancy between the event which had been expected and that which has just occurred. Pearce and Hall (1980) also argue that the gain in associative strength on a conditioning trial depends not only on CS associability, but also on its physical intensity. This idea can be represented in Equation 5:

$$\Delta V_A = S_A \alpha_A \lambda \tag{5}$$

where S is a parameter related to CS intensity. By substitution for α, the change in associative strength to CS_A on trial n is given by Equation 6:

$$\Delta V_A{}^n = S_A |\lambda^{n-1} - V_A{}^{n-1}| \lambda^n \tag{6}$$

Thus, Pearce and Hall's model predicts that during conditioning, increases in the associative strength of a CS will tend to a limit of λ, while there will be a concurrent decline in the associability of the CS to a limit of zero.

Application of the Pearce and Hall (1980) theory to latent inhibition is relatively straightforward. When a CS is preexposed in the absence of a UCS, both λ and associative strength will be zero. During the preexposure phase, the associability of the CS will decline to zero from a starting value presumably determined by prior experience with similar stimuli. Thus, when the CS is subsequently paired with the UCS, little or no conditioning will occur on the first trial, and a difference between the associative strengths acquired by preexposed and non-preexposed CSs will be established. Because the preexposed CS does not predict its consequences on the first acquisition trial, its associability should be restored. Thus, one implication of Pearce and Hall's theoretical analysis is that latent inhibition should be more easily observed early in the acquisition phase.

Pearce and Hall's (1980) model differs from Wagner's (1978) theory in that it does not include an account of habituation. More recently, however, Pearce and Hall (see Hall and Channell, 1985; Kaye and Pearce, 1984) have extended their analysis by arguing that associability (α) can be operationalised in terms of behavioural orienting. This implies that the decline in orienting that occurs as a function of stimulus repetition reflects a decline in stimulus associability, i.e. that habituation and latent inhibition share a common mechanism. Kaye and Pearce (1984) have reported a series of appetitive conditioning studies that provide evidence consistent with this proposal. Thus, both Wagner and Pearce and Hall now argue that the processing decrement thought to underlie habituation is important in producing latent inhibition. However, whereas Wagner assets that a to-be-CS loses associability and is less elaborately processed as it comes to be predicted by contextual cues, Pearce and Hall argue that a preexposed CS loses associability as it comes to predict that it has no consequences.

Despite apparently clear differences between the theories proposed by Wagner (1978) and by Pearce and Hall (1980), it has been difficult to distinguish them at the empirical level (see Mackintosh, 1983). One area that might be important for differentiating the Wagner and the Pearce and Hall accounts of latent inhibition concerns the effects of contextual factors. Whereas contextual cues have a central role in Wagner's (1978) formulation, Pearce and Hall's (1980) theory does not specify any mechanism by which contextual cues might be important in latent inhibition. There are several important questions here, and the most obvious is whether latent inhibition is context-specific. We have already cited evidence which indicates that in transfer-of-training experiments, latent inhibition is attenuated when the CS preexposure and the CS-UCS pairing phases occur in different contexts. This finding seems to hold regardless of whether the context used for CS-UCS pairings is novel (Channell and Hall, 1983; Lubow, Rifkin, and Alek, 1976) or familiar (Hall and Minor, 1984; Lovibond *et al*., 1984). Of equal importance for Wagner's (1978) theory, however, is the prediction that further exposure to context-alone following the CS preexposure phase will result in extinction of context-CS associations and thus lead to an attenuation of latent inhibition. Although some data are consistent with this prediction (Baker and Mercier, 1982; Wagner, 1979; Westbrook *et al*., 1981), others are not (Hall and Minor, 1984).

Even if we could conclude, on the basis of transfer-of-training studies, that latent inhibition is context-specific, this has no special bearing on the theoretically relevant question of whether the processes which underlie habituation also underlie latent inhibition, as required by Wagner's (1978) theory. An interpretation of this sort would be possible if habituation and latent inhibition could be shown to be similarly sensitive to identical contextual manipulations. There are few such direct comparisons of habituation and latent inhibition, but a number of studies have investigated the context-specificity of habituation. Unfortunately, however, the data are equivocal. Although some data suggest that habituation is context-specific (e.g. Evans and Hammond, 1983; Peeke and Veno, 1973), others do not (e.g. Leaton, 1974; Marlin and Miller, 1981, Experiment 3). Moreover, as Mackintosh (1983) has noted, evidence for the context-specificity of habituation does not necessarily imply that associations between context and the stimulus are of prime importance. Mackintosh has suggested that an event plus context might form a perceptual configuration such that presentation of the same event in a different context produces a configural stimulus that is sufficiently different to disrupt habituation. However, Wagner's associative analysis of habituation also predicts that further exposure to the context-alone following habituation training will lead to extinction of the context–stimulus association and thus to an attenuation of latent inhibition. Data of exactly this sort have been reported by Wagner (1976) from an experiment that involved habituation of rabbit peripheral vasoconstriction responses. Animals that were exposed to the context for 24 hours following habituation training displayed *larger* responses to the habituation stimulus (i.e. less habituation) in the test session than did animals that were returned to home cages for the 24 hour period between training and testing. On the other hand, Marlin and Miller (1981, Experiment 4) found no evidence to indicate that long-term habituation of rat startle was disrupted by further exposure to the experimental context between training and testing phases.

A recent series of experiments by Hall and Channell (1985) has provided data that bear directly on the question of whether the same processes are responsible for both habituation and latent inhibition. Using a behavioural measure of orienting in rats, Hall and Channell reported that a familiar stimulus (i.e. a stimulus to which response habituation had occurred) presented in a novel context elicited substantial orienting. To rule out the effects of context novelty, Hall and Channell conducted a second experiment in which they exposed experimental subjects to two contexts (A and B), only one of which (A) was accompanied by the light stimulus to which habituation was measured. A control group was also exposed to both contexts, but not to the light stimulus. Habituation was subsequently tested in context B for both groups. The results showed that presentation of a familiar stimulus in a context in which it had never before occurred, but which was familiar, did not produce dishabituation. Thus, habituation was not context-specific. In Experiment 3, Hall and Channel examined latent inhibition in appetitive conditioning using the animals from Experiment 2 and the habituation stimulus as the CS. They observed that preexposure to the CS in context A produced latent inhibition only when conditioning subsequently occurred in context A. Experimental subjects preexposed to the CS in context A but conditioned in context B conditioned at about the same rate as did control subjects who had not been preexposed to the CS. That is, latent inhibition was context-specific.

What Hall and Channell's (1985) data seem to indicate, therefore, is a dissociation between habituation and latent inhibition. That is, whereas habituated responses were *not* restored when the stimulus was presented in a different but familiar context, latent inhibition was attenuated when the acquisition phase took place in a familiar context which was different from that used during preexposure. However, the conditioning in Experiment 3 was performed in *both* context A and context B. If latent inhibition is context-specific, the design of Hall and Channell's experiment could reveal a context-dependent attenuation of latent inhibition only if conditioning itself is context-specific. That is, for attenuation of latent inhibition to be revealed, there must have been *no* generalization of conditioning from one context to the other. Although it has been argued that the context can act as a cue for conditional relationships that hold in that context (e.g. Bouton and Bolles, 1979), the recent series of well-controlled studies by Lovibond *et al.* (1984) found no evidence for the effect. Given the empirical weakness of the conditional cue account of context-specificity, Hall and Channell's data offer no conclusive evidence of a dissociation between latent inhibition and habituation.[2] Nevertheless, the data reported by Hall and Channell (1985) pose a number of problems for current theories of habituation and latent inhibition. First, the fact that habituated responses were not restored when the stimulus was presented in a different but familiar context is problematical for Wagner's (1978) theory of habituation with its emphasis on context–stimulus associations. Second, the restoration of habituated responses by a familiar stimulus presented in a novel context poses problems for the Pearce and Hall (1980) theory in that it specifies no mechanism by which contextual change can influence the effectiveness of a stimulus.

In addition to the general theories of Pavlovian conditioning discussed above, a rather more specific theory of latent inhibition has been proposed by Lubow (see Lubow *et al.*, 1976; Lubow *et al.*, 1981). Conditioned attention theory asserts simply that any novel stimulus results in a central attention-like response that can be maintained by contiguous stimulation, but which otherwise declines. Thus, non-reinforced preexposure to a CS retards subsequent conditioning to that stimulus because the organism learns, during preexposure, not to attend to it. The rules that govern the maintenance or extinction of the attention response are said to be those of classical conditioning.

In a recent review, Lubow *et al.*, (1981) attempted to demonstrate how conditioned attention theory can account for what is known about latent inhibition. Although space considerations preclude a detailed discussion of Lubow *et al.*'s arguments, conditioned attention theory does seem capable of accounting for much of the data. For example, the positive relationship between CS intensity and latent inhibition, the attenuation of latent inhibition by presentation of a distractor event prior to the acquisition phase, and the attenuation of latent inhibition by presentation of another stimulus immediately following the CS during preexposure, are all consistent with Lubow's theory. On the other hand, it is not clear how conditioned attention theory accounts for the fact that when the CS is followed by another stimulus during preexposure, latent inhibition is attenuated when the second stimulus is omitted at the end of the preexposure phase and immediately prior to acquisition (Hall and Pearce, 1982). Moreover, the theory does not specify a mechanism whereby latent inhibition can be influenced by contextual manipulations, although it does make some predictions about the effects of exposure to the context. Specifically, Lubow *et al.* (1981) have predicted that exposure to the context prior to the CS preexposure phase will increase latent inhibition because context exposure will facilitate the acquisition of conditioned inattention. Wagner's (1978) theory, of course, makes the opposite prediction. Exposure to the context prior to the CS preexposure phase should, through self-generated priming, result in latent inhibition of contextual cues so that they enter less easily into associations with the CS. This, in turn, should result in less latent inhibition during the CS-UCS pairing phase. Although the effects of context exposure prior to the CS preexposure phase provide a way of pitting conditioned attention theory against priming theory, the appropriate experimental work has yet to be performed.

3.2 Human-based theorizing

As the previous section has shown, the experimental analysis of latent inhibition in animals has been intensive and searching. It is somewhat embarrassing, therefore, that a procedure as simple as CS preexposure can produce effects that continue to defy complete explanation (Mackintosh, 1983). Rather more embarrassing, however, is the current level of understanding of the phenomenon in human subjects. As we have already seen, almost all of the human-based research has been demonstrational in nature, and has not, therefore, been designed to bear on important theoretical issues. Unfortunately, much of the research has also failed to provide an adequate demonstration of latent inhibition, in that it has omitted to include one or other of the important control procedures necessary to establish a stimulus-specific and associative effect of preexposure. Where adequate controls have been included, the effects observed have been nothing like as robust as those obtained with animal subjects. The absence of an effective paradigm for inducing reliable preexposure effects makes theory-driven research with human subjects somewhat difficult. At the end of this section, we will discuss some ways in which current experimental methods might be improved. First, however, we will consider what few data there are that bear on the theoretical issues raised by both animal research and by other theoretical accounts of classical conditioning in humans.

The experiments reported by Siddle *et al.* (1985), although essentially demonstrational, provided some data of theoretical relevance. In both studies, the acquisition phase included a trial in which the UCS was omitted, and this trial was followed by a further CS-UCS pairing. To the extent that responding to the absence of the UCS reflects the degree to which the UCS was primed by the CS (Siddle, 1985; Siddle *et al.*, 1983), Wagner's (1978) theory predicts that CS preexposure will result in smaller UCS omission responses. This did not occur in either of the experiments. At the same time, Pearce and Hall's (1980) theory predicts that UCS omission will restore the associability of the CS and lead to increased responsiveness to the CS on the trial following omission. Again, this did not occur in either experiment.

Maltzman *et al.* (1979) have elaborated an account of latent inhibition within Maltzman's (1979, Chapter 6) more general theory of Pavlovian conditioning in humans. Maltzman (1979) conceptualizes Pavlovian conditioning as involving problem-solving activity in which subjects learn the significance of the CS, i.e. that it predicts the UCS. Learning is said to involve the conditioning of attention as reflected by the orienting response (OR), and the discovery by subjects that the CS predicts the UCS is said to lead to what Maltzman has termed a 'voluntary OR'. To account for latent inhibition, Maltzman *et al.* (1979) argued that subjects preexposed to the CS have a more complex problem to solve so that the discovery of CS significance is retarded. In this sense, the introduction of a preexposure phase is seen as equivalent to introducing a masking task (Maltzman *et al.*, 1979, p. 97).

As Maltzman *et al.* (1979) have pointed out, their data might pose some problems for conditioned attention theory. Maltzman *et al.* argued that because the CS+ word was not presented during the preexposure phase, conditioned inattention could not develop to that word. Nevertheless, it might be argued that because latent inhibition can display generalization (Siegel, 1969a), presentation of words *per se* could lead to a retardation of acquisition. If this were the case, however, preexposed groups should have displayed a lower level of responding to all words (including CS− words) during acquisition. This did not occur. In short, conditioned attention theory cannot account for Maltzman *et al.*'s data by recourse to the phenomenon of generalization *and* explain the fact that preexposed and control groups did not differ in terms of CS− responding during acquisition.

Maltzman *et al.*'s (1979) account, although perhaps lacking the scope of animal-based theories, does draw attention to one of the primary problems that arise in attempting to provide a rigorous demonstration of latent inhibition in human Pavlovian conditioning. The rapid learning which typically occurs during simple conditioning obscures the effects of CS preexposure (Lubow, 1973b; personal communication, 1985). Drawing largely upon studies of the effects of stimulus familiarization on reaction time and upon studies of discrimination learning, Lubow has concluded that latent inhibition can be demonstrated more easily in children than in adults (Kaniel and Lubow, in press; Lubow, Alek, and Arzy, 1975; Lubow, Caspy, and Schnur, 1982). On this basis, Lubow has suggested that in adult studies the use of a masking task during the preexposure phase, the conditioning phase, or both, may facilitate a demonstration of latent inhibition.

Human Pavlovian conditioning does occur quickly and is slowed by the use of a masking task. It is possible, therefore, that the addition of a masking task would provide a more sensitive paradigm for a demonstration of latent inhibition. However, we need to consider carefully the reasons why this might be so. It may well be, for example, that a masking task present during acquisition has a retarding effect on conditioning because subjects must detect which of several possible stimuli is functionally related to UCS presentation. If this were so, differences between preexposed and non-preexposed groups which, without masking, would be seen only in early CS-UCS pairings might endure for longer or occur later in the acquisition phase. If masking tasks did exert their effects in this manner, their use during the acquisition, rather than the preexposure, phase of a latent inhibition experiment would be of prime interest. Unfortunately, there are no latent inhibition data which bear directly on the use of masking tasks during Pavlovian acquisition. However, studies which have not used a masking task and which have examined responding across blocks of acquisition trials (e.g. Siddle *et al*., 1985) have obtained only weak latent inhibition effects. In this connection it is interesting to note that the animal data often indicate only a small lag in the progress of conditioning (one to four trials) between preexposed and non-preexposed groups (e.g. Dickinson, 1976; Hall and Pearce, 1979).

An alternative way of using a masking procedure would be to present it during the preexposure phase. On the basis of conditioned attention theory, Kaniel and Lubow (in press) have argued that a masking task during the preexposure phase serves to divert attention from the to-be-CS; a masking task is said to reduce CS salience and thus enhance the occurrence of inattention. There seem to be both logical and empirical problems with this argument. The argument might be that a to-be-CS embedded in a masking task may be perceived as part of the contextual background, and will not, therefore, elicit attentional responses (Ginton, Urca, and Lubow, 1975). However, if a to-be-CS does not elicit attentional responses (i.e. is not processed) during preexposure, it could be argued that a reduction in salience could not occur and, functionally, the stimulus will be relatively novel at the start of the acquisition phase. Latent inhibition would not be expected under these circumstances. If, on the other hand, a reduction in salience does occur, it suggests that inattention has been conditioned, presumably because the masking task did not work effectively! Whatever the merits of these arguments, Ginton *et al*. (1975) presented an auditory to-be-CS to either the ear that was monitored for other events or to the unattended ear during the preexposure phase, and found that latent inhibition occurred regardless of the direction of attention during preexposure.

Although the use of an appropriate masking task may retard the process of conditioning, its effectiveness in revealing latent inhibition effects will be determined largely by experimental ingenuity in finding an appropriate index of the learning process. As Siddle *et al*. (1985) have noted, the integration of human research with animal-based models of conditioning must confront a difficult problem, especially when psychophysiological measures are employed to index conditioning. The difficulty is that in electrodermal conditioning, for example, different constructs such as associability, salience, and associative strength are assumed to be indexed by the same set of peripheral responses. Thus, changes in the magnitude of skin conductance responses may mark changes in CS associability as during the preexposure phase, or changes in associative strength of a CS as a function of its predictive relationship with the UCS as in the acquisition phase. Whether the different electrodermal responses that are observed in long-interval Pavlovian conditioning provide independent measures of associability and associative strength is a matter for debate. Öhman's (1983) comprehensive review suggests that the FAR and SAR are statistically independent and that the FAR is influenced primarily by CS factors such as intensity and fear-relevance. The SAR is more sensitive to UCS probability and the TOR is clearly dependent upon CS-UCS contingency (Öhman, 1974; Siddle *et al*., 1983). Thus FAR responding might index changes in CS associability and changes in associative strength might be reflected by the SAR and the TOR. Because the FAR clearly has a large orienting component (Öhman, 1983), the idea that it reflects associability accords well with the ideas advanced by Hall and Channell (1985) and by Kaye and Pearce (1984).

One way to avoid the problems created by the use of psychophysiological measures that might reflect a number of theoretically important constructs is to employ alternative indices of CS and UCS processing. A promising start in this respect has been made by Dawson, Schell, Beers, and Kelly (1982) with their use of the probe reaction time technique. This requires subjects to respond occasionally to a reaction time cue which may be presented during the ITI, CS, or UCS periods. Increases in reaction time when Pavlovian stimuli are presented or expected are held to reflect the demand for processing elicited by these events. Using this procedure, Dawson *et al*. demonstrated that not only was more processing devoted to CS+ than to CS−, but that a miscued UCS (i.e. a UCS that followed a *CS*−) commanded extra processing resources. A strategy of converging operations that involved psychophysiological and probe reaction time data might not only assist in the integration of animal and human research at a general level, but might provide an incisive manner with which to investigate human latent inhibition.

To conclude this section, it is clear that although the phenomenon of latent inhibition is of considerable theoretical significance, research with human subjects has contributed rather little to the issues raised by the animal work. Moreover, the human literature permits few empirical generalizations. It is possible, however, that research on human latent inhibition has a potentially important role to play. A continuing issue in human research concerns the relationship between conditioned behaviour and orienting, and much of the debate can be framed in terms of the question of whether the relationship between conditioning and orienting is extrinsic or intrinsic (Öhman, 1983). If orienting and conditioning involve different processes (i.e. the relationship is extrinsic), orienting could be removed or controlled for, while leaving the conditioning process unaffected. If, however, orienting and conditioning are related at the process level (i.e. the relationship is intrinsic), modification of orienting would alter the progress of conditioning. Because a good deal is known about human orienting, at least at the level of empirical generalizations (Siddle, 1983), the opportunity exists for a systematic experimental analysis of the relationship between conditioning and orienting in humans. Latent inhibition is clearly a pivotal issue with respect to the understanding of this relationship.

4 Clinical relevance of latent inhibition

In the previous section, we discussed the theoretical importance of latent inhibition. This section is devoted to a brief discussion of the clinical relevance of the phenomenon. The issue of clinical relevance can be addressed in two ways. First, it is possible that the phenomenon of latent inhibition can be exploited as a means of behavioural prophylaxis (Lubow, 1973b). Second, consideration of latent inhibition might help to explain results that are seemingly inconsistent with the view that Pavlovian conditioning plays an important role in the development of maladaptive behaviour.

With regard to behavioural prophylaxis, Lubow (1973b) proposed that the induction of latent inhibition might serve as a means of immunization against the development of maladaptive behaviour that was based on Pavlovian learning. Lubow cited Surwit's (1972) results on the effects of preexposure to aspects of the dental environment on children's responses to dental treatment. Although, as Lubow also noted, the identification of populations at risk and of relevant CSs is difficult, a preexposure procedure might function effectively to reduce acquired fears of any setting in which aversive stimuli are necessarily delivered in the course of medical treatment (e.g. a series of injections). Note, however, that although a procedure which attenuated the acquisition of conditioned fear should reduce the subsequent avoidance of an otherwise threatening environment, it would do nothing to reduce the impact of the aversive UCS at the time of delivery. Such effects may occur (see, for example, Solomon and Corbit, 1974), but they are not normally attributed to latent inhibition. More recently, the relevance of latent inhibition for human taste aversions has been noted. There is evidence of learned taste aversions in humans (Garb and Stunkard, 1974; Logue, Ophir, and Strauss, 1981), and the possible role of such aversions in producing the anorexia seen in some patients who undergo chemotherapy has been noted (e.g. Bernstein, Webster, and Bernstein, 1982). Cannon, Best, Batson, and Feldman (1983) have obtained evidence that flavour preexposure might result in latent inhibition as indexed by an attenuation of food aversion. They examined the effects of preexposure to a novel flavour (cranberry juice) on flavour aversion learning that was supported by an injection of apomorphine. Volunteer subjects underwent preexposure trials three times on each of three consecutive days prior to a single flavour–apomorphine pairing. Preexposure attenuated flavour aversion, as compared with a no-preexposure control condition, when aversion was measured 4 days after conditioning. The effect was not evident 1 month later. Although Cannon *et al*. (1983) were suitably cautious in discussing their findings, they did note that the results have implications for the management of anorexia in chemotherapy patients.

There is one area in which the difficulty in identifying potential CSs against which immunization could be developed (Lubow, 1973b) might be overcome. This relates to the acquisition of phobias in so far as they are the result of conditioning processes. On the basis of Seligman's (1970) criticisms of general-process theories of learning and epidemiological evidence that human phobias are highly selective (e.g. Agras, Sylvester, and Oliveau, 1969), Öhman has argued (Öhman, 1979; Öhman, Dimberg, and Öst, 1985) that small-animal phobias represent an example of prepared learning (see also Seligman, 1971). In a long series of studies on human Pavlovian conditioning with fear-relevant (slides of snakes and spiders) and fear-irrelevant (slides of flowers and mushrooms) CSs, Öhman and his associates have demonstrated that conditioning with 'fear-relevant' CSs is more resistant to extinction, can be established by one CS-UCS pairing, and is less susceptible to instructional manipulation (see reviews by Öhman, 1979, and Öhman *et al*., 1985). Associations between snakes and spiders on the one hand and unpleasant or aversive events on the other are said to be biologically prepared. Leaving aside difficulties inherent in the concept of preparedness (Schwartz, 1974), it does appear, at least at first sight, that the fear-relevant CSs employed by Öhman might be prime candidates for the immunization that should accrue from CS preexposure. However, the prepared learning model holds that it is not stimuli that are prepared, but *associations*. On this basis, it can be argued that preexposure to a fear-relevant CS might be *less* effective in producing latent inhibition than is preexposure to a potential CS whose associations with aversive events are not prepared. Such an assertion would be relatively easy to test using the experimental paradigm employed by Öhman and his associates. On the other hand, the preparedness model was developed, in part at least, on the basis of taste aversion data, and as we have seen earlier, latent inhibition does occur with both flavour and odour aversion after only one preexposure. Despite these uncertainties, it is clear that latent inhibition with fear-relevant CSs is a fertile area for investigation.

The second way in which latent inhibition might have clinical relevance is more indirect and concerns the kind of model of Pavlovian conditioning that is utilized in explanations of psychopathology. For many years, behaviour therapists have used a Pavlovian conditioning model to explain the acquisition of fear-related behaviour and to develop treatment procedures for its elimination. However, doubts have been expressed about the adequacy of the model and some influential advocates of the approach have recently questioned or revised their earlier positions (Eysenck, 1976; Rachman, 1977). Rachman (1977), for example, has reviewed the conditioning model of fear acquisition, and has concluded that it is inadequate on a number of grounds. These include: failure to acquire fear in fear-evoking situations, the difficulty of producing human conditioned fear reactions in the laboratory, the assumption that all potential CSs are equally capable of acquiring fear-evoking properties (the premise of equipotentiality), the distribution of human fears, case histories that are inconsistent with a conditioning model, and the fact that fears can be acquired indirectly.

Öhman's (1979) research and theorizing about conditioning with fear-relevant CSs can be viewed as one attempt to overcome some of the apparent deficiencies associated with the application of general-process learning theory to psychopathology. Specifically, Öhman and his colleagues have addressed the issue of equipotentiality and the unequal distribution of phobias in the general population. They have also examined the question of whether Pavlovian conditioning can occur vicariously (Hygge and Öhman, 1978), and most importantly, the research raises fundamental questions about the relationship between cognition and affect in Pavlovian conditioning.

Öhman's work aside, however, it can be argued that the approach to Pavlovian conditioning adopted by many of those interested in experimental psychopathology involves a model of conditioning that has been rejected by many animal learning theorists for the past 20 years. As Reiss (1980) has noted, there is little mention in the behaviour therapy literature of *current* models of Pavlovian learning and of phenomena such as blocking, inhibitory conditioning, overshadowing, and latent inhibition to which current theorizing is directed. Indeed, the model of Pavlovian conditioning adopted, either explicitly or implicitly, by many behaviour therapists invovles CS-UCS contiguity as the necessary and sufficient factor for the production of conditioning. Reiss (1980) has argued persuasively that consideration of current theories and the phenomena on which they are based has considerable potential for understanding why some CS-UCS contingencies produce conditioning and others do not. Take, for example, a situation in which two cues (A and B) occur together, are followed by a UCS, but in which fear develops only to cue A. Current theories of Pavlovian learning suggest ways by which this outcome might occur. For example, cue A might be more salient than cue B, and the Rescorla–Wagner (1972) theory predicts that not only will the more salient cue (A) gain more associative strength than will the less salient cue (B), but also that cue A will actively prevent cue B from gaining associative strength. The salience difference might arise because cue A is more physically intense than is cue B, or because cue B has been exposed prior to the conditioning episode. Alternatively, the subject's previous history may have involved cue A-UCS pairings. If this were the case, cue A would 'block' cue B from acquiring associative strength (Kamin, 1969). Similarly, current theories of conditioning also have implications for therapeutic procedures. For example, Rescorla (1979) has shown that novel stimuli present during extinction may acquire conditioned inhibitory properties, and may partially protect the CS from extinction. This finding might be relevant to any extinction-based therapy procedure (e.g. flooding) in which the treatment sessions differ markedly from the setting in which the CS is normally encountered. Under these circumstances, preexposure to the therapeutic setting might reduce its associability and thus allow complete extinction of responding to the CS to occur.

In essence, what we are suggesting is that there must be more integration between approaches to psychopathology that utilize a Pavlovian conditioning model and the body of theory and research whose aim is to elucidate the relationships that are learned in conditioning experiments and the rules that govern the formation of associations. If this were to occur, the phenomenon of latent inhibition and theoretical accounts of it may well provide those interested in the understanding and treatment of psychopathology with a powerful explanatory and therapeutic tool.

Notes

1 In fact, the equation we have used is a modification of that provided by Wagner (1978). Wagner's (1978, p. 208) final equation read:

$$\Delta V_i = \alpha[l - (\bar{v} + k)]\beta[\lambda - (\bar{V} + K)]$$

Howevei, because CS representation is reflected by $[l - (\bar{v} + k)]$ which can be considered to be a substitute for α (Pearce and Hall, 1980, p. 535), it seems appropriate to represent the fixed rate learning parameter associated with the CS by the symbol δ.

2 We are indebted to Peter Lovibond for valuable discussion on this point.

Acknowledgements

Preparation of this work was facilitated by Grant A28415689 from the Australian Research Grants Scheme to the first author, a grant from the Committee for Advanced Studies, University of Southampton, to the second author, and Grant GR/6099.6 from the UK Science and Engineering Research Council to both authors.

Thanks are due to Nigel Bond and Muriel Churchill for their critical reading of an earlier draft of this chapter.

References

Agras, W. S., Sylvester, D., and Oliveau, D. (1969). The epidemiology of common fears and phobias, *Comprehensive Psychiatry*, **10**, 151–6.

Anderson, D. C., O'Farrell, T., Formica, R., and Caponigri, V. (1969). Preconditioning CS exposure: Variation in place of conditioning and of presentation, *Psychonomic Science*, **15**, 54–5.

Anderson, D. C., Wolf, D., and Sullivan, P. (1969). Preconditioning exposures to the CS: Variation in place of testing, *Psychonomic Science*, **15**, 233–5.

Baker, A. G., and Mercier, P. (1982). Extinction of the context and latent inhibition, *Learning and Motivation*, **13**, 391–416.

Bernstein, I. K., Webster, M. M., and Bernstein, I. D. (1982). Food aversions in children receiving chemotherapy for cancer, *Cancer*, **50**, 263–5.

Best, M. R., and Gemberling, G. A. (1977). Role of short-term processes in the conditioned stimulus preexposure effect and the delay of reinforcement gradient in long-delay taste-aversion learning, *Journal of Experimental Psychology: Animal Behavior Processes*, **3**, 253–63.

Best, M. R., Gemberling, G. A., and Johnson, P. E. (1979). Disrupting the conditioned stimulus preexposure effect in flavor aversion learning: Effects of interoceptive distractor manipulations, *Journal of Experimental Psychology: Animal Behavior Processes*, **5**, 321–34.

Bond, N., and DiGuisto, E. (1975). Amount of solution drunk as a factor in the establishment of taste aversion, *Animal Learning and Behavior*, **3**, 81–4.

Bouton, M. E., and Bolles, R. C. (1979). Contextual control of the extinction of conditioned fear, *Learning and Motivation*, **10**, 445–66.

Cannon, D. S., Best, M. R., Batson, J. D., and Feldman, M. (1983). Taste familiarity and apomorphine-induced taste aversions in humans, *Behaviour Research and Therapy*, **21**, 669–73.

Carlton, P. L., and Vogel, J. R. (1967). Habituation and conditioning, *Journal of Comparative and Physiological Psychology*, **63**, 348–51.

Channell, S., and Hall, G. (1983). Contextual effects in latent inhibition with an appetitive conditioning procedure, *Animal Learning and Behavior*, **11**, 67–74.

Crowell, C. R., and Anderson, D. C. (1972). Variation in intensity, interstimulus interval, and interval between preconditioning CS exposures and conditioning with rats, *Journal of Comparative and Physiological Psychology*, **79**, 291–8.

Davis, M. (1970). Effects of interstimulus interval length and variability on startle-response habituation in the rat, *Journal of Comparative and Physiological Psychology*, **72**, 177–92.

Davis, M., and Wagner, A. R. (1968). Startle responsiveness after habituation to different intensities of tone, *Psychonomic Science*, **12**, 337–8.

Dawson, M. E., and Furedy, J. J. (1976). The role of awareness in human differential autonomic classical conditioning: The necessary-gate hypothesis, *Psychophysiology*, **13**, 50–3.

Dawson, M. E., and Schell, A. M. (1985). Information processing and human autonomic classical conditioning, in *Advances in Psychophysiology*, vol. 1 (eds. P. K. Ackles, J. R. Jennings, and M. G. H. Coles), 89–165. JAI Press, Greenwich, Conn.

Dawson, M. E., Schell, A. M., Beers, J. R., and Kelly, A. (1982). Allocation of cognitive processing capacity during human autonomic classical conditioning, *Journal of Experimental Psychology: General*, **111**, 273–95.

Dickinson, A. (1976). Appetitive-aversive interactions: Facilitation of aversive conditioning by prior appetitive training in the rat, *Animal Learning and Behavior*, **4**, 416–20.

Dickinson, A. (1980). *Contemporary Animal Learning Theory*, Cambridge University Press, Cambridge.

Domjan, M., and Siegel, S. (1971). Conditioned suppression following CS preexposure, *Psychonomic Science*, **25**, 11–12.

Evans, J. G. M., and Hammond, G. R. (1983). Differential generalization of habituation across contexts as a function of stimulus significance, *Animal Learning and Behavior*, **11**, 431–4.
Eysenck, H. J. (1976). The learning theory model of neurosis—a new approach, *Behaviour Research and Therapy*, **14**, 251–67.
Frey, P. W., and Sears, R. J. (1978). Model of conditioning incorporating the Rescorla–Wagner associative axiom, a dynamic attention process, and a catastrophe rule, *Psychological Review*, **85**, 321–40.
Furedy, J. J., Riley, D. M., and Fredrickson, M. (1983). Pavlovian extinction, phobias, and the limits of the cognitive paradigm, *Pavlovian Journal of Biological Science*, **18**, 126–35.
Garb, J. L., and Stunkard, A. J. (1974). Taste aversions in man, *American Journal of Psychiatry*, **131**, 1204–7.
Ginton, A., Urca, G., and Lubow, R. E. (1975). The effects of preexposure to a nonattended stimulus on subsequent learning: Latent inhibition in adults, *Bulletin of the Psychonomic Society*, **5**, 5–8.
Grant, D. A., Hake, H. W., Riopelle, A. J., and Kostlan, A. (1951). Effects of repeated pre-testing with conditioned stimulus upon extinction of the conditioned eyelid response to light, *American Journal of Psychology*, **54**, 247–51.
Grant, D. A., Hake, H. W., and Schneider, D. E. (1948). Effects of pre-testing with the conditioned stimulus upon extinction of the conditioned eyelid response, *American Journal of Psychology*, **61**, 243–6.
Hall, G., and Channell, S. (1985). Differential effects of contextual change on latent inhibition and on the habituation of an orienting response, *Journal of Experimental Psychology: Animal Behavior Processes*, **11**, 470–81.
Hall, G., and Minor, H. (1984). A search for context-stimulus associations in latent inhibition, *Quarterly Journal of Experimental Psychology*, **36B**, 145–69.
Hall, G., and Pearce, J. M. (1979). Latent inhibition of a CS during CS-US pairings, *Journal of Experimental Psychology: Animal Behavior Processes*, **5**, 31–42.
Hall, G., and Pearce, J. M. (1982). Restoring the associability of a pre-exposed CS by a surprising event, *Quarterly Journal of Experimental Psychology*, **34B**, 127–40.
Hernandez, L. L., Buchanan, S. L., and Powell, D. A. (1981). CS preexposure: Latent inhibition and Pavlovian conditioning of heart rate and eyeblink responses as a function of sex and CS intensity in rabbits, *Animal Learning and Behavior*, **9**, 513–18.
Hulstijn, W. (1978). The orienting reaction during human eyelid conditioning following preconditioning exposures to the CS, *Psychological Research*, **40**, 77–88.
Hygge, S., and Öhman, A. (1978). Modeling processes in the acquisition of fears: Vicarious electrodermal conditioning to fear-relevant stimuli, *Journal of Personality and Social Psychology*, **36**, 271–9.
James, J. P. (1971). Latent inhibition and the preconditioning–conditioning interval, *Psychonomic Science*, **24**, 97–8.
Kalat, J. W., and Rozin, P. (1973). 'Learned safety' as a mechanism in long-delay taste-aversion learning in cats, *Journal of Comparative and Physiological Psychology*, **83**, 198–207.
Kamin, L. J. (1969). Predictability, surprise, attention, and conditioning, in *Punishment and Aversive Behavior* (eds. B. A. Campbell and R. M. Church), pp. 279–96, Prentice-Hall, Englewood-Cliffs, N.J.
Kaniel, S., and Lubow, R. E. (in press). Latent inhibition: A developmental study, *British Journal of Developmental Psychology*.
Kaye, H., and Pearce, J. M. (1984). The strength of the orienting response during

Pavlovian conditioning, *Journal of Experimental Psychology: Animal Behavior Processes*, **10**, 90–109.
Lantz, A. E. (1973). Effect of number of trials, interstimulus interval, and dishabituation during CS habituation on subsequent conditioning in a CER paradigm, *Animal Learning and Behavior*, **1**, 273–7.
Leaton, R. N. (1974). Long-term retention of the habituation of lick-suppression in rats, *Journal of Comparative and Physiological Psychology*, **87**, 1157–64.
Logue, A. W., Ophir, I., and Strauss, K. E. (1981). The acquisition of taste aversion in humans, *Behaviour Research and Therapy*, **19**, 319–33.
Lovibond, P. F., Preston, G. C., and Mackintosh, N. J. (1984). Context specificity of conditioning, extinction, and latent inhibition, *Journal of Experimental Psychology: Animal Behavior Processes*, **10**, 360–75.
Lubow, R. E. (1973a). Latent inhibition, *Psychological Bulletin*, **79**, 398–407.
Lubow, R. E. (1973b). Latent inhibition as a means of behavior prophylaxis, *Psychological Reports*, **32**, 1247–52.
Lubow, R. E., Alek, M., and Arzy, J. (1975). Behavioral decrement following stimulus preexposure: Effects of number of preexposures, presence of a second stimulus, and interstimulus interval in children and adults, *Journal of Experimental Psychology: Animal Behavior Processes*, **104**, 178–88.
Lubow, R. E., Caspy, T., and Schnur, P. (1982). Latent inhibition and learned helplessness in children: Similarities and differences, *Journal of Experimental Child Psychology*, **34**, 231–56.
Lubow, R. E., Markman, R. E., and Allen, J. (1968). Latent inhibition and classical conditioning of the rabbit pinna response, *Journal of Comparative and Physiological Psychology*, **66**, 688–94.
Lubow, R. E., Rifkin, B., and Alek, M. (1976). The context effect: The relationship between stimulus preexposure and environmental preexposure determines subsequent learning, *Journal of Experimental Psychology: Animal Behavior Processes*, **2**, 38–47.
Lubow, R. E., Schnur, P., and Rifkin, B. (1976). Latent inhibition and conditioned attention theory, *Journal of Experimental Psychology: Animal Behavior Processes*, **2**, 163–74.
Lubow, R. E., Weiner, I., and Schnur, P. (1981). Conditioned attention theory, in *The Psychology of Learning and Motivation*, vol. 15 (ed. G. Bower), pp. 1–49, Academic Press, New York.
Mackintosh, N. J. (1975). A theory of attention: Variations in the associability of stimuli with reinforcement, *Psychological Review*, **82**, 276–98.
Mackintosh, N. J. (1983). *Conditioning and Associative Learning*, Clarendon Press, Oxford.
Maltzman, I. (1979). Orienting reflexes and classical conditioning in humans, in *The Orienting Reflex in Humans* (eds. H. D. Kimmel, E. H. van Olst, and J. F. Orlebeke), pp. 323–51, Erlbaum, Hillsdale, N.J.
Maltzman, I., Raskin, D. C., and Wolff, C. (1979). Latent inhibition of the GSR conditioned to words, *Physiological Psychology*, **7**, 193–203.
Marlin, N. A., and Miller, R. R. (1981). Associations to contextual stimuli as a determinant of long-term habituation, *Journal of Experimental Psychology: Animal Behavior Processes*, **7**, 313–33.
Öhman, A. (1974). Orienting reactions, expectancy learning, and conditioned responses in electrodermal conditioning with different interstimulus intervals, *Biological Psychology*, **1**, 189–200.
Öhman, A. (1979). The orienting response, attention, and learning: An information-

processing perspective, in *The Orienting Reflex in Humans* (eds. H. D. Kimmel, E. H. van Olst, and J. F. Orlebeke), pp. 443–71, Erlbaum, Hillsdale, N.J.

Öhman, A. (1983). The orienting response during Pavlovian conditioning, in *Orienting and Habituation: Perspectives in Human Research* (ed. D. Siddle), pp. 315–69, Wiley, Chichester.

Öhman, A., Dimberg, U., and Ost, L.-G. (1985). Animal and social phobias: Biological constraints on learned fear responses, in *Theoretical Issues in Behavior Therapy* (eds. S. Reiss and R. R. Bootzin), 123–75. Academic Press, New York.

Pearce, J. M., and Hall, G. (1980). A model for Pavlovian learning: Variations in the effectiveness of conditioned but not of unconditioned stimuli, *Psychological Review*, **87**, 532–52.

Peeke, H. V. S., and Veno, A. (1973). Stimulus specificity of habituated agression in the stickleback (*Gesterosteus aculeatus*), *Behavioral Biology*, **8**, 427–32.

Perlmuter, L. C. (1966). Effect of CS manipulations on the conditioned eyelid response: Compounding, generalization, the inter-CS interval, and pre-exposure, *Psychonomic Monograph Supplements*, **1**, 271–86.

Rachman, S. (1977). The conditioning theory of fear-acquisition: A critical examination, *Behaviour Research and Therapy*, **15**, 375–87.

Reiss, S. (1980). Pavlovian conditioning and human fear: An expectancy model, *Behavior Therapy*, **11**, 380–96.

Reiss, S., and Wagner, A. R. (1972). CS habituation produces a 'latent inhibition effect' but no active 'conditioned inhibition', *Learning and Motivation*, **3**, 237–45.

Rescorla, R. A. (1969). Pavlovian conditioned inhibition, *Psychological Bulletin*, **72**, 77–94.

Rescorla, R. A. (1971). Summation and retardation tests of latent inhibition, *Journal of Comparative and Physiological Psychology*, **75**, 77–81.

Rescorla, R. A. (1979). Conditioned inhibition and extinction, in *Mechanisms of Learning and Motivation: A Memorial Volume to Jerzy Konorski* (eds. A. Dickinson and R. A. Boakes), pp. 83–110, Erlbaum, Hillsdale, N.J.

Rescorla, R. A., and Holland, P. C. (1976). Some behavioral approaches to the study of learning, in *Neural Mechanisms of Learning and Memory* (eds. M. R. Rosenzweig and E. L. Bennett), pp. 165–92, MIT Press, Cambridge, Mass.

Rescorla, R. A., and Wagner, A. R. (1972). A theory of Pavlovian conditioning: Variations in the effectiveness of reinforcement and nonreinforcement, in *Classical Conditioning II* (eds. A. H. Black and W. F. Prokasy), pp. 64–99, Appleton-Century-Crofts, New York.

Rudy, J. W., and Cheatle, M. D. (1978). A role for conditioned stimulus duration in toxiphobia conditioning, *Journal of Experimental Psychology: Animal Behavior Processes*, **4**, 399–411.

Rudy, J. W., Rosenberg, L., and Sandell, J. H. (1977). Disruption of a taste familiarity effect by novel exteroceptive stimulation, *Journal of Experimental Psychology: Animal Behavior Processes*, **3**, 26–36.

Schnur, P. (1971). Selective attention: Effect of element preexposure on compound conditioning of rats, *Journal of Comparative and Physiological Psychology*, **76**, 123–30.

Schnur, P., and Ksir, C. J. (1969). Latent inhibition in human eyelid conditioning, *Journal of Experimental Psychology*, **80**, 388–9.

Schnur, P., and Lubow, R. E. (1976). Latent inhibition: The effects of ITI and CS intensity during preexposure, *Learning and Motivation*, **7**, 540–50.

Schwartz, B. (1974). On going back to nature: A review of Seligman and Hager's

Biological Boundaries of Learning, *Journal of the Experimental Analysis of Behavior*, **21**, 183–98.
Seligman, M. E. P. (1970). On the generality of the laws of learning, *Psychological Review*, **77**, 406–18.
Seligman, M. E. P. (1971). Phobias and preparedness, *Behavior Therapy*, **2**, 307–20.
Shiffrin, R. M., and Schneider, W. (1977). Controlled and automatic human information processing: II. Perceptual learning, automatic attending, and a general theory, *Psychological Review*, **84**, 127–90.
Siddle, D. (ed.) (1983). *Orienting and Habituation: Perspectives in Human Research*, Wiley, Chichester.
Siddle, D. A. T. (1985). Effects of stimulus omission and stimulus change on dishabituation of the skin conductance response, *Journal of Experimental Psychology: Learning, Memory, and Cognition*, **11**, 206–16.
Siddle, D. A. T., Remington, B., and Churchill, M. (1985). Effects of conditioned stimulus preexposure on human electrodermal conditioning, *Biological Psychology*, **20**, 113–27.
Siddle, D. A. T., Remington, B., Kuiack, M., and Haines, E. (1983). Stimulus omission and dishabituation of the skin conductance response, *Psychophysiology*, **20**, 136–45.
Siegel, S. (1969a). Generalization of latent inhibition, *Journal of Comparative and Physiological Psychology*, **69**, 157–9.
Siegel, S. (1969b). Effect of CS habituation on eyelid conditioning, *Journal of Comparative and Physiological Psychology*, **68**, 245–8.
Siegel, S. (1970). Retention of latent inhibition, *Psychonomic Science*, **20**, 161–2.
Silver, A. I. (1973). Effects of prior CS presentations on classical conditioning of the skin conductance response, *Psychophysiology*, **10**, 583–8.
Solomon, P. R., Brennan, G., and Moore, J. W. (1974). Latent inhibition of the rabbit's nictitating membrane response as a function of CS intensity, *Bulletin of the Psychonomic Society*, **4**, 445–8.
Solomon, R. L., and Corbit, J. D. (1974). An opponent-process theory of motivation: I. The temporal dynamics of affect, *Psychological Review*, **81**, 119–45.
Surwit, R. S. (1972). The anticipatory modification of the conditioning of a fear response in humans. Unpublished doctoral dissertation, McGill University.
Surwit, R. S., and Poser, E. G. (1974). Latent inhibition in the conditioned electrodermal response, *Journal of Comparative and Physiological Psychology*, **86**, 543–8.
Szakmary, G. A. (1977). A note regarding conditioned attention theory, *Bulletin of the Psychonomic Society,* **9**, 142–4.
Wagner, A. R. (1976). Priming in STM: An information-processing mechanism for self-generated and retrieval-generated depression in performance, in *Habituation: Perspectives from Child Development, Animal Behavior, and Neurophysiology* (eds. T. J. Tighe and R. N. Leaton), pp. 95–128, Erlbaum, Hillsdale, N.J.
Wagner, A. R. (1978). Expectancies and the priming of STM, in *Cognitive Processes in Animal Behavior* (eds. S. H. Hulse, H. Fowler, and W. K. Honig), pp. 177–209, Erlbaum, Hillsdale, N.J.
Wagner, A. R. (1979). Habituation and memory, in *Mechanisms of Learning and Motivation: A Memorial Volume to Jerzy Konorski* (eds. A. Dickinson and R. A. Boakes), pp. 53–82, Erlbaum, Hillsdale, N.J.
Westbrook, R. F., Bond, N. W., and Feyer, A. M. (1981). Short- and long-term decrements in toxicosis-induced odor-aversion learning: The role of duration of

exposure to an odor, *Journal of Experimental Psychology: Animal Behavior Processes*, **7**, 362–81.

Westbrook, R. F., Provost, S. C., and Homewood, J. (1982). Short-term flavour memory in the rat, *Quarterly Journal of Experimental Psychology*, **34B**, 235–56.

Zeiner, A. R. (1970). Orienting response and discrimination conditioning, *Physiology and Behavior*, **5**, 641–6.

Cognitive Processes and Pavlovian Conditioning in Humans
Edited by G. Davey

Chapter 6

Pavlovian conditioning and hemispheric asymmetry: A perspective

Kenneth Hugdahl
Department of Somatic Psychology, University of Bergen, Norway

1 Introduction

In the present chapter I will present a perspective on human Pavlovian conditioning relevant to recent theoretical models and empirical data on hemispheric asymmetry, or lateralization, in the intact brain. It will be argued that contemporary theoretical formulations of Pavlovian conditioning and associative learning in terms of orienting and information-processing (Maltzman, 1979; Öhman, 1979a, 1984; Wagner, 1976), memory and expectancy (Estes, 1973; Rescorla, 1972; Whitlow and Wagner, 1984), and attention (Mackintosh, 1975) may be integrated with recent accounts of brain asymmetry and lateralization in terms of higher-order cognitive processing (Moscovitch, 1979; Bradshaw and Nettleton, 1981; Springer, 1977).

The chapter is divided into sections. A general outline of a cognitive view of Pavlovian conditioning is followed by a brief overview of models and methods of hemispheric asymmetry. Then a more detailed account of a lateralized perspective on Pavlovian conditioning is presented including the presentation of empirical data. From these sections, two paradigms developed in our laboratory for the study of lateralized stimulus input in conditioning are presented (the dichotic extinction paradigm and the dichotic acquisition paradigm). The next section deals with the role of awareness in conditioning, and its relation to hemispheric asymmetry, and there is a discussion of relevant animal data for the issue of lateralized effects in conditioning. The chapter ends with a brief summary.

2 Pavlovian conditioning: Theoretical integration

In a restricted sense, Pavlovian conditioning is probably best defined, or described, in empirical terms. Thus, Pavlovian conditioning may be sufficiently defined by four terms: a previously neutral, *conditioned stimulus* (CS) elicits a *conditioned response* (CR) after having been paired in contingency with an *unconditioned stimulus* (UCS) that reflexively elicits an *unconditioned response* (UCR). As argued by Öhman (1984), such a procedurally based definition of conditioning remains completely uncommitted with regard to theoretical interpretations. To take his argument one step further, a definition of conditioning based on a set of empirical manipulations does not even imply that there exists a set of corresponding theoretical concepts. However, in a broader sense, conditioning has traditionally been seen as the result of a close spatial and temporal contiguity between the unconditioned and the conditioned stimulus, resulting in a response to the conditioned stimulus resembling the unconditioned response (e.g. Gormezano and Kehoe, 1975). Conditioning may then be observed as a more or less automatic process inferred from the external contiguity between the CS and the UCS. This S-R view of conditioning not only dominated most of the earlier research, but was also taken as the theoretical foundation for the emerging behaviour therapy methods (e.g. Wolpe, 1958; Eysenck and Rachman, 1965) for the explanation of anxiety disorders. The traditional 'response-oriented' view of conditioning has, however, recently been replaced by a more cognitively based view (e.g. Rescorla, 1967, 1972; Rescorla and Wagner, 1972). Paradoxically, the cognitive reorientation first emerged within animal research (e.g. Rescorla, 1966), and later made its way into human conditioning and clinical applications in behaviour therapy (e.g. Eelen, 1982).

In modern learning theory, contingency rather than contiguity between the CS and the UCS is seen as the necessary prerequisite for conditioning to occur. Thus, it is the correlation between the CS and the UCS, rather than the 'nearness' in time and space that determines the empirical parameters of conditioning. This is to say that a CS must provide *information* about the occurrence of the UCS, meaning that it is the 'predictability' of the CS with regard to the UCS that is important. In addition, Wagner (1976) and Kamin (1969) have stressed that the UCS must in some sense be 'surprising' for the organism. This is illustrated by the 'blocking-paradigm' (Kamin, 1969) where pretraining with a CS_1 and the UCS results in inferior conditioning to a CS_2 during test if the CS_2 has been presented together with the CS_1 as a compound during acquisition. Apparently, the pretraining with the CS_1 'blocks' conditioning to the CS_2 although the CS_2 is paired with the UCS during the compound acquisition.

The implication of the cognitive view of conditioning is that contiguity alone is insufficient as an explanatory concept. The CS must provide information of the 'coming' of the UCS (Rescorla, 1972). This may be illustrated in what might be called 'a diluted' paradigm. Suppose we arrange a situation with simple tones as CSs and white noise as UCS, so that the occurrence of the noise is independent of the occurrence of the CS. That is, the probability of noise is constant at any given time irrespective of whether the CS is present or not. As pointed out by Rescorla (1972), in this situation the CS does not provide unique information about the UCS. However, if the UCS occurs frequently enough there will be some pairings with the CS by sheer chance. Thus, although there is no contingency in the situation, the CS and UCS occur in contiguity on some trials. Figure 6.1 illustrates a situation where the contingency is 'diluted'. In Figure 6.1(b) there are six UCS presentations, with three of them in contiguity with CS presentations, and three in the absence of CS presentations. Thus, although there are three CS-UCS pairings, the CS does not provide unique information for the occurrence of the UCS since the UCS also occurs in the absence of CS. However, if the situation is changed as in Figure 6.1(a), so that all the UCSs in the absence of a CS are

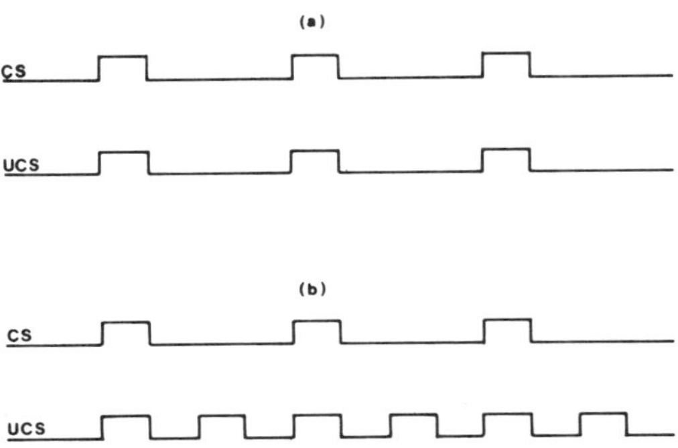

Figure 6.1 Illustration of differences in the amount of information about UCS occurrence provided by the CS. (a) The CS provides unique information of the occurrence of the UCS. (b) Since the UCS also occurs in the absence of the CS, the information about UCS occurrence provided by the CS is reduced compared to the situation in (a)

omitted, then the CS will provide unique information for the UCS occurrence, although the contiguity has not changed.

The purpose of this brief review is to introduce the reader to a cognitive information-processing view of conditioning, stressing such constructs as 'expectancy', 'attention', 'memory', and 'predictability'. From these process-oriented concepts it is a short step to invoke the notion of laterality and brain asymmetry. This is especially true when the basic nature of lateralization is conceptualized in terms of processing strategy (cf. Bradshaw and Nettleton, 1981). Such a view of lateralization stresses the attention and expectancy involved in the task, and how observed asymmetries on the behavioural level may reflect differences in how attention and memory are distributed between the hemispheres. From this it could be inferred that the learning of a contingency between a hemisphere-specific stimulus (e.g. a verbal CS) and a UCS may be related to asymmetrical processing in the brain depending on which hemisphere the stimulus is fed to (cf. Hugdahl, 1984). In fact, Kinsbourne (1973) has argued that observed asymmetries reflect covert shifts of attention to the side of the more activated hemisphere for a particular stimulus or task.

3 Hemispheric asymmetry: Concepts and methods

Only a brief overview of the major concepts and empirical findings concerning hemispheric asymmetry will be made, with no claim of complete coverage. In fact, the number of empirical reports related to the issue of brain asymmetry has long since made any serious attempt at complete review impossible in a single chapter. However, a good introductory text is provided by Springer and Deutsch (1981), and excellent reviews of the entire field of research are provided by Bryden (1982) and by Bradshaw and Nettleton (1983).

Speculations about the relationship between various psychological functions and the specialization of the two cerebral hemispheres in the intact brain have become increasingly popular during the last years. Such speculations are sometimes rather remote from empirical findings. It seems that cerebral asymmetry is used to explain almost every kind of behaviour and psychopathology, from the performance of philharmonics to the attentional span in schizophrenics. It is therefore perhaps sound to take a conservative standpoint concerning behavioural effects of brain asymmetry. However, this 'conservatism' is sometimes carried too far, even questioning the existence of the very phenomenon of functional asymmetry. I agree with Zaidel (1984) who stated that he, in addition to believing that the earth is round, and that the mind is the brain, also asserted a third belief, 'namely that hemispheric specialization exists' (p. 370).

3.1 Functional asymmetry

It is perhaps convenient to start this overview by introducing the distinction between differences in specialization of functions of the two hemispheres (*functional asymmetry*) and the question of whether the hemispheres also differ in shape and form (*structural asymmetry*). Turning first to functional asymmetry, one consistent finding is a superiority for the left hemisphere in processing of language, and language-related stimuli (see Bradshaw and Nettleton, 1981, 1983; Bryden, 1982, for reviews). However, it is important to realize that such a statement does not make a distinction between the expression of speech and perception of language. Most of the existing data indicate the first function to be left hemisphere specialized, or dominant, in most right-handers to a higher degree than the second function. The right hemisphere is mute for the expression of speech (Sperry, 1974; Gazzaniga and LeDoux, 1978). However, as Zaidel (1975; Zaidel and Peters, 1981), among others, has shown, the right hemisphere does have auditory language comprehension, i.e. it possesses some ability for the perception of language. Similarly, although the right hemisphere has a reading lexicon (Zaidel, 1978; Sperry and Gazzaniga, 1967), it seems that it cannot infer the sound of a word from its orthography, i.e. it cannot make grapheme-to-phoneme conversions that are necessary for the mastery of written language (Zaidel, 1984). Thus, both the expression and the perception of verbal stimuli are more specialized in the left hemisphere, although the right hemisphere is not totally devoid of linguistic ability. The terms 'specialized' and 'dominant' are used interchangeably in the present text to denote the concept of superior performance (both motor and sensory) of one hemisphere relative to the other. For a detailed discussion of different definitions of terms and models used in studies of hemispheric asymmetry the reader is referred to Allen (1983). It should be stressed that the left hemisphere dominance for speech expression and language perception is modulated by such factors as handedness (Rasmussen and Milner, 1977), gender (McGlone, 1980), familial sinistrality (Hécaen and Sauguet, 1971), and possibly also hand-posture during writing (Levy and Reid, 1976), although the latter factor has been questioned by Weber and Bradshaw (1981). Thus, all of these factors must be considered and carefully controlled for in all laterality experiments.

Although most theories of laterality and brain asymmetry have been concerned with finding dichotomies and opposites between the hemispheres, it should be clear that just because the left hemisphere is dominant for language, it does not follow a priori that the right hemisphere should be equally as dominant for an opposite, or dichotomous, function (cf. Bryden, 1982). However, although a functional dichotomy may not be inferred a priori, most studies have reported a right hemisphere dominance for the perception and processing of visuo-spatial functions, like the arrangements of block-designs (Galin and Ornstein, 1972), dot enumeration (Kimura, 1966), and perception of tonal patterns (Gordon, 1970), as well as the expression and perception of facial emotions (Suberi and McKeever, 1977; Ley and Bryden, 1979). Thus, a basic, probably biologically based, dichotomous specialization of the two cerebral hemispheres is the ability to communicate with other members of the species, and the ability to orient oneself in space with the help of visual and auditory cues.

3.2 Nature of the stimulus vs. nature of the task

Both Springer and Deutsch (1981) and Bradshaw and Nettleton (1981) (see also Bryden, 1982) have argued that interpreting the basic differences between the hemispheres in terms of the nature and content of the stimulus they are most specialized to process is an oversimplification of hemispheric asymmetry. Rather than focusing on the verbal vs. non-verbal aspects of the stimulus, some studies (e.g. Seamon and Gazzaniga, 1973; Klatzky and Atkinson, 1971) indicate that process-variables like the task to be performed upon the stimulus, or the cognitive strategy used are more important. This way of arguing is then reminiscent of other conceptions of hemispheric asymmetry as 'differences in cognitive style' (Levy-Agresti and Sperry, 1968; Ornstein, 1977) or 'preferred cognitive mode' (Kolb and Whishaw, 1980). When hemispheric asymmetry is conceptualized in terms of differences in process strategy it is also usually assumed that the asymmetry occurs at a later stage in the information-processing chain (Moscovitch, 1979; Butler and Glass, 1976). For example, Sergent (1985) demonstrated a right hemisphere advantage for face recognition only when the information in the stimulus was degraded, thus making it more difficult to perceive the stimulus. However, using lateralized presentations of Stroop-words, Hugdahl and Franzon (1985) found the content of the stimulus to be an important factor in observed asymmetries. Thus, it seems that both the stimulus content and the strategy used by the subject in solving the task are critical variables in the study of hemispheric asymmetry.

3.3 Structural asymmetry

The question of structural asymmetry is related to the view that reported functional asymmetries are the result of differences in the anatomy and structure of the two hemispheres. Although research on hemispheric asymmetry mostly has been concerned with functional asymmetry, important developments within structural asymmetry have been made using autopsy methods as well as more recently developed radiological methods like computerized tomography (CAT) and positron emitted tomography (PET).

In an often cited paper, Geschwind and Levitsky (1968) reported that a small area in the temporal lobe, called planum temporale, close to the Sylvian fissure and Heschl's gyrus, was larger on the left than on the right side of the brain. This area is overlapping the language area in the temporal lobe, and may thus be related to reported functional language asymmetries. Furthermore, the middle cerebral artery leaves the Sylvian fissure at a steeper angle on the left side. The Sylvian fissure is also longer and more horizontally placed than the right fissure (LeMay and Culebras, 1972). A thorough review of structural asymmetries is found in Galaburdao, LeMay, Kemper, and Geschwind (1978).

In order to facilitate comparisons between the studies reviewed in the following sections, a short outline and description of two of the major non-invasive techniques (i.e. the visual half-field (VHF) and the dichotic listening (DL) techniques) will be provided.

3.4 The visual half-field (VHF) technique

Figure 6.2 shows the major projections from the retina in the eye to the primary visual cortex in the occipital lobe. The nasal portion of the retinal inflow of light is projected to the *contralateral* hemisphere due to the overcrossing in the optical chiasma. The temporal portion of the inflow is, however, projected to the *ipsilateral* hemisphere. This means that when the eyes are fixated upon a centrally placed point in the visual field, then stimuli presented to the right of fixation will be projected initially only to the left hemisphere. Similarly, a stimulus presented to the left of fixation will initially be projected only to the right hemisphere. Thus, a verbal stimulus presented in the right half-field will have direct access to the left hemisphere, whereas a stimulus presented in the left half-field must first be transmitted from the right hemisphere through the corpus callosum and other commissures before it can reach the left hemisphere.

Thus, hemispheric differences in the processing of verbal and visuo-spatial stimuli and tasks can be investigated by randomly alternate stimulation in the left and the right half-field. Dependent variables may be either behavioural measures like response latency, response accuracy, and error frequency, or psychophysiological measures like bilateral EEG and event-related potentials (ERPs), or bilateral electrodermal recordings (EDA), and heart-rate (HR) recordings. Stimuli should be flashed briefly (<200 msec) since saccadic eye movements otherwise may distort the unilateral hemisphere projection. Control procedures, like electrooculography (EOG), should be employed to make

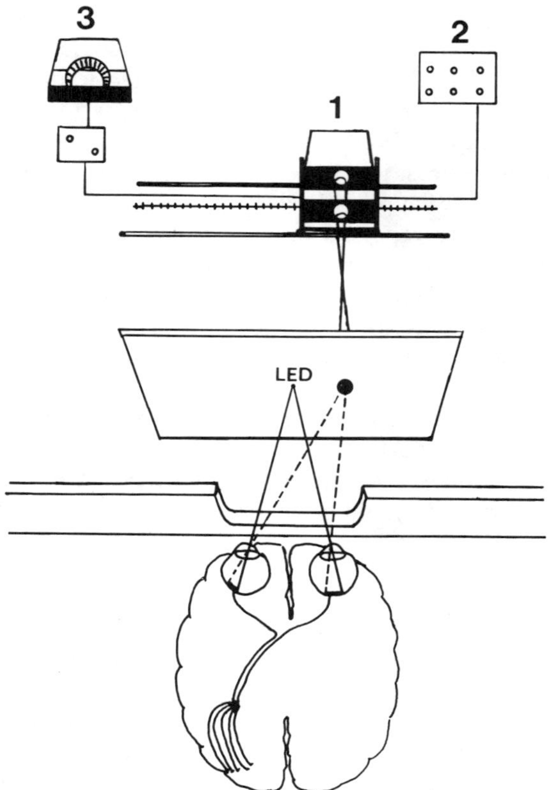

Figure 6.2 Schematic description of the major projections in the visual system, illustrating overcrossing in the optical chiasma. (*From Larsson, Ågren, and Hugdahl, 1983. Reprinted by permission of the publisher*)

sure that the subject actually is fixating the centre of the visual field during stimulation.

It is, however, important to keep in mind that although the visual system is more or less 'perfectly' lateralized in an anatomical sense, stimulation of a single half-field only means an initial advantage for the contralateral hemisphere, since the information rapidly transverses the corpus callosum to reach the other hemisphere. Despite this, superior performance has been obtained for verbal stimuli when presented in the right half-field (called a right field advantage, RFA) (Bryden, 1965; Hugdahl and Franzon, 1985; Bradshaw and Taylor, 1979). Similarly, superior performance has been obtained for nonverbal stimuli presented in the left half-field (Kimura, 1966; Davidoff, 1976; Meyer, 1976).

3.5 The dichotic listening (DL) technique

The general principle for the method of dichotic listening is seen in Figure 6.3.

The theoretical rationale behind the dichotic listening technique is that under conditions of competition between the ears (e.g. when two different auditory stimuli are simultaneously presented, one to each ear), the contralateral projections from the ear to the auditory cortex predominate. That the contralateral pathways are more preponderant than the ipsilateral ones has been established by both electrophysiological techniques, like ERPs (Rosenzweig, 1955; Majkowski, Bochenek, Bochenek, Knapik-Fijalkowska, and Kopec, 1971; Andreassi, DeSimone, Friend, and Grota, 1975; Connolly, 1985), and through monitoring of regional cerebral blood-flow (rCBF) (Maximilian, 1982). The predominance of the contralateral cortical representation of each ear may possibly be a consequence of the ampler projection of second-order neurons to the inferior colliculus on the contralateral than on the ipsilateral side (Brodal, 1981). Although the input to, and the output from, the inferior colliculus are both ipsilateral and contralateral, as a rule, the projection ascending *to* the inferior colliculus is larger from the contralateral than from the ipsilateral ear. However, the pathway ascending *from* the collicle is larger on the ipsilateral side, thus favouring the ultimate representation of the contralateral ear in the auditory cortex (Brodal, 1981).

The contralateral predominance in the auditory system results, according to Kimura (1967), from the fact that a stronger projection from the right ear to the left hemisphere will suppress weaker ipsilateral projection from the left ear. When verbal stimuli are used this suppression by the contralateral

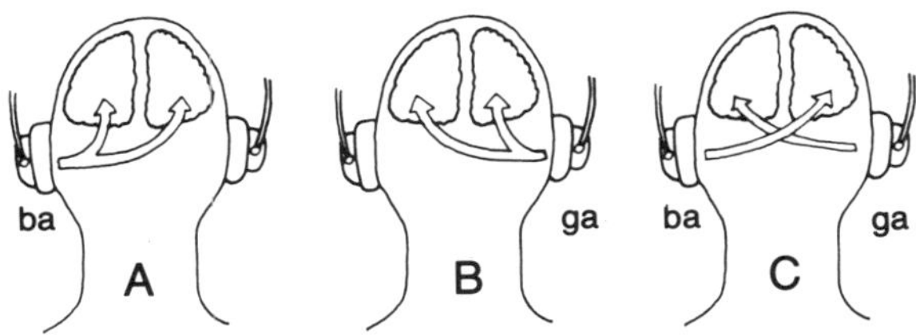

A = Example of monaural stimulation of left ear with the syllable "ba". Note both ipsi- and contralateral projections.

B = Example of monaural stimulation of right ear with the syllable "ga".

C = Example of dichotic stimulation with two different syllables at the same time. The contralateral projections predominate during this condition. Thus, "ga" will be mainly projected to the left hemisphere, and "ba" to the right hemisphere.

Figure 6.3 Schematic description of the principle behind the dichotic listening technique. Contralateral projections are more preponderant than the ipsilateral ones

projection will result in superior recall and recognition of the right ear input. However, some recent evidence (Geffen and Quinn, 1984) argues against Kimura's notion of ipsilateral suppression. The behavioural superiority for the right ear input to verbal stimuli is called a right ear advantage (REA), and taken as an index of hemispheric asymmetry for verbal stimuli. A REA is reported for different kinds of stimuli including digits (Kimura, 1961) and meaningful words (Satz, Achenback, and Fennell, 1967). However, the most frequently used stimuli in DL research are the so called consonant–vowel (CV) syllables including a single consonant paired with a vowel (e.g. Studdert-Kennedy and Shankweiler, 1970). Usually, the stop-consonants, b, d, g, p, t, k together with a vowel are used (e.g. Hugdahl and Andersson, 1984). One of the critical issues in dichotic listening is the synchronization of stimulus onset between channels in order to obtain an exact temporal alignment between the ears. As shown by Berlin (1977), even a 10 msec difference between the ears in the start of the stimuli will result in a disruption of the REA. Therefore, computer generated tapes should be used which allow for exact control of the temporal parameters involved in the technique. One such computer program is the CADDIC—software developed by Hugdahl, Engstrand and Nordstrand (1986).

4 A lateralized perspective on Pavlovian conditioning

A lateralized perspective on Pavlovian conditioning is perhaps most intriguing in the area of human conditioning on the one hand, and language lateralization on the other hand. Even if such a perspective primarily is research-oriented, the successful demonstration of effects of brain asymmetry on conditioning could also have possible clinical value. For example, if lateralized stimulation shows an effect on conditioning in the intact brain, then failure of conditioning in a lesioned brain could be taken as evidence for a deficiency in associative learning at an 'early' stage in the learning process. Thus, the use of a lateralized conditioning paradigm (see section 5 for a description) could be a first step in identifying subtle lesions in the brain which affect learning and memory.

Turning to the research laboratory, it is surprising that so little attention has been paid to the connection between hemispheric asymmetry and conditioning considering the obvious similarities in the concepts used to describe models of asymmetry and models of conditioning. For one thing, if Pavlovian conditioning is couched in information-processing terms (Öhman, 1984; Maltzman, 1979; Dawson, Schell, Beers, and Kelly, 1982) stressing such concepts as 'attention', 'information', and 'expectancy', it is a short step to infer that conditioning to a verbal CS should be differentially affected depending on whether the stimulus is initially fed to the left or to the right hemisphere. Similarly, when the CS is embedded in a masking task making discriminations difficult, superior conditioning should result if the CS is presented initially to the dominant hemisphere and the 'mask' to the other hemisphere, than the other way around. Moreover, if conditioning is said to involve higher-order extraction of information in the CS-UCS contingency (cf. Rescorla, 1980), then the left hemisphere would be at an advantage relative the right hemisphere if the CS is a verbal stimulus. Finally, conditioning to fear-relevant CSs (like pictures of snakes and spiders, Öhman, 1979b; Hare and Blevings, 1975) could be predicted to be more easily acquired and/or more resistant to extinction (cf. Öhman, Fredrikson, Hugdahl, and Rimmö, 1976) if the CSs are initially fed only to the right hemisphere which is believed to be more involved than the left in the processing of emotionally relevant stimuli (Schwartz, Davidson, and Maer, 1975).

In 1970, Seligman proposed that the general laws of learning may not be valid for all kinds of stimuli and responses. Instead he suggested that organisms had evolved a biologically determined 'preparedness' to more easily associate certain stimuli with certain reinforcers. The prototype of the 'prepared paradigm' was the taste-aversion phenomenon (Garcia and Koelling, 1966) where rats easily developed an avoidance response to saccharin-flavoured water if previously paired with injections of lithium chloride (which makes the animal sick), but not when paired with external shocks. However, although critical voices have been raised concerning preparedness (Logue, 1979; Maltzman and Boyd, 1984; McNally, 1981), prepared learning made the way for the introduction of ***stimulus-significance*** as an important factor in conditioning. In the present context, stimulus-significance indicates that conditioning is more easily established when the CS is a non-arbitrary event in relation to the UCS, and to the organism. It is further suggested in the present chapter than stimulus-significance is not only related to biological evolution through 'prepared' contingencies, but that the significance of a verbal CS as compared to a visuo-spatial CS is as biologically important to the organism as is the 'prepared' attribute of the stimulus.

4.1 Asymmetry and orienting: Implications for conditioning

The involvement of functional asymmetry in response systems related to human associative conditioning is most obvious in the electrodermal system. First of all, recent evidence suggests a central role for the temporal and frontal lobes in control of electrodermal activity (EDA) (Wang, 1964; Wilcott and Bradley, 1970; Kimble, Bagshaw, and Pribram, 1965). Second, research has demonstrated bilateral differences in responding with the right and left hands to stimuli that presumably differentially activate the hemispheres (Lacroix and Comper, 1979; Myslobodsky and Rattok, 1977; Boyd and Maltzman, 1982).

These findings should, however, be interpreted with some caution considering that other investigators have failed to report a difference between the hands (Gross and Stern, 1980; Erwin, McClelland, and Kleinman, 1980; Hugdahl, Wahlgren, and Wass, 1982). The issue of bilateral differences in EDA and the relation to hemispheric asymmetry has recently been independently reviewed by Hugdahl (1984) and by Freixa I Baque, Catteau, Miossec and Roy (1984). However, although Hugdahl, Broman, and Franzon (1983a) failed to demonstrate a difference in responding between the hands, significantly larger skin conductance responses (SCRs) were observed from *both* hands when visual verbal stimuli were flashed to the left hemisphere using the VHF technique. Moreover, larger SCRs were observed to visuo-spatial stimuli flashed initially to the right hemisphere. A third area of research relating associative functions and EDA conditioning to hemispheric asymmetry is recent work on both normal and pathological samples showing asymmetry of orienting responses (ORs) and habituation to repeated auditive and visual stimulation. In 1973 Gruzelier reported more spontaneous responses in the right compared to the left hand in institutionalized schizophrenics in a habituation paradigm. This finding is elaborated in a more recent work by Gruzelier (1984) arguing that different schizophrenic syndromes may be related to either left or right hemisphere overactivation. Furthermore, Myslobodsky and Horesh (1978) reported larger amplitudes in the left hand in endogenous depressives compared to normals. Finally, Hugdahl, Wahlgren, and Wass (1982b) found a significant delay in habituation when non-verbal visual stimuli were repeatedly presented only to the right hemisphere.

Considering the close relationship between recent views of orienting and habituation, and of Pavlovian conditioning (see Öhman, 1984; Maltzman, 1979, for reviews), where the OR is said to be crucial to the emergence of a CR, it does not seem too far-fetched to make the inference that conditioning and brain asymmetry are also related. In more detail, Öhman (1984) argues that instead of being a nuisance factor in the process of conditioning, the OR 'provides an important link for the understanding of Pavlovian conditioning, and perhaps learning in general' (p. 317). The point made by Öhman (1984) is that the OR is related to learning in such a way that it habituates only as the subject learns something about the CS-UCS contingency, which is thus seen as a necessary prerequisite for the emergence of a CR (cf. Maltzman, 1971). Since both the evocation of the initial OR on the first trial of stimulation and subsequent habituation upon repeated stimulation have been related to (a) the content of the stimulus in terms of verbal vs. visuo-spatial attributes (Hugdahl, Broman, and Franzon, 1983a; Lacroix and Comper, 1979; Ketterer and Smith, 1982), and (b) the hemisphere which is initially activated by a lateralized stimulus (Hugdahl, Wahlgren and Wass, 1982b; Comper and Lacroix, 1981), then an argument could be raised that conditioning is also related to functional differences between the hemispheres. This will be further discussed in subsequent sections.

However, before leaving the issue of lateralization of orienting behaviour, it may be of interest to note that Maltzman already in 1979 in a paper entitled 'Orienting reflexes and classical conditioning' was aware of the possible relationship between OR and conditioning on the one hand, and brain asymmetry on the other hand. Maltzman (1979) based his arguments on a distinction between involuntary and voluntary ORs (see also Maltzman, 1971). An involuntary OR is a response to a novel stimulus presented for the first time (cf. Sokolov, 1963), whereas a voluntary OR is related to the significance of the stimulus, often manipulated through task-related instructions during the habituation sequence. In his own words, Maltzman argues:

> Our initial hypothesis . . . for the difference between involuntary and voluntary OR stemmed from Pavlov's . . . distinction between the first and second signal system. We assumed that the involuntary OR, the response to novelty in the environment to unexpected changes in physical stimuli, is regulated primarily by the first signal system. Voluntary ORs induced by instructions, speech and generated by the complex cortical processes underlying thinking obviously involve the second signal system. It was then a short step to infer that in dextrals, at least, information processed in the first signal system should be regulated by the *right cerebral hemisphere*, whereas information processed in the second signal system should be regulated primarily by the *left cerebral hemisphere*. We hypothesized therefore that the involuntary OR would be controlled primarily by the right cerebral hemisphere, and the voluntary OR, including its manifestation *in conditioning*, would be regulated primarily by the left cerebral hemisphere. (Maltzman, 1979, p. 329, my italics)

As previously argued, the involuntary OR may not be uniquely related to the right hemisphere as suggested by Maltzman (1979); it may also be related to the left hemisphere depending on the nature of the stimulus and of the task involved (cf. Hugdahl, Broman, and Franzon, 1983a; Hugdahl, Franzon, and Fristorp-Wasteby, 1983c).

4.2 Asymmetry and orienting: Animal data

An important neurophysiological support for the suggestion of lateralization of orienting and conditioning comes from an elegant series of studies on the developing chicken by Rogers and her colleagues (e.g. Rogers and Anson, 1979; Howard, Rogers, and Boura, 1980). By injecting monosodium glutamate, a putative neurotransmitter, and cycloheximide, which inhibits ribosomal protein synthesis, selectively into the left and right forebrain, Rogers has demonstrated lateralized effects for both auditory habituation and visual discrimination learning. The conclusion from her experiments is that both learning of food search in a discriminative paradigm and habituation to a sound during food pecking are retarded after drug treatment of the left forebrain. It is thus quite possible that the left hemisphere is specialized for both learning and habituation. Thus, Maltzman's (1979) suggestion that the OR and its manifestation in conditioning is differentially regulated by the hemispheres is nicely supported by Rogers's data.

4.3 Asymmetry and phasic heart-rate (HR) responses

Before turning to a more detailed discussion of the implications of a lateralized perspective on conditioning, a final source of evidence concerning the relationship between lateralization, and orienting and conditioning, will be touched upon. This is phasic heart-rate changes in response to discrete stimulus events. Typically, a profound deceleration of the heart rate (HR) is observed just prior to UCS onset after CS-UCS pairings (cf. Obrist, Webb, and Sutterer, 1969). In some instances, a multiphasic response pattern is observed in the CS-UCS interval in humans during long interstimulus (ISI) intervals. As can be seen in Figure 6.4, there is a brief first deceleratory peak (called the D1) 1 or 2 sec after CS onset, which is followed by an acceleratory (A1) trend peaking about 3–4 sec after CS onset. Finally, there is a pronounced second deceleration (D2) reaching its peak around the time for the onset of the UCS (or where the UCS should have occurred on UCS-omission trials). The D2 thus 'wanders' with the length of the ISI, being delayed with longer ISIs. However, as pointed out by Bohlin and Kjellberg (1979) in their extensive review of phasic HR changes, the relationship between the D2 peak and the UCS onset reaches a 'ceiling effect' at about 9 sec ISI. If the ISI is increased beyond 9 sec, the D2 'stays' at about the same point in time. This upper limit of the D2 occurrence may be related to physiological and metabolic demands, rather than to behavioural effects. According to Bohlin and Kjellberg (1979), the initial D1 component reflects an OR to the onset of the CS (cf. Connor and Lang, 1969). The accelerative (A1) component, when present, seems to be related to 'significance' in the CS, and to the 'motivational' properties of the UCS (Coles and Duncan-Johnson, 1975). The D2 component, finally, is best described as an 'expectancy' that the UCS will follow the CS at a specific point in time (see also Öhman, 1984, for a detailed discussion of HR changes in conditioning). The D2 component also differentiates between a CS+ (related to UCS occurrence) and an unreinforced CS− (Dawson, Catania, Schell, and Grings, 1979). Thus, both the A1 and the D2 components seem to reflect aspects of conditioning in humans.

The relevance of HR conditioning for the present discussion lies in the fact that several recent investigators, starting from different theoretical and empirical positions, have suggested that phasic changes in cardiac activity in response to external stimuli may be uniquely related to right hemisphere activation. Although such a relationship may intuitively seem somewhat

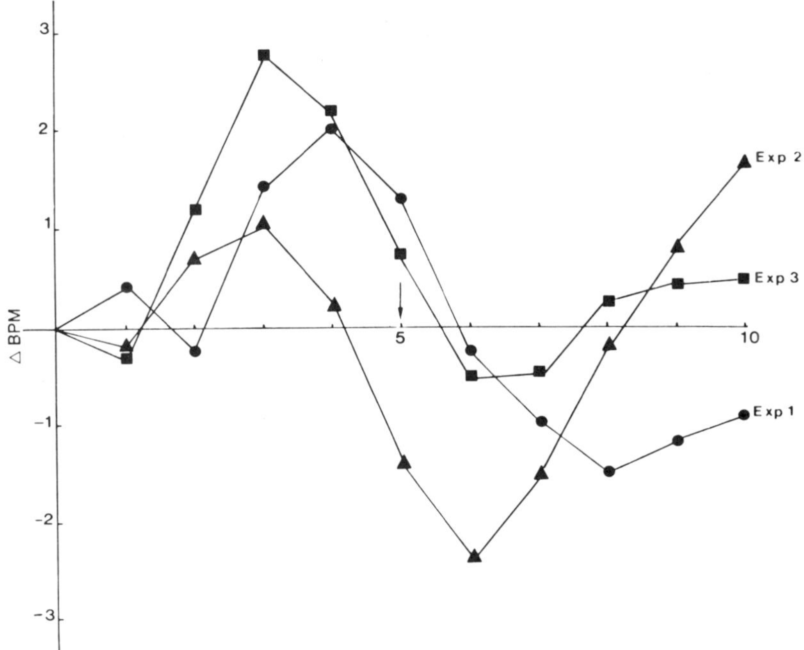

Figure 6.4 Example of phasic heart-rate changes, second by second, from prestimulus baseline in a two-stimulus paradigm. Note onset of second stimulus on sec 5. (*From Hugdahl, Franzon, Andersson, and Walldebo, 1983b. Reprinted by permission of J. B. Lippincott & Co., Philadelphia, Pa.*)

difficult to accept from both a neurophysiological and a neuroanatomical point of view, the available empirical data definitely imply that the suggestion should be taken seriously, promoting further research.

First of all, in 1979 Walker and Sandman recorded event-related potentials (ERPs) separately from the left and right hemispheres when their subjects exhibited spontaneous changes in HR over time. The most interesting finding from the point of view of the present discussion was that ERPs recorded from the right hemisphere were different from the ERPs recorded from the left hemisphere when HR changed. From this Walker and Sandman (1979, p. 727) concluded that 'changes in heart rate are reflected more clearly in the right hemisphere than in the left'. This finding was followed up in another study (Walker and Sandman, 1982) where it was demonstrated that ERPs recorded from the right hemisphere, but not from the left hemisphere, were different in amplitude during systole and diastole of the cardiac cycle. Walker and Sandman (1932, p. 524) thus concluded from their studies that 'the relationship between the heart and the brain is lateralized, and this factor has not been considered in behavioral studies'.

Following the suggestions by Walker and Sandman (1979, 1982), Hugdahl and his co-workers (Hugdahl, Franzon, Andersson, and Walldebo, 1983b) reported essentially a similar relationship between HR and the brain to that found by Walker and Sandman. The important thing is, however, that Hugdahl *et al*. (1983b) performed their experiment from a different point of departure compared to the Walker and Sandman studies. Thus, whereas Walker and Sandman demonstrated differences in electrophysiological activity between the hemispheres when heart rate and blood pressure were 'manipulated', Hugdahl *et al*. demonstrated changes in heart rate when the left and right hemispheres were separately 'manipulated'. In more detail, Hugdahl *et al*. (1983b) presented verbal and spatial visual stimuli initially only to the left or the right hemisphere with the so-called visual half-field (VHF) technique (see section 3.4 for a description of this technique). The stimuli were flashed for 200 msec, either to the left or the right hemisphere. In three consecutive experiments an acceleratory (A1) component with a peak 4 sec after CS onset was found only when the right hemisphere was initially stimulated. Thus, while Walker and Sandman recorded *cortical activity* as the dependent variable when *cardiac activity* was altered or 'manipulated', Hugdahl *et al*. (1983b) reported similar results although they recorded *cardiac activity* when *cortical activity* was manipulated.

Working from quite a different perspective, Katkin and his co-workers (Katkin, 1985; Hantas, Katkin, and Reed, 1984) have reported that the right hemisphere may be uniquely involved in autonomic perception, and especially accuracy of heart-beat detection. This has also been demonstrated by Davidson, Horowitz, Schwartz, and Goodman (1981), who found left hand finger tapping (regulated by the right hemisphere) to be closer to the preceding R-wave in the EKG than were right hand finger tappings (regulated by the left hemisphere). Thus, the findings by Katkin of a right hemisphere superiority for heart-beat perception is supported by the data by Davidson *et al*. (1981) in demonstrating the possibility of special interoceptive abilities of the right hemisphere. Similarly, in a theoretical paper devoted to an analysis of hemispheric differences in the control and maintenance of attention, Jutai (1984) convincingly argued for a right hemisphere dominance of attention and arousal basing his argument on the available empirical literature. Jutai argued further that the empirical data concerning the dominance of the right hemisphere in attention and arousal is most intriguing when cardiac activity is used as an indicator of attentional and arousal behaviour.

Furthermore, Yokoyama, Jennings, Ackles, Hood and Boller (in press) failed to observe anticipatory HR changes in a reaction time task in right hemisphere lesioned patients. Findings like these may further be understood by the observation that it is mainly the right branch of the vagus nerve that innervates the sino-atrial node of the right atrium (Brodal, 1981).

From this somewhat 'scattered' introduction to the main hypothesis that human associative learning in terms of Pavlovian conditioning may be differentially regulated by the cerebral hemispheres, I will now in more detail look at previous attempts to experimentally study lateralization of conditioned behaviour.

5 Asymmetry and conditioning: Experiments

In one of the first attempts to study hemispheric differences in a conditioning paradigm, Hellige (1975) presented semantically meaningful stimuli tachistoscopically with the VHF technique to either the left or to the right hemisphere (see also Saltz, 1973, who may have been the first to use this paradigm). The rationale behind the study was to compare conditioning performance between so called C and V responders to verbal stimuli. The distinction between C and V responders in conditioning was originally introduced by Spence and Taylor (1951), and later elaborated and developed by Grant (e.g. 1968). The C responders are considered to be 'true' conditioned subjects, whereas the V responders are considered to be using voluntary efforts in their CR. Hellige (1975) listed several ways in which C and V responders are believed to differ from each other. It was, for instance, said that the conditioning of Vs is more influenced by the semantic aspects of verbal stimuli, and that Vs are more analytic than Cs during conditioning. Hellige (1975) argued that some of the ways in which C and V form subjects differ from each other parallel some of the ways in which the cerebral hemispheres differ in their processing capacity. Thus, one would expect different rates of conditioning in the two groups of subjects. The ways C and V form subjects are expected to differ include that Vs more than Cs are influenced by the semantic aspects of the CS (see also Bunde, Grant, and Frost, 1970), and that Vs are more active, and especially analytic, than the Cs on a conditioning trial, and thus more able to predict when the UCS will occur. Using a differential eyelid conditioning paradigm, Hellige (1975) reported that the conditioned performance of V subjects was equally influenced by the semantic attributes of the CS regardless of which hemisphere was initially stimulated. However, the conditioning performance of the C subjects was more influenced by the semantic attribute of the CS when it was presented in the right visual half-field (i.e. initially to the left hemisphere), compared to when it was presented in the left half-field (i.e. initially to the right hemisphere). This difference in conditioning between C and V subjects depending on which hemisphere was initially stimulated was replicated in a second experiment in the same study where discriminations between complex polygons and letter naming were used as CS tasks with an air-puff to the eye as the UCS. Thus, the study by Hellige (1975) revealed a left hemisphere advantage for the conditioning to verbal CSs for so-called true conditioned C subjects, but not for the V subjects thought. This is an interesting outcome if we recall that V subjects in general are more influenced by the semantic aspects of the CS. It thus seems that the difference between the groups may be overcome if the CS is fed directly to the left hemisphere in C subjects, but bilaterally to V subjects. From his experiments, Hellige concluded that 'such . . . differences must be incorporated into *both* models of classical eyelid conditioning and models of cerebral hemispheric specialization' (1975, p. 309, my italics). The findings by Hellige were followed up by Benish and Grant (1981) using the same differential eyelid paradigm and VHF technique as used by Hellige. In agreement with one of Hellige's findings Benish and Grant reported overall shorter response latency in C subjects to the CS+ when it was initially presented only to the left hemisphere. However, no other findings were replicated. An interesting difference between the studies that may help explain why not all of Hellige's results were replicated by Benish and Grant is that Benish and Grant had a clear majority of females in their groups. Since females may be less lateralized on tasks requiring linguistic processing than males, (McGlone, 1980; Inglis and Lawson, 1981), having more females than males in a group may confound the experimental variable, thus diluting eventual effects.

Turning to autonomic conditioning, and especially to the conditioning of skin conductance responses (SCRs) in the electrodermal system, Hugdahl, Qundos, and Vaittinen (1982a) used a dichotic listening paradigm with the letters 'p' and 'B' and two piano chords (B major and B flat major) as CSs in a differential conditioning experiment. Hugdahl *et al*. reasoned that since the contralateral auditory pathways are more predominant than the ipsilateral ones (Rosenzweig, 1951; Connolly, 1985), and since the left hemisphere is dominant for verbal stimuli in right-handers, then an auditory verbal CS+ dichotically presented to the right ear should overshadow another verbal stimulus (the CS−) simultaneously presented to the left ear (see section 3.5 for a description of the dichotic listening technique). However, by reversing the earphones for another group of subjects the CS+ would be presented in the left ear, and the CS− in the right ear. Thus, responding should cease non-asymptotically on the very first extinction trial. Following the same logic, it was predicted that a subject presented with a *tonal* CS+ (piano chord) to the left ear (contralateral to the right hemisphere), with the CS− simultaneously in the left ear, should continue responding until asymptote is reached. This was predicted on the basis of right hemisphere dominance for tonal stimuli (Kimura, 1967; Goodglass and Calderon, 1977). By reversing the earphones, with the CS+ in the right ear, and the CS− in the left ear, responding was expected to cease almost immediately. It should be kept in mind, however, that lateralization for music perception is probably less well-developed than lateralization for language. Furthermore, it seems that whether the subjects are musically trained or not plays a crucial role in reported asymmetries to tonal stimuli (Bever and Chiarello, 1974; Schweiger and Maltzman, 1985). The study by Hugdahl, Qundos, and Vaittinen (1982a) is further described below as an example of the so-called dichotic extinction paradigm.

5.1 The dichotic extinction paradigm

The dichotic extinction paradigm consists of three phases (see Figure 6.5). The first phase of the paradigm is a *habituation*, or adaptation, phase where the CS+ and the CS− are presented separately and randomly. During this phase all subjects are treated in an identical manner, and each of the two cues is presented binaurally and in mono (i.e. they are perceived as being 'in the middle of the head'). In the second, *acquisition*, phase the CS+ is followed by the UCS, whereas the CS− is never presented together with the UCS. In the Hugdahl, Qundos, and Vaittinen (1982a) study the UCS was a 95 dB white noise and the (CS)-(UCS) interstimulus interval (ISI) was 4 sec, i.e. trace conditioning following Kimble's (1961) terminology. All stimuli are presented binaurally and separate in time. In the third, *dichotic extinction*, phase, the CS+ and the CS− are presented simultaneously in a dichotic mode. Half of the subjects receive the CS+ in the *right ear* and the CS− in the *left ear*, while the other half of the subjects receive the two cues in a reversed order through turning of the earphones. Thus, one of the unique attributes of the dichotic extinction paradigm is that there is only one single manipulation that is different between the two groups of subjects, i.e. turning of the earphones. A second attribute of the paradigm is that it allows for the presentation of two

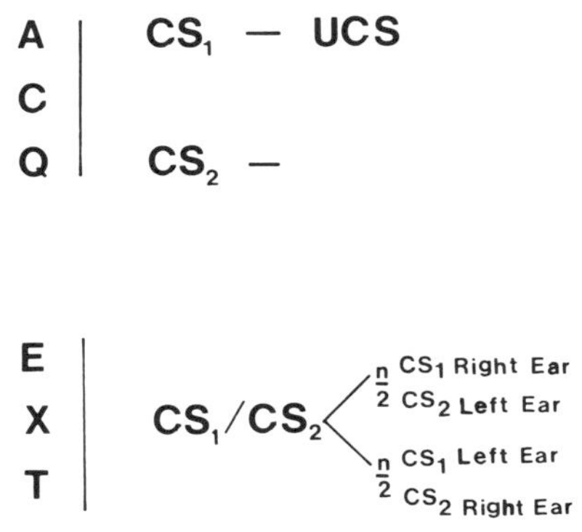

ACQ | CS_1 — UCS
CS_2 —

EXT | CS_1/CS_2
$\frac{n}{2}$ CS_1 Right Ear, CS_2 Left Ear
$\frac{n}{2}$ CS_1 Left Ear, CS_2 Right Ear

Figure 6.5 Schematic outline of the dichotic extinction paradigm (see text for further explanations). $\frac{n}{2}$ = half of the subjects; acq = acquisition phase; ext = extinction phase

stimuli within the same sensory modality exactly at the same point in time. In order to achieve this it is important that stimulus onset in the two channels is carefully synchronized. This may be brought about through the use of computers when preparing dichotic tapes.

The results of the Hugdahl, Qundos, and Vaittinen (1982a) study are seen in Figure 6.6. There is a marked difference in response amplitudes to the verbal CS between the group with the CS+ in the right ear (contralateral to the left hemisphere) during extinction compared to the group with the CS+ in the left ear (contralateral to the right hemisphere). This difference in responding, with almost cessation of responding on the first trials for the CS+ left ear group, is maintained across the entire extinction session (i.e. 32 trials). Note that both 'groups' are treated in an identical manner during habituation and acquisition, and that the only difference during extinction is that the earphones are reversed. For the groups receiving tonal stimuli as CS+ and CS− there was no difference between hemisphere stimulations during

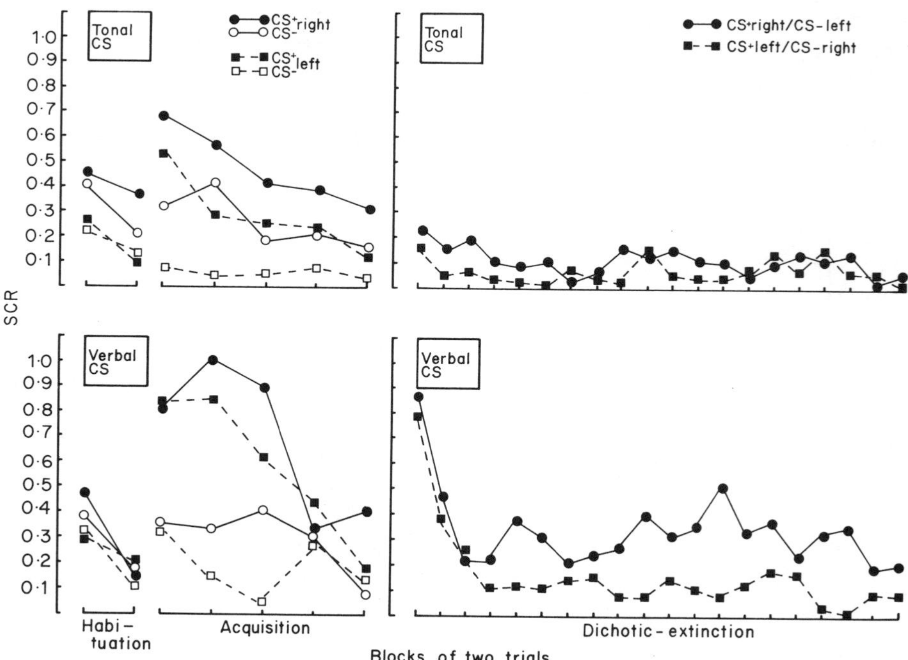

Figure 6.6 Phasic skin conductance responses (SCRs) during habituation, acquisition, and dichotic extinction. (*From Hugdahl, Qundos, and Vaittinen, 1982. Reprinted by permission of J. B. Lippincott & Co., Philadelphia, Pa.*)

extinction. This absence of difference for tonal stimuli may, however, be due to the difficulty in discriminating a B major from a B flat major chord. An alternative is that lateralized conditioning to tonal stimuli is not as effective as the corresponding conditioning to verbal stimuli. A hint to the fact that the tonal stimuli may have been too difficult to separate during the dichotic phase is the responding on the first trial block during dichotic extinction. As seen in Figure 6.6, there is an increase in response magnitude to the verbal stimuli in both groups on the first dichotic trial block compared to the last acquisition trial. This initial increase is not observed in the tonal groups. The initial increase in the verbal groups is probably best described as a perceptual disparity response (Grings, 1960) which is triggered because of the unexpected introduction of the dichotic mode of stimulus presentation. In other words, the subjects in the verbal groups recognize that the stimulus pattern they hear during dichotic extinction is different from the pattern heard during habituation and acquisition. This then reinstates the orienting response (OR) on the first dichotic presentation which should habituate on the next few trials. The absence of a perceptual disparity response, or OR, in the tonal groups may therefore be taken as evidence for a failure of discrimination between the CS+ and the CS−. If the two chords are not perceived as separate stimuli but as a whole, there is no reason to predict a reinstated OR on the first dichotic trial during extinction. In other words, these subjects are not perceiving the introduction of the dichotic presentation mode as different from the mode of presentation during the habituation and acquisition phases of the experiment.

The finding of a lateralized effect for conditioning to the verbal CSs in the Hugdahl, Qundos, and Vaittinen (1982a) study was replicated in a second experiment in our laboratory (Hugdahl and Brobäck, in press). The general outline of the Hugdahl and Brobäck experiment was identical to the outline of the Hugdahl *et al.* (1982a) study with the exception that the two CS cues were the syllables ‘Ba’ and ‘Pa’, and that the UCS was a 106 dB white noise with a constant amplitude. Finally, a non-reinforced control group was added with only CS presentations. The results of the Hugdahl and Brobäck experiment are seen in Figure 6.7. The most interesting aspect of the data in Figure 6.7 is that the CS+ right ear group once again is superior to the CS+ left ear group across the entire extinction session. Of further interest is that not only phasic skin conductance responses (SCRs) in response to CS presentations were different between the groups, but also tonic skin conductance levels (SCLs) differed in the same direction during dichotic extinction. In their conclusion Hugdahl, Qundos, and Vaittinen (1982a) wrote that before their findings are related to hemispheric asymmetry more research should be performed, perhaps on other subjects with a proposed different cerebral organization. If the findings by Hugdahl *et al.* (1982) and by Hugdahl and Brobäck (in press) are attenuated or eliminated in such a group of subjects, then perhaps one

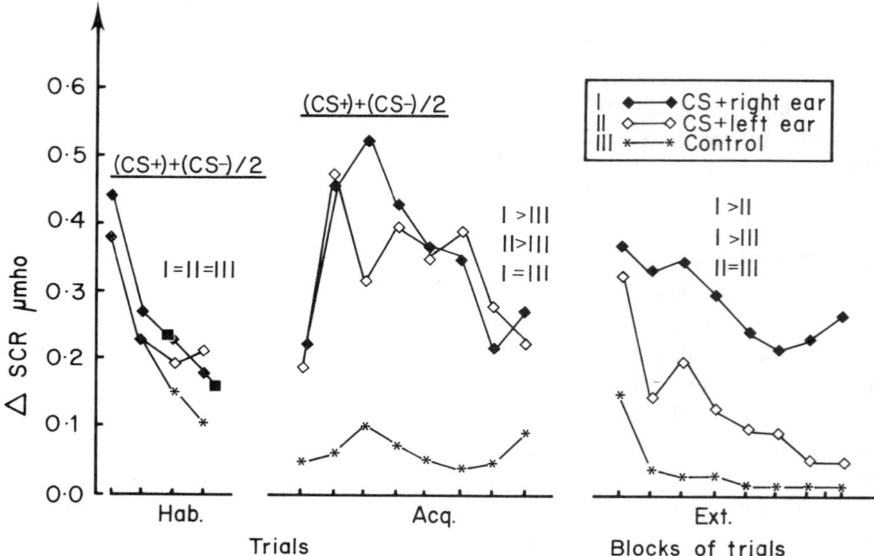

Figure 6.7 Phasic skin conductance responses (SCRs) during habituation, acquisition, and dichotic extinction. (*From Hugdahl and Broback*, in press)

may with better accuracy conclude that the reported data do link associative mechanisms to hemispheric asymmetry.

In another experiment in our laboratory (Hugdahl, Kvale, Nordby, and Overmier, submitted) visual stimuli presented with the VHF technique were used as CSs, and with bilateral SCRs as dependent measures. The stimuli were incongruent colour-words, i.e. colour-words written in an incongruent colour, like the word RED written in green. During acquisition, incongruent colour-words were simultaneously presented one to the left and one to the right of centre fixation, i.e. with initial right and left hemisphere inputs, with a 106 dB white noise as the UCS. During extinction, the words were presented in white against a black background, and the colours were presented without the words. The rationale for the experiment was as follows. When an incongruent colour-word is presented to the right of fixation (left hemisphere) together with an aversive UCS, then the semantic component, and not the colour, would predominate and become conditioned to the UCS. Conversely, when the same stimulus is presented to the left of fixation (right hemisphere), then the colour component, and not the semantic component, would predominate. When the semantic and the colour components are taken apart during extinction, by presenting the word in white against a black background, and the colour without the word then slower extinction would be revealed to the word for right field presentations during acquisition compared to left field presentations. Preliminary analyses of the data have basically confirmed the predictions, similarly, slower extinction would be revealed to the colour for left field presentations. This experiment is not strictly speaking an example of a lateralized extinction paradigm, but rather an example of a lateralized acquisition paradigm, since the lateralization of CS input occurs during the acquisition phase of the experiment. In the next section another example of a lateralized acquisition paradigm will be described.

5.2 The dichotic acquisition paradigm

Figure 6.8 depicts the logic behind the dichotic acquisition paradigm. The major difference between the dichotic extinction and acquisition paradigms is that the dichotic mode of CS presentation occurs during the acquisition phase in the dichotic acquisition paradigm, but during the extinction phase in the dichotic extinction paradigm. I will describe the dichotic acquisition paradigm by reference to a recent experiment in our laboratory.

The CV syllables ‘Ba’ and ‘Pa’ were used as CSs, and a 106 dB white noise was used as the UCS. In the first phase of the experiment (see Figure 6.8),

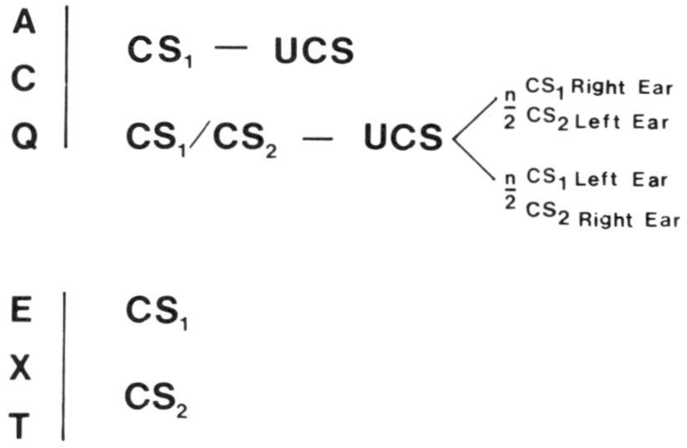

ACQ | CS_1 — UCS
ACQ | CS_1/CS_2 — UCS: $\frac{n}{2}$ CS_1 Right Ear, CS_2 Left Ear; $\frac{n}{2}$ CS_1 Left Ear, CS_2 Right Ear

EXT | CS_1
EXT | CS_2

Figure 6.8 Schematic outline of the dichotic acquisition paradigm (see text for further explanations). $\frac{n}{2}$ = half of the subjects; acq = acquisition phase; ext = extinction phase

either the syllable 'Ba' or the syllable 'Pa' was 100 per cent reinforced with UCS presentations contingent upon CS presentation. Half of the subjects had the 'Ba' presented together with the UCS, and the other half had the 'Pa' presented together with the UCS in a counterbalanced manner. During this phase, all stimuli were presented binaurally and in mono. The UCS was presented 4 sec after CS onset on each trial. During the next phase, dichotic acquisition, 'Ba' and 'Pa' were presented simultaneously, one to each ear. The CS that had been paired with the UCS during the first phase will in the following be called CS_1, and the CS that had not been presented in the first phase will be called CS_2, i.e. for half of the subjects 'Ba' was the CS_1 and 'Pa' was the CS_2, while for the other half of the subjects the order was reversed.

During the dichotic acquisition phase, one group of subjects had the CS_1 presented in the *right ear* (contralateral to the left hemisphere), and the CS_2 simultaneously presented in the *left ear* (contralateral to the right hemisphere). Another group of subjects had the earphones reversed, i.e. the CS_1 in the right ear, and the CS_2 in the left ear. Thus, as with the dichotic extinction paradigm, the only difference between groups is the reversal of earphones.

During the third, extinction, phase all subjects in both groups were treated identically, with the CS_1 and the CS_2 presented separately on each trial, binaurally and in mono (see Figure 6.8). Order of presentation of the CS_1 and the CS_2 was randomized.

The following predictions were made. The group with the CS_1 in the right ear during the dichotic acquisition phase should demonstrate larger response amplitudes to this cue than to the CS_2 during extinction. The group with the CS_2 in the right ear during dichotic acquisition should, however, demonstrate equal response amplitudes to the CS_1 and the CS_2 during extinction. The rationale for these predictions is as follows. The CS_1 right ear group is both pretrained with CS_1-UCS trials during the first phase of the experiment *and* has the CS_1 in the ear contralateral to the speech dominant left hemisphere during dichotic acquisition. Such an arrangement should then 'block' out conditioning to the CS_2. Thus, the result should be larger responses during extinction to the CS_1 compared to the CS_2. However, the group with the CS_2 in the right ear during dichotic acquisition is first pretrained with CS_1-UCS trials during the first phase, and then they receive the CS_2 during the next phase in the ear contralateral to the left hemisphere. Since the UCS is presented during both the first and the second phases, this group would then develop a CS-UCS contingency for both the CS_1 and the CS_2. Thus, equal responding should occur to both cues. The results are seen in Figure 6.9.

As revealed in Figure 6.9, the paradigm yields different response amplitudes during extinction, depending on which ear the CS_1 is presented in during the dichotic acquisition phase of the experiment. Thus, effects of lateralized stimulus input are again demonstrated in a conditioning context,

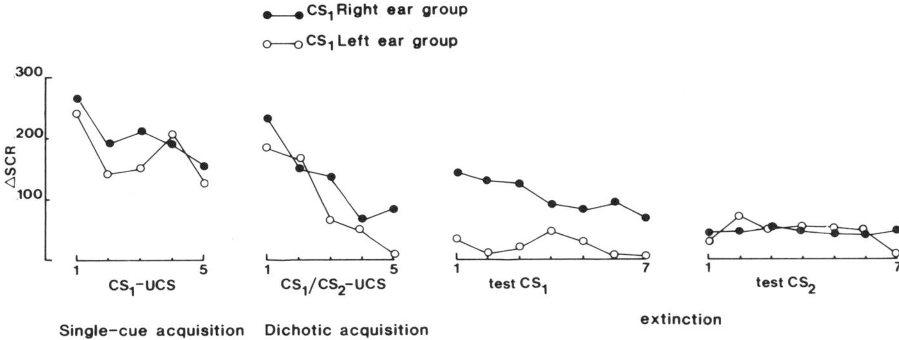

Figure 6.9 Phasic skin conductance responses (SCRs) during habituation, dichotic acquisition, and extinction. (*The help of Elisabeth Henriksson and Osamha Qundos in collecting the data is greatly appreciated*)

although the results for the dichotic acquisition paradigm are not as clear-cut as the results for the dichotic extinction paradigm (cf. Hugdahl, Qundos, and Vaittinen, 1982; Hugdahl and Brobäck, in press).

6 Asymmetry and awareness of conditioning

In a frequently cited paper, Corteen and Wood (1972) showed that a conditioned electrodermal response to city names, presented via earphones, could be elicited without the subject being aware of the presentation of the CS. In a first phase of the Corteen and Wood experiment, subjects received an electric shock as the UCS contingent upon the presentation of the verbal CS (the city name). During this phase, the subject's attention was directed towards the words they heard in the earphones. In a second phase, the conditioned words were presented in the left ear while prose passages were presented in the other ear in a dichotic shadowing task. The subjects were instructed to attend only to the prosa-passages in the right ear, ignoring the left ear input. The results showed that the previously shocked city names elicited more electrodermal responses than control words when presented in the non-attended ear during the dichotic phase of the experiment. Corteen and Wood interviewed their subjects after the experiment to make sure that they had not been aware of the city names presented in the non-attended left ear. Although post experimental interviewing techniques for good reasons may be questioned as measures of awareness (see Dawson, 1973), the results by Corteen and Wood (1972) indicate that the elicitation by a CS of a previously learned CR is possible without the subject being aware of the occurrence of the CS. This finding was later replicated by Wright, Andersson, and Stenman (1975), Dawson and Schell (1982), and Martin, Stambrook, Tartaryn, and Biehl (1984). However, Wardlaw and Kroll (1976) failed to replicate the original Corteen and Wood (1972) experiment. What is important in the present context is the remarkable fact that previous interpreters of the discrepancy between the original Corteen and Wood (1972) study and the replication by Wardlaw and Kroll (1976) have failed to notice the procedural differences, and especially the relation of such differences to hemispheric asymmetry. Thus, as also pointed out by Martin *et al*. (1984), Corteen and Wood (1972) presented the critical CSs in the *left ear* on all trials for all subjects, with the prose passages in the right ear, whereas Wardlaw and Kroll (1976) *counterbalanced* CS presentations between the ears. From what has been argued in the previous section, paying attention to a verbal passage presented under dichotic competition should be more effective in the right ear (initial left hemisphere input), whereas conditioning to a shock-reinforced CS having an emotional aspect should be more effective in the left ear. Thus, by counterbalancing the presentation of the CSs and the prose passages between the ears, it is not surprising that Wardlaw and Kroll (1976) failed to find evidence of unaware conditioning.

This line of reasoning is further substantiated by a closer analysis of the data reported by Wright *et al*. (1975). These investigators used two-syllable words as CSs that were paired with shock-UCSs during acquisition. During a test phase, approximately half of the subjects had the unattended CS in the *left ear* and the other half had the CS in the *right ear*. Although, overall, significantly larger EDA responses were obtained to the critical CSs compared to control stimuli, it is interesting to note that only 9 out of 20 subjects who shadowed the *left* ear message conditioned reliably, whereas 21 out of 24 subjects who shadowed the *right* ear message conditioned well. That brain asymmetry may play a role in unaware conditioning in humans was first suggested by Dawson and Schell (1982) who found that when the unattended words (CSs) were presented in the right ear there were indications of a different mode of responding related to attentional shifts, from when the same CSs were presented in the left ear. This was commented upon in a note by Öhman (1984, p. 357) who stated that: 'While this finding may indicate a different relationship between verbal awareness and orienting *depending on what hemisphere is activated*, more data are certainly needed before firmer statements can be made' (my italics). I agree with Öhman that more data are necessary, and that adequately designed experiments hopefully can further elucidate the role played by the cerebral hemispheres in unaware and aware conditioning in the intact human.

7 Asymmetry and learning: Animal data

Turning to the animal level, an example of the role played by asymmetry and lateralization in conditioning is a recent report by Stokes and McIntyre (1985) on a lateralized effect on state-dependent learning in the rat. State-dependent learning means that the psychological 'state' of the organism at the time of testing matches the 'state' at the time of acquisition (Overton, 1964). Usually, a drugged state is used contingent on CS exposure. Tests for a CR are then performed under both a drugged and a non-drugged state, with better conditioning in the drugged state. Stokes and McIntyre (1985) produced state-dependency through eliciting kindled seizures in the left or right hippocampus in the split-brain operated animal. When later tested in an avoidance conditioning paradigm it was shown that those animals that were kindled in the left side of the brain showed better evidence of conditioning when the 'state' of seizure during training and testing was the same, while showing impaired conditioning when the state during training and testing were different. Kindled seizures in the right side of the brain displayed good evidence of a conditioned avoidance response irrespective of whether or not the training and testing states were the same. Thus, the study by Stokes and McIntyre (1985) has demonstrated an interesting effect of brain asymmetry on learning in the animal which supports previous findings described by Rogers (e.g. Rogers and Anson, 1979) on the effects of lateralized administration of drugs in the developing chicken brain.

7.1 Asymmetry of brain transmitters

The discussion of brain asymmetry and learning may be put one step further by also including a discussion of recent reports of asymmetrical distribution of neurotransmitters in the brain on both the human and the animal level. Starting with the human brain, Oke, Keller, Mefford, and Adams (1977) found higher concentrations of noradrenaline in the right somatosensory input area of the thalamus. As also pointed out by Jutai (1984), this area of the thalamus has important cortical connections in the parietal lobe, an area critical for attention (cf. Mesulam, 1981). This finding may thus be linked to learning and conditioning considering the importance of noradrenaline in avoidance conditioning recently reported by Archer (1982). By using a noradrenaline-selective neurotoxin, called DSP4, Archer and colleagues (e.g. Archer, Mohammed, and Järbe, 1983) have convincingly demonstrated the involvement of noradrenaline in avoidance conditioning in the rat brain. In addition, Glick and his co-workers (e.g. Glick, Ross, and Hough, 1982) have reviewed data showing asymmetries in several other transmitter systems, and brain areas. Among other things, both gamma-aminiobutyric acid (GABA) and dopamine (DA) have been found to be asymmetrically distributed. The reports of DA asymmetry are especially noteworthy in the present context since Mintz and Myslobodsky (1983) have suggested that it is the dopaminergic circuitry of the right hemisphere that may be responsible for bilateral control of electrodermal orienting and habituation. Mintz and Myslobodsky studied the electrodermal orienting response to simple visual stimuli in Parkinsonian patients with either a left- or a right-sided extrapyramidal lesion syndrome. Among their many findings was that absence of an electrodermal OR was correlated with a right hemisphere dysfunction, and that the dysfunction was caused by a dopamine deficit. Asymmetry of the nigrostriatal dopamine system was also reported by Jerussi and Taylor (1982) with higher dopamine metabolites in the contralateral striatum to the dominant direction of rotation in haloperidol (a DA-antagonist) treated animals. It is thus possible that the motor laterality imbalance found in schizophrenics (e.g. Gur, 1977) with a pronounced left-sidedness on most tests for asymmetry is a reminiscence of an unequal distribution of dopamine in the two halves of the brain.

Whether asymmetry of the distribution of neurotransmitters in both the animal and human brain is actually related to conditioning, including CSs that presumably differentially activate the hemispheres, is at present an open question. However, considering the intimate relationship between the orienting response and attention on the one hand, and Pavlovian conditioning on the other hand (Öhman, 1979a, 1984; Maltzman, 1979), every demonstration of asymmetry of brain functions related to orienting and attention (Mintz and Myslobodsky, 1983; Jutai, 1984; Gruzelier, 1984; Gruzelier, Brow, Perry, Rhonder, and Thomas, 1984) is of relevance for a lateralized perspective on Pavlovian conditioning. The issue of asymmetry of neurotransmitters in the brain and their importance for learning could perhaps be tested by developing adequate animal models where either unilateral depletions of transmitters are preformed, or the effects of unequal distributions of transmitters between the two halves of the brain otherwise are manipulated while the animals are undergoing a conditioning experience. The DSP4 technique as used by Archer (e.g. 1982) seems a promising method in this respect.

8 Summary and conclusions

A perspective on human Pavlovian conditioning is presented which argues for a functional relationship between associative learning and hemispheric asymmetry in the intact brain. Experimental work is reviewed demonstrating effects of lateralization on both eyelid and electrodermal conditioning. In particular, superior performance is usually observed when verbal CSs are initially presented only to the left hemisphere, thought to be dominant for the processing of linguistic material. However, although the results are compelling, it is important to keep in mind that the stress in the present chapter is on a *perspective* rather than on ready formulated hypotheses and existing data. The empirical data are sometimes conflicting on the human level, urging for the need to develop adequate animal models where the effects of cerebral asymmetry on conditioning can be further investigated.

The most obvious area on the human level to be the subject for future research is autonomic conditioning. As argued previously, this is especially true when conditioning is framed in information-processing terms, stressing conditioning as the result of extracting information in the CS about UCS occurrence (e.g. Rescorla, 1980; Öhman, 1984). It is argued that the cerebral hemispheres are differentially sensitive in extracting such information depending on the nature and content of the conditioned stimulus. Conditioning to semantically meaningful CSs should be primarily regulated by the left hemisphere, whereas conditioning to emotionally and visuo-spatially relevant CSs should be primarily regulated by the right hemisphere. It is the hope that the present chapter may be instrumental in inspiring future research concerning hemispheric asymmetry and Pavlovian conditioning.

Acknowledgement

This research was financially supported by the Swedish Council for Research in the Humanities and the Social Sciences, and by the Norwegian Council for Research in the Social Sciences. Critical comments on earlier drafts of the manuscript by J. Bruce Overmier are greatly acknowledged.

References

Allen, M. (1983). Models of hemispheric specialization. *Psychological Bulletin*, **93**, 73–104.

Andreassi, J. L., DeSimone, J. J., Friend, M. A., and Grota, P. A. (1975). Hemispheric amplitude asymmetries in the auditory evoked potential with monaural and binaural stimulation. *Physiological Psychology*, **7**, 169–71.

Archer, T. (1982). DSP4, a new noradrenaline neurotoxin, and the stimulus conditions affecting acquisition of two-way active avoidance. *Journal of Comparative and Physiological Psychology*, **96**, 476–90.

Archer, T., Mohammed, A. K., and Järbe, T. U. C. (1983). Latent inhibition following systemic DSP4: Effects due to presence and absence of contextual cues in taste-aversion learning. *Behavioral and Neural Biology*, **38**, 287–306.

Benish, W. A., and Grant, D. A. (1981). Hemispheric processing in differential classical eyelid conditioning. *Bulletin of the Psychonomic Society*, **15**, 433–4.

Berlin, C. I. (1977). Hemispheric asymmetry in auditory tasks. In *Lateralization in the nervous system* (eds. S. Harnad, R. W. Doty, L. Goldstein, J. Jaynes, and G. Krauthamer). Academic Press, New York.

Bever, T. G., and Chiarello, R. J. (1974). Cerebral dominance in musicians and nonmusicians. *Science*, **185**, 537–9.

Bohlin, G., and Kjellberg, A. (1979). Orienting activity in two-stimulus paradigms as reflected in heart rate. In *The Orienting Reflex* (eds. H. D. Kimmel, E. H. van Olst, and J. F. Orlebeke). Erlbaum Associates, Hillsdale, N.J.

Boyd, G. M., and Maltzman, I. (1982). Skin conductance response and muscle activity during auditory, visual and memory tasks (Abstract). *Psychophysiology*, **19**, 308.

Bradshaw, J. L., and Nettleton, N. C. (1981). The nature of hemispheric specialization in man. *The Behavioral and Brain Sciences*, **4**, 51–91.

Bradshaw, J. L., and Nettleton, N. C. (1983). *Human Cerebral Asymmetry*. Prentice-Hall, Englewood Cliffs, N.J.

Bradshaw, J. L., and Taylor, M. J. (1979). A word-naming deficit in non-familial sinistrals? Laterality effects of vocal responses to tachistoscopically presented letter strings. *Neuropsychologia*, **17**, 21–32.

Brodal, A. (1981). *Neurological Anatomy*, 3rd edition. Oxford University Press, New York.

Bryden, M. P. (1965). Tachistoscopic recognition, handedness and cerebral dominance. *Neuropsychologia*, **3**, 103–5.

Bryden, M. P. (1982). *Laterality—Functional asymmetry in the intact brain*. Academic Press, New York.

Bunde, D. C., Grant, D. A., and Frost, M. R. (1970). Differential conditioning to stimuli that express a response-related command or convey reinforcement-related information. *Journal of Verbal Learning and Verbal Behavior*, **9**, 346–55.

Butler, S. R., and Glass, A. (1976). EEG correlates of cerebral dominance. In *Advances in Psychobiology* (eds. A. H. Riesen and R. F. Thompson). John Wiley & Sons, London.

Coles, M. G. H., and Duncan-Johnson, C. C. (1975). Cardiac activity and information-processing: The effects of stimulus significance, and detection and response requirements. *Journal of Experimental Psychology: Human Perception and Performance*, **1**, 418–28.

Comper, P., and Lacroix, J. M. (1981). Further evidence of lateralization in the electrodermal system as a function of relative hemispheric activation (Abstract). *Psychophysiology*, **18**, 149.

Connolly, J. F. (1985). Stability of pathway-hemispheric differences in the auditory event-related potential (ERP) to monaural stimulation. *Psychophysiology*, **22**, 87–96.

Connor, W. H., and Lang, P. J. (1969). Cortical slow-wave and cardiac rate response in stimulus orientation and reaction-time conditions. *Journal of Experimental Psychology*, **82**, 310–20.

Corteen, R. S., and Wood, B. (1972). Autonomic response to shock-associated words in an unattended channel. *Journal of Experimental Psychology*, **94**, 308–13.

Davidoff, J. (1976). Hemispheric sensitivity differences in the perception of color. *Quarterly Journal of Experimental Psychology*, **28**, 387–94.

Davidson, R. J., Horowitz, M. E., Schwartz, G. E., and Goodman, D. M. (1981). Lateral differences in the latency between finger tapping and the heart beat. *Psychophysiology*, **18**, 36–41.

Dawson, M. E. (1973). Can classical conditioning occur without contingency learning? A review and evaluation of the evidence. *Psychophysiology*, **10**, 82–6.

Dawson, M. E., Catania, J. J., Schell, A. M., and Grings, W. W. (1979). Autonomic classical conditioning as a function of awareness of stimulus contingencies. *Biological Psychology*, **9**, 23–40.

Dawson, M. E., and Schell, A. M. (1982). Electrodermal responses to attended and nonattended significant stimuli during dichotic listening. *Journal of Experimental Psychology: Human Perception and Performance*, **8**, 82–6.

Dawson, M. E., Schell, A. M., Beers, J. R., and Kelly, A. (1982). Allocation of processing capacity during human autonomic classical conditioning. *Journal of Experimental Psychology: General*, **111**, 273–95.

Eelen, P. (1982). Conditioning and attribution. In *Learning Theory Approaches to Psychiatry* (ed. J. Boulougouris). John Wiley & Sons, London.

Erwin, R. J., McClelland, B. A., and Kleinman, K. M. (1980). Effects of level of arousal and type of task on bilateral skin conductance asymmetry and conjugate lateral eyemovements. *Pavlovian Journal of Biological Science*, **15**, 59–67.

Estes, W. K. (1973). Memory and conditioning. In *Contemporary Approaches to Conditioning and Learning* (eds. F. J. McGuigan and D. B. Lumsden). V. H. Winston & Sons, Washington, D.C.

Eysenck, H. J., and Rachman, S. (1965). *The Causes and Cures of Neurosis*. Routledge & Kegan Paul, London.

Freixa I Baque, E., Catteau, M.-C., Miossec, Y., and Roy, J.-C. (1984). Asymmetry of electrodermal activity: A review. *Biological Psychology*, **18**, 219–39.

Galaburda, A. M., LeMay, M., Kemper, T. L., and Geschwind, N. (1978). Right–left asymmetries in the brain. *Science*, **199**, 852–6.

Galin, D., and Ornstein, R. (1972). Lateral specialization of cognitive mode: An EEG study. *Psychophysiology*, **9**, 412–18.

Garcia, J., and Koelling, R. A. (1966). Relation of cue to consequence in avoidance learning. *Psychonomic Science*, **4**, 123–4.

Gazzaniga, M. S., and LeDoux, J. E. (1978). *The Integrated Mind*. Plenum Press, New York.

Geffen G. and Quinn K. (1984). Hemispheric specialization and ear advantages in processing speech. *Psychological Bulletin*, **96**, 273–91.

Geschwind, N., and Levitsky, W. (1968). Left–right asymmetries in temporal speech region. *Science*, **161**, 186–7.

Glick, S. D., Ross, D. A., and Hugh, L. B. (1982). Lateral asymmetry of neurotransmitters in human brain. *Brain Research*, **234**, 53–63.

Goodglass, H., and Calderon, M. (1977). Parallel processing of verbal and musical stimuli in right and left hemispheres. *Neuropsychologia*, **15**, 397–407.

Gordon, H. W. (1970). Hemispheric asymmetries in perception of musical chords. *Cortex*, **6**, 387–98.

Gormezano, I., and Kehoe, E. J. (1975). Classical conditioning: Some methodological conceptual issues. In *Handbook of Learning and Cognitive Processes*, vol. 2. *Conditioning and Behavior Theory* (ed. W. K. Estes). Erlbaum Associates, Hillsdale, N.J.

Grant, D. A. (1968). Adding communication to the signalling property of the CS in classical conditioning. *Journal of General Psychology*, **79**, 147–74.

Grings, W. W. (1960). Preparatory set variables related to classical conditioning of autonomic responses. *Psychological Review*, **67**, 243–52.

Gross, J. S., and Stern, J. A. (1980). An investigation of bilateral asymmetries in electrodermal activity. *Pavlovian Journal of Biological Science*, **15**, 74–81.

Gruzelier, J. H. (1973). Bilateral asymmetry of skin conductance orienting activity and levels in schizophrenia. *Biological Psychology*, **1**, 21–41.

Gruzelier, J. H. (1984). Hemispheric imbalances in schizophrenia. *International Journal of Psychophysiology*, **1**, 227–40.

Gruzelier, J. H., Brow, T., Perry, A., Rhonder, J., and Thomas, M. (1984). Hypnotic susceptibility: A lateral predisposition and altered cerebral asymmetry under hypnosis. *International Journal of Psychophysiology*, **2**, 131–9.

Gur, R. C. (1977). Motoric laterality imbalance in schizophrenia. *Archives of General Psychiatry*, **34**, 33–7.

Hantas, M. N., Katkin, E. S., and Reed, S. D. (1984). Cerebral lateralization and heart beat discrimination. *Psychophysiology*, **21**, 274–8.

Hare, R. D., and Blevings, G. (1975). Conditioned orienting and defensive responses. *Psychophysiology*, **12**, 289–97.

Hécaen, H., and Sauguet, J. (1971). Cerebral dominance in left-handed subjects. *Cortex*, **7**, 19–48.

Hellige, J. B. (1975). Hemispheric processing differences revealed by differential conditioning and reaction time performance. *Journal of Experimental Psychology: General*, **104**, 309–26.

Howard, K. J., Rogers, L. J., and Boura, A. L. A. (1980). Functional lateralization of the chicken forebrain revealed by use of intracranial glutamate. *Brain Research*, **188**, 369–82.

Hugdahl, K., Engstrand, O., and Nordstrand, L. (1986). A graphic-interactive CAD system for dichotic stimulus alignment–CADDIC. Psykologisk Rapportsevle, University of Bergen, **7**, no. 3.

Hugdahl, K. (1984). Hemispheric asymmetry and bilateral electrodermal recordings: A review of the evidence. *Psychophysiology*, **21**, 371–93.

Hugdahl, K., and Andersson, L. (1984). A dichotic listening study of differences in cerebral organization between dextral and sinistral subjects. *Cortex*, **20**, 135–41.

Hugdahl, K., and Brobäck, C.-G. (in press). Effects of brain asymmetry on conditioning in a dichotic extinction paradigm.

Hugdahl, K., Broman, J.-E., and Franzon, M. (1983a). Effects of stimulus content and brain lateralization on the habituation of the electrodermal orienting reaction (OR). *Biological Psychology*, **17**, 153–68.

Hugdahl, K., and Franzon, M. (1985). Visual half-field presentations of incongruent color-words reveal mirror-reversal of language lateralization in dextral and sinistral subjects. *Cortex*, **21**, in press.

Hugdahl, K., Franzon, M., Andersson, B., Walldebo, G. (1983c). Heart rate responses (HRR) to lateralized visual stimuli. *Pavlovian Journal of Biological Science*, **18**, 186–98.

Hugdahl, K., Franzon, M., and Fristorp-Wasteby, E. (1983c). Electrodermal orienting responses to verbal and geometrical visual stimuli projected to the left or right retinal half-fields: Sex effects. *Acta Psychologica*, 141–54.

Hugdahl, K., Kvale, G., Nordby, H., and Overmier, J. B. (submitted). Lateralized presentation of visual CSs: Effects on electrodermal conditioning.

Hugdahl, K., Qundos, O., and Vaittinen, J. (1982a). Effects of hemispheric asymmetry on electrodermal conditioning in a dichotic listening paradigm. *Pavlovian Journal of Biological Science*, **17**, 120–8.

Hugdahl, K., Wahlgren, C., and Wass, T. (1982b). Habituation of the electrodermal orienting reaction is dependent on the cerebral hemisphere initially stimulated. *Biological Psychology*, **15**, 49–62.

Inglis, J., and Lawson, J. S. (1981). Sex differences in the effects of unilateral brain damage on intelligence. *Science*, **212**, 693–5.

Jerussi, T. P., and Taylor, C. A. (1982). Bilateral asymmetry in striatal dopamine metabolism: implications for pharmacotherapy of schizophrenia. *Brain Research*, **246**, 71–5.

Jutai, J. W. (1984). Cerebral asymmetry and the psychophysiology of attention. *International Journal of Psychophysiology*, **1**, 219–25.

Kamin, L. (1969). Predictability, surprise, attention, and conditioning. In *Punishment and Aversive Behavior* (eds. B. A. Campbell and R. M. Church). Appleton-Century-Crofts, New York.

Katkin, E. S. (1985). Blood, sweat, and tears: Individual differences in autonomic self-perception. *Psychophysiology*, **22**, 125–37.

Ketterer, M. W., and Smith, B. D. (1982). Lateralized cortical/cognitive processing and electrodermal activity: Effects of subject and stimulus characteristics (Abstract). *Psychophysiology*, **19**, 238.

Kimble, D. P., Bagshaw, M. H., and Pribram, K. H. (1965). The GSR of monkeys during orienting and habituation after selective ablations of the cingulate and frontal cortex. *Neuropsychologia*, **3**, 121–8.
Kimble, G. A. (1961). *Hilgard and Marquis' Conditioning and Learning*. Appleton-Century-Crofts, New York.
Kimura, D. (1961). Cerebral dominance and the perception of verbal stimuli. *Canadian Journal of Psychology*, **15**, 166–71.
Kimura, D. (1966). Dual functional asymmetry of the brain in visual perception. *Neuropsychologia*, **4**, 275–85.
Kimura, D. (1967). Functional asymmetry of the brain in dichotic listening. *Cortex*, **3**, 163–78.
Kinsbourne, M. (1973). The control of attention by interaction between the cerebral hemispheres. In *Attention and Human Performance*, vol. IV (ed. S. Kornblum). Academic Press, New York.
Klatzky, R., and Atkinson, R. (1971). Specialization of the cerebral hemispheres in scanning for information in short-term memory. *Perception and Psychophysics*, **10**, 335–8.
Kolb, B., and Whishaw, L. Q. (1980). *Fundamentals of Human Neuropsychology*. Freeman & Co., San Francisco.
Lacroix, J. M., and Comper, P. (1979). Lateralization in the electrodermal system as a function of cognitive/hemispheric manipulations. *Psychophysiology*, **16**, 116–29.
LeMay, M., and Culebras, A. (1972). Human brain-morphologic differences in the hemispheres demonstrable by carotid arteriography. *New England Journal of Medicine*, **287**, 168–70.
Levy, J., and Reid, M. (1976). Variations in writing posture and cerebral organization. *Science*, **194**, 337–9.
Levy-Agresti, J., and Sperry, R. W. (1968). Differential perceptual capacities in major and minor hemispheres (Abstract). *Proceedings of the National Academy of Sciences*, **61**, 337–9.
Ley, R. G., and Bryden, M. P. (1979). Hemispheric differences in recognizing faces and emotions. *Brain and Language*, **7**, 127–38.
Logue, A. W. (1979). Taste aversion and the generality of the laws of learning. *Psychological Bulletin*, **86**, 276–96.
McGlone, J. (1980). Sex differences in human brain asymmetry: A critical survey. *Behavioral and Brain Sciences*, **3**, 215–63.
Mackintosh, N. J. (1975). A theory of attention: Variations in the associability of stimuli with reinforcement. *Psychological Review*, **82**, 276–98.
McNally, R. L. (1981). Phobias and preparedness: Instructional reversal of electrodermal conditioning to fear-relevant stimuli. *Psychological Reports*, **48**, 175–80.
Majkowski, J., Bochenek, W., Bochenek, Z., Knapik-Fijalkowsa, A., and Kopec, J. (1971). Latency of averaged evoked potentials to contralateral and ipsilateral auditory stimulation in normal subjects. *Brain Research*, **25**, 416–19.
Maltzman, I. (1971). The orienting reflex and thinking as determiners of conditioning and generalization to words. In *Essays in Neobehaviorism* (eds. H. H. Kendler, and J. T. Spence). Appleton-Century-Crofts, New York.
Maltzman, I. (1979). Orienting reflexes and classical conditioning in humans. In *The Orienting Reflex* (eds. H. D. Kimmel, E. H. van Olst and J. F. Orlebeke). Erlbaum Associates, Hillsdale, N.J.
Maltzman, I., and Boyd, G. (1984). Stimulus significance and bilateral SCRs to potentially phobic pictures. *Journal of Abnormal Psychology*, **93**, 41–6.
Martin, D. G., Stambrook, M., Tataryn, D. J., and Biehl, H. (1984). Conditioning in the unattended left ear. *International Journal of Neuroscience*, **23**, 95–102.

Maximilian, V. A. (1982). Cortical blood flow asymmetry during monaural verbal stimulation. *Brain and Language*, **15**, 1–11.
Mesulam, M. M. (1981). A cortical network for directed attention and unilateral neglect. *Annals of Neurology*, **10**, 309–25.
Meyer, G. E. (1976). Right hemisphere sensitivity for the McCullogh effect. *Nature*, **264**, 751–3.
Mintz, M., and Myslobodsky, M. S. (1983). Two types of hemisphere imbalance in hemi-Parkinsonianism coded by brain electrical activity and electrodermal activity. In *Hemisyndromes: Psychobiology, Neurology, Psychiatry* (ed. M. S. Myslobodsky). Academic Press, New York.
Moscovitch, M. (1979). Information processing and the cerebral hemispheres. In *Handbook of Neurobiology*, vol. 2 (ed. M. S. Gazzaniga). Plenum Press, New York.
Myslobodsky, M. S., and Horesh, N. (1978). Bilateral electrodermal activity in depressive patients. *Biological Psychology*, **6**, 111–20.
Myslobodsky, M. S., and Rattok, J. (1977). Bilateral electrodermal activity in waking man. *Acta Psychologica*, **41**, 273–82.
Obrist, P. A., Webb, R. A., and Sutterer, J. R. (1969). Heart rate and somatic changes during aversive conditioning and a simple reaction time task. *Psychophysiology*, **5**, 696–723.
Öhman, A. (1979a). The orienting response, attention and learning: An information-processing perspective. In *The Orienting Reflex* (eds. H. D. Kimmel, E. H. van Olst, and J. F. Orlebeke). Erlbaum Associates, Hillsdale, N.J.
Öhman, A. (1979b). Fear relevance, autonomic conditioning, and phobias: A laboratory model. In *Trends in Behavior Therapy* (eds. P. O. Sjöden, S. Bates, and W. S. Dockens). Academic Press, New York.
Öhman, A. (1984). The orienting response during Pavlovian conditioning. In *Orienting and Habituation—Perspectives in Human Research* (ed. D. Siddle). John Wiley & Sons, London.
Öhman, A., Fredrikson, M., Hugdahl, K., and Rimmö, P. A. (1976). The premise of equipotentiality in human classical conditioning: Conditioned electrodermal responses to potentially phobic stimuli. *Journal of Experimental Psychology: General*, **105**, 313–37.
Oke, A., Keller, R., Mefford, I., and Adams, R. N. (1977). Lateralization of norepinephrine in human thalamus. *Science*, **200**, 1411–13.
Ornstein, R. (1977). *The Psychology of Consciousness*. Harcourt Brace Jovanovich, New York.
Overton, D. A. (1964). State-dependent or 'dissociated' learning produced with pentobarbital. *Journal of Comparative and Physiological Psychology*, **57**, 3–12.
Rasmussen, T., and Milner, B. (1977). The role of early left-brain injury in determining lateralization of cerebral speech functions. *Annals of the New York Academy of Sciences*, **299**, 355–69.
Rescorla, R. A. (1966). Predictability and number of pairings in Pavlovian fear conditioning. *Psychonomic Science*, **4**, 383–4.
Rescorla, R. A. (1967). Pavlovian conditioning and its proper control procedures. *Psychological Review*, **74**, 71–80.
Rescorla, R. A. (1972). Information variables in Pavlovian conditioning. In *Learning and Motivation*, vol. VI (ed. G. H. Bower). Academic Press, New York.
Rescorla, R. A. (1980). *Pavlovian Second-order Conditioning*. Academic Press, New York.
Rescorla, R. A., and Wagner, A. R. (1972). A theory of Pavlovian conditioning: Variations in the effectiveness of reinforcement and nonreinforcement. In *Classical*

Conditioning II: Current Theory and Research (eds. A. Black and W. F. Prokasy). Appleton-Century-Crofts, New York.

Rogers, L. J., and Anson, J. M. (1979). Lateralization of function in the chicken fore-brain. *Pharmacology, Biochemistry and Behavior*, **10**, 679–86.

Rosenzweig, M. R. (1955). Representation of two ears at the auditory cortex. *American Journal of Physiology*, **167**, 147–58.

Saltz, E. (1973). Higher mental processes as the bases for the laws of conditioning. In *Contemporary Approaches to Conditioning and Learning* (eds. F. J. McGuigan and D. B. Lumsden). V. H. Winston & Son, Washington, D.C.

Satz, P., Achenbach, K., and Fennell, E. (1967). Correlations between assessed manual laterality and predicted laterality in a normal population. *Neuropsychologia*, **5**, 295–310.

Schwartz, G. E., Davidson, R. J., and Maer, F. (1975). Right hemisphere lateralization for emotion in the human brain: Interaction with cognition. *Science*, **190**, 266–8.

Schweiger, A., and Maltzman, I. (1985). Behavioral and electrodermal measures of lateralization for music perception in musicians and nonmusicians. *Biological Psychology*, **20**, 129–45.

Seamon, J., and Gazzaniga, M. S. (1973). Coding strategies and cerebral laterality effects. *Cognitive Psychology*, **5**, 249–56.

Seligman, M. E. P. (1970). On the generality of the laws of learning. *Psychological Review*, **77**, 400–18.

Sergent, J. (1985). Role of input and task factors in asymmetric hemispheric processing of faces. *Journal of Clinical and Experimental Neuropsychology*, **7**, 158–9.

Sokolov, E. N. (1963). *Perception and the Conditioned Reflex*. Pergamon Press, London.

Spence, K. W., and Taylor, J. A. (1951). Anxiety and strength of the UCS as determiners of amount of eyelid conditioning. *Journal of Experimental Psychology*, **42**, 183–8.

Sperry, R. W. (1974). Lateral specialization in the surgically separated hemispheres. In *The Neurosciences: Third Study Program* (eds. F. O. Schmitt and F. G. Worden). MIT Press, Cambridge, Mass.

Sperry, R. W., and Gazzaniga, M. S. (1967). Language following surgical disconnection of the hemispheres. In *Brain Mechanisms Underlying Speech and Language* (ed. F. L. Darley). Grune & Stratton, New York.

Springer, S. P. (1977). Tachistoscopic and dichotic listening investigations of laterality in normal human subjects. In *Lateralization in the Nervous System* (eds. S. Harnad, R. W. Doty, L. Goldstein, J. and G. Krauthamer). Academic Press, New York.

Springer, S. P., and Deutsch, G. (1981). *Left Brain, Right Brain*. Freeman & Co., San Francisco.

Stokes, K. A., and McIntyre, D. C. (1985). Lateralized state-dependent learning produced by hippocampal kindled convulsions: Effects of split-brain. *Physiology and Behavior*, **34**, 217–24.

Studdert-Kennedy, M., and Shankweiler, D. (1970). Hemispheric specialization for speech perception. *Journal of the Acoustical Society of America*, **48**, 579–94.

Suberi, M., and McKeever, W. F. (1977). Differential right hemisphere memory storage for emotional and non-emotional faces. *Neuropsychologia*, **5**, 757–68.

Wagner, A. R. (1976). Priming in STM: An information-processing mechanism for self-generated or retrieval-generated depression in performance. In *Habituation: Perspectives from Child Development, Animal Behavior, and Neurophysiology* (eds. T. J. Tighe and R. N. Leaton). Erlbaum Associates, Hillsdale, N.J.

Walker, B. B., and Sandman, C. A. (1979). Human visual evoked responses are related to heart rate. *Journal of Comparative and Physiological Psychology*, **93**, 717–29.

Walker, B. B., and Sandman, C. A. (1982). Visual evoked potentials change as heart rate and carotid pressure change. *Psychophysiology*, **19**, 520–7.

Wang, G. H. (1964). *Neural Control of Sweating*. University of Wisconsin Press, Madison, Wis.

Wardlaw, K. A., and Kroll, N. E. (1976). Autonomic responses to shock-associated words in a nonattended message: A failure to replicate. *Journal of Experimental Psychology: Human Perception and Performance*, **2**, 357–60.

Weber, A. M., and Bradshaw, J. L. (1981). Levy and Reid's neurological model in relation to writing hand/posture: An evaluation. *Psychological Bulletin*, **90**, 74–88.

Whitlow, J. W. Jr, and Wagner, A. R. (1984). Memory and habituation. In *Habituation, Sensitization, and Behavior* (eds. H. S. Peeke and L. Petronovitch). Academic Press, New York.

Wilcott, R. C., and Bradley, H. H. (1970). Low-frequency electrical stimulation of the cat's anterior cortex and inhibition of skin potential responses. *Journal of Comparative and Physiological Psychology*, **69**, 351–5.

Wolpe, J. (1958). *Psychotherapy by Reciprocal Inhibition*. Stanford University Press, Stanford, Calif.

Wright, J. M. von, Andersson, K., and Stenman, U. (1975). Generalization of conditioned GSRs in dichotic listening. In *Attention and Performance*, vol. V (eds. P. M. Rabbit and S. Dornic). Academic Press, London.

Yokoyama K., Jennings, R., Ackles, P., Hood P., and Boller, F. (in press). Lack of heart rate changes during an attention-demanding task after right hemisphere lesions. *Neurology*.

Zaidel, E. (1975). A technique for presenting lateralized visual input with prolonged exposure. *Vision Research*, **15**, 283–9.

Zaidel, E. (1978). Lexical organization in the right hemisphere. In *Cerebral Correlates of Conscious Experience* (eds. P. Buser and A. Rougeul-Buser). Elsevier, Amsterdam.

Zaidel, E. (1984). Some plans and paradoxes in the interface of behavioral and ERP indices of hemispheric asymmetries. In *Cognitive Psychophysiology—Event-related Potentials and the Study of Cognition* (ed. E. Donchin). Erlbaum Associates, Hillsdale, N.J.

Zaidel, E., and Peters, A. M. (1981). Phonological encoding and ideographic reading by the disconnected right hemisphere: two case studies. *Brain and Language*, **14**, 205–34.

Cognitive Processes and Pavlovian Conditioning in Humans
Edited by G. Davey

Chapter 7

Conditioning and perception

Peter Davies
University of Bradford

1 The cognitive approach to perception and a challenge to it

1.1 The cognitive approach

Neisser (1966) in his approach to visual cognition started from the assumption that 'the world of experience is produced by the man who experiences it'. He presented an argument in favour of perceptual synthesis based upon the reinterpretation of empirical evidence while ignoring the underlying physiological activity. This was not an unintentional oversight but the result of the considered judgement that we know too little of underlying physiological mechanisms to make any theory more than speculative; his main concern was to demonstrate the need to look at the whole process in cognitive terms. His central assertion was that 'seeing, hearing, and remembering are all acts of *construction*, which may make more or less use of stimulus information depending on circumstances'.

1.2 Prologue: the limitations of sensory physiology

The present chapter seeks to challenge part of this view. There is no doubt that perception does not equate with reception. Nor is there any reason to question his assertion that 'seeing, hearing, and remembering are all acts of construction'. We do not have direct access to the world and our perceptions of it are mediated by both the limitations of our sensory systems and the even greater limitations of our information processing capacity. In order to function and survive in the middle of the vast torrent of environmental information which makes up our individual universe we need efficient strategies to select environmentally relevant stimuli and processes to convert those which are selected into behaviourally relevant responses. It will be argued that conditioning, in all its aspects, provides both strategies and processes. However, before turning to this it may be useful to consider briefly what Neisser probably had in mind when he considered underlying physiological activity and decided that insufficient was known to make any theory other than speculative.

An excellent example for this purpose is to consider the question of colour vision. From the time of Helmholtz it has been recognized that the retinal layer possesses at least three types of cones, each maximally sensitive to lights of different wavelengths. Elaborate theories of colour perception have been built upon the physiological structures involved in colour perception which account for nearly all the empirical data other than some types of colour-blindness and Land's data. In a series of experiments Land demonstrated that normal colour vision may occur given adequate brightness ratio information and the superimposition of white and a monochromatic light (Land, 1959a, 1959b). Given such stimulation an observer should, on the basis of the physiology of the eye, perceive a monochromatic range of various degrees of saturation plus greys and black. However, the observed result is close to normal full colour vision and it occurs when both the original model and the photographs of the model are displayed side by side. This result is intriguing as the photographs are lit in the special way and the model by normal room lighting. To see both in normal colour simultaneously implies that the processes underlying Land's demonstrations are not incompatible with those underlying normal vision. However there is no simple explanation for this compatability as in the Land demonstrations only one cone type is stimulated by coloured light, i.e. light of a wavelength to which a cone type is maximally sensitive.

These data may be compared with the well-known facts of retinal perimetry which indicate that the cone types, presumed to be the physiological basis for colour discrimination, are distributed over the retina in such a way that the full colour spectrum should only be perceived over a small region approximately 20° to 30° about the fixation point (Boring, Langfeld, and Weld, 1948). Thus only a small region around the fovea is served by all three cone types and colour vision based on all three cone types should be possible only within this region. In the more peripheral retinal regions served by only two, or even one, cone types colour vision should be confined to colours obtainable by mixing the appropriate lights. Thus red and green should not be perceived much beyond 20° to 30° from the point of fixation with a surrounding aura of blue up to some 50° to 60°. If the trichromatic theories of perception, any of them, accounted for normal colour vision not one of the Land experiments could produce the results reported and normal colour vision should be 'normal' only within 20° to 30° of the point of fixation. Moreover, if visual perception was entirely dependent upon peripheral receptors being stimulated then closure of one eye would lead to a hole in the remaining field of vision as each eye has a blind spot devoid of any type of receptor cells. Thus, without any weight of consideration of the rival merits of rival theories it may be asserted confidently that normal perception does not depend solely upon a simple causal chain of photo receptors, neural connections, and associated photochemical and biochemical processes.

1.3 Sensory physiology and percepts

However, this does not mean that we can ignore the basic facts of physiology nor the wealth of information that has been accumulated concerning them. The physiological bases of visual and auditory perception are undoubtedly the bases of our visual and auditory percepts. My argument is that this physiological substrate is merely the base upon which normal percepts are built. It is assumed that the physiological structures responsible for reception and processing provide the most accurate source of knowledge that we have regarding the nature of the world. However, they do so at the expense of making inordinate demands upon processing and attention. Normal environmental interactions are assumed to take place upon the basis of learned associations rather than detailed processing. Only when such associations fail to act as reliable predictors do we fall back upon our primary data source. Thus both our most accurate knowledge of the world and our secondary, derived, knowledge of the world are limited ultimately to the fidelity and integrity of the physiological substrate. Nothing could be learned which was not available at this level, e.g. a colour-blind individual will never learn to perceive colours. However, learning may frequently transcend reality by including in any given percept features not present in a particular input if such features are normally associated with such an input. Examples of such 'misperceptions' are legion, most do not probably come to our attention unless behavioural consequences follow from acting upon assumed, but not actually present, features of the input. On this basis perceptions must be seen as the product of both learning and the physiological substrate.

There are several objections to regarding the physiological substrate as the sole determinant of perception. Perhaps the most crucial is that of individual differences in perception as consequences of differences in interest or training. Assuming a normal physiology in two observers then the same physical stimulus must provide the same stimulation to both of them and result in the same, or very similar, physiological activity. If this activity was the sole determinant of perception then the resulting percepts would be the same, or very similar, in both observers. The biological imperative to interact with the world in a survival oriented way does ensure commonality of most percepts in terms of gross features, but what each individual perceives—the meaning, significance, and interpretation put on the input—differs and frequently differs widely.

Such differences can be explained largely in terms of selective attention which has long been of interest to psychologists. The necessity to apportion our attention is imposed upon us by our limited capacity to process information. According to Miller (1956) the information processing capacity of man is limited to 7 ± 2 bits. This conclusion is based upon psychophysical discrimination data, i.e. the raw material from which knowledge of the environment must be built. A second major problem is that information processing must take time. If our perceptions were dependent solely upon their physiological substrate we would be unable to make simple decisions such as figure/ground (informational overload) and would live in our own immediate past (information processing lag). Moreover, percepts would be truly common in that all organisms with intact physiological substrates would have the same percepts of any given input. On the whole none of these considerations applies. We cope with input selection, we predict outcomes to perceive a world in which behaviour is appropriate to the environmental imperatives, and we have minor differences in our perceptions of the world.

On the whole these considerations have been recognized by perceptual theorists and there are a plethora of perceptual theories. The earliest suggested that man received faint copies of the world via his sensory systems, later views suggested that some association of ideas was necessary, others that immediate experiences occurred against a context by which they could be evaluated, yet others that perception was probabilistic in the statistical sense, or that needs, attitudes, and values interacted with the sensory input to produce percepts. Not one of these views other than the eidola theory (faint copies) is manifestly wrong. Moreover, all can be reformulated in terms of conditioning. For the moment the argument will be confined to Helmholtz's notion of unconscious inference as this embraces the majority of the facts that demand explanation.

2 Perception as a product of conditioning

2.1 Helmholtz and unconscious inference

Helmholtz argued that sensory input was symbolic (Helmholtz, 1879) by which he meant that the input does not have to share an identity with the external referent but only an invariant relationship with it. He also argued that the experience of such regular relations allowed an 'unconscious inference' to be made and that perception was the aggregate of unconscious inferences.

Sechenov worked in Helmholtz's laboratory for a time during the period he spent in the West from 1856 to 1863 and became familiar with the concept of 'unconscious inference'. Pavlov was influenced subsequently by Sechenov from whom he probably acquired his knowledge of Helmholtz's concept. Thus, in 1928, Pavlov wrote:

> Evidently, what the genius Helmholtz referred to as 'unconscious conclusion' corresponds to the mechanism of the conditioned reflex. When, for example, the physiologist says that for the formation of the conception of the actual size of an object there is necessary a certain length of the image on the retina and a certain action of the internal and external muscles of the eye, he is stating the mechanism of the conditioned reflex. When a combination of stimuli, arising from the retina and ocular muscles, coincides several times with the tactile stimulus of a body of a certain size, this combination comes to play the role of a *signal*, and this becomes the conditioned stimulus for the real size of the object. From this hardly contestable point of view, the fundamental facts of the psychological part of physiological optics are physiologically nothing else than a series of conditioned reflexes, i.e., a series of elementary facts concerning the complicated activity of the eye analyzer. (Pavlov, 1928, emphasis in the original, cited in Warren and Warren, 1968, p. 18).

If, as Helmholtz maintained, perception is largely a matter of unconscious inference and this in turn is, as Pavlov suggested, only another name for the classically conditioned response, then it should be possible to demonstrate the formation of classically conditioned percepts within the laboratory. It is not possible to demonstrate that all percepts are conditioned responses, nor that any individual, normal, response has been acquired through conditioning. However, for reasons stated earlier, conditioning would serve to overcome two problems, namely the information bottleneck and the processing time lag, as well as fitting well with the evidence on perceptual development and studies of perceptual deprivation. Provided that there is evidence that percepts may be conditioned then a theoretical case may be made for conditioning being a major determinant of perception.

2.2 Why hasn't this been said before?

As Wolpe points out, 'the role of conditioning in the development of perception has received very little notice from psychologists despite the long availability of a brilliant monograph on the subject by James G. Taylor (1962). Two problems are contained in the statement above. First, we have

(3.4.2) A_3, A_4, A_5, A_6, A_7, and A_8 are the sets of angles in terms of which the position of the eyes in their sockets and the position of the head relative to the trunk can be described.

(3.4.3) $O \equiv [(a_3, a_5, a_6, a_7, a_8);\ t_{a3} = t_{a5} = t_{a6} = t_{a7} = t_{a8}]$
describes all physically possible orientations of the left eye and the head. There is a corresponding set for the right eye.

(3.4.4) $K \subset \Delta \times O$
describes all pairs, (δ,o), that result in retinal stimulation.

(3.4.5) A_1 is the set of all horizontal angular deviations of rays of light from the optic axis. A_2 is the set of vertical deviations.

(3.4.6) $H \subset A_1 \times A_2$
defines the positions of all retinal points.

(3.4.7) $R \equiv H \times \Psi$
is the set of all proximal stimuli applied to the retina.

(3.4.8) $N \sim R$
is the set of afferent neural processes induced by R.

(3.4.9) $V_1 \equiv [(k,n);\ k \in K,\ n \in N,\ k \rightarrow r \rightarrow n]$
defines the afferent process in the left optic nerve as a joint function of the positions of objects in the environment, the energy of the light they reflect, and the orientation of eye and head. V_2 is similarly defined for the right eye.

(3.4.10) V_3 to V_8 are the sets of afferent impulses generated in the lateral rectus muscles of the left eye (V_3), and of the right eye (V_4), in the superior and inferior rectus muscles of both eyes (V_5), in the muscles that rotate the head about its vertical axis (V_6), backward and forward (V_7) and sideways (V_8). These are all joint functions of the angles, A_3 to A_8, and the time during which the position has been held.

(3.4.11) V_9, V_{10}, and V_{11} are the proprioceptive functions of the position of the hand.

(3.4.12) $S \equiv [(v_1, v_2, \ldots v_{11});\ t_{v1} = t_{v2} = \ldots = t_{v11}]$
is the set of all possible states of the afferent system, V_1 to V_{11}, as determined jointly by the environment, the orientation of eyes and head, and the position of the hand.

(3.4.13) $\Sigma \equiv [s \in S;$ for every s_i, $s_j \in \Sigma$, $t_{si} = t_{sj}]$
defines the complete state of the system as determined by the subset of Δ that is operating on the retinas at any moment of time.

(3.4.14) $Z(E) \subset A_3 \times A_4 \times A_5$
is the set of all physically possible positions of the eyes.

(3.4.15) $M(E) = Z(E) \times Z(E)$
is the set of all movements of the eyes.

(3.4.16) $M(H) = Z(H) \times Z(H)$
is the set of all movements of the head.

(3.4.17) $M(A) = Z(A) \times Z(A)$
is the set of all movements of the hand.

(3.4.18) $M \equiv [(m(E), m(H), m(A); t_{m(E)} = t_{m(H)} = t_{m(A)}]$
is the set of all simultaneous movements of eyes, head, and hand.

(3.4.19) D is the set of all drive stimuli.

(3.4.20) $Q \equiv [(s,d); s \in S, d \in D, t_s = t_d]$
is the set of all states of the system as determined jointly by S and D.

(3.4.21) $Q(\delta) \equiv [q \in Q;$ for every $q_i, q_j \in Q(\delta), \delta(q_i) = \delta(q_j)]$
is an equivalence class of Q as determined by a specific $\delta \in \Delta$. No two elements of $Q(\delta)$ can occur simultaneously.

(3.4.22) $Q(z) \equiv [q \in Q(\delta);$ *for every* $q_i, q_j \in Q(z), z(q_i) = z(q_j)]$
is an equivalence class of $Q(\delta)$ as determined by the initial position, z(A) of the hand.

(3.4.23) $U \equiv [(q,m); q \in Q, m \in M, o < (t_m - t_q) \leqslant 10$ sec.]
is the set of all conjunctions of states $q \in Q$ with movements $m \in M$. U is not a function. It describes an irregular and unstable system.

(3.4.24) $F \equiv [(q,m); q \in Q, m \in M, q \rightarrow m]$
is the set of all conjunctions of states $q \in Q$ with conditioned responses $m \in M$.

(3.4.25) $F' \sim F$
is the set of neural structures or engrams mediating the conditioned responses, $q \rightarrow m$, of F.

(3.4.26) E″ is the set of energies applied to the elements of E′.

(3.4.27) $E = E' \times E''$
is the set of engrams in action.

(3.4.28) $\Phi \equiv [(q,e); q \in Q, e \in E, q \rightarrow e]$
is the set of states of the system including active engrams but not movements.

(3.4.29) $\Pi \equiv [\phi \in \Phi;$ *for every* $\phi_i, \phi_j \in \Pi, t_{ei} = t_{ej}]$.

3.5 We may begin by observing that an element of Φ defines

Figure 7.1 (*Reproduced by permission of Yale University Press from J. G. Taylor,* The Behavioural Basis of Perception, *Yale University Press, New Haven, Conn., and London, 1962*)

the incontrovertible fact the role of conditioning in perception has received very little notice from psychologists, just how little will become apparent in a later section when this work is summarized. Secondly, there is the almost monumental disinterest in Taylor's undoubtedly brilliant book. This is almost certainly due to the rigour with which he approached his subject and his desire for precision which led to him couching his theory in what he describes as 'a special notation derived from set theory' (Taylor, 1971). This has had the effect of concealing his insights rather than making them available and testable. His aim was to make his propositions so precise that they would be amenable to experimental verification. Unfortunately many of his factors remain mysterious and imprecise despite being given a precise set notation. The specimen page (Figure 7.1) will probably illustrate this point better than any word of mine.

2.3 Adaptation studies

When Taylor wrote his monograph he lacked any direct evidence of sensory conditioning and relied instead upon adaptation, or relearning, studies using adult subjects. What emerged from these studies was that adaptation occurred not as a consequence of exposure time but as a consequence of environmental feedback. To put this into the terminology of conditioning the device to which the subject was required to adapt, e.g. displacing prisms or vision inverters, provided sensations which acted as the CSs and the environmental consequences of the resulting percepts would act as the UCSs. When the device was first worn the abnormal percept which was experienced gave rise to a UCS which was always aversive as the behavioural consequence of acting upon a false premise about the nature of the environment. As adaptation (conditioning) occurred and the resulting modified percept was acted upon, the UCS was appetitive in that environmental interaction of an adaptive nature resulted from such percepts. For example, in one experiment with inverting spectacles Taylor described how the subject was equipped with a short board to use as a shield while an accomplice experimenter stabbed at the subject's ribs with an umbrella. For so long as the subject reacted on the basis of the physical input, a laterally inverted image, they were stabbed in the ribs, which is quite clearly an aversive event. Once they learned to compensate for the image inversion they were able to block the blows, and finally their percepts came into line with the consequences of having such an adaptive strategy, i.e. they perceived the world in its normal relationships despite the experimental device.

Initially it was thought that continual wearing of such a device would be necessary if adaptation was to occur. However, this proved not to be the case. Periods of normal vision do not prevent adaptation, nor does prolonged wearing of a device lead to adaptation unless feedback occurs as a consequence of environmental interaction.

Some years ago one of my own students repeated Stratton's work (Stratton, 1897) on bicoloured lenses, which formed a crucial part of Taylor's experimental evidence, using bicoloured contact lenses. Over a 3 month period of wearing bicoloured red/green contact lenses during all waking hours he adapted to almost normal colour vision. This was tested using a colour naming task based on Munsell colours to control for non-colour cues such as relative brightness. Moreover, he was able to live a full and normal life including driving a car. Other subjects were tested using bicoloured spectacle lenses and they too adapted whether they wore them over all daylight hours or only for mornings or afternoons. I was a subject in the partial wearing group and can testify to how terrifying it is to attempt to drive a car while wearing such a device at night. All headlights from oncoming traffic look like advancing brake lights and orientation is quickly lost. I tried this activity but once as I felt that the potential aversive feedback was likely to result in permanent adaptation! The fact that Mr Robinson, my student, was able to drive regularly and at any time of the day or night after 6 weeks of wearing his bicoloured contact lenses is a very telling testimony to his level of adaptation.

2.4 The roles of operant and classical conditioning

Returning to Taylor, one of the points which he makes quite clearly is that when he refers to conditioning he has no particular type of conditioning in mind. In some cases the conditioning would be classical, in other operant. There are at least two ways of looking at this: (a) that there are two distinct forms of conditioning or (b) that both operant and classical conditioning are subsets of the same type of learning. Not wishing to join the lists on behalf of these causes, I would wish to associate myself with Taylor's views, i.e. (a) conditioning is the basis of perception and (b) it is relatively immaterial which form of conditioning is involved in any given situation. Sometimes it will be operant, at others classical, and quite frequently in complex environmental transactions there will be contributions from both types.

The first of these statements is strong and needs some justification. The second is debatable as one of the implications is that there are no real differences other than procedural ones in these two types of conditioning. Let me start with the first one: 'conditioning is the basis of perception'. Conditioning in the classical sense is producing an appropriate response in advance, or even the temporary absence, of the appropriate unconditioned stimulus. As such it is clearly an associative process in that the production of the appropriate response depends upon a regularly associated, and predictive, stimulus. This mechanism jumps the temporal hurdle raised earlier in that only the predictive stimulus (the CS) need be processed and the response (the CR) can occur well before the UCS has been either received or processed. However, when the associative link between the CS and UCS is broken frequently, the predictive value of the CS is lost and extinction occurs. Nevertheless, in the world outside the laboratory stimulus relations tend to be remarkably constant, e.g. in fruit, redness goes with ripeness and sweetness, and smoke accompanies fire. Thus once an association is learned it is unlikely to be extinguished owing to the poor predictive value of the CS. On the contrary, the high predictive value of naturally occurring associations is likely to be highly rewarding in that responses to such CSs are likely to be environmentally appropriate. Conditioning, of the classical type, would also serve to minimize information processing especially as not all stimuli need be processed prior to initiating the appropriate response.

Turning to the second statement, it is difficult to find any direct experimental evidence for operant conditioning being a factor in perception. However, it is implicit in Helmholtz's notion of unconscious inference that the resulting inferences are reliable, i.e. reinforced by environmental interaction, and it is equally true that classically conditioned percepts extinguish when the UCS is not presented over a large number of trials. Predicting the UCS in a classical paradigm appears to equate with reinforcing emitted behaviour in the operant one.

One of the major problems with conditioning as the basis of perception is the apparent simplicity of conditioning. I say 'apparent' as conditioning should be taken to include all related behaviours such as habituation, orientation, sensitization, and pseudo conditioning as well as higher order, compound, and configured conditioning. Sokolov (1963) wrote a book entitled *Perception and the Conditioned Reflex*. In this book he concentrates more or less exclusively upon the orienting response. When the full gamut of conditioning and conditioning-like behaviours are considered there is more than adequate complexity to account for both the commonalities and diversities of perception.

This last point is an important one as any adequate theory of perception must account not only for the commonalities of shared perceptual experiences but also for individual diversities. These may arise from at least three sources, (a) physiological abnormality such as a retinal cone deficiency, (b) physiological malfunction such as vitamin deficiency (see Spies, Aring, Gelperin, and Bean, 1938), or (c) attitudes and values or, to put it another way, past experience. The Directive State and probabilistic functionalist literature is replete with examples in this third category though only one reference is given here (McClelland and Atkinson, 1948). It is in this last category, under the heading of experience, that conditioning comes into its own.

2.5 Synethesia and studies involving hypnosis

On the whole there is very little direct experimental evidence to show that percepts can be conditioned though this notion has been around for quite a long time. Marks (1975) in a review of 'coloured-hearing' considers the possibility that colour tone synesthesia may arise from a conditioning process and he discusses the history of attempts at creating artificial, or deliberately learned, synesthesia. He argues that in nature 'experienced conjunctions are . . . *fortuitous*' and 'it is difficult to see how they can lead to the regularities that are observed in synesthesia'. Nevertheless, in an experimental setting the conjunctions are not fortuitous but contrived and they should therefore demonstrate whether or not synesthesia can be learned. Marks cites a report by Binet (1893) in which Binet artificially paired colours and sounds until his proficiency at naming colours in response to sound stimuli became equal to that of a synesthete. However, Marks notes that when Kelly (1934) presented eighteen subjects with eight pairs of colours and accordion notes 'there was no tendency for the subjects to actually "see" the colors when the notes were played'. He also notes experiments by Leuba (1940) and Leuba and Dunlap (1951) in which auditory conditioning was conducted while the subjects were under hypnosis. The subjects came to experience sensations of touch and smell, conditioned to sound, which came on automatically and involuntarily. These experiments will not be relied upon in the present context for a number of reasons. Binet's study is really little more than paired associate memory which may or may not be considered to be an example of conditioning. The Leuba studies involve hypnosis and this raises its own problems as the status of hypnosis itself is in doubt. According to Edmonston (1972) conditioning is not, on the whole, facilitated by hypnosis, and Platanov (1959) claims that deep hypnotic states inhibit the evocation of even previously learned CRs. However, light stages of hypnosis seem to facilitate the acquisition of CRs. This whole area defies description. I am interested in hypnosis and especially interested in the relation between hypnosis and conditioning. Most of my current research involves using hypnotically induced subjects in perceptual conditioning experiments. However, it is from this deeply and personally involved position that it seems prudent to discount all perceptual conditioning reports based upon hypnosis. This is not to say that they are sham, nor that hypnosis distorts the results. Quite frankly, the case for the conditioning of percepts and the role of conditioning in perception can be established without reference to hypnosis. To introduce evidence which could invite criticism on the grounds that a non-validated procedure, or an ill-understood phenomenon, was involved would be to weaken the case. However, hypnosis does seem to have a role in perception. Both negative and positive hallucinations can be induced (provided the way in which the subject behaves in response to his own percepts is regarded as evidence of such percepts; as no one can enter any other subject's head, behaviour and/or subject reports seem to be the best source of evidence as to what is perceived by any given subject). The literature and practice of hypnosis is replete with examples of perceptual realignment, redefinition, or distortion. In therapy these can range from redefining phobic stimuli as neutral or even affective, to redefining pain as 'healing sensations'. In some cases attention is drawn to sensations which have never hitherto been noticed while in other situations sensations are excluded from the final percept. All this evidence argues strongly for perception being superordinate to reception and modifiable by cognitive (or subconscious) factors. Fascinating as this evidence is it has no place in the present argument unless hypnosis turns out to be a manifestation of verbal conditioning. This is not unlikely. Through association words evoke their referents. (Provided one accepts Skinner's view of language acquisition (Skinner, 1957) this is not a difficult proposition to accept. The alternative view that man contains an 'innate language acquisition device' seems tautologous in that man speaks and he could not, regardless of reinforcement contingencies, unless he was innately equipped to do so.) So, if we accept that words evoke their referents, i.e. that the meaning of words is largely conditioned, then responses to hypnotic instructions must be higher order conditioned responses and any influences upon percepts must be consequences of conditioning. However, this argument must be seen as speculative in that Skinner's view of language acquisition has not been accepted universally nor has hypnosis been shown to be higher order conditioning using verbal CSs. Given time these views may become established psychological 'truths'. Until such time the argument for the role of conditioning in perception must rest upon other evidence. The following section reviews briefly a number of experiments which demonstrate the actual conditioning of percepts.

3 Conditioned percepts

3.1 Earlier studies

The earliest reference to conditioned percepts occurs in a charmingly titled paper, 'Visual, cutaneous, and kinaesthetic ghosts', by Swindle in 1917. His knowledge of conditioning was somewhat limited, e.g. Pavlov appears as Pawlaw, but he advances a hypothesis to account for the appearance of diurnal ghosts based upon classical conditioning of positive afterimages of long duration. This hypothesis rests upon his own results concerning positive afterimages (Swindle, 1916). This experiment, upon which Swindle bases his theory of ghosts, is seriously flawed; nevertheless his theory may well account for some of the reported sightings. The validity of this work is not vital to the current case and it is included only for the sake of completeness.

In the 1917 paper Swindle refers to a conditioned cutaneous response. In his first experiment Swindle discovered the stimulus properties of the cessation of a habituated response. Using a pair of dividers he stimulated the subject's arm with one point only and noticed that even though he did not remove the stimulus the subject would alternate his reports between 'one point' and 'no points'. When the second point was presented during the habituation period the report was 'one (point), and you shifted it', but when the first (habituated) point was removed the subject responded 'two' before changing his response to 'now it's only one'. This simple experiment was later elaborated to use 315 nail heads, profiled to fit the subject's forearm at 0.4 cm centres, as the source of the UCS. The nailed block was applied repeatedly for

20 second periods over 30 minutes. After this training a single nail point applied to the trained area evoked responses such as 'Many, at least half a dozen'. This effect had disappeared when retested 1 week after the training, but with a period of training in each of 3 successive weeks the effect began to persist. As Swindle remarks, 'Perhaps not all of the 315 nail heads appeared in the revived cutaneous pattern.' It would indeed be surprising if any subject could ever, under any circumstances, provide an accurate estimate of the number of nail heads applied. This experiment is probably a demonstration of sensitization or pseudo conditioning. Without repeating it and applying suitable tests it is quite impossible to say. It is difficult to identify a CS unless this is the application of the block of nails to the arm with the UCS being the sensations arising therefrom. However, it is here that we encounter a major difficulty with all perceptual conditioning experiments. Conditioning is not necessary to explain why a feeling of 'nails on the arm' should result from someone placing nails on the arm. Intramodal experiments are very difficult to devise as the responses, whether conditioned or not, will always be what uninstructed common sense would expect them to be. The effect of the single nail does defy a common-sense explanation but does not prove a case for conditioning.

The first serious, and incontrovertible, account of perceptual conditioning appears to be a report by Ellson (1941) who established an auditory response to a visual stimulus. This experiment paired an auditory stimulus of indeterminate onset and offset with a light CS. The auditory UCS was ramped up from a subthreshold level at the rate of 2 dB per second (i.e. below the j.n.d. for auditory change) until the subject reported hearing it. The level was then maintained for 2 seconds before the ramp was reversed and the tone became inaudible. Subjects conditioned to the light CS in that they reported auditory sensations even in the absence of the auditory stimulus. However, it is interesting to note that Ellson is not prepared to regard the resulting percepts as percepts but prefers to call them 'hallucinations'. This implies (a) that the effects experienced by subjects were not contingent upon an external stimulus event, (b) that the subjects were 'mistaken' in some way, and (c) an implicit suggestion that normal auditory responses are in some way 'real'.

3.2 Conditioned percept or hallucination

If we take these assumptions in turn we can learn quite a lot about the ways in which percepts are conceived by psychologists. A percept is normally regarded as being the experiential correlate of an external event which gives rise to this percept. This suggests, in turn, that visual stimuli are required to produce visual percepts, auditory stimuli to produce auditory percepts, and so on throughout our sensory systems. That anyone should treat this position seriously is surprising as the notion of direct conduction of 'images' via the nerves was rejected by Johannes Mueller when he published his doctrine of the specific energies of the nerves. It is not the nature of the input which matters, but the region of the brain stimulated as a consequence of the input.

The second assumption implied by 'hallucination' is that the subjects' percepts were not originating from the world, and could in principle be distinguished from percepts which did so. This argument is discussed by Hirst who gives the following example, 'as the drunkard looks first at the pink rat and then at the real bed on which it sits, there is a smooth transition. Consequently in both kinds of case—illusory and seemingly genuine perceptions—we must be directly aware of the same kind of entity, namely sense-data'. If we accept Hirst's argument, and that of the other philosophers whose position he is summarizing, it is clear that hallucinations are valid percepts for their percipients.

The third assumption is that normal auditory (or visual, or olfactory) percepts are in some way 'real' and correspond to events in the external world. In one sense they must do so as if they had no correspondence with the world they would indeed be arbitrary and meaningless. However, they are not copies of the world nor direct representations of it. The notion of Naïve Realism has long been rejected by philosophers and psychologists alike.

At this point, or possibly long before, the reader may well be asking, Why this diversion into philosophical considerations in a section on experimental evidence? One reason is that psychologists will not talk about conditioned percepts. Even today the percepts arising from a CS, which would not otherwise apart from its experimentally created association give rise to the percepts experienced, are regarded as less than genuine. This point is best illustrated by a yet to be published paper based on the Ellson experiment discussed earlier. The title of this paper, which is a conditioning study and which refers frequently to 'sensory conditioning', is 'Scopalamine and the sensory conditioning of hallucinations' (Warburton, Wesnes, Edwards, and Larrad, 1985). It may be that this title is justified because of the close link with the methodology of Ellson or it may reflect a reluctance to grasp the nettle and talk of conditioned percepts. This I can understand as there is little precedent for doing so. Taylor, in his book, was able to discuss the behavioural basis of perception but the studies he reported were not conditioning experiments. It is only recently that I have had the courage to talk about conditioned percepts rather than conditioned processes or conditioned afterimages. To regard the latter as 'conditioned images' was a conceptual shift which I may yet live to regret. Provided conditioning is limited to peripheral activities and epiphenomena of little interest it is regarded as a harmless eccentricity. To try to make it a central process in human cognition is to deny, to some minds, human freedom and dignity; and to regard it as the central process in human cognition is to challenge the fundamental beliefs of the majority, including fellow psychologists. However, this is the position from which I now approach the relation between conditioning, perception, and consciousness (Davies, 1984). Having made this much clear let us return to the experimental evidence which led me to this position.

3.3 Chronology of some major perceptual conditioning experiments

Howells (1944) reported the experimental establishment of colour–tone synesthesia. This paper originated from an accidental misconnection of a set of American traffic lights where tonal signals accompanied the red/green lights. The resulting spate of accidents was sufficiently interesting to Howells for him to investigate the possibility that colour perception could be, in such circumstances as a regularly linked tone–light signal, tone dependent. This experiment is interesting not only as an experiment but especially because it has its origins in 'the real world', i.e. people were behaving as if conditioned to perceive colours to tone stimuli as a consequence of (hitherto) invariate pairings. If conditioning occurred only in the laboratory it would be of little interest, if perception is based on conditioning then it should be all-pervasive and the origins of this experiment illustrate such pervasiveness.

Howells established colour-tone synesthesia in a well-controlled laboratory experiment which incorporated both a verbal response and a colour comparitor task to control for response–demand characteristics (Howells, 1944). In this experiment the subjects were exceedingly well motivated to make objectively accurate responses. They were all US 'veterans' who needed a satisfactory 'experimental participation report' in order to maintain their financial support as students. They were presented with two auditory–visual pairs, say high tone–red, low tone–green, with 10 per cent of the pairings being inappropriate, e.g. high tone–green. Accuracy of reporting was stressed but after 5000 trials they reported the colour of the light as being that indicated by the tone and, using desaturated lights as the UCS, they would match the perceived light with a comparator light based upon tonal indications. This experiment does not appear to have been replicated. This could be for either of two reasons. First, there is the sheer length of the experiment. Secondly, stimulus parameters do seem to be critical, especially so during the test trials.

Some years ago one of my research students tried to extend this result without replicating it first. The experimental arrangement involved clusters of red, green, and white lights arranged so as to produce both foveal stimulation and stimulation at 30°, 60°, and 90° from the fovea in both the temporal and nasal visual fields. It was hypothesized that conditioning would occur earlier in the periphery (where sensory input for colour is less compelling than at the fovea) as a result of foveal pairings. It was assumed that the peripheral colour responses would produce a perceptual effect comparable to foveally presented unsaturated colours. After some 20 subjects and 6000 trials each this experiment was abandoned without any evidence of conditioning. In retrospect this may well have been a mistake. The initial experiment involved 5000 trials with but a single light source in the fovea; my student's experiment used seven locations in all. Furthermore, the assumptions were that sensory information about wavelength was less good in the periphery than at the fovea, and that peripheral URs would give way to CRs more readily than the foveal URs. The first of these may have been reasonable but the second one may well be unreasonable. However, in Howells's experiment the critical UCS was a desaturated light whereas in this experiment it was a saturated one in one of several non-foveal locations. For the moment the validity of Howells's findings has to be accepted as even though the work has not been replicated no one has refuted his findings.

Chronologically the next reports are those of two Russians, Nicholas and Catherine Popov, who reported a whole series of afterimage conditioning experiments in the 1950s (Popov and Popov, 1953a, 1953b, 1953c, 1954a, 1954b, 1954c, 1954d). These reports are less than complete in that the exact methodology is never described. However, it is clear that they succeeded in pairing various CSs such as words (the word 'light' repeated), tones, and flute notes with the presentation of a visual stimulus (probably a coloured shape) to subjects in a totally dark environment. They recorded image durations and verbal descriptions of the images which included colour effects and mobility. They also compared these data for both conditioned and unconditioned images as well as the effects of alcohol and caffeine upon both unconditioned and conditioned images. These experiments cannot be replicated as the precise details of procedure are obscure. However, all their major results have been reproduced (with the exception of caffeine which does not seem to have been tried). For many years I have paired various tones or words with various visual stimuli and found that subjects seated in complete darkness would report visual sensations to auditory input after an adequate number of pairings (Davies 1974a, 1974b, 1976; Davies, Bennett, and Davies, 1983). The earliest experiment, carried out in 1969 and which was never published, was probably closest to that of the Popovs. The subject sat in a photographic darkroom while the experimenter, who was seated outside the room, shouted 'Light-light' at 3–4 minute intervals before triggering a photographic flash gun. Afterimage data were recorded by key press for duration and tape recorder for description. After 5 hours no results had been obtained. At this point the experimenter was just about to despair and stop the experiment when the subject said, 'The flash has failed again but I am seeing something. Do you want me to report it?' You can imagine the answer! Subsequent questioning revealed that similar CRs had occurred for at least 2 hours but the subject believed that he should only report visual sensations whenever the light had flashed. This cautionary tale is included because the instructions to the subject are critical. If they are too stringent no reports are obtained; too lax and they could well be seen as facilitating. As a footnote it should be said that this experiment should not have worked. Very few subjects show conditioning on this task when subjected to massed practice at approximately 20–30 trials per hour. However, had it not done so I think I would have abandoned this line of research as the Popovs' papers do not inspire confidence and at that time my interests lay more with afterimages than with conditioning.

The next publication to which we must turn our attention is that of Doty and Giurgea (1965) who report conditioned reflexes established by direct electrical stimulation of cortical areas in infrahuman subjects. The areas were the motor cortex and those associated with visual and auditory perception. The results indicate that after an adequate number of direct, coupled, presentations the activation of one area alone would evoke responses from the other areas. Thus an excitation in an auditory area of the cortex would produce activity within a visual area and vice versa. However, for obvious reasons, no subjective reports were obtained so it is impossible to know what sort of percepts were associated with either the inputs or the evoked activity.

In the same year Bzhalava published the results of an afterimage conditioning experiment (Bzhalava, 1965) which in many ways is not unlike that of the Popovs except that the conditioning paradigm was both unusual and sophisticated. The exact procedures are again difficult to uncover but this time because of the language in which their report is written (Georgian). The work is summarized in Razran (1971), reported again in Russian (Bzhalava, 1971), and a translation of various portions of yet another book by Bzhalava is available in English (National Lending Library, JPRS: 40, 522). For the moment we may stay with the Razran summary as it contains the essentials of the methodology and an outline of the results.

The procedure is clearly that of classical conditioning in that a tone was used as the CS and the illumination of a visual target (circle or triangle) as the UCS. The subjects were tested individually in complete darkness and the UR was the afterimage sequence which was both described and reported by key press coupled to a timing device. Each subject received 300 trials at the rate of 10 a day.

This procedure differs from conventional conditioning experiments in that there are no test trials as such. Each trial provides two opportunities to detect the effect of the CS. The first is indirect evidence of conditioning as the afterimage sequence after the light UCS presentation increases in duration. This increase is quite rapid with duration of sequence doubling after eight sessions, i.e. 80 trials (NB in his summary Razran says 18 trials but this is incorrect). After 30 sessions the duration of the image sequence was reported as having reached 180 seconds, a nine fold increase on the baseline. The second opportunity to observe conditioning is provided by visual responses reported after CS onset, and prior to the UCS presentation. As this is a long period of time (30 seconds) and the CR is slow to develop over trials, it is possible to study the aetiology of the CR. Five levels are described by Razran using Bzhalava's own descriptions and criteria.

> Evidence of fully formed direct conditioning—the sound clearly evoking the light percept—was reported by all subjects . . . Bzhalava's . . . subjects apprised him of five evolving levels of conditioning, the tone evoking consecutively: (a) fleeting amorphous light sensations 'resembling moving clouds', which the experimenter labels 'retinal', (b) relatively stable sensations of an 'amorphously illuminated gray field', (c) 'square outlines of the field' (perception), (d) 'varying outlines of a number of geometrical figures', and (e) clear perception of 'the illuminated circle or triangle'—the UCS. (Razran, 1971, p. 250)

I have obtained an independent translation (courtesy of Dr Ludmilla Rickwood of Plymouth Polytechnic) of the relevant sections from Bzhalava (1971) and it is clear that Bzhalava's writings are 'very involved, with a lot of deviations, so the thoughts are somewhat unclear unless one reads the book twice over'. I think this may account for what I assume to be a second error in the Razran summary, i.e. '(e) clear perception of "the illuminated circle or triangle"'. None of my subjects are over 15 years of doing similar experiments has ever reported clear perception of the UCS itself. The light flash is not reported unless it occurs and in the Bzhalava paradigm it does so on every trial. What is reported, and what I take (e) to mean, is 'clear perception of images of circles or triangles', i.e. images indistinguishable in size, shape, or colour sequences from the afterimage sequence which forms the UR. This is commonly achieved though, in my experience, not by all subjects. Approximately half to two thirds of subjects show this but about 15–20 per cent of them show few signs of conditioning within 300 trials. Indeed two subjects even reported no visual afterimages whatsoever in response to the light flash, i.e. there was no UR. One was 'conditioned' for 500 trials by which time he reported an image sequence of 20 seconds which was about the same as the baseline UR for normal subjects. I dismissed the second subject without further ado once I found this abnormal lack of an unconditioned response!

These minor criticisms aside, the Bzhalava study represents very strong evidence for the conditioning of visual percepts. Over many years I have run experiments based upon what I conceived as being the Popov and Popov approach and, later, Bzhalava's paradigm. The latter method provides the most reliable, the most informative, and the most provocative data. Conditioning can be seen to occur as it is occurring, i.e. indirect evidence is available long before any unequivocal CRs are emitted. One of my earlier papers (Davies, 1976) focuses upon the advantages of this paradigm both in terms of speed of acquisition as a consequence of not using normal test trials and in terms of the additional information derived from the levels of conditioning identified by Bzhalava. The latter, levels of conditioning, also proved useful in establishing the extent of generalization when exploring semantics using a conditioned visual response (Davies, Bennett, and Davies, 1983). Generalization could be judged not only on the basis of whether or not a response had occurred but the strength of the association also was reflected in the qualitative components of that response.

4 The practicalities of sensory conditioning

4.1 Acquisition time

Probably the first thing to strike anyone reading the above literature is the length of the conditioning procedures required. To condition a visual percept seems to demand 200–300 trials and auditory percepts require 80–100 trials. This point will be referred to later in the context of ecological validity. For the moment it should merely be noted that these experiments are time consuming.

4.2 Status of data

The next problem is the status of the data which is not unrelated to the instructions given to the subject. The data are of necessity subjective. One cannot get into the head of the observer and one cannot be certain that any report is genuine. However, the same argument applies to even the reaction time experiment; what proof can be given that the subject's button press is a response to the critical stimulus? On any one trial the subject may have conformed to experimental imperatives, experimenter demands, or merely pressed the button out of curiosity or because it was there. Of course, it is highly improbable that any one subject should continue to do this over 100 trials or that any two subjects should behave in a similar manner. In the visual conditioning experiments the subject must be given instructions which extract the maximum information without biasing the subject to generate responses to non-existent sense data. Subjects are actually reluctant to report visual effects to auditory stimuli, many do not do so until the effects are so compelling that they cannot be avoided, and the first reports are often at the fifth level of Bzhalava's hierarchy. The best evidence that the reports are genuine, not manifestations of demand characteristics, is (a) that Bzhalava's hierachy is always followed from the level at which the subject starts reporting; (b) that at the geometric shape stage the reports refer to all sorts of geometric figures ranging from circles, lines, and angles to the target figure in different orientations. Simultaneous negative and positive images are reported frequently. These *cannot* occur under normal circumstances provided UCS presentations are sufficiently separated in time. A typical schedule is ten trials per hour and without a CS this rate of UCS presentation produces very, very few reports of this nature. Rotations of the target figure and totally different configurations never occur in the absence of the CS. It is on these grounds that I believe the reports to be genuine.

A recent line of argument has been that these reports reflect a lowering of criterion in a signal detection experiment. Appealing as this may be it is an unlikely explanation of the subjective reports. First, there is no reason why a criterion shift should be associated with a hierarchical shift in the quality of the reports. Secondly, as this literature is not widely known subjects are unlikely to know what is expected of them. Thirdly, there is no explanation in Signal Detection Theory as to why response duration should increase on every trial. In non-conditioning experiments I have presented unpaired UCS presentations at 15 minute intervals over 10 to 12 hour periods and found that after an initial increase in the imagery reports durations shorten again and return to around baseline after some 40 trials. This contrasts with the conditioning data where subjects typically report sub-baseline durations on the first block of paired trials before commencing the increased duration reports. It would also, on the basis of SDT, be difficult to account for the behaviour of control subjects who do not change their reports in any significant way over trials (Davies, 1974).

4.3 Practical considerations

The actual experimental procedure to induce visual perceptual conditioning does not appear to be unduly critical. It is necessary to have a defined CS which is not readily available in any other circumstances otherwise non-reinforced 'trials' will occur out of the experimental situation. The 1000 Hz tone is quite good except that the BBC close-down signal is this frequency. Ex-subjects have reported seeing circles and triangles on their otherwise blank screens, and at least one of them believed these to have been transmitted! The conditioning should be in the normal forward direction and accompanied by appropriate instructions. It is also a mistake to assume that the subject's verbal reports are necessarily comprehensible. What would the reader make of 'A Christmas tree on a rocking horse'? (It turned out to be an inverted kite shaped figure with two sides of a triangle surmounting a semicircle with the diameter upwards.) One way of finding what subjects report is to use only one dark adapted eye for training purposes and to obtain coloured drawings of image sequences after designated trials. In order to do this the subjects' own descriptions are played back to them on selected trials, the test eye is covered by an eye patch, and low level illumination is provided; subjects then draw what they have described.

One of the difficulties is to decide whether or not the image sequence duration increase is merely a prolonged UR or a UR plus CR. In one experiment I sought to test this using a new UCS once the sequence duration had increased. The argument was that if the long image sequences were made up of UR + CR than a differently shaped UCS would produce about baseline UR figures of the new shape and the additional duration would show as a CR attributable to the original UCS. No such result was found; the images combined to produce compound figures throughout the series. Moreover, duration times decreased, presumably as a consequence of competing responses.

Duration data are difficult to record in that no external criterion can be imposed. Subjects must be asked to maintain similar standards and to release their response key at a similar point on every trial. This may be when the image breaks into random, unstructured, blobs of light or the moment when no sensations of a visual nature can be observed. Almost certainly the wide range of differences which can be observed between individual subjects reflects not only physiological individual differences but also differences in the reporting criteria adopted.

Once an initial CR has been established, higher order conditioning is easy, and second order responses have been established in as few as three trials, and third order responses in as little as one trial after the second order response has been established (Davies, Bennett, and Davies, 1983). These results are almost certainly due to the transfer from a tonal CS_1 to first a verbal CS_2 and then to a semantically meaningful CS_3.

One of the biggest problems with the visual conditioning is the persistence of normal afterimages. To this end low intensity light sources are required and long intertrial intervals. The resulting low density of activity makes subjects difficult to retain. Not many people are prepared to sit in a totally dark room on their own for 1 hour on 30 different days. Subject wastage is a very real problem. However, extraverts who take up the challenge actually seem to condition better than introverts which is contrary to expectation. True, this is based on $N = 3$, but it was very surprising to have three EPI tested extreme extraverts staying the course let alone conditioning well. One possible explanation is that in the situation employed *the only* way of keeping up a level of stimulation is to generate images in response to the tone. The alternative is to sit in total darkness in a quiet environment which is not typical of extraverts.

The choice of visual stimulus is also of some importance. The literature suggests that a variety of images, i.e. images differing from the UCS in significant ways such as colour, shape, or orientation, occur prior to the reliable evocation of an identifiable CR similar to the UR in these characteristics. The Popovs' experiments seem to have suffered in this respect as the UCS seems to have been an illuminated rectangular surface and the responses may never have exceeded the third level of the hierarchy identified by Bzhalava.

Image distortions could arise as a consequence of peripheral stimulation. Given that subjects are usually conditioned in complete darkness it is likely that the image falls off the fovea and consequently, in the lack of a frame of reference in the form of a background, seems distorted. I have used two controls for this. The initial control was to use a synoptophore which presents separate images to both eyes and to use one channel for a fixation light and the other for the UCS presentation. This is far from perfect as image fusion in the synoptophore cannot be guaranteed in the absence of two images, one to each eye, and time to achieve fusion. The second control was to use a light emitting diode (LED) as a fixation point. This suffers from the defect, as does the synoptophore, that the fixation point itself becomes an integral part of the CS sequence, i.e. a compound conditioning paradigm is imposed. Neither procedure influences the number of distorted images reported by subjects.

Multiple images could arise as a consequence of prolonged UCS presentation. Where this exceeds the latency of an eye movement (100 msec) it is always possible that these images arise from eye movements. However, even 1 msec presentations of the UCS will result in multiple images during the fourth stage of the Bzhalava hierarchy. Invertions of images and rotating images cannot arise as a consequence of UCS presentation whatever its duration. However, such reports are frequent. Hence, it is unlikely that the duration of the UCS is a critical factor so far as the quality of reported images is concerned.

The suggestion that the choice of visual stimulus is important is made only so that when any of these effects are observed it is possible to say where they may have originated. Examination of many hundreds of hours data recording suggests that the CR evolves as a prolongation of the normal sequence of visual events, i.e. a normally fragmenting afterimage sequence is prolonged with images of the same kind. The visual responses occurring between CS onset and the UCS onset tend to occur just prior to UCS onset as 'amorphous clouds' and 'grey clouds' and then move back to UCS onset over trials. In other words, the first indications of CRs prior to UCS onset tend to be non-structured visual events which occur close to the UCS onset. With additional trials these experiences occur closer to the CS onset and the period between UCS onset and CS onset is filled with experiences following the Bzhalava hierarchy. A few subjects reach the point where almost immediately after the CS onset they report images such as those normally contingent upon the UCS presentation and continue to do so for as long as the CS is presented, i.e. the tonal CS now produces images similar to those produced initially by the light flash. The majority of subjects report other less well-structured images over this period. Within the constraints of any experiment, say 200–500 trials at the rate of 10 trials per hour, not all subjects produce CRs which are indistinguishable from UCSs. However, the descriptions of what is experienced by these subjects are sufficiently convincing to establish that conditioning occurs.

4.4 Ecological validity

The ecological validity of such conditioning must now be examined. If all the experiments showed was that a visual experience could occur to auditory input or an auditory experience to a visual input, then they would indeed be trivial. It is probably possible to condition almost any response to any stimulus given appropriate conditions. However, if it is believed that conditioning is the fundamental mechanism of the action of the sensory modalities, a view congruent with Helmholtz and his concept of unconscious inference, and Pavlov's comment on the Helmholtz model, then it is necessary to look more closely at the procedure and the responses.

4.5 The case for cross-modal studies

If conditioning is the *modus operandi* of the modalities it is clearly very difficult to demonstrate this using visual stimuli to produce visual responses. To turn on the light and have subjects say 'I see' is clearly inappropriate. Light produces vision and this is what 'everybody knows'. It is almost impossible to devise a conditioning experiment in which an intramodal stimulus produces a response which is unequivocally a conditioned response; if sound gives rise to audition and light to vision this evidence is hardly likely to promote thought about the nature of the perceptual systems themselves. An experiment in which a visual CS was used to generate a visual CR is on record (Davies, 1974b). Subjects were presented with a visual stimulus, consisting of a circle with inscribed cross, illuminated for 1msec at 60 J. They were asked to observe the resulting images and record their duration. Each subject had 40 presentations over a prolonged period, often with several days elapsing between trials. They were tested with both unstructured light flashes, i.e. illumination of the closed eyes, and with illumination of a circle only. Both tests yielded reports of afterimages of circles, or circles with inscribed crosses. In one case these results were obtained 43 days after the last training trial which should preclude any normal retinal persistence of the training target.

This experiment, which was derived from Swindle (1916) on positive afterimages of long duration, shows that both the light flash itself and a flashed partial target are adequate stimuli to generate CRs. As both tests involved a similar light flash it is likely that this was a CS in both cases. However, the compound CS of light flash plus circle produced the more convincing results. It should be said that there have been anecdotal reports of conditioning to light flashes. The late C. R. Evans, during lecture tours, used to demonstrate stabilized visual imagery using powerfully illuminated figures to produce visual afterimages. By his account, more than one member of his audiences reported experiencing images of the figures up to months later when dramatic light intensity changes were encountered. The majority of my own subjects have also reported this effect when not preoccupied or concentrating, e.g. as passengers in cars at night when oncoming headlights would give rise to images of circles or triangles. However, Evans's reports are of one trial learning which makes them more surprising than reports from subjects who have received 200–300 trials.

Earlier it was noted that cross-modal conditioning is remarkably slow to establish. The literature reveals a range of 80 to 5000 trials being required. Now if we assume that conditioning is the basis of perception then we must consider two types of stimuli. Intramodal stimuli would normally be relevant stimuli. However, such conditioning is difficult to demonstrate, hence there is little experimental evidence other than perceptional adaptation studies. Even these cannot demonstrate the full efficacy of conditioning as by their very nature they demand extinction of the normal responses prior to the establishment of the new, adapted, response. However, stimuli arising from the environment must normally do so in multimodal configurations. The sight and smell, or sight and sound, of events tend to go together, e.g. the odour of ripe strawberries or the crackling of a fire. In cross-modal conditioning studies the aim is to make only one stimulus of a concatenation of stimuli appropriate and adequate to trigger the response. If the task was learned too readily then normal perception would indeed be difficult as accidental coincidences of multimodal stimuli would lead to the establishment of spurious responses. In short, the difficulty in establishing cross-modally conditioned responses reflects the stability of our perceptual systems while the fact that such responses can be established reflects the adaptability and predictive nature of these systems when faced with environmental invariates in the form of concatenations.

4.6 Evolutionary isomorphism

There is no doubt that conditionability, i.e. the range of conditionable responses and complexity of paradigms which are effective, is related to both ontological and phylogenetic ascent. It would indeed be surprising if this was merely an accidental correlate of such ascent. My view is that this susceptibility to conditioning underpins the ascent and that conditioning is the mechanism by and through which increasingly complex interactions with the world can be undertaken within the informational limits of the neurological system. The basic physiological receptor systems provide an inefficient basis for environmental interaction which is accurate but slow; the resulting experiences through association provide the basis for conditioning which provides a basis for rapid, but potentially inaccurate, responding. Interestingly enough most perception is inaccurate in terms of the received input. The normal textbook on perception devotes whole sections to phenomena such as illusions, size–distance constancy, constancy of form, and constancy of colour. If the input gave rise directly to the percepts the world would be an unstable, kaleidoscopic place of constantly changing sizes, shapes, and colours. However, if certain aspects of the world are reliably associated with the world, just as Helmholtz described in 'unconscious inference', then conditioning could well be *the* fundamental mechanism of perception. The experimental evidence supports the proposition that percepts can be conditioned but it is examination of the facts of perception which provides a strong case for believing that this may be so.

If perception is largely a function of conditioning, i.e. only the basic information upon which learning is based being provided by the receptor systems as well as cues (the CSs) for conditioned responses, then conditioning may be seen as the process underlying the majority of behaviour. Perception, what we interpret the world to be, clearly determines our consciousness. We can be conscious only of what we perceive, or conceive that we might perceive. For many years many psychologists have eschewed mental events such as consciousness on the grounds that such events and their underlying processes were covert and unobservable. Should it be accepted that they too can be explained on the basis of a fairly well-understood process, i.e. conditioning, much of the mystery surrounding them should disappear. There is, of course, an unbridgeable gulf between demonstrating that in the special circumstances of the psychologist's laboratory certain percepts may be conditioned and the proposition that all normal percepts are CRs. However, deprivation studies have consistently revealed that in the absence of suitable environmental experience normal perception fails to develop. When the nature of 'experience' is examined it turns out to be exposure to environmental concatenations of events or, to put it another way, the patterns of associations occurring over time. Conditioning is nothing more than learning appropriate responses to such patterns. If this really is the case most behaviour can be explained on the basis of memory for such associations, with conditioning as the process which transforms memory into activity. Thus the fundamental fact of psychology would be memory, and the fundamental process determining both what is stored and how stored information is used would be conditioning. To many this may well seem unduly simplistic. However, the facts of conditioning are well established and cannot be denied. If additional processes are postulated it becomes necessary to explain under what conditions conditioning operates and what may prevent it from doing so. In the past it has often been suggested that higher order cognitive activity may override conditioned behaviour. However, perception is a higher order mental activity and the evidence is that this itself may be subject to conditioning. If the process works well in certain cases, and 300 or 5000 experimental trials are as nothing to the experienced regularities of the world over a lifetime, then why should it be limited to only such cases? The Law of Parsimony would suggest that if a system works well on one principle any other principles are superfluous. Thus, on the somewhat limited experimental evidence which is available it is a reasonable assumption that conditioning underlies all normal perception and, indirectly, determines consciousness.

References

Boring, E. G., Langfeld, H. S., and Weld, H. P. (1948). *Foundations of Psychology*. Wiley, New York, p. 287.

Bzhalava, I. T. (1965). *Perception and Set*. Tbilisi: Metsniyerba.

Bzhalava, I. T. (1971). *Set and the Machinery of the Brain*. Tbilisi: Metsniyerba.

Davies, P. (1974a). Conditioned after-images I. *British Journal of Psychology*, **65**, 191–204.

Davies, P. (1974b). Conditioned after-images II. *British Journal of Psychology*, **65**, 377–93.

Davies, P. (1976). Conditioning after-images: A procedure minimizing the extinction effect of normal test trials. *British Journal of Psychology*, **67**, 181–9.

Davies, P. (1984). Conditioning: The underpinning of consciousness. *Speculations in Science and Technology*, **7** (3), 133–40.

Davies, P., Bennett, S., and Davies, G. L. (1983). Semantic conditioning investigated using second-order conditioned visual afterimages. *Perceptual and Motor Skills*, **57**, 703–9.

Doty, R. W., and Giurgea, C. (1965). Conditioned reflexes established by coupling electrical excitation of two cortical areas. In *Cognitive Processes and the Brain* (eds. P. Milner and M. Glickman). D. van Nostrand Co., New Jersey, Toronto and London.

Edmonston, W. E. (1972). In *Hypnosis, Research Developments and Perspectives* (ed. E. Eromm, and R. E. Shor). Paul Elek (Scientific Books) Limited, London.

Ellson, D. G. (1941). Hallucinations produced by sensory conditioning. *Journal of Experimental Psychology*, **28**, 1–20.

Helmholtz, H. von (1879). The facts of perception. Founder's Day address at Berlin University, 3 August 1878. August Hirschwald, Berlin, 1879. Reprinted in Warren, R. M., and Warren, R. P. (1968), *Helmholtz on Perception: Its Physiology and Development*. Wiley, New York.

Howells, T. H. (1944). The experimental development of color-tone synesthesia. *Journal of Experimental Psychology*, **34**, 87–103.

Kelly, E. K. (1934). An experimental attempt to produce artificial chromaesthesia by the technique of conditioned response. *Journal of Experimental Psychology*, **17**, 315–41.

Land, E. H. (1959a). Colour vision and the natural image I. *Proceedings of the National Academy of Science*.

Land, E. H. (1959b). Colour vision and the natural image II. *Proceedings of the National Academy of Science*, pp. 636–44.

Leuba, C. (1940). Images as conditioned sensations. *Journal of Experimental Psychology*, **26**, 345–51.

Leuba, C., and Dunlap, R. (1951). Conditioning imagery. *Journal of Experimental Psychology*, **41**, 352–5.

McClelland, D. C., and Atkinson, J. W. (1948). The projective expression of needs. I. The effect of different intensities of hunger drive on perception. *Journal of Psychology*, **25**, 205–22.

Marks, L. E. (1975). On coloured-hearing synesthesia: cross-modal translations of sensory dimensions. *Psychological Bulletin*, **3**, 303–31.

Miller, G. A. (1956). The magical number seven, plus or minus two: some limits on our capacity for processing information. *Psychological Review*, **63**, 81–97.

Neiser, U. (1966). *Cognitive Psychology*. Appleton-Century-Crofts, New York.
Platanov, K. I. (1959). *The Word as a Physiological and Therapeutic Factor: Problems of Theory and Practice of Psychotherapy on the Basis of the Theory of I. P. Pavlov*. Translated from 2nd Russian edition (1955) by D. A. Myshne; Moscow, Foreign Languages Publishing House.
Popov, N. A, and Popov, C. (1953a). Contribution a l'étude des fonctions corticales chez l'homme; par la méthode des refléxes conditionnès électrocorticaux. Action de l'alcool sur les images consécutives et leur conditionnement. I. *Compte Rendus hebdomadaires Séances Académie Science*, Paris, **237**, 930–2.
Popov, N. A., and Popov, C. (1953b). Contribution a l'étude des fonctions corticales chez l'homme par la méthode des refléxes conditionnès électrocorticaux. II. De la modification par l'alcool des couleurs des images consécutives et des images consécutives conditionnées. *Compte Rendus hebdomandaires Séances Académie Science*, Paris, **237**, 1439–41.
Popov, N. A., and Popov C. (1953c). Le Conditionnement dans l'écorce cérébrale chez l'homme étudie par la méthode électroencephalographique. III. La différenciation des refléxes conditionnès électrocorticaux et le conditionnement des images consécutives. *Compte Rendus hebdomandaires Séances Académie Science*, Paris, **238**, 744–6.
Popov, N. A., and Popov, C. (1954a). Contribution a l'étude des fonctions corticales chez l'homme. IV. Action du café sur les images consécutives et les images consécutives conditionèes. *Compte Rendus hebdomandaires Séances Académie Science*, Paris, **238** (II), 2026–8.
Popov, N. A., and Popov, C. (1954b). Contribution a l'étude des fonctions corticales chez l'homme par la méthode des refléxes conditionnès électrocorticaux. V. Deuxième système de signalisation. *Compte Rendus hebdomadaires Séances Académie Science*, Paris, **238**, 2118–20.
Popov, N. A., and Popov, C. (1954c). Contribution a l'étude des fonctions corticales chez l'homme. VI. Inhibition externe, étudièe par la méthode électroencephalographique et la méthode des images consécutives. *Compte Rendus hebdomandaires Séances Académie Science*, Paris, **239**, 1859–62.
Popov, N. A., and Popov, C. (1954d). Contribution a l'étude de l'extinction des refléxes conditionnès électrocorticaux chez l'homme. Role du stéréotype dynamique et la cyclochronie dans la genèse des neuroses. *Compte Rendus hebdomandaires Séances Académie Science* Paris, **238**, 1912–14.
Razran, G. (1971). *Mind in Evolution*. Houghton Mifflin Company, Boston, Mass.
Skinner, B. F. (1957). *Verbal Behaviour*, Appleton, New York.
Sokolov, Ye. N. (1963). *Perception and the Conditioned Reflex* (trans. S. W. Waydenfeld; eds. R. Worters and A. D. B. Clarke), Pergamon Press, Oxford and London.
Spies, T. D., Aring, C. D., Gelperin, J., and Bean, W. B. (1938). The mental symptoms of pellagra: Their relief with nicotinic acid. *American Journal of Medical Science*, **196** (15), 1–132.
Stratton, G. M. (1897). Vision without inversion of the retinal image. *Psychological Review*, **4**, 341–60 and 463–81.
Swindle, P. F. (1916). Positive afterimages of long duration. *American Journal of Psychology*, **28**, 349–72.
Swindle, P. F. (1917). Visual, Cutaneous, and kinaesthetic ghosts. *American Journal of Psychology*, **28**, 349–72.
Taylor, J. G. (1962). *The Behavioural Basis of Perception*. Yale University Press, New Haven, Conn., and London.
Taylor, J. G. (1971). Personal communication.

Warburton, D. M., Wesnes, K., Edwards, J., and Larrad, D. (1985). Scopalamine and the sensory conditioning of hallucinations. *Neuropsychobiology* (in press).

Warren, R. M., and Warren, R. P. (1968). *Helmholtz on Perception: Its Physiology and Development*. Wiley, New York.

Cognitive Processes and Pavlovian Conditioning in Humans
Edited by G. Davey

Chapter 8

A neo-Pavlovian interpretation of the OR and classical conditioning in humans: With comments on alcoholism and the poverty of cognitive psychology

Irving Maltzman
University of California, Los Angeles

1 Introduction

Four problems will be considered in the present chapter:

(a) the philosophy of psychology, including the nature of behaviourism and its variations; and the nature of cognitive psychology and its variations;
(b) the retreat towards cognitive psychologies of classical conditioning, their poverty, in particular their inadequate treatment of traditional problems such as awareness and expectancy;
(c) one kind of classical conditioning will be examined, conditioning the OR, and the proposal that there is more than one kind of classical conditioning in humans; there are no universal laws of classical conditioning;
(d) an examination of an aspect of a critical social problem, alcohol addiction, in terms of classical conditioning.

2 Behaviourism, S-R psychology, and cognitive psychology

Before considering the area of classical conditioning in humans, it is important to step back and evaluate the larger scene of psychology, its basic assumptions, its past and possible future directions.

Science is more than a body of verifiable knowledge, empirical generalizations, and abstract theories that integrate diverse sets of established generalizations. Bodies of knowledge are inextricably influenced, related, and set in one direction or another by value judgements, by volitional decisions that are neither true nor false, and by the conventions that are based upon such decisions. Reichenbach (1938) noted that some volitional decisions lead to equivalent systems based upon different conventions, e.g. different systems of measurement. They are equivalent in that for any unit in one system there is a unit in the alternative system which can be substituted for it. Although based upon conventions and logically equivalent, conventional differences are not trivial, as suggested by the enormous social resistance and expense encountered in an effort to switch from one conventional system of measurement to another.

Reichenbach (1938) suggests that there is another, more fundamental, kind of volitional decision in science. It is the volitional bifurcation, a decision that leads to divergent systems. Volitional bifurcations involve the most fundamental aims or goals a science may adopt. Alternative systems diverge following such a decision because different problems, techniques, and related theories develop that are congruent with the widely different aims of the divergent systems. It is inconceivable, for example, that Wundt would invent the Skinner box.

Introduction of a volitional bifurcation represents a revolutionary change based upon a value judgement, since it is a decision concerning the aims or goals of science one ought to adopt. There has been only one such revolution, volitional bifurcation, in the 2000 year history of psychology: the behaviouristic revolution (Watson, 1913). Behaviourism stated that the goal of the science of psychology ought to be the study of behaviour not mind. Behavourism as a systematic position resting upon a volitional decision is neither true nor false. Nor was the older consciousness centred mentalistic structural psychology disproven. No critical experiment was conducted demonstrating its falsity. Behaviourism rested upon a decision made, and adopted, by a large number of psychologists. It determined the future direction of psychology. A current movement back towards mentalistic psychology in similar fashion is not based upon the falsification of behaviourist aims.

Behaviourism rests upon a value judgement that the purpose of psychology is to provide an explanation of behaviour in terms of conditions and laws that are physical in nature. In place of mentalistic conceptions there will be behavioural dispositions, principles of physiology and neuroscience generally, and the commonly accepted descriptions of environmental events. Translation of mentalistic conceptions into behavioural or physiological ones is not the goal of behaviourism. Its goal is to explain the behaviour in question. Theoretical concepts that refer to events that are not directly observable are entirely legitimate; it is a decision to limit oneself only to environmental variables and observable behaviour. A behaviourism can take advantage of all natural science knowledge, genetics, neuroendocrinology, neurochemistry, physiology, etc., as well as objective social science knowledge, epidemiology, etc. There is no methodological reason for behaviourism to be limited to molar behaviour, gross behavioural changes, or the products of gross behaviour changes such as bar presses, or to muscle twitches. One must distinguish between stylistic decisions and empirical hypotheses of behaviourists on the one hand and fundamental decisions constituting the basis of the systematic position on the other. Molar and operant behaviourism are unnecessarily restrictive and are not entailed by the basic assumption of behaviourism. These variations are based upon relatively specific decisions as to how one ought to proceed in reaching the common goal of predicting and explaining behaviour.

Decisions, which are neither true nor false, must be distinguished from hypotheses with empirical content, hypotheses that are in principle falsifiable. Watson, who made the revolutionary decision to change the goal of psychology from the study of the average normal adult human mind to the study of behaviour, also formulated a number of empirical hypotheses. Any one or all of them could be rejected, falsified, or accepted, confirmed, and one would still remain a behaviourist. These hypotheses do not characterize the behaviourist. They characterize Watson the theorist. He held to a frequency theory of learning, a motor theory of thinking, a particular theory of emotions, and, generally, nurture rather than nature as a determiner of behaviour. Most, if not all of his hypotheses are false, or too ambiguous to falsify. Their truth status is irrelevant to the basic thesis of behaviourism. One can adopt a drive reduction theory of learning, a drive induction, or a contiguity theory, and still remain a behaviourist. A particular theory of learning does not constitute the criterion of a behaviourist, nor does a position on the question of nature vs. nurture, etc. One can accept the evidence that there is a genetic component in schizophrenia or not, and remain a behaviourist. One can accept the evidence that there is a genetic component accounting for some of the variance in gamma alcoholism, as I do, or not, and remain a behaviourist. In the latter case, I believe, it is a mistaken behaviourist, but still a behaviourist.

Unfortunately, some clinical psychologists, who align themselves with some variant of behaviourism, fail to understand the conventional bases of behaviourism, and that questions of fact or adopting particular empirical hypotheses do not characterize the essential nature of behaviourism. They erroneously assume that if one is a behaviourist one must believe that alcoholism is learned, that controlled drinking is a feasible treatment goal, etc. What characterize behaviourism are the decisions concerning the fundamental goals of psychology, not particular hypotheses or prejudice with respect to any given problem.

Cognitive and non-cognitive psychologies are distinguished on the basis of their manner of dealing with the issue of intentionality. But there are different kinds of cognitive psychologies, as there are different kinds of behaviourisms. Brentano (1874/1973), one of the founders of modern psychology, and a leading act psychologist, presented the basic issue in its modern form. By so doing, he changed the issue of mental vs. physical from a metaphysical problem into a problem of conceptual analysis. Brentano argued that mental terms are intentional. They always refer to an object. Physical terms do not. This property of intentionality suggests that mental concepts cannot be reduced to physical terms. Intentional concepts, acts, constitute the unique subject matter of psychology, distinguishing it from the physical and biological sciences. These latter sciences do not ordinarily employ intentional concepts. Brentano thus carved out, delineated, a unique subject matter for study by the new discipline of psychology. He argued that the act of seeing is mental, the subject matter of psychology. The content or object of the act, what is seen, is the subject matter of physics, etc.

Sentences including intentional terms such as 'I expect the UCS' are irreducible to physical terms in the sense that they cannot be replaced by an equivalent sentence with no intentional terms, e.g. 'There is a UCS'. The latter sentence does not contain intentional terms; it contains only grammatical terms and a term for a physical event. But it cannot be used in all circumstances in which one would employ the first sentence. The two sentences do not have the same meaning.

Presence of intentional terms in a psychological theory characterizes that theory as cognitive. A cognitive psychology utilizes many of these terms in its theories and usually does not attempt to define, explicate, or specify these terms further. Intentional terms are often used in a manner which suggest that their author assumes that everyone knows the meaning of the terms, and the conditions under which they are to be employed. Furthermore, the author usually assumes that there are general principles governing these terms. In fact, there usually are none. Use of intentional terms in such a manner is mischievous and a detriment to the advance of scientific knowledge, regardless of their status in philosophy. Presumably, the goal of a science of psychology is to explain. For behaviourists, it is to explain and predict behaviour. In order to achieve this end there must be laws, generalities, or the delineation of the physical events leading from antecedents to consequent events. If consciousness centred psychologists state that they wish to explain mind, or consciousness, then it is encumbent upon them to specify what they are explaining and how. Within our area of discussion, the problem is simple: they wish to explain phenomena of conditioning. How can they accomplish this end with unspecified laws of expectancy or metaphors referring to central processing units of computers?

It is commonly overlooked that Brentano considered his act or intentional psychology a descriptive psychology. It was a cataloguing of the various kinds of intentional terms. According to Brentano explanatory psychology which he planned to cover, but never did, has recourse to physiological laws. Explanatory psychology ultimately would indicate the genesis or origins of acts and in that sense explain the psychological phenomena.

Methodological behaviourism accepts the special status of intentional terms in the philosophy of mind but does not recognize any special status for these concepts in its science, its psychology. If methodological behaviourism uses mentalistic concepts in a theory, it specifies their use in physical terms. They are used as defined terms. When mentalistic or conscious centred psychologists use intentional terms, they are usually undefined. Methodological behaviourism recognizes that behaviourism is basically the science of the 'behaviour of the other one' and is concerned with the prediction and explanation of the behaviour of another person. The consciousness centred cognitive psychologist is interested in explaining how the mind works. Mentalistic psychologists mistakenly believe they are *inferring* mental processes from the behaviour of another individual. A behaviourist, if using similar terms, *defines* them in terms of that behaviour.

Among the more specific goals of the behaviourist is the explanation of behaviour that is loosely referred to by notions such as 'purpose'. The purpose of behaviourism is not to explain 'purpose', which can only be explicated by an analysis of language or epistemology, but to explain the behaviour described by that term. We wish to explain purposive or expectant behaviour.

Tolman, the first cognitive behaviourist (e.g. Tolman, 1925a/1951), 1925b/1951, 1932) took the explanation of purposive behaviour as his goal. He was a methodological behaviourist, along with Clark L. Hull. They differed in the nature of their theories of learning in general, as well as in the particulars of their theories of goal directed or purposive behaviour. Tolman showed that there is no contradiction between behaviourism and cognitive psychology, as long as one properly defines the theoretical terms employed. Tolman was concerned with explaining purpose, consciousness, ideas, cognition, etc., in a molar behaviouristic manner. His programme of research and theory began in the early 1920s. His analyses are as cogent today as they were then.

He states,

> orthodox psychology maintains that . . . mind exhibits 'purpose,' whereas body does not. Purpose is held to be essentially a mentalistic category. . . . it will be the thesis of the present paper that a behaviourism . . . finds it just as easy and just as necessary to include the descriptive phenomena of 'purpose' as does a mentalism. Purpose, adequately conceived . . . is itself but an objective aspect of behavior. When an animal is learning a maze, or escaping from a puzzle box, or merely going about his daily

> business of eating, nest building, sleeping, and the like, it will be noted that in all such performances a certain *persistence until* character is to be found. Now it is just this *persistence until* character which we will define as purpose. . . . upon further analysis, we discover that such a description appears whenever in order merely to *identify* the given behavior a reference to some 'end object' or 'situation' is found necessary. (Tolman, 1925a/1951, pp. 32–3)

Again, Tolman states,

> whenever, in merely describing a behavior, it is found necessary to include a statement of something either *toward which* or *from which* the behavior is directed, there we have purpose. But we may analyze further. Just when is it we find a statement of a 'toward whichness' or of a 'from whichness' thus necessary? We find it necessary, whenever, by modifying the various attendant circumstances, we discover that the same goal is still there and still identifying the given response. . . . In short, purpose is present, descriptively, whenever a statement of the goal object is necessary to indicate (1) constancy of goal object in spite of variations in adjustment to intervening obstacles, or (2) variations in final direction corresponding to differing positions of the goal object, or (3) cessation of activity when a given goal object is entirely removed. (Tolman, 1925a/1951, pp. 34–5)

Radical behaviourism, currently the branch of behaviourism that is most active and visible, is often erroneously equated with behaviourism *per se* by its critics. It is in fact only one form of behaviourism. Identification of all of behaviourism with one of its several forms, radical behaviourism, is undoubtedly due to the wide acclaim and recognition received by its founder, B. F. Skinner, and his relatively large number of followers. Another reason is that philosophers find it vulnerable to attack because of its philosophy of mind (e.g. Dennett, 1978; Malcolm, 1964) and because of excessively simplistic and distorted notions promulgated by adherents who call themselves some form of behaviourist. This is especially true among some clinical psychologists, who appear to have little basic understanding of the systematic position of behaviourism (e.g. Cummings, Gordon, and Marlatt, 1980).

Methodological and radical behaviourism differ most fundamentally in their philosophy of mind. Methodological behaviourism remains aloof from technical philosophical problems, leaving them to the philosophers. If pressed, methodological behaviourists would find psychophysical parallelism the most congenial form of philosophy of mind. Radical behaviourism, in contrast, adopts a materialistic philosophy of mind, a philosophy of mind which as they present it does not work. It has not accomplished what the philosophers have failed to do, demonstrate the reducibility of intentional to non-intentional terms. Radical behaviourists have failed to provide a satisfactory translation for a sentence such as 'I am aware of the UCS' into an equivalent sentence that does not contain intentional terms.

However, the methodological behaviourist does not consider this failure of radical behaviourism in its philosophy critical to the enterprise of a behaviouristic psychology. Radical behaviourism presents itself as a philosophy of science and philosophy of mind (Skinner, 1974). Methodological behaviourism is more modest in its goals, proposing only a philosophy of psychology. It therefore is more in keeping with the spirit of early Watson than is radical behaviourism. Our goal ought to be the description, explanation, and prediction of observable behaviour. Furthermore, there ought to be no restriction upon theorizing or the nature of theorizing provided it meets scientific canons.

It is important to distinguish between S-R psychology and behaviourism. Every S-R psychologist in the field of learning is a behaviourist; but not every behaviourist is an S-R psychologist. We have noted one already, Tolman. Many of the criticisms of behaviourism are pertinent only to S-R theories. Critics are often unaware of the fundamental distinction between the two. It must also be noted that radical behaviourists such as Skinner and his followers are not S-R psychologists. Pavlov, who I would consider a methodological behaviourist, was not an S-R psychologist. He theorized about states of excitation and inhibition, not implicit Ss and Rs. Lashley, one of the founders of behaviouristic physiological psychology, was not an S-R psychologist. What characterizes S-R psychology is the nature of its theoretical terms. They are most often couched as implicit responses and response produced stimuli, fractional anticipatory goal responses, rg-sg, drive stimuli, etc. Associations or habit strength develops between Ss and Rs. Hull, Guthrie, and Spence were leading S-R psychologists who were behaviourists and learning theorists. Skinnerian radical behaviourists are not S-R psychologists, because (a) they eschew theory as much as possible, and it is the kind of theoretical terms used that makes one an S-R theorist or not, and (b) radical behaviourists emphasize operant conditioning, the emission of responses, rather than response elicitation which requires specifiable stimuli.

Since radical behaviourism is by far the most active and visible current form of behaviourism, many of the criticisms aimed at radical behaviourism have mistakenly been taken as criticisms of behaviourism as a whole. Thus, cognitive behaviour therapists are rebelling against behaviour therapy and behaviour analysis and calling their rebellion, which consists of introducing the use of theoretical intervening variables such as thoughts, a revolutionary change, a paradigm shift. Actually, it is a return to methodological behaviourism—if they are behaviourists at all. If they are, they are cognitive behaviourists. Methodologically, this is a return to Tolman of more than 50 years ago.

As I have previously noted (Maltzman, 1968), 'a cognitive psychology can just as well be behavioristic as . . . mentalistic. It all depends upon the status of intentional terms within their psychology: are they translated into behavioral and physical terms, or not. If the former is the case, it is a cognitive behaviourism. If the latter is the case, it is a consciousness-centered cognitive psychology' (p. 275).

It was also noted that there is a variety of different kinds of experimental research suggesting that an S-R theory of human conditioning and learning is untenable. Research contrary to and incompatible with S-R theory is not necessarily incompatible with other kinds of theory formulated within a framework of methodological behaviourism (Maltzman, 1968). Such research is perfectly compatible with a behaviouristic theory which is neither cognitive nor S-R, a neo-Pavlovian theory of conditioning and learning. A theory of the latter type takes advantage of its roots in biobehavioural science, evolutionary theory, and developments in research on classical conditioning conducted in the spirit of Pavlov, conducted with a biological orientation. If we turn to cognitive psychology and its attempts to deal with the phenomena of classical conditioning, we find a different picture.

3 The poverty of cognitive psychology

3.1 Awareness

It is more than a decade since Brewer (1974) forcefully wrote that there is no convincing evidence of classical or operant conditioning in adult humans. Awareness was the apparent Waterloo of behaviouristic theories of conditioning. He suggested that since verbal reports of the relevant stimulus contingencies were present whenever conditioning occurred, true, non-mediated, conditioning was not obtained. It must be noted that the mere presence of a verbal report describing the contingency of CS and UCS was taken as an index of awareness. It has been repeatedly found that such a verbal report is a concomitant of many kinds of human adult conditioning. But it must be noted that the cognitive psychologist further assumes that the awareness in some sense 'caused' the conditioning. Yet there are no laws of 'awareness'; there is no explication of what 'awareness' in some sense is, how it works, why some people in an experiment manifest it and others do not. There are no principles of awareness other than the principles associated with the verbal report defining awareness.

There is no explanation by cognitive psychologists why infants, animals, schizophrenics, etc., who cannot provide reports of verbal awareness may nevertheless condition. There is no explanation why awareness may interfere with conditioning (e.g. Razran, 1949). Cognitive psychologists ignore instances of classical conditioning of the GSR that occur in the absence of the verbal report of stimulus contingencies (Brandeis and Lubow, 1975). For the methodological behaviourist these are experimental problems to be studied. They are not givens or phenomena to be ignored. Verbal awareness is only one kind of awareness that may, or may not, accompany learning (Maltzman, 1979a). Verbal reports of stimulus contingencies occur because the typical classical conditioning experiment of the GSR employing college students as subjects is essentially a problem solving task. Subjects engage in extensive implicit verbal problem solving. When the problem of 'what leads to what' is solved, an OR occurs to the newly discovered significant stimulus, the CS, and the subject can verbalize the sequence of events that led to this discovery. That OR is taken as the GSR-CR. But not all classical conditioning is of this kind, conditioning the GSR-OR, and therefore need not be accompanied by verbal awareness, the ability to report the stimulus contingencies (Maltzman, 1979a). Or, if stimulus contingencies are reported, verbal awareness is present, it need not be accompanied by radical changes in the dependent measure of conditioning. The latter would be the case when the dependent measure of conditioning is not a measure of the OR (e.g. Eaglen and Mackenzie, 1982). Since the verbal report is not a mirror of presumptive mental phenomena as implicitly assumed by consciousness centred cognitive psychologists, but is itself a dependent variable, it is manipulable and subject to a variety of experimental events. Thus, interference, distractibility, and a variety of motivational states may influence the verbal report independently of the biobehavioural measure of the CR. Also, the test for verbal awareness may elicit a response at the time of the test, knowledge and reconstruction of events that are indicative of verbal awareness, but the discovery of the appropriate CS-UCS contingency occurred in the test situation not the original conditioning situation.

An advantage of semantic conditioning of the GSR is that the test for verbal awareness may be conducted without the above potential contaminating factors (e.g. Maltzman, Gould, Pendery and Wolff, 1977; Pendery and Maltzman, 1977). On the other hand, a precise report of stimulus contingencies, 'insight', need not lead to conditioning, as psychotherapists since Freud have known. This lack of causal efficacy on the part of verbal awareness is not surprising once we recognize that (a) verbal awareness does not cause conditioning, it is a concomitant of conditioning under certain circumstances; and (b) conditioning of the GSR-OR is a special kind of conditioning; there are no universal laws of human classical conditioning.

In the hands of cognitive psychologists, from Brewer (1974) to Öhman (1983), there has been no progress in the examination of awareness or other intentional terms. There has been no progress towards developing laws of awareness or laws of intentionality by cognitive psychologists interested in classical conditioning. Furthermore, cognitive psychologists fail to mention a variety of embarrassing phenomena. They ignore evidence of classical conditioning in the absence of verbal awareness, despite the fact that every effort was made to obtain such reports (Brandeis and Lubow, 1975; Gorn, 1982; Martin, Stambrook, Tataryn, and Beihl, 1984). Verbal reports of a contingency between CS and UCS account for a major portion of variance in the typical laboratory experiment of classical conditioning of the GSR. In more than 1000 participants in our classical conditioning experiments on semantic conditioning of the GSR, no one who failed to give a verbal report of awareness showed evidence of conditioning. However, not every subject who verbalized the CS-UCS contingency showed conditioning. Why the individual differences? What variables may be independently related to verbal awareness? There is some evidence that individual differences in magnitude of the initial index of the OR may predict verbal awareness (Maltzman and Raskin, 1965). What does awareness, however defined by the cognitive psychologist, have to do with the conditioning effects present in an addiction, the immune system, or the pituitary-adrenal axis under stress, etc.? All of these phenomena occur outside of the laboratory and to an increasing degree are being studied in the laboratory. Cognitive psychology is silent concerning the role of awareness in conditioning as it occurs outside the laboratory. In general those cognitive psychologists, primarily so-called cognitive behaviour therapists or cognitive social learning theorists, do very poorly in their efforts to interpret addictions in terms of learning, as we shall see. They are forsaking principles of classical conditioning for vague but voguish intentional notions such as expectancy (e.g. Marlatt, 1979). The acquisition of an addiction and the role played in this by conditioning is very different from the conditioning characteristically studied in the laboratory. Today that is typically conditioning the GSR, conditioning a manifestation of the OR.

Guthrie's (1935) criticism of the cognitive psychology of Tolman is as apt today as it was some 50 years ago. Guthrie commented that Tolman left his animals buried in thought. In its modern version cognitive psychology leaves the organism buried in a computer or its software as well as thoughts and expectancies. There is no connection with the biological bases of behaviour or the behaviour itself. How are allocations of resources, subroutines, or awareness, etc., translated into a GSR, action, addictions, neuroses, the release of neuropeptides, etc.?

A striking example of this lacuna in cognitive theory as it relates to classical conditioning in humans is evident in Öhman's (1983) effort to formulate an information processing interpretation of classical conditioning. Among other serious inadequacies, it lacks an adequate discussion of awareness. Experiments by Öhman (1979) and his associates purporting to demonstrate the biological preparedness of classical conditioning of phobias do not obtain verbal reports of awareness. For conditioned phobias to be a manifestation of biological preparedness, according to the implications of cognitive folk psychology, they must be non-mediated, primitive, or primary. One must demonstrate that such conditioning occurs independently of awareness. Öhman and other cognitive psychologists are enmeshed in their web of suppositions, because they assume implicitly that awareness causes conditioning. It is necessary, therefore, for the conditioned analogue of phobias to occur in the absence of verbal awareness. Yet Öhman and his colleagues never attempt to obtain verbal reports of awareness from their subjects in these conditioning experiments.

Research that has obtained reports of verbal awareness of CS-UCS contingencies in the analogue conditioned phobia situation contradicts Öhman's theory (Dawson and Schell, 1981). Other evidence convincingly demonstrates that Öhman's laboratory analogue of biologically prepared conditioned phobias is in error (Deitz, 1982; Maltzman and Boyle, 1984; McNally, 1981).

In principle, a behaviouristic neo-Pavlovian approach has no difficulty with the problem of verbal awareness, because it is not accorded fundamental explanatory status. Awareness does not cause conditioning. Awareness does not 'explain' conditioning as some cognitive psychologists imply (e.g. Brewer, 1974). In the present formulation verbal awareness is a consequence of much the same conditions that lead to conditioning in the first place (Maltzman, 1979a, 1979b). Conditioning the salivary response can occur in the absence of verbal awareness, in the absence of the verbalization of the relevant stimulus contingencies, contrary to verbal awareness; or it can be facilitated by verbal awareness (Razran, 1949).

Outside the laboratory verbal awareness is an arcane issue when profoundly important and powerful effects of conditioning are considered, e.g. conditioned components of the immune system (Ader and Cohen, 1981) or addictive behaviours (Ludwig, Wikler, and Stark, 1974; Wikler, 1980). Nevertheless, we assume that cortical sets, dominant foci, direct and influence the course of conditioning that is not accompanied by verbal awareness just as they influence conditioning accompanied by verbal awareness, although not necessarily in precisely the same manner. We would not expect them to, since conditioning the GSR-OR and conditioning T cells must occur in a very different way. We cannot generalize from the principles of conditioning the GSR-OR to the conditioning of other systems, even to other autonomic responses that are not measures of the OR.

Verbal awareness is intimately related to conditioning of the GSR. Occurrence of a voluntary OR is closely related to the discovered significance of the CS in classical conditioning, and to discovery in problem solving generally (Maltzman, 1979a). Articulate college students characteristically engage in implicit verbal problem solving during a classical conditioning experiment. They therefore can verbally report upon their discovery, if it occurs, of the contingency between CS and UCS. Occasion of the discovery is correlated with the elicitation of a voluntary OR which is taken as the GSR-CR by the experimenter.

Verbal awareness is intimately related to verbal operant conditioning for somewhat similar reasons. Implicit problem solving of a verbal nature occurs during the course of the 'conditioning'. Subjects can therefore report their verbal behaviour that culminated in the solution of the problem. If they conform to the demands of the situation, verbal conditioning is manifested. Reports of their implicit verbal problem solving are taken as evidence of verbal awareness. We are arguing, of course, that use of a conditioning procedure does not guarantee that 'laws of conditioning' are operating to determine the observed behaviour. There are very different principles operating in the acquisition of different kinds of behaviour changes all of which may be observed in a conditioning procedure.

The preceding arguments imply that when a response that is not a measure of the OR is employed as the CR and when it is relatively free of verbal regulation, then verbal awareness will not be intimately related to acquisition or extinction of the response. Evidence related to this problem has been reported by Eaglen and Mackenzie (1981, 1982). Digital vasoconstriction and digital vasodilation were conditioned with cold and warm temperature as the UCSs. In Sokolov's (1963a) terms, adaptive reflexes were conditioned. Extinction following a relatively small number of trials could be induced by verbal instructions that the UCS would no longer be presented. Verbal instructions, however, did not facilitate extinction following a large number of conditioning trials. These results suggest that elicitation of an OR produced discriminative inhibition of the adaptive CR when a relatively small number of conditioning trials were administered. Two factors were operating to reduce the effects of verbal instructions after a large number of trials: automatization of conditioning and habituation of the OR. These interesting experiments need to be replicated with independent measures of the OR in a different response system from the one serving as the dependent measure of conditioning. Nevertheless, they illustrate, again, that verbal awareness is not some 'thing' or process that automatically inhibits or facilitates CRs, as cognitive psychologists suggest (Brewer, 1974).

A striking example of the dissociation of awareness and the GSR-OR to significant stimuli has been described by Tranel and Damasio (1985). They reported results of two cases of prosopagnosia, the inability to verbally recognize, show evidence of verbal awareness, of familiar faces. Nevertheless, these patients manifested significantly larger GSRs to familiar than unfamiliar faces. Stable visual prosopagnosia in these patients was caused by bilateral occipitotemporal damage, as verified by computerized tomography and nuclear magnetic resonance imaging. According to cognitive folk psychology, appearance of ORs under such circumstances would be impossible, since the OR is caused by the awareness process.

These findings by Tranel and Damasio contradict the cognitive formulation of Bernstein (Bernstein and Taylor, 1979) that significance is a consequence of a process of appraisal or judgement. These patients cannot manifest verbal awareness or an appraisal. Nevertheless, they show a GSR-OR to significant stimuli. An inherent difficulty in a cognitive formulation such as Bernstein's is that there is no independent criterion of, definition of, or means of measuring 'appraisal'. Bernstein's conception is therefore either false or untestable. In either case, it does not advance our knowledge of the complex processes determining selective orienting. Cognitive psychologists such as Siddle and Spinks (1979) fail to appreciate the fundamental differences between Maltzman (1979a, 1979b) and Bernstein's (Bernstein and Taylor, 1979) theories of significance. According to Maltzman's theory, significance is a consequence of dominant foci or cortical sets established *prior* to the presentation of the stimulus or event designated or discovered as significant. Independent measures are available for assessing significance of stimuli such as evaluative scales of the semantic differential (Maltzman, 1979a; Maltzman, Raskin, and Wolff, 1979). Finally, electrocortical and other kinds of measures are available for independently assessing the presence of cortical sets, dominant foci, and their distribution (Maltzman, 1979a).

3.2 Expectancy or conditioned anticipation

Expectancy or anticipation is a favoured concept in cognitive theories. It is especially common in the literature concerned with classical conditioning of the GSR. Multiple responses usually occur when a long CS-UCS interval is employed. A common convention is to score the largest response in the first half of the total interval, e.g. the first 4 sec in an 8 sec CS-UCS interval, and also score the largest response in the second interval.

Grings (1965) has non-committally labelled these first and second interval responses. Others, however, have followed Stern (1972) and labelled the response in the first interval conditioned OR, assuming that it is a response to the CS. A response in the second interval is called the conditioned anticipatory response, assuming that it is in anticipation of the UCS. These responses are taken to represent fundamentally different processes and are assumed to function in fundamentally different ways (Öhman, 1983). First interval responses are responses to the novel CS. Initially they were thought to be a bothersome artifact, but they were subsequently considered conditionable. It was assumed that, as in the case of ORs generally, their manifestation as first interval GSRs would habituate. Following Soviet theorists, it was assumed that as the OR habituated, true conditioning would develop as reflected by a conditioned anticipatory response (Gale and Ax, 1968). Expectancy will increase in the second interval as orienting habituates, decreases in the first interval.

Öhman (1983) attempts to accumulate an array of studies purporting to demonstrate that second interval, so-called conditioned anticipatory responses, vary in a different manner from first interval responses. In so doing, he ignores alternative interpretations of the differences (Biferno and Dawson, 1978), and ignores obvious contradictory evidence (Gale and Ax, 1968; Maltzman *et al*., 1978). He argues that absence of a relationship between first and second interval responses (Prokasy and Ebel, 1967) supports the hypothesis that these responses reflect different processes, but ignores the reported correlation of 0.74 between first and second interval CRs found by Biferno and Dawson (1978) although he comments on experimental operations that differentially affect the two responses. The latter ambiguous effects are open to a variety of interpretations. Finally, he cites some of his own unpublished data as support for differential processes producing first and second interval CRs (Öhman, 1983, p. 33). Purportedly less habituation in second than in first interval CRs is taken as the critical evidence. He neglects to mention that the *sine qua non* of anticipation is an increase in responsivity with reinforced trials. His second interval responses show less habituation than his first interval responses because of a floor effect in the latter. They are smaller responses from the outset, therefore there is less to habituate, hardly evidence for an expectancy process.

There is one kind of critical evidence necessary to support an expectancy interpretation of second interval GSRs: a demonstration that first interval responses increase during the course of conditioning followed by their decrease and a concomitant increase in second interval responses which remain at a high level of responsivity as long as the UCS occurs in a predictable manner. Ideally, these results should be demonstrated within the same individual, because group results often do not accurately depict the sequence of events within any individual member of the group (Pendery and Maltzman, 1977). Nevertheless, even with group data which are ordinarily presented, the essential characteristic of conditioned anticipation is an increasing magnitude of response obtained in the second interval, immediately prior to the UCS. Ideally, its shape should be a mirror image of the response in the first interval. Evidence pertinent to this problem, but consistently ignored, is contained in an experiment by Gale and Ax (1968).

They administered 300 discriminative conditioning trials, 60 trials per day for 5 days. High and low tones were used as a CS+ and a CS− (T+ and T−), respectively. The CS+ was always followed by electric shock as the UCS. A 9.5 sec CS-UCS interval was employed with a scoring convention that labelled GSRs an OR if they occurred within 1.0–4.5 sec after onset of the CS. Responses were labelled anticipatory if they occurred with a latency of 4.5–10.5 after onset of the CS, that is, if they occurred immediately prior to the UCS. Responses reaching their maximum amplitude shortly after the UCS were also considered anticipatory responses, since the long latency of the GSR suggests that they were initiated prior to the appearance of the UCS.

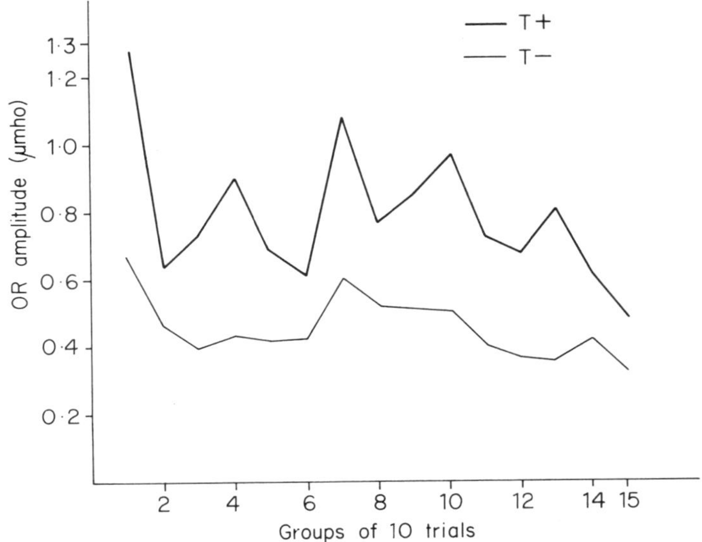

Figure 8.1 Mean magnitude of the first interval ('orienting') GSR to the reinforced CS+ (T+) and the non-reinforced CS− (T−) averaged over blocks of ten trials. (*From E. N. Gale and A. F. Ax, Long term conditioning of orienting responses,* Psychophysiology, **5** *(1968), 307–15. Copyright 1968 by the Society for Psychophysiological Research. Reprinted by permission of the Society and the authors*)

Figure 8.1 shows the results of the GSRs scored in the first interval averaged over blocks of ten trials, the response they call the OR because they believe it occurs to the CS.

Conditioned discrimination occurred as indicated by the consistent and statistically significant difference in the magnitude of the GSR to the CS+ and CS−. Maximum responsivity occurred on the first trial block with subsequent significant and parallel habituation in responsivity to the CS+ and CS−. Gale and Ax report that the magnitude of the GSR-OR did not differ on the first presentation of the CS+ and CS−. Differential responsivity to the CS+ and CS− developed within the first trial block.

Figure 8.2 shows the differential conditioning for responses scored in the second interval. These are assumed to reflect a process of growing anticipation or expectancy for the UCS. Significantly greater responsivity occurred to CS+ as compared to CS−, but there is no evidence of a gradual development of responsivity to CS+ and a decline in responsivity to CS− with continued trials.

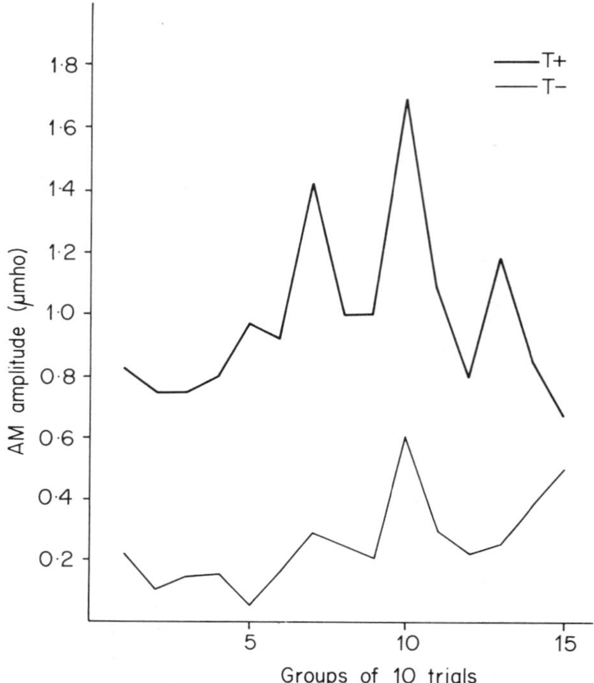

Figure 8.2 Mean magnitude of the second interval ('anticipatory') GSR to the reinforced CS+ (T+) and the non-reinforced CS− (T−) averaged over blocks of ten trials. (*From E. N. Gale and A. F. Ax, Long term conditioning of orienting responses,* Psychophysiology, **5** *(1968), 307–15. Copyright 1968 by the Society for Psychophysiological Research. Reprinted by permission of the Society and the authors*)

A comparison of Figures 8.1 and 8.2 fails to show a reciprocal relationship between responses scored in the first and in the second interval, so-called conditioned ORs and conditioned anticipatory responses. According to cognitive theory, there should have been a decline of conditioned GSR-ORs and a gradual increase in conditioned anticipation or expectancy for the UCS. Obviously these results did not occur. Gale and Ax's findings contradict the cognitive conception that a process of anticipation develops and is reflected in second interval responses. Particularly damaging to the expectancy notion is the decline, habituation, in second interval responses paralleling the habituation of first interval responses. Such results are precisely what should obtain if these are all manifestations of ORs as Maltzman has hypothesized (e.g.

Maltzman, 1979a). Such contradictory evidence, long available, has consistently been ignored by cognitive psychologists (e.g. Öhman, 1983).

Rapid habituation despite 100 per cent reinforcement—that is, rapid habituation once the CS-UCS contingency is predictable, once learning has occurred—conforms to the implications of a neuronal model of an OR. It is entirely out of keeping with the cognitive folk psychology of anticipation. There is no reason for a CR that is consistently reinforced to habituate, if it reflects a hypothetical process of anticipation, other things being equal. There is good reason for it to habituate if second interval responses are a reflection of an OR. Predictable stimuli represent a match between the neuronal model of past stimulation and present stimuli. GSR-ORs, whether they are labelled CRs or not, are less likely to occur under such circumstances, in the absence of novelty.

Further evidence contradicting the conception of conditioned anticipation has been obtained in a study of repeated semantic conditioning sessions (Maltzman, Weissbluth, and Wolff, 1978). Male college students participated in five successive daily semantic conditioning sessions of 40 conditioning trials. Different common words were presented where one, the CS word, was always followed in 10 sec by a 0.5 sec loud white noise that served as the UCS. Neutral unrelated words were interspersed between conditioning trials, and a habituation list of common words preceded conditioning trials each day.

Figure 8.3 shows the mean GSRs in the first and second intervals induced by the CS word on each of the 40 conditioning trials for each of the five daily sessions. Responses to control words preceding and following each conditioning trial were scored and analysed, but are omitted from Figure 8.3 for the sake of clarity. It is apparent that first interval GSRs are significantly larger than second interval GSRs despite the rapid habituation, inhibition of reinforcement, culminating in a low level of responsivity well before the completion of the 40 trials each day. It is apparent that an asymptote of responsivity was reached well within the first 10 trials on the first day, and that first and second interval GSRs parallel each other. There is no evidence of the growth of second interval responses implying the development of an expectancy or conditioned anticipation of the UCS. Again, the experimental evidence contradicts the cognitive folk psychology of anticipatory processes or expectancies.

Further contradictory evidence is provided by Burstein and Smith (1972). They present extensive data which fail to show systematic increases in latency, magnitude, or frequency of second interval responses over trials. Their results, as do ours shown in Figure 8.3, suggest that second interval responses are simply longer latency responses induced by the CS. Until evidence is presented to the contrary, the most parsimonious interpretation of second interval conditioned GSRs is that they are simply manifestations of continued orienting to the CS. Experiments by Gale and Ax (1968) and Maltzman *et al.*

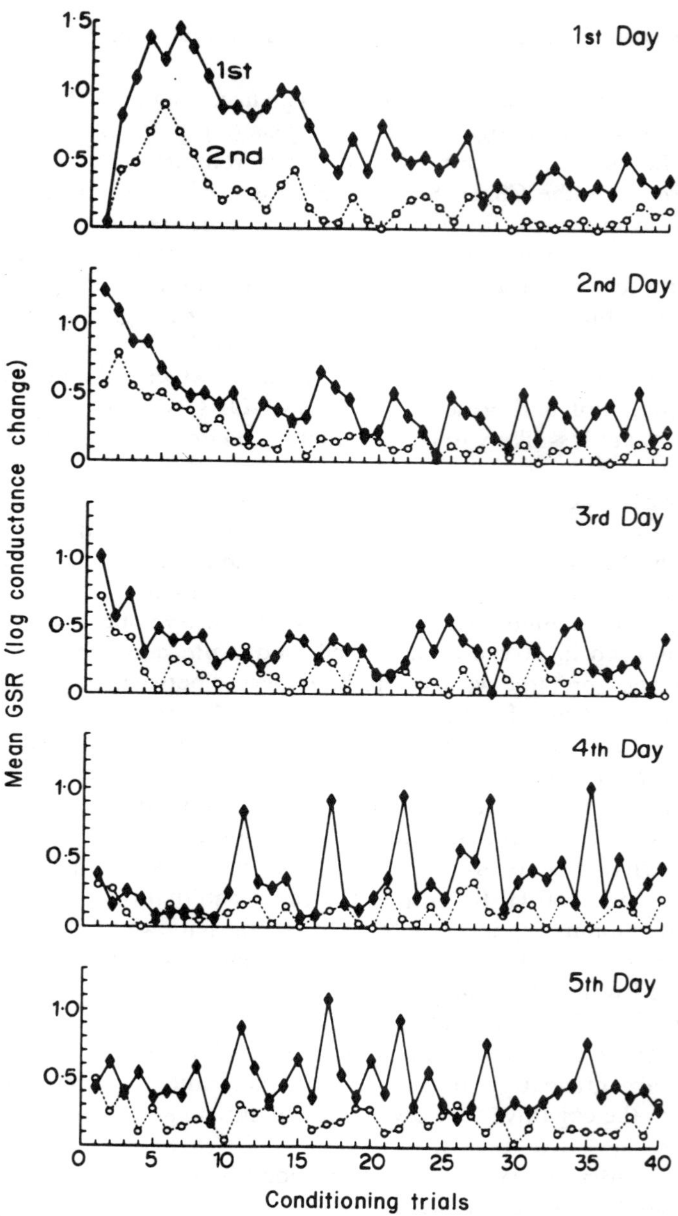

Figure 8.3 Mean magnitude of first and second interval GSRs induced by the critical word, CS, on each of the 40 conditioning trials for each of the daily conditioning sessions. An extraneous stimulus change was introduced on trials 11, 17, 22, 26, and 35, on Day 4 and Day 5. Mean GSRs to the control words immediately preceding and following CS are omitted for the sake of clarity. (*From I. Maltzman, S. Weissbluth, and C. Wolff, Habituation of orienting reflexes in repeated GSR semantic conditioning sessions,* Journal of Experimental Psychology: General, **107** *(1978), 309–33. Copyright 1978 by the American Psychological Association. Reprinted by permission of the Association*)

(1978) used different UCSs and different CSs. They employed far more conditioning trials than the usual human classical conditioning experiment, providing ideal conditions for the growth of expectancies. Both experiments produced results contradicting the notion of conditioned anticipation or expectancy. Implications of these findings therefore have considerable generality.

Öhman's espousal of expectancy is an example of the fallacy of affirming the consequent. This fallacy indicates the importance of the falsifiability of hypotheses as a criterion of scientific meaning, and is the reason why the notion of expectancy as formulated by Öhman and other cognitive psychologists is false. The hypothesis 'if a bird is a swan, it is white' may serve as an example. A white bird is found in a pond. This is in accord with the hypothesis that swans are white. But it may also be a pigeon; other interpretations are possible. But if a black swan is found, we know necessarily that the hypothesis that swans are white is false. Studies by Gale and Ax and by Maltzman *et al.* show that the folk psychology of expectancy is not a swan.

It must also be observed that anticipation, descriptively, has repeatedly been noted in what essentially are first interval responses (a) during habituation (Pendery and Maltzman, 1977; Maltzman, Weissbluth, and Wolff, 1978) and (b) in response to control filler words in semantic conditoning with highly noxious stimuli (Maltzman, Langdon, Pendery, and Wolff, 1977; Maltzman, Gould, Barnett, Raskin, and Wolff, 1977). According to Öhman's theory of expectancy in conditioning, first interval responses are expressions of ORs and cannot show anticipation, only second interval responses are expressions of expectancy. Our results, again, long in the literature, demonstrate that Öhman's theoretical conception of ORs as first interval responses is false, as well as his conception of second interval responses as anticipatory. The former conception is false because he fails to integrate ORs with a theory of a neuronal model and match/mismatch as a basis for the occurrence of ORs. The latter conception of the OR has the power of accounting for anticipation in non-intentional terms.

4 Classical conditioning of the orienting reflex

For some 30 years the theoretical interpretation of human classical conditioning in the West has been dominated by Hull's (1943) S-R theory of behaviour and Spence's (1956) variation. Classical conditioning of autonomic activity in the form of its most commonly used variable, the GSR, was dominated by Mowrer's (1938, 1939) conception: the GSR is a manifestation of the emotional response to a noxious stimulus. It was assumed that the GSR in its unconditioned form was a manifestation of a response to pain elicited by a noxious stimulus. In its conditioned form, the GSR was a manifestation of anxiety, an anticipatory fractional component of the emotional response to a noxious stimulus. Variations of this form of theoretical interpretation and the related research were used in the analysis of clinical phenomena. Mowrer's research and theoretical formulation of verbal conditioning of anxiety and the classic experiment by Cook and Harris (1937) were particularly attractive to a learning theory oriented clinical psychology. Verbal conditioning of anxiety involves instructing subjects that a painful UCS will follow a particular innocuous stimulus. Presentation of that innocuous signal, prior to its pairing with the noxious UCS, results in a large GSR induced by the innocuous stimulus. An anxiety response has been verbally conditioned to the UCS. According to social learning theory, cognitive activity mediates the transfer of the anxiety response from the UCS to the CS (Bandura, 1969).

Our view of human classical conditioning has a different emphasis than past theories of human classical conditioning as formulated by Hull, Spence, and Mowrer. It is not an S-R theory, although it is behaviouristic. It also differs radically from the orientation of social learning theory, cognitive social learning theory, and current efforts at interpreting human classical conditioning in terms of information processing metaphors, and cognitive 'folk psychology' (Stich, 1983).

The present formulation recognizes that human behaviour, even the simplest human behaviour, is a manifestation of an enormously complex biological organism. Conditioning does not occur in a black box, an empty shell, or a buffer. We do not condition a disembodied response. We condition an organism, usually an inquiring, suspicious, curious, bored—all of these and more, or none—college sophomore. The conditioned response is a small sample of the complex behavioural, physiological, and neurochemical changes occurring at the moment. It is produced in a person with a variety of cortical sets, dominant foci, interests, attitudes, etc., present at the moment the CS and UCS are presented which influence and direct the nature of the CR.

Our formulation has an affinity with neo-Pavlovian developments over the years (e.g. Anokhin, 1974; Asratyan, 1965; Beritoff, 1965; Konorski, 1967; Sokolov, 1963b). It is in the tradition emphasized by Garcia (Garcia, McGown, and Green, 1972) and Lashley (1923, 1951). We must always consider that, as Lashley emphasized,

> input is never into a quiescent or static system, but always into a system which is already actively excited and organized. In the intact organism behavior is the result of interaction of this background of excitation with input from any designated stimulus. Only when we can state the general characteristics of this background of excitation, can we understand the effects of a given input. (Lashley, 1951, p. 112)

Lashley concluded his classic paper on the problem of serial order in behaviour with the following statement: 'Attempts to express cerebral function in terms of the reflex arc, or of associated chains of neurons, seem to me doomed to failure because they start with the assumption of a static nervous system. Every bit of evidence available indicates a dynamic, constantly active system, or rather a composite of many interacting systems' (Lashley, 1951, p. 135). I might add that a static central processing unit is as inadequate as a static nervous system.

Lashley offered several suggestions concerning fruitful directions to be taken in an examination of the problem of serial order in behaviour. One such suggestion was the examination of the implications of one of the oldest and, I believe, best established empirical phenomena in the area of complex processes, the phenomenon of mental set or determining tendency (Maltzman, 1955). It is interesting that by the time Lashley offered his suggestion that set or determining tendency is a fruitful notion to pursue, considerable work of which he apparently was unaware had already been conducted coordinating the notion of set with a physiological conception of great importance. Unfortunately, much of this work and its theoretical significance has been unduly neglected in the West.

I am referring to the conception of a dominant focus, a conception introduced by Ukhtomsky and which has been under investigation for many years in the USSR (e.g. Bykov, 1958; Bechterev, 1933; Livanov, 1977; Razran, 1961; Rusinov, 1970). I have used the term cortical set to refer to the same phenomena. It is immensely important in accounting for a variety of classical conditioning phenomena peculiar to humans as well as many of the characteristics of the OR. These include the role of significance in relation to the OR, the influence of instructions, and interests and attitudes (e.g. Maltzman, 1979a, 1979b; Maltzman, Langdon, and Feeney, 1970; Maltzman, Gould, Pendery, and Wolff, 1982; Wingard and Maltzman, 1980; Schweiger and Maltzman, 1985). It is an acquired system that integrates and directs the flow of behaviour and the direction of flow of information within and among physiological systems. It is the very basis of classical conditioning. There are at least three general biological systems that organize and direct behaviour: the appetitive, aversive, and orienting systems. Dominant foci develop within and among each of these. They form functional systems (Anokhin, 1974) which integrate and direct behaviour, including the direction of attention and the OR. Cortical sets or dominant foci provide the basis for the significance of stimuli, interests, attitudes, and dispositions. When a dominant focus involves multiple physiological systems, it may serve as the basis for addictions.

Before turning to the nature of conditioning of the GSR-OR we must consider some of the characteristics of the OR (e.g. Maltzman, 1971, 1975, 1977, 1979a, 1979b; Maltzman and Mandell, 1968; Maltzman and Raskin, 1965; Pendery and Maltzman, 1977; Sokolov, 1960, 1963a, 1963b, 1969; Schweiger and Maltzman, 1985; Wingard and Maltzman, 1980).

The OR is a defined or abstract concept. It is not the GSR or changes in sweat glands, no more than arousal is low voltage fast wave activity in the

EEG, or anxiety the sweat on my palms. A number of general characteristics are ascribed to the OR (Sokolov, 1963b). First, it is an organismic response. It involves widespread changes throughout the organism, in contrast to adaptive reflexes which are relatively localized in nature. Changes representing the OR vary in duration. They may be relatively brief, phasic, in nature, or relatively long in duration. One of their distinctive characteristics is that ORs are non-specific. No particular stimulus quality is necessary for their occurrence. They have no one adequate stimulus for their initiation. A novel auditory stimulus as well as a novel visual or tactual stimulus may apparently induce the same organismic changes. A striking feature of the OR is that repeated elicitations result in relatively rapid habituation. A decrement in its response measures, magnitude, amplitude, or relative frequency of response occurs. All response systems show some degree of habituation with repeated elicitations (Razran, 1971). Response decrements are particularly rapid in measures of the OR, especially when they are initiated by predictable, innocuous, and non-significant stimuli. Relatively rapid habituation of GSR-CRs and UCRs with 100 per cent reinforcement from high noxious UCSs indicates that these responses are manifestations of ORs (Maltzman, Weissbluth, and Wolff, 1978).

There are additional, and unduly neglected, characteristics of ORs: they may be voluntary or involuntary and conditioned or unconditioned. 'Voluntary' and 'involuntary' refer to the extent to which the OR is under verbal regulation, the extent to which it is influenced by speech, either covert or overt, either on the part of the experimenter or the subjects themselves. 'Conditioned' and 'unconditioned', of course, indicate that they may be learned or unlearned. These different forms are characteristically evoked during the course of an experiment. Initial presentation of the CS prior to pairing with a UCS is a novel stimulus. It evokes a phasic involuntary, unconditioned, OR. When classical conditioning of the GSR is successfully manifested in a laboratory experiment with human subjects, the GSR-CR characteristically is a reflection of a conditioned voluntary OR.

It must be remembered that 'conditioning' is used in two senses: (a) as a name for a procedure, and (b) a particular kind of learning. We are using the term here in the sense of a procedure. As a procedure it involves presenting a CS, a relatively innocuous neutral stimulus, followed by a UCS, a stimulus which evokes a large UCR on the first trial. After varying numbers of trials the CS evokes a larger response than it did prior to conditioning, or a response larger than the one evoked by a stimulus unpaired with the UCS. In our semantic conditioning experiments, there is always a within-subject control stimulus, words, so that the CS word followed by the UCS must evoke a significantly larger response that the preceding and following control words that are never followed by the UCS. Classical conditioning is an enormously flexible procedure that has been employed with a vast number of different species and response systems from the single cell to an array of different behavioural and physiological changes in subjects ranging from college sophomores to a vast array of clinical populations. Because the basic experimental procedure is the same does not mean that the laws of behavioural change, the laws governing the appearance of a differential response to the CS+ as compared to the CS−, are the same. Garcia (Garcia *et al*., 1972) has shown that the laws are different in the case of conditioned taste aversions from those in exteroceptive conditioning. There is biological preparedness for certain kinds of CS-UCS acquisitions. There are different kinds of principles involved when different response and physiological systems are engaged. Classical conditioning of the OR system differs fundamentally from, for example, conditioning the immune system.

Conditioning the OR, as reflected in the GSR which is its most commonly employed and perhaps most sensitive measure, differs fundamentally from conditioning or learning motor responses (Grings and Lockhart, 1966) or verbal learning (Brown, 1937). Principles of conditioning differ depending upon the biological system that is acted upon and measured. In the case of learning a motor response, the conditioned voluntary OR reaches a maximum before the conditioned motor response is acquired. Conditioned discrimination must occur before conditioned or learned differentiation. Once motor learning is successful, the situation is predictable and the OR habituates.

Figure 8.4 depicts conditioned response curves strikingly different from those seen in Figures 8.1 and 8.2. It shows the mean GSR evoked during semantic conditioning with different UCSs. The UCS followed one particular word after 10 sec where that word was interspersed among different common words. Responses to preceding, C_1, and following, C_2, control words are also plotted.

Reasons for the profound difference in the kinds of conditioning curves depicted in Figure 8.4 as compared to such as those shown in Figures 8.1 and 8.2 have been discussed elsewhere (Maltzman, 1977, 1979a; Pendery and Maltzman, 1977). Laboratory classical conditioning of the GSR with college students is a procedure that induces problem solving in the typical inquisitive college student. If, and when, the student discovers the significance of the CS as a signal for the UCS, an OR, a form of attention, is induced to the discovered significant stimulus. This is not the OR to novelty or stimulus change, but an OR induced by the problem solving process, an OR generated by the subject. These have been called voluntary ORs (e.g. Maltzman, 1979a) in order to distinguish them from involuntary ORs. The two kinds of ORs differ in terms of their initiating conditions, functional relations to other variables, as well as morphology. Classical conditioning of the GSR is thus a situation which provides an exquisitely sensitive measure of the changes in the OR, a form of attention, during the course of a problem solving situation of varying difficulty. Its difficulty varies depending upon the

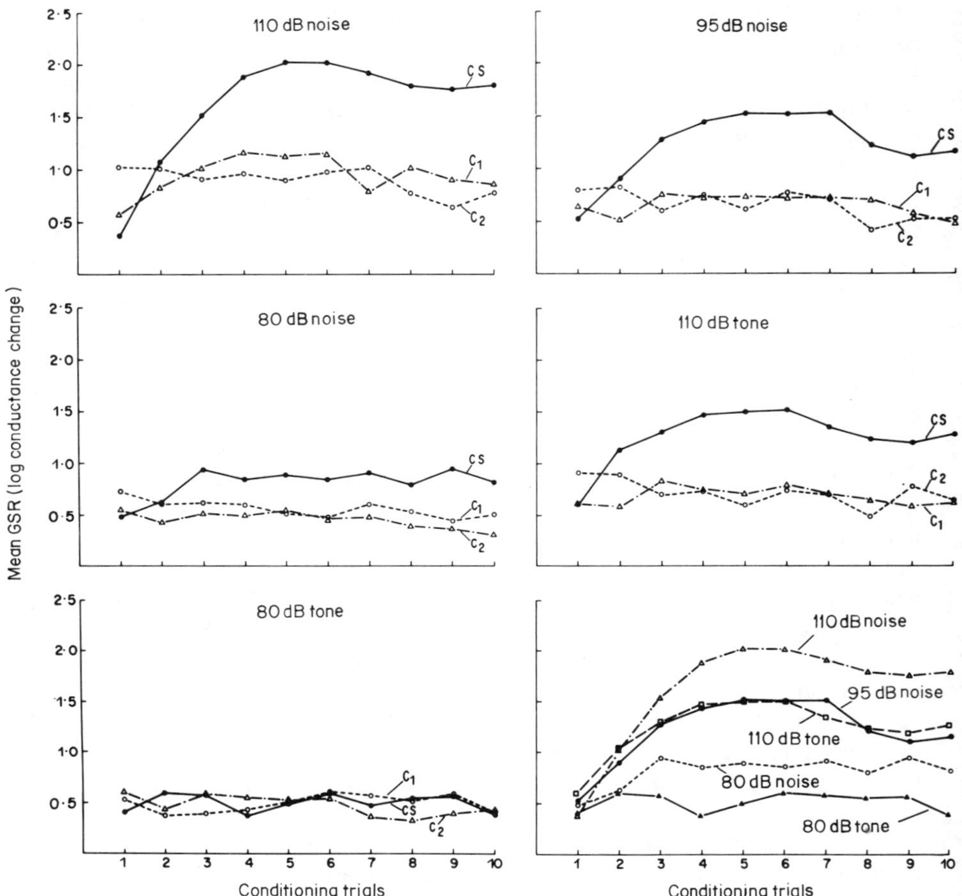

Figure 8.4 Differential semantic conditioning of the GSR to a CS word with different UCSs, and different immediately preceding, C_1, and following, C_2, control words. (*From I. Maltzman, B. Langdon, M. Pendery, and C. Wolff, Galvanic skin response-orienting reflex and semantic conditioning and generalization with different unconditioned stimuli,* Journal of Experimental Psychology: General, **106** *(1977), 141–72. Copyright 1977 by the American Psychological Association. Reprinted by permission of the Association*)

number of different kinds of potential CSs presented, the extent of 'masking'. Simple conditioning, or discriminative conditioning with a CS+ and a CS−, is learned within two or three trials, if learned at all. Conditioning of the GSR-OR in the individual subject appears to be an all-or-none process. Either they orient differentially or do not. Conditioning in a situation such as the one employed by Gale and Ax (1968) is therefore complete for most subjects within the first trial block. Since the pattern of reinforcement is 100 per cent and does not change, a neuronal model coincident with the pattern of stimulation is quickly formed. Decline in the GSR-CR occurs as it would in any other kind of OR where there is a match between past and present stimulation patterns or where the problem is solved.

Figure 8.4, in contrast to Figures 8.1 and 8.2, depicts conditioning following presentation of a list of innocuous words designed to habituate the GSR-OR to words in general. Conditioning trials consist of one common word, a CS word, interspersed among other common words. It is a more difficult problem to solve 'what signals what' than in a simple classical conditioning task. Individual differences are greater, subjects learn at different rates and show their maximum response on different trials. When response magnitude is averaged over a large number of subjects who are dispersed over several trials in the display of their maximum GSR-OR, the relatively smooth conditioning curves shown in Figure 8.4 are produced. No individual subject shows a comparable growth curve (Maltzman, Langdon, Pendery and Wolff, 1977).

Much of the misunderstanding on the part of cognitive psychologists concerning the role of the OR in classical conditioning of the GSR and the nature of expectancy has been due to their failure to distinguish between observation and theoretical statements, between description and explanation. Under some circumstances an increase in responsivity of the GSR scored in the second interval of the CS-UCS interval may be observed. An analogous increase in responsivity was found following the UCS in Maltzman *et al.* (1978). The logic of cognitive folk psychology suggests that the hypothetical unobservable process of expectancy was expressed by this observed increase. But attributing the observed increase in responsivity to a hypothetical expectancy is untenable because there was nothing to anticipate following the UCS. An alternative interpretation in keeping with established principles is that the increase in second interval responsivity accompanied the decreases in magnitude of the UCR during the course of its habituation; latency and magnitude are negatively correlated. As a consequence, the increase in latency and decrease in magnitude with continued conditioning trials cast more small responses into the second scoring interval. Clearly, an observed increase in responsivity in the second interval following a UCS is not identical with 'anticipation' or 'expectancy', a theoretical conception. On the contrary, such an increase, once more, contradicts the 'common sense' assumed by cognitive psychologists in their folk psychology of anticipation.

It must also be noted that conceptions of the neuronal model and match/mismatch between past and present stimulation leading to the expression of an OR can account for changes in responsivity that may be described as 'anticipation' or 'expectancy' (Maltzman *et al.*, 1978; Maltzman, Gould, Barnett, Raskin, and Wolff, 1977; Pendery and Maltzman, 1977). A neuronal model and related conceptions therefore permit the explanation in non-intentional terms of what descriptively is intentional in character. What may be *described* as an expectancy or anticipation can be *explained* in non-expectancy terms. An account of this sort is reductionistic in one sense and therefore of considerable power. 'Anticipation' in long delayed conditioning was first described by Pavlov. In long CS-UCS interval conditioning the conditioned salivary response eventually occurs just prior to the UCS. It may be described as anticipating the UCS. But it is explained by Pavlov in terms of principles of inhibition. What may, again, be described intentionally as an expectancy, is explained in non-intentional terms.

5 Alcoholism

Alcoholism is the major preventable disease in the United States. It is the third or fourth leading cause of death. Costs to society of alcoholism and alcohol misuse are estimated to be between $40 billion and $60 billion a year (Institute of Medicine, 1980). To a striking degree, alcohol addiction manifests the fundamental role of conditioning, learning, and motivation, goal directed behaviour. It is a problem that includes aspects of experimental, social, and clinical psychology, as well as neuroscience, sociology, anthropology, epidemiology and medicine. A discussion of all of the ramifications of the problem, experimental and theoretical, is beyond the scope of this chapter; it certainly is beyond the scope of the few remaining pages to this chapter. A specific issue will therefore be briefly considered: relapse.

An immediate question is, relapse to and from what? An alcoholic has serious interpersonal, professional, and, very often, medical problems. Alcoholics may literally destroy themselves and those around them for a drink. Verbal awareness of the CSs and the UCs and the consequent behaviour usually does not change the destructive goal directed behaviour. It is purposive and irrational. Alcoholics can often explicitly state that they have a problem, are trying to control it, and yet continue to drink, relapse, and find themselves in serious medical, social, and professional difficulties. Repeated cycles of this sort are not uncommon.

An alcoholic according to Jellinek (1960), a pioneer in the modern scientific study of alcoholism in the United States, is anyone whose drinking does damage to themselves or to others. Jellinek added that there are different types of alcoholics. For convenience we will classify them as problem drinkers and alcoholics. Both types may have serious social, professional, and medical problems as a consequence of their drinking. More alcohol may be consumed by the former than the latter. Mere amount consumed is not an adequate criterion for distinguishing among heavy drinkers, problem drinkers, and alcoholics, because of enormous individual differences in the reaction to alcohol.

There are several explicit behavioural indices that distinguish an alcoholic from a problem drinker. They form the syndrome of alcoholism: (a) physical dependence as defined by repeated experiences of withdrawal following an extended drinking period; signs of withdrawal include increased anxiety, profuse perspiration, abnormal EEG recordings, hallucinations, fever, nausea, vomiting, diarrhoea, generalized seizures, and delirium tremens (Wikler, Pescor, Fraser, and Isbell, 1956; (b) a high degree of tolerance, behavioural and physiological habituation, to the effects of alcohol; (c) a loss of control as manifested by an inability to consistently choose not to drink when alcohol is available, and an inability to consistently choose to stop after starting to drink. Consistency of choice is the critical criterion, because clinical experience suggests that every alcoholic at some time or another has stayed sober for a period of time or has practised moderation in their drinking. They cannot, however, consistently choose to drink in moderation over the long term as several long term follow-up studies have dramatically demonstrated (Edwards, 1985; Helzer, Robins, Taylor, Carey, Miller, Combs-Orme, and Farmer, 1985; Pendery, Maltzman, and West, 1982).

An individual addicted to alcohol is consumed by thoughts of drinking, when and where will they be able to get a drink, will they run dry, will their supply be sufficient to get through the day, etc. They cover up, lie, deny their problems and the consequences of their drinking. Their life style changes; every aspect of their life comes to centre around their drinking practices. Alcohol literally becomes the dominant focus of their life. The need to drink influences, directs, every waking and sleeping hour, every aspect of the alcoholic's life.

Elimination of a dominant focus of such organismic breadth, a focus that governs literally every aspect of behaviour, asleep as well as awake, requires another dominant focus. Since an addiction to alcohol produces a style of life centred around alcohol, a new life style is needed to inhibit the dominant focus of the addiction. Alcoholics Anonymous has had the success it appears to have had with alcoholics (e.g. Alford, 1980) either as the sole source of treatment, or as an adjunct to other treatments, because it literally offers, makes possible, a new way of life. If offers new friends who do not drink. For the chronic alcoholic this may be an entirely new social life, new values, new ways of evaluating people and events, and new goals. Its structure, meetings, and fellowship provide a new focus that can occupy an individual during the critical early period of abstinence, and whenever and wherever necessary thereafter for the remainder of their life.

Craving, which increases the disposition to drink and may increase the probability of loss of control, may produce relapse when the cues associated with drinking and withdrawal are present. A classical conditioning analysis of the kind proposed by Ludwig and Wikler (1974) suggests that there is a profound qualitative difference between problem drinkers and alcoholics. Individuals who have never experienced withdrawal will not develop conditioned craving and therefore are at much less risk of loss of control and relapse. Problem drinkers are not as driven to drink as the alcoholic who must drink in order to avoid the pain of withdrawal. If a return to moderate drinking after treatment is possible, it would be possible for the problem drinker and not the alcoholic. These are precisely the results obtained in treatment follow-up studies that have obtained independent measures of severity of dependence (e.g. Orford, Oppenheimer, and Edwards, 1976). Therefore, contrary to the views of those who insist that problem drinkers and alcoholics are on a continuum distinguished only by the amount consumed, there is a good theoretical basis in terms of conditioning principles for distinguishing between the classes of problem drinker and alcoholic. Additional evidence for the distinction from pathophysiology, behavioural genetics, and measurement theory will not be considered here.

6 Priming alcoholics: expectancy and conditioning interpretations

A basic problem in the treatment of alcoholics is the relapse from treatment. Abstinence, the treatment goal of probably all established alcoholism treatment programmes in the United States, is not always attained after a single period of treatment. Many times it never is attained. Relapse, and repeated slips, are common. A basic theoretical and practical problem is the understanding and possible avoidance of relapse once abstinence has been achieved. There are two current analyses of the phenomenon of relapse and some related research and theory. One is an expectancy theory (Cummings, Gordon, and Marlatt, 1980; Marlatt, 1979), the other is a theory based upon classical conditioning and related principles of learning (Ludwig and Stark, 1974; Ludwig and Wikler, 1974; Ludwig, Wikler, and Stark, 1974).

Ludwig and his associates have offered a classical conditioning interpretation of relapse that has testable implications. According to these investigators, craving may develop following a period of abstinence and, if so, it increases the disposition to drink, loss of control over the drinking, and relapse. They interpret craving as the cognitive–symbolic correlate of the subclinical withdrawal syndrome. It is the verbal expression of conditioned components of withdrawal. In other words, the UCR is the syndrome of hyperexcitability and the painful behavioural and physiological changes that occur when abstinence is introduced following extended heavy drinking. Some components of the withdrawal syndrome become conditioned to accompanying exteroceptive and interoceptive cues. One of the latter is the taste and smell of alcohol, a cue that occurred in the presence of withdrawal, since an alcoholic usually drinks in order to avoid or reduce withdrawal as well as to get high. Interoceptive cues of dysphoria are also conditioned to the withdrawal syndrome. Conditioned craving is a source of motivation for the alcohol directed behaviour which is reinforced by a reduction of the subclinical withdrawal syndrome, the dysphoric state. A wide range of dysphoric states may come to evoke the conditioned subclinical withdrawal syndrome, craving, via generalization.

This conditioning analysis suggests that the alcoholic is unlikely to be able to return to moderate social drinking. Abstinence is the only viable treatment goal. Furthermore, moderate drinking will partially reinforce, and therefore increase, the resistance to extinction of the conditioned withdrawal syndrome. It will increase the resistance to extinction of craving and increase the probability of loss of control of drinking and concomitant relapse.

An obvious basic implication of this conditioning hypothesis is that there must be a relationship between the strength of craving and the frequency and intensity of withdrawal experiences. Ludwig and Stark (1974) examined the latter hypothesis by constructing a questionnaire assessing the frequency and intensity of withdrawal experiences as well as situations in which craving was reported as experienced. Patients at a VA alcoholism treatment facility were administered the two questionnaires. A significant correlation of 0.48 was obtained, confirming the conditioning hypothesis.

The traditional view of alcoholism emphasizes abstinence as a treatment goal, and that alcoholism is qualitatively different from problem drinking, distinguished in part by withdrawal experiences and loss of control (e.g. Royce, 1981). Revisionist critics cite a number of different kinds of evidence purporting to contradict traditional views on the acquisition and treatment of alcoholism (e.g. Marlatt and Nathan, 1978; Miller, 1976; Pattison, Sobell, and Sobell, 1977). This is not the place to critically review the purported evidence cited by the revisionists. One kind of evidence is pertinent, however, to the consideration of classical conditioning vs. expectancy, cognitive, theories of relapse. This is the experimental study of priming.

Marlatt, Demming, and Reid (1973) have conducted a widely cited study purporting to support an expectancy theory of alcoholic behaviour and relapse. It is also taken as a critical contradiction to the traditional view of alcoholism (e.g. Marlatt, 1983; Peele, 1984). A balanced placebo factorial design was employed in the experiment. Half the participants received an alcoholic beverage and half received a non-alcoholic tonic. Half the participants in each of these two conditions were informed that they received alcohol whereas half were informed that they received tonic. There were two groups of participants receiving these treatments, so that there were eight subgroups in all. One group consisted of social drinkers whereas the second group were non-abstinent alcoholics according to the criteria of the investigators. All participants were asked to taste and rate three different drinks. A priming dose was administered to all subjects prior to the rating task. Subjects receiving alcohol in the rating task received a primer of 1 oz vodka mixed with 5 oz tonic. Participants receiving the non-alcoholic beverage received 6 oz tonic. Priming was administered approximately 20 minutes before the experimental task. Subjects were asked to rinse their mouths with a mouthwash which was modified to contain a 30 per cent solution of 100 proof (50 per cent) alcohol before consuming a beverage.

Results indicated that alcoholics and social drinkers drank more during the test if they were told that they were drinking alcohol whether or not they received alcohol. The interpretation was that the expectancy of alcohol determined the amount consumed not the actual beverage. In addition, there was no evidence of loss of control or significantly more drinking by alcoholics who received alcohol than by alcoholics who received tonic, a placebo. Under both conditions alcoholics drank more than social drinkers. Cummings *et al.* (1980) ascribe enormous significance to such findings. They state,

> the role of expectancy in the perceived effects of alcohol may have important implications for the control and prediction of alcoholic relapse insofar as it pinpoints the significance of psychological factors as they interact with the pharmacological action of alcohol. According to this view, the reinforcing quality of alcohol for the experienced user may not be based on the satiation of biochemical mediated craving but rather on the expectation of certain behavioral effects. This has important treatment implications, for if the determinants of alcohol use . . . are not primarily physiological, then cognitive–behavioral intervention would be the treatment of choice as compared to drug therapies which risk pharmacological side effects and additional drug dependence. Equally significant, the treatment goal of controlled social use clearly becomes a viable alternative to abstinence when psychological factors are seen to play a primary role in mediating pharmacological effects. (Cummings *et al.*, 1980, pp. 295–6)

There are serious shortcomings in the above theorizing, especially the *non sequitur* of the last sentence. We shall pass them by in order to consider the serious shortcomings in the research (Marlatt *et al.*, 1973) as follows.

(a) There is no independent measure of severity of dependence in the alcoholics. It ignores the traditional distinction between gamma alcoholics and problem drinkers. Loss of control applies to alcoholics who have had repeated and severe withdrawal experiences. That the participants in this group have a history of problems as a consequence of excessive drinking is no guarantee that they are addicted to alcohol. If they are not addicted, have not experienced repeated withdrawal, they would not experience craving and loss of control. They therefore would not be expected to drink more with a priming dose than without.

(b) A single priming dose was employed. A parametric study is needed, since the amount employed as a primer may be too small to induce a conditioned response, components of the withdrawal syndrome, craving, and an increased disposition to drink. This is especially true because of the next shortcoming in the study.

(c) Administering a mouthwash prior to consuming a drink may have had the effect of a local anaesthetic. It reduced sensitivity to the cues of alcohol, the interoceptive cues most likely to elicit the conditioned components of the craving response (Garcia *et al*., 1972).

Fortunately, some of the above shortcomings in the Marlatt *et al*. study have been avoided in a series of experiments conducted by a group of British investigators (e.g. Hodgson, Rankin, and Stockwell, 1979; Rankin, Hodgson, and Stockwell, 1974; Stockwell, Hodgson, Rankin, and Taylor, 1982). Unfortunately, these studies have not received the attention their importance merits. Results obtained by the British investigators contradict Marlatt's expectancy conception and its purported implications for the theory and treatment of alcoholism. Absence of a priming effect in the Marlatt *et al*. (1976) study is also explained by these British experiments. They show the robustness of a conditioning theory creatively applied by investigators with a knowledge of clinical problems as well as a knowledge of conditioning principles.

A first step in the research was the development of a questionnaire (Stockwell, Hodgson, Edwards, Taylor, and Rankin, 1979) related to the alcohol addiction syndrome (Edwards and Gross, 1976). Self-reported ratings of frequency and severity of withdrawal experiences, among other characteristics of the dependency syndrome, are obtained by the questionnaire.

A next step was the development of a behavioural measure of craving (Rankin, Hodgson, and Stockwell, 1979). Outpatient alcoholics all rated as severely dependent participated as volunteers in the experiment which was conducted in their homes. Participants had to be drinking at home all day and be willing to be visited by the experimenter.

A within-subject design was employed in which all subjects participated in a high and low craving condition on successive days. The test of craving consisted of giving the participants two glasses each containing vodka and tonic upon arrival of the experimenter in the subject's home and 3 hours later, at the end of the session. Subjects were told that they could drink the alcohol at their own rate. The purported purpose was to obtain the participant's judgement of how pleasurable they thought the drink was. Speed of consuming the drink was recorded. Participants rated on a five point scale their level of anxiety, desire for a drink, and difficulty in resisting alcohol at the start and completion of a session. Measures of body temperature, pulse and blood alcohol levels, and finger tremor were also obtained.

Participants in the high craving condition were asked to drink normally before the experimenter arrived. They were given the initial two drinks and then asked to refrain from taking any alcohol until the final test 3 hours later.

Subjects in the low craving condition were also asked to drink normally prior to the arrival of the experimenter. However, they were allowed to continue drinking for the first 2½ hours of the experiment and were asked to refrain only for the last half hour.

Significant differences between the high and low craving conditions were obtained on a number of measures. Of major concern here, the subjects under the high craving condition showed a significant increase in their speed of consuming the drink at the end of the session. Finger tremor and self-rated craving and inability to resist a drink also increased in the high but not the low craving condition.

Given validated objective measures of the severity of alcohol dependence and of craving, Hodgson, Rankin, and Stockwell (1979) turned to the study of the priming effect. Volunteer participants were all hospitalized alcoholics. Following a period of at least 10 days of abstinence in the hospital, all subjects were given either a high (150 ml vodka), a low (15 ml vodka), or no priming dose in the morning and asked to consume the drink, which was a mix of alcohol and tonic, or solely tonic, within 45 minutes. A within-subject design was employed so that each subject participated in each of the three conditions with at least 1 day between each condition. In the afternoon of the priming day subjects were presented with five drinks. They were asked to consume at least one of them so that speed of consumption of the first drink would be available for all subjects, since not all wished to consume all five drinks. Subjects rated their desire to drink on a five point scale. Pulse and blood alcohol levels were obtained before and after each session.

A significant interaction was obtained between the questionnaire measure of dependency and the behavioural measure of craving, the speed of consuming one drink in the afternoon. Severely dependent alcoholics reported a significantly stronger desire to drink than the moderately dependent alcoholics, consumed the first drink more quickly, and consumed significantly more alcohol during the test. The larger the priming dose, the faster the severely dependent alcoholic consumed the first drink. Exactly opposite results were obtained with the moderately dependent alcoholics. The larger the priming dose, the slower their consumption. They showed a satiation effect whereas the severely dependent alcoholic showed an appetizer or priming effect. If the two groups are averaged together, if severity of dependence is ignored, there is no priming effect, precisely the result reported by Marlatt *et al*. (1976). Contrary to Marlatt *et al*., when severity of dependency is considered, when alcoholics are differentiated from problem drinkers, alcoholics show a priming effect. Although this study demonstrates why Marlatt and earlier investigators failed to obtain a priming effect, it did not employ placebo conditions. All of the participants received accurate information concerning the nature of their drinks.

A subsequent study employed the balanced placebo design as well as measures of severity of dependence (Stockwell, Hodgson, Rankin, and Taylor, 1982). Hospitalized alcoholics who participated in the study were categorized as either moderately or severely dependent. Half of each condition received alcohol and tonic and half received only tonic. Half of each of these two conditions were informed they were receiving tonic and half were informed they were receiving an alcoholic beverage. A within-subject design was employed so that each participant served in each of the four different priming conditions: (a) given tonic, told tonic, (b) given alcohol, told tonic, (c) given tonic, told alcohol, (d) given alcohol, told alcohol.

Briefly, the results showed that alcohol had a priming effect upon severely dependent alcoholics regardless of whether they were informed it was alcohol or tonic. Expectancy had no effect upon their consummatory behaviour. Being told that they received alcohol increased the speed of consumption in the moderate alcoholics as compared to their being told they received tonic. A so-called expectancy effect was obtained with problem drinkers but not with alcoholics. Whether any such effect would be obtained if subjects were not required to rinse their mouths with an astringent wash is not known at present. Given the experimental conditions employed, there was a significant interaction between priming and the severity of dependence. These results contradict Cummings *et al.*'s (1980) sweeping statement concerning the importance of expectancy.

Stockwell *et al*. (1982) demonstrated that there is a fundamental difference between problem drinkers and alcoholics. Priming, loss of control, and craving characterize alcoholics but not problem drinkers. These behavioural effects are related to the past history of the frequency and severity of withdrawal symptoms and are therefore in accord with the classical conditioning theory suggested by Ludwig and his colleagues. Results obtained by Stockwell *et al*. (1982) support an interpretation of craving and loss of control as classically conditioned components of the withdrawal syndrome. Distinguishing between problem drinkers and alcoholics is therefore valid and valuable, theoretically as well as practically for treatment purposes. Results obtained by Stockwell *et al*. contradict the poorly specified cognitive notions of expectancy and the attempt by revisionists (e.g. Heather and Robertson, 1983; Marlatt, 1983) to introduce a treatment goal of moderate drinking for individuals addicted to alcohol. If moderate drinking is a viable treatment goal, then it is only for clearly defined problem drinkers who do not suffer loss of control, craving, or are subject to the effects of priming. Abstinence is the only viable treatment goal for alcoholics who may be independently defined on the basis of the frequency and severity of withdrawal symptoms and who are characterized by behavioural symptoms of loss of control and craving. The efficacy of a classical conditioning approach to the analysis of problem drinking and alcoholism is thus supported in striking fashion by the experimental literature. Vaguely specified expectancy interpretations are contradicted by the available experimental evidence, provided that *all* of that evidence is examined.

7 Conclusion

I wish to make myself clear on one point. Although I have criticized efforts at cognitive formulations, I believe these specific formulations warrant attack because they are contrived and poorly formulated, based upon loose metaphors, ignore pertinent embarrassing results, or are derived from folk psychology with no accompanying empirical principles.

Cognitive folk psychology is especially vacuous when it is applied to complex human behaviour outside of the laboratory, when it is used in an effort to explain complex social and clinical phenomenon. Cognitive concepts are especially vacuous under such circumstances, because the phenomena are so apparently complex. Clinical and field data do not have the constraints of clearly defined laboratory experimental variables and relatively standardized experimental procedures that may serve to delimit the meaning of the concepts employed.

There is no logical reason why behaviouristic cognitive psychology cannot be effective. But in the field of classical conditioning with its long history of biobehavioural research, unfortunately ignored all too often by many investigators in the field of human conditioning, a cognitive 'theory' is arcane.

The most exciting and fundamental relevant developments are occurring in the neurosciences overlapping with psychology. Investigators of human conditioning should be seeking points of contact with these developments, not with computer metaphors or folk psychology. It is revealing that neuroscientists are studying classical conditioning at the level of the cell or even the level of molecular biology, whereas psychology persists in constructing fanciful metaphors relating to research already at hand that was produced by a tradition of biobehavioral research and theory beginning with Pavlov.

References

Ader, R., and Cohen, N. (1981). Conditioned immunopharmacologic responses. In *Psychoneuroimmunology* (ed. R. Ader), pp. 281–319, Academic Press, New York.

Alford, G. S. (1980). Alcoholics Anonymous: An empirical study. *Addictive Behaviors*, **5**, 359–70.

Anokhin, P. K. (1974). *Biology and Neurophysiology of the Conditioned Reflex and its Role in Adaptive Behavior*. Pergamon, Oxford.

Asratyan, E. A. (1965). *Conditoned Reflex and Compensatory Mechanisms*. Pergamon Press, London.

Bandura, A. (1969). *Principles of Behavior Modification*. Holt, Rinehart, & Winston, New York.

Bechterev, V. M. (1933). *General Principles of Human Reflexology*, 4th edn. Jarrolds, London.

Beritoff, J. S. (1965). *Neural Mechanisms of Higher Vertebrate Behavior*. Little, Brown, & Company, Boston, Mass.

Bernstein, A. S., and Taylor, K. W. (1979). The interaction of stimulus information with potential stimulus significance in eliciting the skin conductance orienting response. In *The Orienting Reflex in Humans* (eds. H. D. Kimmel, E. H. van Olst, and J. F. Orlebeke), pp. 499–519, Erlbaum, New York.

Biferno, M. A., and Dawson, M. E. (1978). Elicitation of subjective uncertainty during vasomotor and electrodermal discrimination classical conditioning. *Psychophysiology*, **15**, 1–8.

Brandeis, R. C., and Lubow, R. E. (1975). Conditioning without awareness—again. *Bulletin of the Psychonomic Society*, **5**, 36–8.

Brentano, F. (1874/1973). *Psychology from an Empirical Standpoint*. Routledge & Kegan Paul, London.

Brewer, W. F. (1974). There is no convincing evidence for operant or classical conditioning in adult humans. In *Cognition and the Symbolic Processes* (eds. W. B. Weimer and D. S. Palmero), pp. 1–42, Wiley, New York.

Brown, C. H. (1937). The relation of magnitude of galvanic skin responses and resistance levels to the rate of learning. *Journal of Experimental Psychology*, **20**, 262–78.

Burstein, K. R., and Smith, B. D. (1972). The latency distribution of the skin conductance response as a function of the CS-UCS interval. *Psychophysiology*, **9**, 14–20.

Bykov, K. M. (ed.) (1958). *Text-book of Physiology*. Foreign Languages Publishing House, Moscow.

Cook, S. W., and Harris, R. E. (1937). The verbal conditioning of the galvanic skin reflex. *Journal of Experimental Psychology*, **21**, 202–10.

Cummings, C., Gordon, J. R., and Marlatt, G. A. (1980). Relapse: Prevention and prediction. In *The Addictive Behaviors* (ed. W. R. Miller), pp. 291–321, Pergamon Press, Oxford.

Dawson, M. E., and Schell, A. M. (1981). Electrodermal classical conditioning with potentially phobic CSs: Cognitive/autonomic dissociations? Paper presented at the meeting of the Society for Psychophysiological Research, Washington, D.C., October.

Deitz, S. (1982). Individual differences in electrodermal response conditioning and self-report of discomfort: A phobia analogue. *Physiological Psychology*, **10**, 239–45.

Dennet, D. C. (1978). *Brainstorms*. Bradford Brooks, Cambridge, Mass.

Eaglén, A., and Mackenzie, B. (1981). Partial reinforcement and extinction in vasomotor conditioning: A test of cognitive and two-factor theories. *Pavlovian Journal of Biological Science*, **16**, 108–17.

Eaglen, A., and Mackenzie, B. (1982). Overlearning and instructional control of extinction of vasomotor responding. *Behaviour Research and Therapy*, **20**, 41–8.

Edwards, G. (1985). A later follow-up of a classic case series: D. L. Davies's 1962 Report and its significance for the present. *Journal of Studies on Alcohol*, **46**, 181–90.

Edwards, G., and Gross, M. M. (1976). Alcohol dependence: provisional description of a clinical syndrome. *British Medical Journal*, **1**, 1058–61.

Gale, E. N., and Ax, A. F. (1968). Long term conditioning of orienting responses. *Psychophysiology*, **5**, 307–15.

Garcia, J., McGown, B. K., and Green, K. F. (1972). Biological constraints on conditioning. In *Classical Conditioning II: Current Research and Theory* (eds. A. H. Black and W. F. Prokasy), pp. 3–27, Appleton-Century-Crofts, New York.

Gorn, G. J. (1982). The effects of music in advertising on choice behavior: A classical conditioning approach. *Journal of Marketing*, **46**, 94–101.

Grings, W. W. (1965). Verbal-perceptual factors in the conditioning of autonomic responses. In *Classical Conditioning* (ed. W. F. Prokasy), pp. 71–89, Appleton-Century-Crofts, New York.

Grings, W. W., and Lockhart, R. A. (1966). Galvanic skin response during avoidance learning. *Psychophysiology*, **3**, 29–34.

Guthrie, E. R. (1935). *The Psychology of Learning*. Harper, New York.

Heather, N., and Robertson, I. (1983). *Controlled Drinking*. Methuen, London.

Helzer, J. E., Robins, L. N., Taylor, J. R., Carey, K., Miller, R. H., Combs-Orme, T., and Farmer, A. (1985). The extent of long-term moderate drinking among alcoholics discharged from medical and psychiatric treatment facilities. *New England Journal of Medicine*, **312**, 1678–82.

Hodgson, R., Rankin, H., and Stockwell, T. (1979). Alcohol dependence and the priming effect. *Behaviour Research and Therapy*, **17**, 379–87.

Hull, C. L. (1943). *Principles of Behavior*. Appleton-Century, New York.

Institute of Medicine (1980). *Alcoholism, Alcohol Abuse, and Related Problems: Opportunities for Research*. National Academy Press, Washington, D.C.

Jellinek, E. M. (1960). *The Disease Concept of Alcoholism*. Hillhouse Press, New Brunswick, N.J.

Konorski, J. (1967). *Integrative Activity of the Brain*. University of Chicago Press, Chicago.

Lashley, K. S. (1923). The behavioristic interpretation of consciousness. *Psychological Review*, **30**, 237–72 and 329–53.

Lashley, K. S. (1951). The problem of serial order in behavior. In *Cerebral Mechanisms in Behavior* (ed. L. A. Jeffress), pp. 112–36, Wiley, New York.

Livanov, M. N. (1977). *Spatial Organization of Cerebral Processes*. Wiley, New York.

Lockhart, R. A. (1973). Cognitive processes and the multiple response phenomenon. *Psychophysiology*, **10**, 112–18.

Ludwig, A. M., and Stark, L. H. (1974). Alcohol craving: Subjective and situational aspects. *Quarterly Journal of Studies on Alcohol*, **35**, 899–905.

Ludwig, A. M., and Wikler, A. (1974). 'Craving' and relapse to drink. *Quarterly Journal of Studies on Alcohol*, **35**, 108–30.

Ludwig, A. M., Wikler, A., and Stark, L. H. (1974). The first drink: psychobiological aspects of craving. *Archives of General Psychiatry*, **30**, 539–47.

McNally, R. J. (1981). Phobias and preparedness: Instructional reversal of electrodermal conditioning to fear-relevant stimuli. *Psychological Reports*, **48**, 175–80.

Malcolm, N. (1964). Behaviorism as a philosophy of psychology. In *Behaviorism and Phenomenology* (ed. T. W. Wann), pp. 141–62, University of Chicago Press, Chicago.

Maltzman, I. (1955). Thinking from a behavioristic point of view. *Psychological Review*, **62**, 275–86.

Maltzman, I. (1968). Theoretical conceptions of semantic conditioning and generalization. In *Verbal Behavior and General Behavior Theory* (eds. T. R. Dixon and D. L. Horton), pp. 291–339, Prentice-Hall, Englewood Cliffs, N.J.

Maltzman, I. (1971). The orienting reflex and thinking as determiners of conditioning and generalization to words. In *Essays in Neobehaviorism: A Memorial Volume to Kenneth W. Spence* (eds. H. H. Kendler and J. T. Spence), pp. 89–111, Appleton-Century-Crofts, New York.

Maltzman, I. (1975). Comments on conditioning and psychopathology. In *Experimental Approaches to Psychopathology* (eds. M. O. Kietzman, S. Sutton, and J. Zubin), pp. 325–44, Academic Press, New York.

Maltzman, I. (1977). Orienting in classical conditioning and generalization of the galvanic skin response to words: An overview. *Journal of Experimental Psychology: General*, **106**, 111–19.

Maltzman, I. (1979a). Orienting reflexes and classical conditioning in humans. In *The Orienting Reflex in Humans* (eds. H. D. Kimmel, E. H. van Olst, and J. F. Orlebeke), pp. 323–51, Erlbaum, New York.

Maltzman, I. (1979b). Orienting reflexes and significance: A reply to O'Gorman. *Psychophysiology*, **16**, 274–83.

Maltzman, I., and Boyle, G. (1984). Stimulus significance and bilateral SCRs to potentially phobic pictures. *Journal of Abnormal Psychology*, **93**, 41–6.

Maltzman, I., Gould, J., Barnett, O. J., Raskin, D. C., and Wolff, C. (1977). Classically conditioning components of the orienting reflex to words using an innocuous and noxious UCS under different CS-UCS intervals. *Journal of Experimental Psychology: General*, **106**, 185–212.

Maltzman, I., Gould, J., Pendery, M., and Wolff C. (1977). Semantic conditioning and generalization of the GSR orienting reflex with overt and covert activity. *Journal of Experimental Psychology: General*, **106**, 172–84.

Maltzman, I., Gould, J., Pendery, M., and Wolff, C. (1982). Task instructions as a determiner of the GSR index of the orienting reflex. *Physiological Psychology*, **10**, 235–8.

Maltzman, I., and Langdon, B. (1969). Semantic generalization of the GSR as a function of semantic distance or the orienting reflex. *Journal of Experimental Psychology*, **80**, 289–94.

Maltzman, I., Langdon, B., and Feeney, D. (1970). Semantic generalization without prior conditioning. *Journal of Experimental Psychology*, **83**, 73–5.

Maltzman, I., Langdon, B., Pendery, M., and Wolff, C. (1977). The GSR orienting reflex and semantic conditioning and generalization with different unconditioned stimuli. *Journal of Experimental Psychology: General*, **106**, 141–71.

Maltzman, I., and Mandell, M. P. (1968). The orienting reflex as a predictor of learning and performance. *Journal of Experimental Research in Personality*, **3**, 99–106.

Maltzman, I., and Raskin, D. C. (1965). Effects of individual differences in the orienting reflex on conditioning and complex processes. *Journal of Experimental Research and Personality*, **1**, 1–16.

Maltzman, I., and Raskin, D. C. (1979). Selective orienting and habituation of the GSR as a consequence of overt and covert activity. *Physiological Psychology*, **7**, 204–8.

Maltzman, I., Raskin, D. C., and Wolff, C. (1979). Latent inhibition of the GSR conditioned to words. *Physiological Psychology*, **7**, 193–203.

Maltzman, I., Vincent, C., and Wolff, C. (1982). Verbal conditioning, task instructions, and inhibition of the GSR measure of the orienting reflex. *Physiological Psychology*, **10**, 221–8.

Maltzman, I., Weissbluth, S., and Wolff, C. (1978). Habituation of orienting reflexes in repeated GSR semantic conditioning sessions. *Journal of Experimental Psychology: General*, **107**, 309–33.

Marlatt, G. A. (1979). Alcohol use and problem drinking: A cognitive-behavioral analysis. In *Cognitive-behavioral Interventions. Theory, Research, and Procedures* (eds. P. C. Kendall and S. D. Hollon), pp. 319–55, Academic Press, New York.

Marlatt, G. A. (1983). The controlled-drinking controversy: A commentary. *American Psychologist*, **38**, 1097–1110.

Marlatt, G. A., Demming, B., and Reid, J. B. (1973). Loss of control drinking in alcoholics. An experimental analogue. *Journal of Abnormal Psychology*, **81**, 233–41.

Marlatt, G. A., and Nathan, P. E. (eds.) (1978). *Behavioral Approaches to Alcohol*. Rutgers Center of Alcohol Studies, New Brunswick, N.J.

Martin, D. G., Stambrook, M., Tataryn, D. J., and Beihl, H. (1984). Conditioning in the unattended left ear. *International Journal of Neuroscience*, **23**, 95–102.

Miller, P. M. (1976). *Behavioural Treatment of Alcoholism*. Pergamon, Oxford.

Mowrer, O. H. (1938). Preparatory set (expectancy)—a determinant in motivation and learning. *Psychological Review*, **45**, 62–91.

Mowrer, O. H. (1939). A stimulus–response analysis of anxiety and its role as a reinforcing agent. *Psychological Review*, **46**, 553–65.

Öhman, A. (1979). Fear relevance, autonomic conditioning, and phobias: A laboratory model. In *Trends in Behavior Therapy* (eds. P.-O. Sjoden, S. Bates, and W. S. Dockens, III), pp. 107–33, Academic Press, New York.

Öhman, A. (1983). The orienting response during Pavlovian conditioning. In *Orienting and Habituation* (ed. D. Siddle), pp. 315–69, Wiley, Chichester.

Orford, J., Oppenheimer, E., and Edwards, G. (1976). Abstinence or control: The outcome for excessive drinkers two years after consultation. *Behaviour Research and Therapy*, **14**, 409–18.

Pattison, E. M., Sobell, M. B., and Sobell, L. C. (eds.) (1977). *Emerging Concepts of Alcohol Dependence*. Springer, New York.

Peele, S. (1984). The cultural context of psychological approaches to alcoholism. *American Psychologist*, **39**, 1337–51.

Pendery, M., and Maltzman, I. (1977). Instructions and the orienting reflex in 'semantic conditioning' of the galvanic skin response in an innocuous situation. *Journal of Experimental Psychology: General*, **106**, 120–40.

Pendery, M. L., Maltzman, I. M., and West, L. J. (1982). Controlled drinking by alcoholics? New findings and a reevaluation of a major affirmative study. *Science*, **217**, 169–75.

Prokasy, W. F., and Ebel, H. C. (1967). Three components of the classically conditioned GSR in human subjects. *Journal of Experimental Psychology*, **73**, 247–56.

Rankin, H., Hodgson, R., and Stockwell, T. (1979). The concept of craving and its measurement. *Behaviour Research and Therapy*, **17**, 389–96.

Razran, G. (1949). Attitudinal determinants of conditioning and of generalization of conditioning. *Journal of Experimental Psychology*, **39**, 820–9.

Razran, G. (1961). The observable unconscious and the inferable conscious in current Soviet psychophysiology: Interoceptive conditioning, semantic conditioning, and the orienting reflex. *Psychological Review*, **68**, 81–147.

Razran, G. (1971). *Mind in Evolution*. Houghton Mifflin, Boston, Mass.

Reichenbach, H. (1938). *Experience and Prediction*. University of Chicago Press, Chicago.

Royce, J. E. (1981). *Alcohol Problems and Alcoholism*. The Free Press, New York.

Rusinov, V. S. (1970). *Electrophysiology of the Central Nervous System*. Plenum, New York.

Schweiger, A., and Maltzman, I. (1985). Behavioural and electrodermal measures of lateralization for music perception in musicians and nonmusicians. *Biological Psychology*, **20**, 125–45.

Siddle, D. A. T., and Spinks, J. A. (1979). Orienting response and information-processing: Some theoretical and empirical problems. In *The Orienting Reflex in Humans* (eds. H. D. Kimmel, E. H. van Olst, and J. F. Orlebeke), pp. 473–97, Erlbaum, New York.

Sokolov, E. N. (1960). Neuronal models and the orienting reflex. In *The Central Nervous System and Behavior* (3rd conference) (ed. M. A. B. Brazier), pp. 187–276, Josiah Macy, Jr Foundation, New York.

Sokolov, E. N. (1963a). Higher nervous functions: The orienting reflex. *Annual Review of Physiology*, **25**, 545–80.

Sokolov, E. N. (1963b). *Perception and the Conditioned Reflex*. Macmillan, New York.

Sokolov, E. N. (1969). The modeling properties of the nervous system. In *Handbook of Contemporary Soviet Psychology* (eds. M. Cole and I. Maltzman), pp. 671–704, Basic Books, New York.

Spence, K. W. (1956). *Behavior Theory and Conditioning*. Yale University Press, New Haven, Conn.

Stern, J. A. (1972). Physiological response measures during classical conditioning. In *Handbook of Psychophysiology* (eds. N. S. Greenfield and R. A. Sternbach), pp. 197–228, Holt, Rinehart, & Winston, New York.

Stich, S. (1983). *From Folk Psychology to Cognitive Science*. MIT Press, Cambridge, Mass.

Stockwell, T., Hodgson, R., Edwards, G., Taylor, C., and Rankin, H. (1979). The development of a questionnaire to measure severity of alcohol dependence. *British Journal of Addictions*, **74**, 79–87.

Stockwell, T. R., Hodgson, R. J., Rankin, H. J., and Taylor, C. (1982). Alcohol dependence, beliefs, and the priming effect. *Behaviour Research and Therapy*, **20**, 513–22.

Tolman, E. C. (1925a/1951). Behaviorism and purpose. In *Collected Papers in Psychology*. pp. 32–37, University of California Press, Berkeley.

Tolman, E. C. (1925b/1951). Purpose and cognition: The determiners of animal learning. In *Collected Papers in Psychology*. pp. 38–47, University of California Press, Berkeley.

Tolman, E. C. (1932). Purposive behavior in animals and men. Appleton-Century-Crofts, New York.

Tranel, D., and Damasio, A. R. (1985). Knowledge without awareness: An autonomic index of facial recognition by prosopagnosics. *Science*, **228**, 1453–4.

Watson, J. B. (1913). Psychology as the behaviorist views it. *Psychological Review*, **20**, 158–77.

Watson, J. B. (1930). *Behaviorism*. Norton, New York.

Wikler, A. (1980). *Opioid Dependence*. Plenum, New York.

Wikler, A., Pescor, F. T., Fraser, H. F., and Isbell, H. (1956). Electroencephalographic changes associated with chronic alcoholic intoxication and the alcohol abstinence syndrome. *American Journal of Psychiatry*, **113**, 106–14.

Wingard, J. A., and Matlzman, I. (1980). Interest as a predeterminer of the GSR index of the orienting reflex. *Acta Psychologica*, **46**, 153–60.

Cognitive Processes and Pavlovian Conditioning in Humans
Edited by G. Davey

Chapter 9

The interaction of neurohormones with Pavlovian A and Pavlovian B conditioning in the causation of neurosis, extinction, and incubation of anxiety

H. J. Eysenck and **M. J. Kelley**
Institute of Psychiatry, University of London

1 Watson's theory of neurosis and its critics

Watson and Rayner (1920) pioneered a theoretical account of the origins and treatment of neurosis in terms of Pavlovian conditioning and extinction, and Mary Cover Jones (1924) demonstrated the practical usefulness of the theory in her treatment of a number of childhood neuroses. In spite of the very incidental way in which Watson presented his theory (more or less as an appendage to the case of 'little Albert'), and the relative ignorance at the time of the principles of conditioning (Pavlov's book had not yet been translated into English), the theory has been very influential in the development of modern behaviour therapy. While there are many criticisms of the theory as originally stated, deriving both from clinical and experimental observations, it is possible to reformulate the theory to bring it into line with modern developments in learning theory and the neurobiology of anxiety. Eysenck (1979) proposed one possibility. We will expand upon it here.

Major theoretical developments have occurred since the days of Watson. For instance, there is now a greater recognition of the biology of individual differences in behaviour and that such differences are critical to the construction of theories. In the model of neuroses proposed here, genetic and neuroendocrine factors will be considered. A second development is that learning theory has changed. The 'principles' by which associations are formed and modified have never been laid down in any final form (except maybe in the minds of critics of behaviour therapy) but are in a state of conceptual evolution based upon ongoing experimental investigation. For example, there is now greater recognition that strong excitatory associations are readily formed between only certain combinations of cues and consequences. This selective associability or 'preparedness' is not reducible to the UCS and CS having characteristics in common (Kelly, in press, a; Mackintosh, 1984), and applies also to humans (Seligman, 1971; Öhman, 1980) and to conditioned inhibitory associations as well (LoLordo and Jacobs, 1983). The second development is that general principles of conditioning may interact with the particular motivational systems involved and with individual differences. In this regard, we will here initially focus on differences between Pavlovian A and Pavlovian B conditioning (Grant, 1964) and then show how the importance of this distinction can be combined with propositions about individual differences in the neurohormones which modulate anxiety. It will be argued that neuroses develop as an interaction of two *permissive* factors, conditioning and neurohormones, both of which are necessary for the development of neurotic disorders. To elucidate this we will primarily consider phobias, and only briefly comment upon other possible applications of this model.

As Eysenck has pointed out (Eysenck, 1982a), there are three problems with Watson's theory which require recourse to genetic and 'preparedness' factors, i.e. the notion that some stimulus or response events are more easily conditioned than others. In the first place, Watson's experiment with little Albert has been found difficult to replicate. In the second place, phobias tend to be very restricted in the range of stimuli which call them forth—open spaces, small animals, closed spaces, etc.; this provides external validity for the importance of selective associability (Arrindell *et al*., 1984). Finally, associative conditioning usually requires very precise CS-UCS timing; this is not likely to happen in everyday life situations which might generate neurotic conflicts. Theories invoking genetic factors and associative 'preparedness' can explain these anomalies. Watson and Rayner used rats as a CS, which may be regarded as a 'prepared' stimulus, but those who tried to replicate his work used wooden ducks and other non-prepared stimuli. The precise timing of CS-UCS relations can be considerably degraded with 'prepared' stimuli; e.g. in rats long periods of time may elapse between CS and UCS presentation in the acquisition of taste aversions (Garcia, McGowan, and Green, 1971). Finally, the preparedness of responses and CSs in conditioning can most readily be explained in genetic terms (Glickman and Morrison, 1969; Krechevsky, 1933; Grossen and Kelley, 1972; Kelley, in press, b). There are good reasons to believe such factors also apply to primate phobias (Mineka *et al*., 1984) including those of humans, as we shall see presently.

Actually Watson and Rayner (1920) appeared to have been aware of the necessity of introducing genetic factors into their scheme when they said that 'such persistence of early conditioned responses may be found only in persons who are constitutionally inferior' (p. 14). We certainly now have considerable evidence from the work of Rose and Ditto (1983) and Torgersen (1979) that there is a strong genetic component in the causation of phobic fears, and that this genetic component is both general and specific, i.e. contributing to the appearance of all types of fears as well as predisposing an individual to develop a specific kind of fear. It should also be remembered that the personality variables of introversion and neuroticism are related to the easy development of anxiety and have been shown by twin, adoptive and familial studies to have a strong genetic component (Eaves and Eysenck, 1975, 1985; Eysenck, 1956; Eysenck and Prell, 1951). Specificity for a particular type of conditioned anxiety simply presents a lesser degree of genetic predisposition.

We must now turn to the possibility that answers to the second lot of criticisms, both experimental and clinical, which have been directed towards Watson's theorizing can be found by distinguishing between Pavlovian A and Pavlovian B conditioning. First of all, let us list briefly the difficulties with Watson's account of the origin of neurotic disorders. As Eysenck (1979, 1982a) has pointed out, Watson's theory (like Freud's) is based on the occurrence of a traumatic fear-producing event, constituting the UCS, which is followed by fear/pain responses which constitute the UCR. Neutral stimuli accidentally present at the time will become conditioned through contiguity, thus being made into CSs which from then on will evoke CRs similar in nature to the UCR, i.e. feelings of fear and pain. These CRs continue indefinitely, unless deconditioned along the lines discussed by Watson and Rayner, and exemplified in the work of Mary Cover Jones. What is wrong with this account?

The first problem is a clinical one. War neuroses often do begin with a traumatic event, such as the person in question being buried alive by an explosion, or coming in contact with death or mutilation of friends and colleagues. However, in civilian neuroses such events are very rare, and in the majority of cases the initiating event is not excessively traumatic, and does not produce an immediate, strong CR. Rather, there appears to be an insidious increase in the anxiety produced by the CS which may take years, or even decades, before a full-blown phobia becomes apparent, or a clinical state of anxiety is reached. This is the major clinical objection to the theory.

From an experimental point of view, a second objection is the simple one that on this account extinction should set in almost immediately, making impossible the development of any long-lasting neurosis. Whatever the CS may be, the subject is likely to encounter it quite frequently and without attending reinforcement. This should produce relatively quick extinction of the CR. Let us consider a person suffering from a cat phobia; he or she is likely to encounter cats in non-threatening situations quite frequently, and each such encounter should foster extinction. The phobia should thus quite soon disappear. The fact that this does not seem to happen is a powerful argument against Watson's theory.

A third point which is of importance is that in ordinary Pavlovian conditioning there is no way in which the CR could be stronger than the UCR. Yet if we look at clinical cases, as mentioned above, the initiating conditioning experience often leads to UCRs and CRs which are rather mild; it is only after the insidious development of the neurosis has taken place that the CRs become so strong as to constitute an actual mental illness. Hence in these quite typical cases of neuroses and phobias, the CR becomes much stronger than the original UCR; on ordinary Pavlovian principles this would seem to be impossible.

What these three objections have in common, of course, is a reference to the development of the CR over time, when the subject is exposed a number of times to the CS only, i.e. to the CS without simultaneous reinforcement. Classical conditioning theory would expect *extinction* under these conditions, but what happens in the case of the development of a neurotic illness seems to be the opposite, i.e. an *incrementation* of the CR. To explain this anomaly, Eysenck followed up Grant's (1964) suggestion that there was an important distinction between Pavlovian A and Pavlovian B conditioning, and proposed that the consequences of this distinction are important in regard to extinction.

2 Pavlovian A and Pavlovian B conditioning

Pavlovian A conditioning is exemplified by the textbook example of classical conditioning, i.e. salivation on the part of the dog to the sound of a bell which had been repeatedly presented shortly before food was given to the hungry dog. Of the many UCRs presented by the dog (approach to the food, ingestion, etc.), Pavlov chose only to measure one, namely buccal salivation. As Zener (1937) pointed out, it is noteworthy that the CR did not include approach to and attempts to feed upon the bell or other source of the CS. Any approach and reorientation movements were directed to the food source, showing that the CS does not substitute for the UCS, as S-R theorists have often stated. Pavlov maintained that the CS serves as a signal that the food is about to be presented, and this position is also taken by S-S theorists. This approach is now almost universally recognized as being more in line with the facts than the old-fashioned S-R approach (Mackintosh, 1984).

Pavlovian B conditioning is directly linked by Grant (1964) to the Watson and Rayner (1920) experiment, but as he points out, Pavlov has priority. A reference experiment for Pavlovian B conditioning could be that in which an animal is given repeated injections of morphine. The UCR in this case involves severe nausea, profuse secretion of saliva, vomiting, and then profound sleep. After repeated daily injections, Pavlov's dogs were found to show severe nausea and profuse secretion of saliva at the first touch of the experimenter (Pavlov, 1927, p. 35–6).

In what way does this paradigm differ from that for Pavlovian A conditioning? There are several differences. Some are more important from our point of view than others. First, in Pavlovian B conditioning, stimulation by the UCS is not contingent on the subject's instrumental acts. Buccal stimulation by the UCS requires ingestion, an instrumental act by the subject. There is no such dependence in the case of Pavlovian B conditioning. Secondly, in Pavlovian B conditioning there is little or no dependence on the motivational state of the organism. Pavlovian A conditioning is only possible when the subject is in a suitable state (e.g. hunger in the case of salivary conditioning in dogs). In the case of Pavlovian B conditioning the UCS provides the drive or motivation. Related to this, in Pavlovian B conditioning the UCS elicits the complete UCR, whereas in Pavlovian A conditioning the organism emits the UCR of approaching and ingesting the food. Finally, and most important, in Pavlovian B conditioning the CS appears to act as a partial substitute for the UCS; this, as we have seen, is not true of Pavlovian A conditioning. To express it in different terms, in Pavlovian A conditioning typically the CR and the UCR are different (salivation as opposed to approach to and ingestion of food). In Pavlovian B conditioning they are similar or identical (nausea, profuse secretion of saliva, etc.). As Grant (1964) points out, many components of the UCR in Pavlovian conditioning 'are readily seen as components of the CR which will be evoked by the preparations for the injection after repeated daily morphine injections' (p. 5). A great deal of interoceptive conditioning (Bykov, 1957; Razran, 1961) and autonomic conditioning (Kimble, 1961) appears to follow the Pavlovian B paradigm.

These differences between Pavlovian A and Pavlovian B conditioning can be used to argue that the consequences of CS-only presentations may be quite different in the two paradigms (Eysenck, 1976). In Pavlovian A conditioning, it is meaningful for both the subject and experimenter to talk about 'CS-only presentation' as the presentation of the CS which is not followed by the UCS. However, in Pavlovian B conditioning this is difficult to accomplish because the CR, which follows the CS, is for all purposes identical to the UCR! Consequently the phrase 'CS-only presentation' is meaningful for the experimenter, who controls the presentation of the UCS, but not for the subject, who experiences the CR as identical with the UCR. In Pavlovian B conditioning, if it be true that the CS-only condition is not necessarily fulfilled (as far as the subject of the experiment is concerned), then it would seem to follow that the ordinary laws of extinction might not always apply. Although the experimenter has arranged the contingencies in such a way that CS is not followed by UCS, under certain conditions (to be specified later) the CR itself might act as a reinforcement equivalent to the UCR, thus producing not extinction but an increment in the strength of the CR. This incrementation has been called *incubation* and has led to a revised conditioning theory of neurosis (Eysenck, 1968, 1976). Before discussing other theoretical details of this model, let us consider whether there are any experimental studies supporting this possibility. The concept of incubation certainly agrees with the observations of a gradual development of neurotic symptoms noted in the clinical literature, but experimental work would obviously be preferable as proof.

3 Incubation theory and neurosis

The best example showing the development of incubation is possibly the work of Napalkov (1963), who worked with dogs and used an increase in blood pressure (in millimetres) as his response measure. The UCS was a pistol shot fired behind the ear of the dog, and the CS was a touch of a feather on the dog's ear. Figure 9.1 shows the results of the experiment. The lower curve (marked UCS) shows habituation of the UCR when no CS was given. It will be seen that the original UCR is well below the traumatic level; increases in blood pressure of 50 millimetres occur quite frequently in the daily life of a dog. Note that the UCR quickly habituates; after 25 trials there is no more reaction on the part of the dog.

Note also how very different is the fate of the CR. Here only one pairing of CS-UCS is given (single-trial conditioning) and afterwards the dog is only

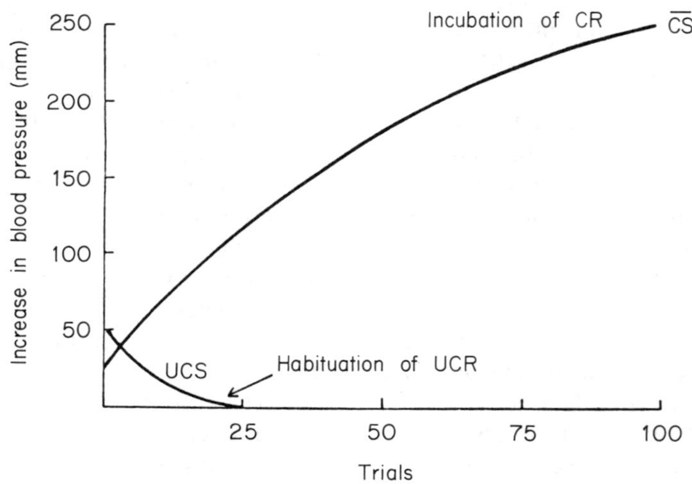

Figure 9.1 Incubation of CR and habituation of UCR. (*Eysenck, 1967*)

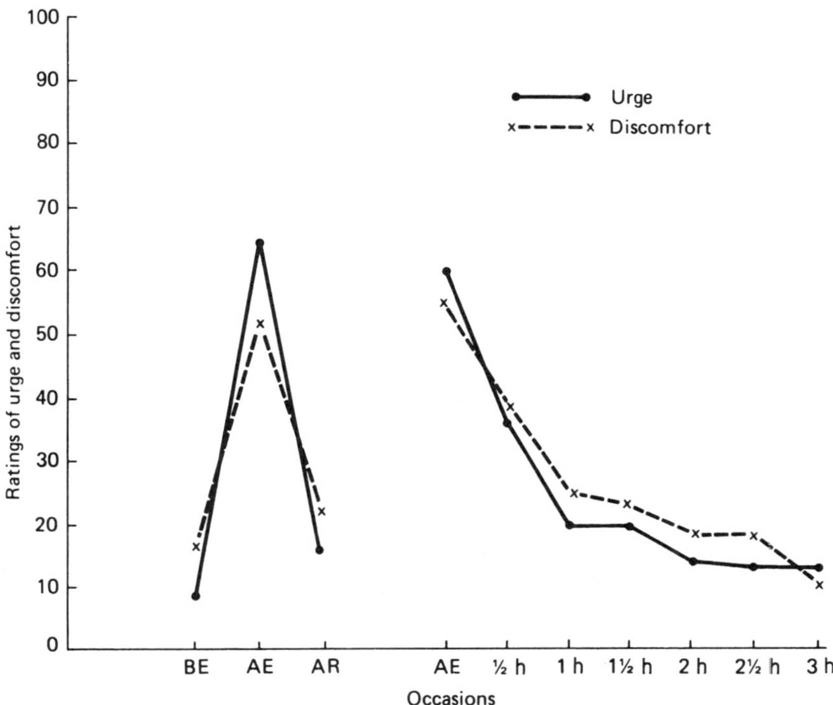

Figure 9.2 Urge of discomfort ratings before exposure (BE) and after exposure (AE) to dirt, and after cleaning ritual (AR). (*Rachman and Hodgson, 1980*)

exposed to the CS. What is found, as the figure shows, is a tremendous incrementation of the CR, rising to a mean increase in blood pressure of 250 millimetres after 100 trials—the opposite of extinction! Napalkov found that this increase was often *chronic*; in other words, the dogs retain the high blood pressure even without CS presentation. This may be a good analogue of psychosomatic disorders. This experiment exemplifies the mechanism outlined in our discussion of the origins of incubation. There are many other supportive studies in the animal literature, mostly using rats but also other types of animals. These have been discussed elsewhere (Eysenck, 1968, 1976, 1982b) and will not be reviewed again here. Instead, we will later on consider some of the literature relating neurohormones to the manifestions of extinction and incubation. Prior to doing this we must first consider other aspects of Pavlovian B conditioning which are critical to the model.

A critical variable determining whether extinction or incubation will occur is the duration of CS-only exposure. Data bearing upon this using human phobics have been collected in our laboratories by Rachman and Hodgson

(1980). The data consist of ratings of urge and discomfort for obsessive–compulsive patients using a hand-washing ritual to reduce their anxiety (similar data are available for physiological measures of anxiety). These patients were exposed to urns containing dirt and rubbish into which they were asked to dip their hands. On the left of Figure 9.2 we see ratings before exposure (BE), after their anxiety was increased by exposure to the dirt and rubbish (AE), and after they were allowed to reduce their anxiety by engaging in the hand-washing ritual (AR). On the right of the graph we see again the high degree of anxiety after exposure, but this time subjects were not allowed to wash their hands. This exposure to the CS over a period of 3 hours produced exactly the kind of curve, mirroring the reduction of anxiety over time, which is shown in Figure 9.3. Thus *protracted* exposure to the feared object without reinforcement leads to extinction even in Pavlovian B conditioning paradigms.

This outcome is highly dependent upon the duration of CS-only exposure. At the clinical level, this is well illustrated by the research of Rachman (1966) on spider phobics. In contrast to the above study by Rachman and Hodgson (1980), where the length of CS exposure was 1–3 hours, these patients were exposed to the phobic stimulus (spiders crawling about on a table top) for only 2 minutes. With this duration of CS-only exposure, not only did therapeutic extinction not occur, but some of the subjects in fact got worse, i.e. their fears increased in strength (incubation).

This interaction between duration of CS-only exposure and change in the strength of the CR is represented in Figure 9.3; however, it should be carefully noted that the incrementation in the strength of the CR with a short duration CS is expected to occur only in certain individuals. In this regard Morley (1977) has found that incubation occurs in Maudsley emotionally reactive but not in the Maudsley non-reactive strain of rats, and Eysenck (1979, 1982b) has suggested that incubation effects are more likely to occur in individuals high on neuroticism and introversion. The basis of this relationship is discussed in more detail by Eysenck and Eysenck (1985).

This dimension of CS-only duration, which is a critical variable determining whether incubation will occur, is not fixed but varies with the strength of the CR. The interaction between these two factors is depicted in Figure 9.3. Curve A illustrates the declining strength of the CV with long-continued exposure to the CS-only. Data substantiating the shape of this curve have been published from animal laboratories under conditions of flooding with response prevention, i.e. exposure to the anxiety-producing CS by making it impossible for the animal to escape from the testing chamber (e.g. Solomon and Wynne, 1953; Solomon, Kamin, and Wynne, 1953). There is a critical point on the graph of curve A. If the strength of the CR is *above* that point at cessation of exposure (critical strength), then *incubation* will ensue. If it is *below* the critical point, *extinction* will ensue. This clearly makes *duration of*

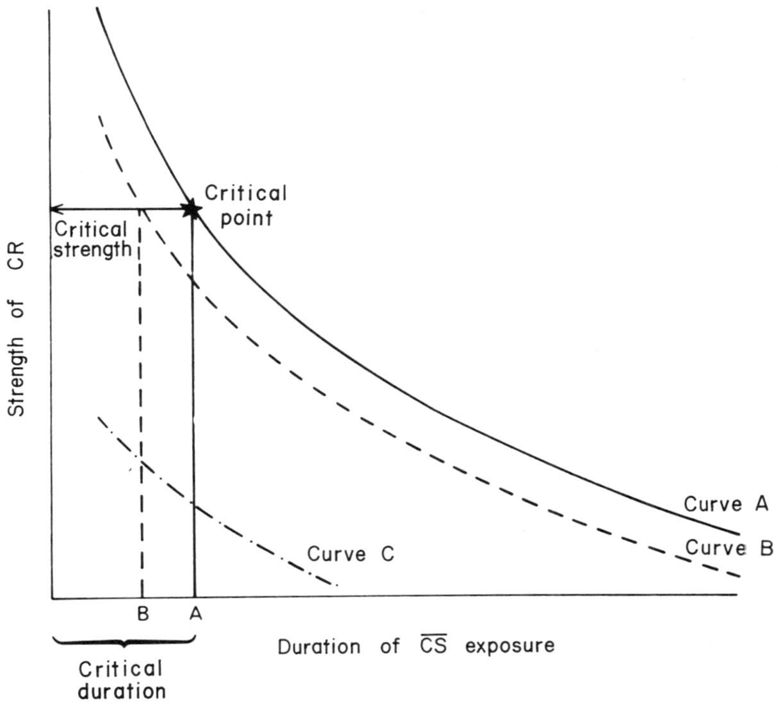

Figure 9.3 Incubation of anxiety as a function of duration of CS-only exposure. (*Eysenck, 1968*)

CS exposure a crucial element; Short-term duration, particularly when the Cr is rather strong, will lead to incubation, long-term duration to extinction. Curve B suggests what would happen once the patients had extinguished part of their anxiety through exposure to 'flooding with response prevention', and have gone to the bottom of curve A; the effect of this extinction is shown by displacement of the curve downwards, to the position of curve B. Several such repetitions of the extinction process would lead to curve C, and eventually to complete extinction. The method of therapy often called 'desensitization' would start with exposing the patient to anxiety-producing stimuli where the strength of the CR is well below the critical point, as in curve C, and would continue to go up the hierarchy of CSs, taking care that the critical point was never reached. The important point to pick up from Figure 9.3 is that to reach the critical point for incubation to occur a shorter duration of CS-only exposure is required for curve B than for curve A.

Shortly we will turn to recent research which suggests that we may soon be able to identify some of the physiological factors which mediate these individual differences, but first it should be pointed out that the theory, as so far presented, already makes testable clinical predictions; for instance, why desensitization or flooding with response prevention will sometimes have good and sometimes bad consequences (Eysenck, 1978a). Wolpe (1958) described how, when in the process of desensitization, the therapist makes a mistake and exposes the patient to too-strong UCSs leading to too-strong UCRs, this affects the treatment very badly; he recommends the therapist to stop treatment immediately, to go back to relaxation and then to use lower-level stimuli. In spite of this it has often been reported that when such a mistake occurs and the therapist responds as recommended, the patient nevertheless often gets much worse. This is precisely what would be predicted; the critical duration of CS-only exposure is too short to produce extinction, and hence incubation results. The obvious suggestion, therefore, is that when such an error is made, the therapist should immediately cease to use desensitization and switch over to flooding with response prevention. The present theory predicts that such a course would obviate the evil consequences of error. Such testable clinical predictions would seem to be crucial to the evaluation of the theory (Eysenck, 1978a).

4 The generality of the conditioning theory of neurosis

This theory, it is suggested, is in good accord with both clinical and experimental data, and would constitute a unified theory of neurosis, psychotherapy, behaviour therapy, and spontaneous remission (Eysenck, 1980). What are the main facts that require to be accounted for? In the first place, it seems clear from the meta-analysis carried out by Prioleau, Murdock, and Brody (1983) that psychotherapy is not superior in its effects to placebo treatment. In the second place, it seems clear that behaviour therapy does have significantly better effects than psychotherapy, particularly with more severe cases of neurosis (Kazdin and Wilson, 1978; Rachman and Wilson, 1980). In the third place, it seems that psychoanalysis frequently produces negative effects, i.e. it makes patients worse (Strupp, Handley, and Gomes-Schwartz, 1977). In the fourth place, it seems clear that spontaneous remission is a very powerful factor, consistently demonstrating effects strikingly rivalling the effect of psychotherapy and psychoanalysis (Rachman and Wilson, 1980). How does our theory succeed in accounting for these varied results?

Our theory states that the treatment of neurotic disorders is dependent entirely on Pavlovian extinction, which can be produced in a variety of ways (desensitization, modelling, flooding with response prevention, etc.). The only treatment to use the method consistently and to its best advantage is behaviour therapy; this would seem to account for the superiority of behaviour therapy as far as effectiveness is concerned. The different varieties of psychotherapy and psychoanalysis implicitly make use of methods rather similar to desensitization, i.e. the use of imagery and speech to produce CS-only representions of feared objects, in an atmosphere that is relaxed and friendly, and usually going on from less feared to more feared topics. They should be less successful than behaviour therapy because the use of the method is only implicit, and frequent errors are made. Much the same may be said of spontaneous remission; patients discuss their problems with friends, priests, teachers, relatives, etc., in a relaxed and friendly atmosphere, and this will be predicted to have similar effects to doing so in the presence of psychotherapists.

Why is it that psychoanalysis in particular often seems to have negative effects on patients? The answer may lie in the general lowering of anxiety and other CRs which can be produced by relaxation, empathy, friendliness, and warmth in the therapist (Truax, 1963; Truax, Frank, and Imber, 1966). Traditional psychoanalysts exhibit exactly the opposite tendencies, i.e. they are remote, non-supportive, intent on interpretation rather than on advice and help. Under these conditions the anxiety (CR) of the patient can be increased disastrously, raising it well above the critical point, and thus leading to incubation rather than to extinction. Descriptively there is ample evidence for this hypothesis in the accounts given by former patients (Sutherland, 1976; York, 1966). Thus it would appear that all the relevant phenomena can be accounted for successfully by this revamped conditioning theory of neurosis.

Zillmann (1984) has provided theoretical and experimental support for the hypothesis of additivity of therapist-produced anxiety and symptoms-related CR anxiety in his excitation-transfer paradigm, which is a development of his three-factor theory of emotion, and its dispositional, excitatory, and experiential components. This paradigm, according to Zillmann, applies to potentially unrelated successive emotional reactions and to emotional reactions elicited by simultaneously present, yet potentially unrelated, stimuli. 'In the former case, the paradigm projects the intensification of any emotional reaction that is evoked during the presence of residual sympathetic excitation from antecedent reactions; in the latter, it projects the intensification of any emotional reactions by sympathetic excitation due to stimuli other than those that elicited the emotional reaction proper' (p. 147). As Zillmann puts it: 'The paradigm is applicable to all emotional reactions associated with sympathetic dominance in their excitatory component' (p. 148). Thus the paradigm would seem to apply to therapist-produced anxiety adding to symptom-related CR anxiety.

Cognitive theorists have often criticized conditioning theories on the ground that cognitive factors are neglected, that they are seriously oversimplistic, and that important elements are missing. Most of these objections result from a misunderstanding of the nature of modern learning theory (Mackintosh, 1984), which is much more in line with S-S than with S-R types of theory, and which incorporates 'representations' of stimuli in its account. The first writer has dealt with this issue at some length elsewhere (Eysenck, 1978; in press). Criticisms of the Watsonian model are not appropriate to the revised model here presented, which includes such extinction methods as modelling, and also incorporates observational methods of conditioning (Mineka *et al*., 1984).

In addition to direct conditioning and vicarious acquisition, i.e. observing a fearful model, Rachman (1977) recognizes acquisition of fear by transmission of information. This model, too, can be recognized as a mode of conditioning when it is recalled that Pavlov insisted on the importance of the second signalling system and maintained that words can be conditioned stimuli as well as conditioned responses. The empirical literature certainly recognizes that while direct conditioning plays a major part in the acquisition of phobic fears and anxieties, observational acquisition of fears, and transmission of information, also play minor parts (Kleinknecht, 1982; Lautsch, 1971; Liddell and Lyons, 1978; Murray and Foote, 1979; Ost and Hugdahl, 1981, 1983, 1985; Rimm *et al*., 1977; Wolpe, 1981). In all these cases genetic factors, of course, play a strong predisposing role (Oauls *et al*., 1980).

It was one of the unfortunate consequences of Watson's original advocacy of methodological behaviourism that some of his personal beliefs, strictly irrelevant to the logic of his scientific system, became widely accepted by behaviourists. These beliefs included a strong environmentalism, the dislike of personality and individual difference factors, and the neglect of physiological and biochemical variables as determinants of behaviour. The change from methodological to radical and dialectical behaviourism (Davey, 1983) did little to change these irrational and irrelevant associations. The present emphasis on genetic, personality, and neurobiological factors may seem to some to contradict the tenets of behaviourism, but this is not so. As long as these variables can be shown experimentally to be determinants of human conduct or animal behaviour, there can be no a priori reasons for rejecting them.

5 The neurobiology of incubation: ACTH and the opioids

The remainder of this chapter will focus upon the thesis that neurosis is an outcome of individual differences in levels of neurohormones and the occurrence of conditioning. We will suggest that these two elements of this equation must both be present for the development of neurotic behaviour. This hypothesis largely stems from 35 years of animal research which has shown that neurohormones can have a profound modulating influence on resistance to extinction; hence the straightforward theoretical question is whether individual differences in these hormones mediate the persistence characteristic of disorders such as phobias and the absence of persistence typical of depression. It will be seen that considerable experimental and clinical work with humans is consistent with this possibility. In the framework of the incubation concept, it will be argued that individual differences in levels of hormones allow the fearful CS to dramatically increase in excitatory strength, or to decrease, depending upon the hormones *and* duration of CS exposure. We will review the literature which shows that hormonal mediation of incubation is a reliable phenomenon. At the level of psychological processes, we will suggest that incubation occurs by hormones influencing mechanisms of attention so as to produce changes in CS associability or in the absolute capacity of a CS to have inhibitory or excitatory strength. At the level of psychological treatment of neuroses, this model predicts that an intervention strategy involving both hormones *and* conditioning may have more impact than manipulation of only one of these factors.

As considerable genetic evidence suggests that predispositions to neuroses are largely inherited, it is to be expected that further advances in understanding the process of incubation will come from an understanding of individual differences in neurobiological factors such as neurohormones (Eaves and Eysenck, 1987). Apart from peripheral endocrine functions, hormones are present in the central nervous system (CNS) and affect emotions by the modulation of activity in the limbic system. It is established that at least patients with panic attacks have limbic abnormalities (Reiman *et al*., 1984) and that the behavioural effects of hormones are dependent upon the integrity of limbic structures (Wimersma Greidanus *et al*., 1983; Wied and Jolles, 1982). In addition, hormone-induced changes in hippocampal theta occur which show some correspondence with anxiety-related behavioural outcomes (Urban, 1984; Gray, 1982; Urban and Wied, 1978). This modulation of limbic activity is a balanced outcome of many hormones.

There is evolutionary, anatomical, cellular, and physiological evidence that hormones have preceded, and are of at least equal importance to, the better studied neurotransmitters (Le Roith *et al*., 1982; Krieger, 1983; Iversen, 1984). In contrast to theoretical models of anxiety which are based largely upon pharmacological effects of benzodiazapines, the neurohormonal hypothesis has many putative ligands which are naturally released during stress. This neurohormonal approach to anxiety is developed in more detail elsewhere (Kelley, in preparation), but even the sketch supplied here can more adequately explain anxiety than an account which relies solely upon traditional neurotransmitters; moreover, because it is based upon the development and causation of anxiety, as it naturally occurs, it will perhaps lead to better psychopharmacological approaches for enhancing the effect of behaviour therapy. This is not to say that the effects of neurohormones are always independent of catecholamines (Dunn and Kramarcy, 1984; Carpenter and Gruen, 1982); moreover, some peptide hormones satisfy many of the requirements for themselves being called neurotransmitters (Buijs, 1983).

At this stage in the development of a conditioning-neurohormone model of neuroses, it is entirely unclear whether hormones originating from the peripheral endocrine glands, ectopic tumours, lymphocytes, or the gut should be assigned any less importance than those from the CNS. However, a distinction needs to be made between the control of peripheral circulating and intracerebral hormone levels: for instance, in the case of hormones such as vasopressin and oxytocin, the cell bodies which radiate to the posterior pituitary and those which radiate down to the brain stem (and affect CSF levels) are different and are not necessarily controlled by the same mechanisms. Nevertheless, much of what follows is based upon peripheral levels of hormones, but it is important to realize that circumventricular organs within the brain (which are outside of the blood–brain barrier) are 'sensors' of blood-borne hormones. In addition, steroid hormones readily pass the blood–brain barrier. This also appears to be true of at least some of the stable metabolic fragments of the peptide hormones with psychological properties.

As with our earlier discussion of Pavlovian B conditioning, it may be of advantage to begin at a place which gives some external validity to our approach. One of the bits of information which suggests that there may be a relationship between neurohormones and neurosis is that there are similarities in the symptoms of anxiety neuroses and withdrawal from opiate addiction (Redmond, 1981; Hall, 1979). This observation is consistent with the finding that there is a strong (0.67) negative correlation between levels of trait neuroticism and opioid peptides in the cerebrospinal fluid (Post *et al*., 1984). This correlation is even higher (−0.91) with a measure of state anxiety. From this relationship and the well-established relationship between analgesia and CNS opioids it is possible to argue that *low levels of opioids in the brains of neurotics may make them more susceptible to incubation effects*.

The well-documented analgesic properties of exogenous opiates have natural counterparts in the brain which play a similar role in response to stress. This endogenous opioid analgesia is subject to associative conditioning (Sherman *et al*., 1984; Fanselow, 1984; Terman *et al*., 1984). Intracerebral injections of beta-endorphin attenuate passive avoidance, and random shocks produce an endogenous release of endorphins of the same magnitude (Izquierdo *et al*., 1981, 1982). These effects are not dependent upon the use of electric shock; opioid analgesia also occurs in intraspecific aggressive encounters in rats and mice (Miczek *et al*., 1982, 1984; Fanselow and Sigmundi, 1982). A word of caution must be introduced, however, because the endogenous opioids are in fact a very diverse group of peptides where not only is the nomenclature just beginning to be agreed upon but the behavioural properties of pharmacological injections are in fact quite diverse (Kitchen, 1984; Wied and Jolles, 1982). Nevertheless, the above properties remain as one of principal functions of the endogenous opioids in the CNS (Tricklebank and Curzon, 1984; Bechara and Kooy, 1985).

These analgesic effects of opioids interact with another peptide hormone, adrenocorticotropin (ACTH). The opioids dampen neuronal excitation, cholinergic and norandrenergic turnover rates, and behavioural performance in aversive conditioning, but ACTH has the opposite effects (Bertolini and Gessa, 1981; Redmond and Huang, 1979; Redmond and Krystal, 1984; Charney and Redmond, 1983; Markely and Sze, 1984). In the ACTH-mediated incubation effects, which we will discuss in detail shortly, the opioids have a competitive affinity with ACTH for the same receptors. If we block these receptors with the opioid antagonist, naloxone, ACTH (and also vasopressin) loses its capacity to induce incubation effects or prolong extinction (Smock and Fields, 1981; Concannon et al., 1980a, 1980b; Vito and Brush, 1984). This reciprocal relationship between ACTH and the opioids, in conjunction with the negative correlation between CSF opioids and anxiety, suggests that ACTH may play an active role in the occurrence of incubation effects.

A tie between experimentally produced changes in emotionality (defecation) as a trait, and the capacity for stress-induced changes in ACTH levels, has been recently demonstrated by Armario *et al*. (1984). This observation can be combined with the findings of Morley (1977) who showed that emotional animals are more likely to show incubation effects. This is also consistent with the suggestion of Eysenck (1979, 1982b) that incubation effects are likely to be stronger in subjects high on neuroticism (N) and introversion (I). The reasons for this suggestion can be deduced from the nature of these two major personality dimensions, and need not be detailed here. We will now turn to direct experimental evidence that hormones such as ACTH can modulate incubation.

In a series of aversive conditioning studies by Riccio and his students, ACTH or epinephrine injections (which increases ACTH in the rat) were given to rats prior to a 1-minute presentation of the CS during a forced-exposure trial following acquisition training. This procedure repeatedly resulted in a large permanent increase in fear of the CS when animals were tested 24 hours later for resistance to extinction *without* an injection. Mere presentation of the CS or elevation of ACTH levels alone did not produce such effects (Haroutunian and Riccio, 1977, 1979). Kelley (in press, c) has provided an additional control. In this experiment rats were first given three 0.5 mA foot shocks during two direct placements in the black side of a shuttle-box with a closed guillotine door and never shocked during two placements on the white side. In the second phase, the different groups of rats were re-exposed to the black side and either given (a) a prior 0.02 mg injection of adrenaline (epinephrine) or (b) saline, or (c) epinephrine injection 5 hours later. The latency to cross from the white to the black side 24 hours later was found to be several-fold longer in the groups given an epinephrine injection shortly before re-exposure. The findings thus demonstrate that *contiguity* between the presence of the fear cue and high levels of hormones is required to produce incubation effects in the rat. The importance of this contiguity has also been demonstrated by other investigators (Rigter, Elbertse, and Riezen, 1975; Weinberger *et al*., 1984). While ACTH released by acute exogenous injections is one possible explanation of this, it is also possible that peripheral epinephrine itself is important (McGaugh, 1983; Borrell *et al*., 1983).

The capacity of ACTH to produce incubation effects is supported by an extensive body of evidence from many laboratories showing that ACTH will enhance resistance to extinction. This occurs with a variety of aversive conditioning procedures and with ACTH (4–10) which has CNS but no peripheral endocrine properties (Wied and Jolles, 1982). There is also evidence that physiological levels of ACTH can have modulatory effects on extinction (Endroczl *et al*., 1977; Wimersma Greidanus *et al*., 1977, 1983; Pagano and Lovely, 1972; Bohus *et al*., 1982). While these properties of ACTH have been observed in Pavlovian A conditioning, they are more readily observed with Pavlovian B conditioning. Consistent with this is the well-established observation that sexual behaviour is the other motivational system where ACTH has a robust effect (Bertolini and Gessa, 1981; Bertolini *et al*., 1984; Wied and Jolles, 1982). Eysenck (1982a) has suggested that sexual drives are the equivalent on the appetitive side to anxiety on the aversive side for the production of incubation effects.

These findings are consistent with other open-field research suggesting that injections of ACTH or its releasing factor (CRF) may be 'anxiogenic' in rats (Britton and Britton, 1981; Britton *et al*., 1982; File and Vellucci, 1978). Some support for this hypothesis also exists from studies on the effect of CRF in rhesus monkeys (Kalin *et al*., 1983a, 1983b); however, these 'anxiogenic' properties of CRF and ACTH are only seen in situations which are already fearful. For instance, in the study by Haroutunian and Riccio (1979) exposure to one side of a novel shuttle-box contiguous with an ACTH injection was not itself sufficient to produce later spatial avoidance of that side of the apparatus; thus it would appear that an ACTH injection is not, by itself, an aversive UCS. Considerable evidence suggests that the actions of ACTH are on the CS not the UCS or UCR. When ACTH levels are increased by adrenalectomy, the immediate behavioural responses to foot shock (flinch, jerk, vocalization) are not increased (Borrell *et al*., 1983). In addition, while reduced open-field ambulation is sometimes observed after adrenalectomy, this is not influenced by injections of dexamethasone which should reduce ACTH levels. Similarly, effects on exploratory behaviour are not reliably found after injections with ACTH (4–10) (Bohus *et al*., 1982). The open-field apparatus has been shown to be a potent releaser of fear (Blanchard *et al*., 1974) but that might be dependent upon the strain of rats which would account for some of the ambiguity in the open-field findings with ACTH. Finally, the results of experiments with humans also suggest that injections of CRF or ACTH are not themselves anxiogenic (Beckwith and Sandman, 1978, 1982; Gold *et al*., 1984b). In contrast, the anxiogenic properties of the ACTH in rats are readily observed when a CS for fear is present; then, as we have just seen, ACTH enhances the excitatory properties of the cue.

It is not understood how ACTH produces an increase in excitatory strength of cues. It has been suggested that these instances of incubation are best explained by memory retrieval mechanisms (Riccio and Concannon, 1981), but it should be pointed out that such an inference is unwarranted. In the context of Haroutunian and Riccio's incubation experiments, the retrieval hypothesis, as they outline it, requires that state-dependent learning occurs during the initial acquisition of the CR, i.e. the endogenous release of ACTH has become one of the CSs, which is then represented by the later exogenous injection given during the CS-only trial. The fallacy here is that state-dependent learning only occurs in the absence of more salient environment cues. In the above incubation experiments a salient spatial environmental cue was present. This relationship with environmental cues is also true of human state-dependent learning (Eich, 1980).

Another possible explanation is that incubation effects are mediated by selective attention: ACTH and other neuromodulators of anxiety may enhance the capacity of a CS to show an increment in the level of excitatory strength by influencing its associability. Unfortunately, the effects of ACTH and other peptides have not as yet been investigated upon 'blocking' and 'overshadowing' (Mackintosh, 1984) indices of selective attention in rats, thus direct evidence for this possibility awaits testing. Nevertheless, Beckwith and Sandman (1978, 1982) using reversal learning and intradimensional and extradimensional shift experiments have argued that ACTH influences selective attention. These older behavioural assays for selective attention, however, are subject to alternative interpretations (Sutherland and Mackintosh, 1971; Mackintosh, 1974). If hormones influence the occurrence of incubation effects by increasing the associability of the CS, then when associability *per se* is increased there should not only be an increased capacity for larger increments in excitatory strength but also an increased capacity for decrements in excitatory strength when the parametric conditions are favourable for extinction (long CS-only duration). Under these circumstances, ACTH should then facilitate extinction. While this theoretical deduction is seemingly contradicted by the findings of a large number of avoidance experiments in which ACTH increased resistance to extinction, the prediction in fact has not been tested. We will soon consider the actions of vasopressin on incubation, and then see that the deduction has some empirical support.

It is also possible that ACTH enhances the capacity for increments in the excitatory strength of the CS, not by affecting its associability, but by simply extending the upper limit of excitatory (or inhibitory) strength which the cue can potentially obtain. This possibility can be thought of as still 'attentional' but not specifically 'selective attention' or enhanced cue associability in the sense outlined by Mackintosh (1975, 1984). Pigache and Rigter (1981) have discussed this possibility. A third, and possibly more parsimonious possibility is that ACTH may only enhance the excitatory strength of the CR. By this mechanism the increase in CS excitatory strength after a CS-only trial in which ACTH levels are elevated may be a passive outcome of increased CR strength on the trial. These various theoretical alternatives are consistent with (a) the selective action of ACTH on the CR but not the UCR, (b) Napalkov's (1963) results showing a decline of the UCR while the CR increases (c) the ACTH extinction and incubation findings.

6 Vasopressin and cortisol

We will return to a further discussion of ACTH and the opioids, but first some other hormones need also to be considered which may play a role in human neurotic behaviour. We will review here some of the animal evidence that cortisol and vasopressin (AVP) are also involved in the mediation of extinction and incubation effects.

Like ACTH and the opioids, AVP has modulatory properties on neuronal activity in the limbic system and effects on resistance to extinction in aversive conditioning preparations. The large pharmacological doses of AVP used in earlier experiments may have produced enhanced resistance to extinction by inducing aversive states (Ettenburg *et al.*, 1983); however, more recent evidence argues that physiological changes in CNS levels of AVP can produce such changes (Laczi *et al.*, 1983a, 1983b, 1984; Wimersma Greidanus *et al.*, 1983; Kovács *et al.*, 1981; Weid *et al.*, 1984a, 1984b; Hamburger-Bar, Ebstein and Belmaker, 1984; Schulz *et al.*, 1974). Short-term motivational effects of AVP injected intracerebroventricularly into mice have been shown to occur with doses as low as one nanogram (Boakes *et al.*, 1985; Meisenburg, 1981; Meisenburg and Simmons, 1982). Recently an AVP-like peptide in the sympathetic nervous system has been identified, suggesting that many of the effects attributed to circulating AVP may be neurally evoked (Hanley *et al.*, 1984). Like ACTH, the effects of AVP on extinction can be found with peptide fragments of the natural parent compound, DG-AVP and DG-LVP for instance, which have CNS properties but are virtually devoid of tropic effects. Again like ACTH (4–10), these fragments have robust effects on sexual and fear motivational systems—the systems where Pavlovian B conditioning primarily operates (Bohus, 1977)—but little if any effect upon appetitively reinforced behaviour (Strupp *et al.*, 1984).

Using a three-stage experimental design similar to that used in the studies by Haroutunian and Riccio (1977, 1979), Krejci *et al.* (1983) found that some peptide fragments of arginine vasopressin (dD-AVP and DG-dDAVP) could produce incubation effects if the rats were injected prior to a 5-minute forced exposure trial with the previously established aversive CS. While the effect was not strong, this is consistent with the long cS duration they used. A finding which is of equal or greater theoretical interest is that with 10 minutes of exposure to the CS a highly reliable attenuation of the excitatory properties occurred, *the opposite of incubation*. This was also found with lysine vasopressin (LVP) and a fragment of arginine vasopressin (DG-AVP) which has virtually no peripheral endocrine properties in the body. Again, such an interaction is consistent with the importance of CS duration that we have stressed as critical to the occurrence of incubation. It is important to realize that most of the conditioning studies where vasopressin has been shown to increase extinction have used a short duration CS, and that considerable dispute has occurred in regard to the reliability of the extinction effect (Sahgal, 1984; Weid, 1984; Gash and Thomas, 1984). The experiments by Krejci *et al.* (1983) indicate that CS duration may account for some of this variation. Equally important, the experiments by Krejci *et al.* suggest that the selective attention hypothesis discussed earlier may be applicable to the effects of vasopressin, i.e. by changing the associability of the CS with hormones, and excitatory properties of the cue may then more readily increase or decrease, depending upon duration of CS exposure.

Many neurohormones reduce resistance to extinction. This appears to be true of some stable naturally biograded metabolities of AVP (Burback *et al.*, 1983a, 1983b), and of cortisol and corticosterone (in the rat). These latter steroids are produced by the adrenal cortex and readily pass across the blood–brain barrier to modulate extinction and produce anxiolytic effects (Bohus *et al.*, 1982; File, 1978; File *et al.*, 1979). Endroczi (1975) has reported a very high correlation (0.89) between an extinction measure (habituation) and uptake of corticosterone in the hippocampus, a primary receptor target for corticosterone. The importance of hippocampal corticosteroids for the success of forced-exposure therapy has been demonstrated. Bohus (1974) found, like many before him, that providing rats with extended forced exposure to fear cues will greatly attenuate the fear of those cues as measured on later extinction tests; however, if the level of ACTH was driven up by adrenalectomy prior to the exposure, the rats behaved as if they had no forced exposure. Supplying replacement corticosterone to the adrenalectomized animals prior to exposure resulted in extinction being normalized. This leaves open the question of whether the absence of corticosteroids or an increase in ACTH produced this effect. Both are outcomes of adrenalectomy. Further research with this experimental preparation by Bohus and Kloet (1981) has implicated the importance of corticosterone. Dexamethasone is a potent synthetic steroid which like corticosterone suppresses the release of

CRF from the hypothalamus and also ACTH and beta-endotrophin from the pituitary; however, unlike corticosterone it does not bind to receptors in the hippocampus. In contrast to corticosterone, replacement doses of dexamethasone did not normalize the extinction. Further evidence that corticosterone has a specific effect apart from its effects on ACTH comes from direct implants of this steroid in the limbic and mid-brain structures. This procedure does not suppress ACTH but produces similar effects on extinction to peripheral injections (Bohus, 1968, 1973).

7 Clinical consequences of the hormone—incubation theory

We have seen that individual differences in endogenous hormones affect extinction, and that experimental manipulation of hormone levels can mediate the occurrence of the incubation of anxiety in animals. Now we will turn to a further consideration of the clinical literature. While there is only a limited amount of human experimental research which directly bears upon our hypothesis, an abundant literature is consistent with our model.

The relationship between attention and hormones that we have seen in the animal literature also appears to occur in humans. Endroczi *et al*. (1970) and Miller *et al*. (1974) have shown that ACTH (4–10) will substantially retard EEG habituation. More recently, Timsit-Berthier *et al*. (1982, 1983) have reported similar results using EEG measures and AVP. Anderson *et al*. (1979) have shown that passive avoidance learning in Lesch-Nyhan patients is greatly improved after the administration of AVP. Miller *et al*. (1977) only found a weak effect of ACTH (4–10) on human avoidance conditioning but this result is probably due to a ceiling effect in the control group. Brunia and Boxtel (1978) found that ACTH (4–10) would enhance sympathetic arousal but only during a stressful task; and Breier *et al*. (1979) showed that these effects interact with the personality dimension of introversion–extraversion. This can also occur in natural disorders: an increase in attention occurs when ACTH levels are increased by congenital adrenal hyperplasia (Vieth *et al*., 1985). Gaillard (1981) has reviewed the human ACTH literature where attention, memory, and psychophysiological measures have been used and concluded that the peptide acts upon 'task-orientated motivation and sustained attention' (p. 194). Other groups have reached similar conclusions for ACTH and AVP-related peptides (Rockstroh *et al*., 1981, 1982, 1983; Fehm-Wolfsdorf *et al*., 1981; Pigache and Rigter, 1981; Strupp *et al*., 1984; Legros and Lancranjan, 1984; Born *et al*., 1984). As might be expected from our earlier discussion of the effects of hormones on incubation and extinction, cortisol has the opposite effect on psychophysiological measures of attention, and the involvement of the opioid receptors has been implicated (Arnsten *et al*., 1983, 1984; Kopell *et al*., 1970). While consistent, these psychological findings are not robust; however, based upon our earlier discussion of Pavlovian A and Pavlovian B conditioning, it might be expected that if emotionally 'prepared' stimuli were used, such as used by Öhman (1980) in his phobic analogue studies, very robust effects might occur.

The above effects with ACTH and AVP on humans are observed with large pharmacological doses. Recently we have found evidence that physiological levels of plasma AVP can have psychological consequences for humans. The amount of AVP released by smoking a single strong cigarette is inversely related to the self-report and signal-detection measures of difficulties in concentration when chronic smokers abstain from smoking for 24 hours. In view of the evidence that genetic factors are related to the occurrence of neuroticism, it is of some interest that, at least in the case of osmotic challenge with normal volunteers, the level of AVP is a stable, reproducible characteristic which is genetically determined (Gold *et al*., 1984a).

It is possible to raise many hypotheses concerning how differences in levels of neurohormones may provide the permissive circumstances for various conditioning factors to then become operational in the production of phobic fears and depression. For instance, the low persistence and cognitive state of depressives are certainly not caused by unpredictable or uncontrollable life events *per se*. Such factors may only be some important determinants of neuroses if the appropriate hormonal conditions are also present. Such possibilities are beginning to be systematically explored. Gold *et al*., (1984a) have produced evidence that changes in levels of AVP fluctuate with changes in depressive states, and that drugs which affect depression also affect levels of AVP. In the above study by Kelley *et al*., (1985), we also found a relationship between low AVP and depression. The smokers with low AVP were more neurotic, as measured by the Eysenck Personality Inventory, than those with high AVP levels and also rated themselves as more depressed on a withdrawal symptom inventory. As further evidence that the hormonal state may be only a *permissive* condition in the causation and treatment of psychological disorders, Gold *et al*. (1984a) found that supplying a replacement AVP peptide fragment (DD-AVP) only helped two out of seven depressed patients.

Other evidence can be cited which supports these relationships between conditioning, AVP levels, and neurotic disorders. Corson and O'Leary Corson (1983) have found that after aversive electro-cutaneous conditioning, the dogs which showed persistent poor adaptation (tachycardia, polypnea, profuse salivation, high energy metabolism, high urinary catecholamines) during re-exposure to the conditioning room also had very high levels of vasopressin in the urine they excreted. The development of learned helplessness in rats can be blocked by an intraventricular injection of antivasopressin serum (Leshner *et al*., 1978). Moreover, injections of ACTH or AVP can enhance experimentally induced defeat in mice (Roche and Leshner, 1979). The defeat here is created by having the mouse (or rat) be attacked in forced encounters with another mouse in the latter's territory (Blanchard *et al.*, 1975; Flannelly *et al.*, 1984). The opioid consequences of this defeat are conditionable, and the development of tolerance to this analgesia is enhanced by AVP and oxytocin (Miczek *et al.*, 1982; Miczek and Thompson, 1984; Ritzmann *et al.*, 1984).

Of course, AVP is not the only hormone which may be clinically important in the causation and treatment of neurosis. In view of the research showing that high levels of ACTH are necessary for the occurrence of incubation effects, it should come as no surprise that some older evidence (see Lader, 1980) suggests that anxious neurotics have a hyperactive adrenocortical system, which is suggestive of high levels of ACTH and its hypothalamic releasing factor (CRF). The evidence is, however, far from clear. Much of this earlier work is based upon plasma cortisol levels, which now can be reliably and unobtrusively assayed by saliva samples (Riad-Fahmy *et al.*, 1982); but the difficulty with cortisol as a marker of pituitary or hypothalamic activity is that it is only an indirect index of ACTH and CRF levels. As we shall see shortly, the ambiguity in the evidence regarding cortisol may be of considerable importance.

Curtis *et al.* (1976, 1978) have done some research which substantially bears upon our neuroendocrine-conditioning hypothesis of neurosis. They exposed patients to phobic stimuli for a few hours using conventional *in vivo* flooding therapy. A variety of subjective and objective measures indicated that the patients were intensely afraid during, but not before and after, the periods of exposure. What is of interest is that plasma cortisol levels did not increase during the flooding periods but actually dropped slightly. While the release of corticosteroids is very low in animals when exposed to a CS after mastering an avoidance task, this occurs because the avoidance response is available. The trauma of these phobics when given forced exposure with *no* escape possible is not the same; in fact, it is the very condition where one would expect extensive activation of the hypothalamic-pituitary-adrenal system!

These studies by Curtis *et al.* are subject to several interpretations. Recall that the work of Bohus and Kloet (1981) showed that hippocampal corticosterone is critical for extinction to occur during flooding. This finding can be combined with the evidence that stress causes a down regulation in these corticosteroid receptors in the hippocampus and amygdala (Sapolsky *et al.*, 1984), and that these corticosteroids are critical for the opioid form of stress-induced analgesia (MacLennan *et al.*, 1982). This may be particularly important given the negative correlation between CNS opioids and neuroticism (Post *et al.*, 1984).

There are other possible interpretations. Since elevations in cortisol serve a negative feedback function in the control of the continued release of CRF and

ACTH from the hypothalamus and pituitary (Jones *et al.*, 1982), one interpretation of the studies by Curtis is that levels of CRF or ACTH are possibly very elevated during exposure. The physiology of the adrenal glands is still not well understood, and an increasing amount of evidence suggests cortisol secretion is also determined by extra-pituitary mechanisms (Fehm *et al.*, 1984a, 1984b). As it has only been recently discovered that enkephalins are secreted by the adrenals under stress, their absence during 'flooding' may also be influencing the persistence of phobias (Hanbauer *et al.*, 1982; Plotnikoff *et al.*, 1976). Yet another possibility is that CRF levels are high in phobias but there is no increase in ACTH because of a desensitization of ACTH-secreting cells in the pituitary (Rivier and Vale, 1983). Vasopressin levels could be important here; not only does it interact with CRF to potentiate the stress-induced release of ACTH, but it also works synergistically with CRF to facilitate this desensitization of pituitary cells in the release of ACTH (Hoffman *et al.*, in preparation—cited by Axelrod and Reisine, 1984).

Gold *et al.* (1984b) have recently investigated the properties of CRF with volunteers and depressed patients. As with ACTH and AVP, they found no change in 'psychological state' after injections of CRF, but no one has investigated CRF in humans under anxiety-provoking circumstances. Their preliminary results with depressives suggest that the negative feedback mechanism by which cortisol reduces ACTH secretions is active in the subgroup of depressives showing less suppression of ACTH after dexamethasone, and that the hypercortisolism of this subpopulation of depressives is a function of high levels of CRF and an increase in ACTH. This has also been demonstrated by Holsboer *et al.* (1985). While the reduced suppression of cortisol levels after dexamethasone is thought to be more typical of endogenous depressions, there is evidence that both reactive and endogenous depressions are outcomes of natural conditioning (Finlay-Jones and Brown, 1981; Matussek and Wiegand, 1985; Dolan *et al.*, submitted).

CRF also dampens the appetite, thus it may be involved in the development of anorexia nervosa (Britton *et al.*, 1984; Morley and Levine, 1982). Another peptide, cholecystokinin (CCK), has also been implicated in anorexia nervosa (Shillar and Davison, 1984; Stacher *et al.*, 1979; Collins *et al.*, 1983), and in the development of tolerance to opioids (Ben-Horin *et al.*, 1984; Tang *et al.*, 1984; Watkins *et al.*, 1984). Gold *et al.* (1984c, in press) have shown that AVP levels are elevated and oxytocin levels are depressed in the cerebrospinal fluid of anorexic patients. Oxytocin, a sister neurohypophyseal hormone to AVP, has traditionally been thought only to affect lactation and parturition, but more recent evidence suggests it is also a stress hormone in females and that exogenous injections can modulate extinction (Williams *et al.*, 1985; Legros *et al.*, 1982, 1984; Lange *et al.*, 1983; Kovács *et al.*, 1978). Its release can be conditioned in female rats (Kelley, submitted, a). A naturally occurring metabolite of oxytocin is stable to further degradation and readily passes the blood–brain barrier (Hoffman *et al.*, 1977; Burbach *et al.*, 1983a; Griffiths and McDermott, 1984).

In summary, there is considerable direct and indirect evidence that individual differences in the balanced neurohormonal system affecting anxiety may provide the permissive basis by which the incubation process occurring with Pavlovian B conditioning may then operate to create neurotic behaviour. While behaviour therapy has made considerable advances independent of the medical profession and without taking individual differences into account, the hypothesis 'that differences in physiology are not important' is undoubtedly wrong. To change this statement into a constructive theory of just how neuroendocrine processes contribute to the causation of neuroses (and the varying success of exposure therapy) will require psychologists to work with clinical pharmacologists and physiologists in the testing of specific hypotheses. There is every reason to believe this will be a lively interdisciplinary area in the near future. In this regard the possibility exists that the administration of hormones, or synthetic fragments or competitive antagonists to natural hormones, may facilitate the extinction process during exposure therapy (Sawyer and Manning, 1985, 1984; River *et al.*, 1984). At the very least, the time is ripe to try some alternatives to the GABA hypothesis of anxiety and the benzodiazepines (Sartory, 1983).

This brings to an end our revision of Watson's theory of neurosis and its treatment. We have retained the fundamental notions introduced by Watson, namely that neurotic disorders are produced by Pavlovian conditioning and can be cured by Pavlovian extinction, but we have made many additions and alterations to the theory which bring it in line with recent experimental work. We have added elements such as the influence of genetic factors and associative 'preparedness', the influence of personality and individual differences, and the determination of extinction and incubation phenomena by neurohormones which did not form part of the original theory but which have been found to play an important part in the preservation of fear and anxiety. The theory is sufficiently detailed to be experimentally testable, both in the laboratory and in the clinic. Whether such tests, when properly conducted, will support the theory is, of course, something which cannot be predicted at the moment; but certainly the pioneer neuroendocrinologist, Pavlov, would be pleased with our attempts to delineate specific propositions on pathological 'psychic secretions' which are clearly capable of confirmation or disconfirmation.

Acknowledgement

The authors are indebted to the R. J. Reynolds Tobacco Company for a grant which made the completion of this chapter possible.

References

Anderson, D. C., Crowell, C., Koehn, D., and Lupo, P. (1976). Different intensities of unsignalled inescapable shock treatments as determinants of non-shock-motivated open field behavior: A resolution of disparate results. *Physiology and Behavior*, **17**, 391–4.

Anderson, L. T., David, R., Bonnet, K., and Dancis, J. (1979). Passive avoidance learning in Lesch-Nyhan disease: Effect of 1-desamino-8-arginine-vasopressin. *Life Sciences*, **24**, 905–10.

Armario, A., Castellanos, J. M., and Balasch, J. (1984). Effect of crowding on emotional reactivity in male rats. *Neuroendocrinology*, **39**, 330–3.

Arnsten, A. F. T., Neville, H. J., Hillyard, S. A., Janowsky, D. S., and Segal, D. S. (1984). Naloxone increases electrophysiological measures of selective information processing in humans. *Journal of Neuroscience*, **4**, 2912–19.

Arnsten, A. F. T., Segal, D. S., Neville, H. J., Hillyard, S. A., Janowsky, D. S., Judd, L. L., and Bloom, F. E. (1983). Naloxone augments electrophysiological signs of selective attention in man. *Nature*, **304**, 725–7.

Arrindell, A., Emmelkamps, M. G., and Ende, J. van der (1984). Phobic dimensions: 1. Reliability and general reliability across samples, gender and nations. *Advances in Behaviour Research and Therapy*, **6**, 207–53.

Axelrod, J., and Reisine, T. D. (1984). Stress hormones. Their interaction and regulation. *Science*, **224**, 452–9.

Banerjee, U. (1956). *Psychopharmacology*, **22**, 133–47.

Bechara, A., and Kooy, D. van der (1985). Opposite motivational effects of endogenous opioids in brain and periphery. *Nature*, **314**, 533–4.

Beckwith, B. E., and Sandman, C. A. (1978). Behavioral influences of the neuropeptides ACTH and MSH: A methodological review. *Neuroscience and Behavioural Reviews*, **2**, 311–38.

Beckwith, B. E., and Sandman, C. A. (1982). Central nervous system and peripheral effects of ACTH, MSH, and related neuropeptides. *Peptides*, **3**, 411–20.

Ben-Horin, N., Ben-Horin, E., and Frenk, H. (1984). The effects of proglumide on morphine induced motility changes. *Psychopharmacology*, **84**, 541–3.

Bertolini, A., Fratta, W., Gessa, G. L., Montaldo, S., and Serra, G. (1984). Penile erection during morphine withdrawal: possible role of ACTH-MSH peptides. In E. E. Müller and A. R. Genazzani (eds.), *Central and Peripheral Endorphins Basic and Clinical Aspects* (pp. 229–35). New York: Raven Press.

Bertolini, A., and Gessa, G. L. (1981). Behavioral effects of ACTH and MSH peptides. *Journal of Endocrinological Investigation*, **4**, 241–51.

Blanchard, R. J., Fukunaga, K. K., Blanchard, D. C., and Kelley, M. J. (1975). Conspecific aggression in the laboratory rat. *Journal of Comparative and Physiological Psychology*, **89**, 1204–9.

Blanchard, R. J., Kelley, M. J., and Blanchard, D. C. (1974). Defensive reactions and exploratory behavior in rats. *Journal of Comparative and Physiological Psychology*, **87**, 1129–34.

Boakes, R. J., Ednie, J. M., Edwardson, J. A., Keith, A. B., Sahgal, A., and Wright. C. (1985). Abnormal behavioral changes associated with vasopressin-induced barrel rotations. *Brain Research*, **326**, 65–70.

Bohus, B. (1968). Pituitary ACTH release and avoidance behavior of rats with cortisol implants in mesencephalic reticular formation and median eminence. *Neuroendocrinology*, **3**, 355–65.

Bohus, B. (1973). Pituitary-adrenal influences on avoidance and approach behaviour of the rat. *Programme of Brain Research*, **39**, 407–20.

Bohus, B. (1974). Hormones and the forced extinction of a passive avoidance response in the rat. *Brain Research*, **66**, 366–7.
Bohus, B. (1977). Effect of desglycinamide-lysine vasopressin (DG-LVP) on sexually motivated T-maze behavior of the male rat. *Hormones and Behavior*, **8**, 52–61.
Bohus, B., and Kloet, E. R. de (1981). Adrenal steroids and extinction behavior: Antagonism by progesterone, deoxycorticosterone and dexamethasone of a specific effect of corticosterone. *Life Science*, **28**, 433–40.
Bohus, B., Kloet, E. R. de, and Veldius, H. D. (1981). Adrenal steroids and behavioural adaptation: Relationship to brain corticosteroid receptors. In D. Ganten and D. Pfaff (eds.), *Adrenal Actions on Brain* (pp. 107–48). New York: Springer-Verlag.
Born, J., Fehm-Wolfsdorf, G., Schiebe, M., Rockstroh, B., Fehm, H.-L., and Voigt, K. H. (1984). Dishabituating effects of an ACTH 4–9 analog in a vigilance task. *Pharmacology Biochemistry and Behavior*, **21**, 513–19.
Borrell, J., Kloet, E. R., de, Versteeg, D. H. G., and Bohus, B. (1983). Inhibitory avoidance deficit following short-term adrenalectomy in the rat: The role of adrenal catecholamines. *Behavioral and Neural Biology*, **39**, 241–58.
Breier, C., Kain, H., and Konzett, H. (1979). Personality dependent effects of the ACTH 4–10 fragment on test performances and on concomitant autonomic reactions. *Psychopharmacology*, **65**, 239–45.
Britton, D. R., and Britton, K. T. (1981). A sensitive open-field measure of anxiolytic drug activity. *Pharmacology Biochemistry and Behavior*, **15**, 577–82.
Britton, D. R., Hoffman, D. K., Lederis, K., and Rivier, J. (1984). A comparison of the behavioral effects of CRF, sauvagine and urotensin I. *Brain Research*, **304**, 201–5.
Britton, D. R., Koob, G. F., Rivier, J., and Vale, W. (1982). Intraventricular corticotropin-releasing factor enhances behavioral effects of novelty. *Life Sciences*, **31**, 363–7.
Brunia, C. H. M., and Boxtel, A. van (1978). MSH/ACTH 4–10 and task-induced increase in tendon reflexes and heart rate. *Pharmacology Biochemistry and Behavior*, **9**, 615–18.
Buchsbaum, M. S., Davis, G. C., and Bunny, W. E. (1977). Naloxone alters pain perception and somatosensory evoked potentials in normal subjects. *Nature*, **270**, 620–2.
Buijs, R. M. (1983). Vasopressin and oxytocin—their role in neurotransmission. *Pharmacology Therapy*, **22**, 127–41.
Burbach, J. P. H., Bohus, B., Kovács, G. L., Nispen, J. W. van, Greven, H. M., and Wied, D. de (1983a). Oxytocin is a precursor of potent behaviourally active neuropeptides. *European Journal of Pharmacology*, **94**, 125–31.
Burbach, J. P. H., Kovács, G. L., and Wied, D. de (1983b). A major metabolite of arginine vasopressin in the brain is a highly potent neuropeptide. *Science*, **221**, 1310–12.
Bykov, K. M. (1957). *The Cerebral Cortex and the Internal Organs*. New York: Chemical Publication Company.
Carpenter, W. T., and Gruen, P. H. (1982). Cortisol's effect on human mental functioning. *Journal of Clinical Psychopharmacology*, **2**, 91–101.
Charney, D. S., and Redmond, D. E., Jr (1983). Neurobiological mechanisms in human anxiety. *Neuropharmacology*, **22**, 1531–6.
Collins, S., Walker, D., Forsyth, P., and Belbeck, L. (1983). The effects of proglumide on cholecystokinin-, bombesin-, and glucagon-induced satiety in the rat. *Life Sciences*, **32**, 2223–9.
Concannon, J. T., Riccio, D. C., and McKelvey, J. (1980a). Pavlovian conditioning of

fear based upon hormonal mediation of prior aversive experience. *Animal Learning and Behavior*, **8**, 75–80.

Concannon, J. T., Riccio, D. C., Maloney, R., and McKelvey, J. (1980b). ACTH mediation of learned fear: Blockade by naloxone and naltrexone. *Physiology and Behavior*, **23**, 977–9.

Corson, S. A., and O'Leary Corson, E. (1983). From bromides to peptides: The role of chemicals in conditioning and learning theory. In A. Krakokowski (ed.), *Psychosomatic Medicine: Theoretical, Clinical, and Transcultural Aspects* (pp. 189–200). New York: Plenum Publishing Corp.

Curtis, G., Buxton, O. M., Lippman, D., Nesse, R., and Wright, J. (1976). 'Flooding *in vivo*' during the circadian phase of minimal cortisol secretion: Anxiety and therapeutic success without adrenal cortical activation. *Biological Psychiatry*, **11**, 101–7.

Curtis, G. C., Nesse, R., Buxton, M., and Lippman, D. (1978). Anxiety and plasma cortisol at the crest of the circadian cycle: Reappraisal of a classical hypothesis. *Psychosomatic Medicine*, **40**, 368–70.

Davey, G. (ed.) (1983). *Animal Models of Human Behavior*. New York: Wiley.

Dolan, R. J., Calloway, S. P., Fonagy, P., De Souza, F. V. A., and Wakling, A. (submitted). Life events, depression and the hypothalamic–pituitary–adrenal axis.

Dunn, A. J., and Kramarcy, J. R. (1984). Neurochemical responses in stress. Relationships between the hypothalamic–pituitary–adrenal and catecholamine systems. In L. L. Iversen, S. D. Iversen, and S. H. Snyder (eds.), *Handbook of Psychopharmacology*, vol. 18: *Drugs, Neurotransmitters and Behavior* (pp. 455–515). New York: Plenum Press.

Eaves, L., and Eysenck, H. J. (1975). The nature of extraversion: A genetical analysis. *Journal of Personality and Social Psychology*, **32**, 102–12.

Eaves, L., and Eysenck, H. J. (1987). *The Genetics of Personality*. New York: Academic Press.

Eich, J. E. (1980). The cue-dependent nature of state-dependent retrieval. *Memory and Cognition*, **8**, 157–73.

Endroczi, E. (1975). Mechanisms of steriod actions on motivated behavioral reactions. In W. H. Gispen, Tj. B. van Wimersma Greidanus, B. Bohus, and D. de Wied (eds.), *Progress in Brain Research*, vol. 42: *Hormones, Homeostasis and the Brain*. Amsterdam: Elsevier.

Endroczi, E., Hracher, A., Nyakas, C., and Szabo, G. (1977). Correlation between passive avoidance learning and plasma ACTH response in adrenalectomised rats. *Acta Physiologica Academiae Scientiarum Hungaricae Tomus*, **50**, 35–7.

Endroczi, E., Kissak, K., Fekete, T., and Weid, D. de (1970). Effects of ACTH on EEG habituation in human subjects. In D. de Weid and J. A. W. M. Weijnen (eds.), *Pituitary, Adrenal and the Brain*. Amsterdam: Elsevier.

Ettenberg, A., Kooy, D. van der, Le Moal, M., Koob, G. F., and Bloom, M. (1983). Can aversive properties of (peripherally-injected) vasopressin account for its putative role in memory? *Behavioural Brain Research*, **7**, 331–50.

Eysenck, H. J. (1956). The inheritance of extraversion–introversion. *Acta Psychologica*, **12**, 95–110.

Eysenck, H. J. (1967). Single trial conditioning neurosis and the Napalkov phenomenon. *Behaviour Research and Theory*, **5**, 63–5.

Eysenck, H. J. (1968). A theory of the incubation of anxiety/fear responses. *Behaviour Research and Therapy*, **6**, 309–21.

Eysenck, H. J. (1976). The learning theory model of neurosis—a new approach. *Behaviour Research and Therapy*, **14**, 251–67.

Eysenck, H. J. (1978a). What to do when desensitization goes wrong? *Australian Behaviour Therapist*, **5**, 15–16.

Eysenck, H. J. (1978b). Expectations as causal elements in behavioural change. *Advances in Behaviour Research and Therapy*, **1**, 171–5.

Eysenck, H. J. (1979). The conditioning model of neurosis. *Behavior and Brain Science*, **2**, 155–99.

Eysenck, H. J. (1980). A unified theory of psychotherapy, behaviour therapy and spontaneous remission. *Zeitschrift für Psychologie*, **188**, 43–56.

Eysenck, H. J. (1982a). Neobehavioristic (S–R) theory. In G. T. Wilson and C. M. Franks (eds.), *Contemporary Behaviour Therapy* (pp. 205–76). New York: Guildford Press.

Eysenck, H. J. (1982b). Why do conditioned responses show incrementation, while unconditioned responses show habituation? *Behavior Psychotherapy*, **10**, 217–22.

Eysenck, H. J. (in press). Psychotherapy to behaviour therapy: A paradigm shift. In D. Lishman, F. Rotgers, and C. Franks (eds.), *Paradigms in Behavior Therapy: Present and Promise*.

Eysenck, H. J., and Prell, D. B. (1951). The inheritance of neuroticism: An experimental study. *Journal of Mental Science*, **97**, 441–65.

Fanselow, M. S. (1984). Shock-induced analgesia on the formalin test: Effects of shock severity, naloxone, hypophysectomy and associative variables. *Behavioral Neuroscience*, **98**, 79–95.

Fanselow, M. S., and Sigmundi, R. A. (1982). The enhancement and reduction of defensive fighting by naloxone pretreatment. *Physiological Psychology*, **10**, 313–16.

Fehm, H. L., Holl, R., Steiner, K., Klein, E., and Voigt, K. H. (1984b). Evidence for ACTH-unrelated mechanisms in the regulation of cortisol secretion in man. *Klinische Wochenschrift*, **62**, 19–24.

Fehm, H. L., Klein, E., Holl, R., and Voigt, K. H. (1984a). Evidence for extrapituitary mechanisms mediating the morning peak of plasma cortisol in man. *Journal of Clinical Endocrinology and Metabolism*, **58**, 410–14.

Fehm-Wolfsdorf, G., Elbert, T., Lutzenberger, W., Rockstroh, B., Birbaumer, N., and Fehm, H. L. (1981). Effect of an ACTH 4-9 analog on human cortical evoked potentials in a two-stimulus reaction time paradigm. *Psychoneuroendocrinology*, **6**, 311–20.

File, S. E. (1978). ACTH, but not corticosterone impairs habituation and reduces exploration. *Pharmacology Biochemistry and Behavior*, **9**, 161–6.

File, S. E., and Vellucci, S. V. (1978). Studies on the role of ACTH and 5-HT in anxiety using an animal model. *Journal of Pharmacy and Pharmacology*, **30**, 105–10.

File, S. E., Vellucci, S. V., and Wendlandt, S. (1979). Corticosterone—an anxiogenic or an anxiolytic agent? *Journal of Pharmacy and Pharmacology*, **31**, 300–5.

Finlay-Jones, R., and Brown, G. W. (1981). Types of stressful life event and the onset of anxiety and depressive disorders. *Psychological Medicine*, **11**, 803–15.

Flannelly, K. J., Blanchard, R. J., and Blanchard, D. C. (1984). *Biological Perspectives on Aggression*. New York: Alan R. Liss.

Gaillard, A. W. K. (1981). ACTH analogs and human performance. In J. L. Martinez, Jr, R. A. Jensen, and R. B. Messing (eds.), *Endogenous Peptides and Learning and Memory Processes* (pp. 181–96). New York: Academic Press.

Garcia, J., McGowan, B. K., and Green, K. F. (1971). Biological constraints on conditioning. In A. W. Black and W. F. Prokasy (eds.), *Classical Conditioning: Current Theory and Research*. New York: Appleton-Century.

Gash, D. M., and Thomas, G. J. (1984). Reply from Don M. Gash and Garth J. Thomas. *Trends in Neuroscience*, March, 64–6.

Glickman, S. E., and Morrison, B. J. (1969). Some behavioral and neural correlates of predation susceptibility in mice. *Communications in Behavioral Biology*, **4**, 261–7.

Gold, P. W., Ballenger, J. C., Robertson, G. L., Weingartner, H., Rubinow, D. R., Hoban, M. C., Goodwin, F. K., and Post, R. M. (1984a). Vasopressin in affective illness: Direct measurement, clinical trials, and response to hypertonic saline. In R. M. Post and J. C. Ballenger (eds.), *Neurobiology and Mood Disorders* (pp. 323–39). London: Williams & Wilkins.

Gold, P. W., Chrousos, G., Kellner, C., Post, R., Roy, A., Augerinos, P., Schulte, H., Oldfield, E., and Loriaux, D. L. (1984b). Psychiatric implications of basic and clinical studies with corticotropin-releasing factor. *American Journal of Psychiatry*, **141**, 619–27.

Gold, P. W., Kaye, W., Robertson, G. L., and Ebert, M. (1984c). Abnormal regulation of arginine vasopressin in plasma and cerebrospinal fluid of patients with anorexia nervosa. *New England Journal of Medicine*, **308**, 1117–23.

Gold, P. W., Rubinow, D., Post, R. M., Kaye, W., Strupp, B. J., Fisher, D., Artman, A., and Goodwin, F. K. (in press). Presence of oxytocin in human cerebrospinal fluid: Comparison of levels found in normal controls and patients with affective illness and anorexia nervosa. *Journal of Clinical Endocrinology Metabolism* (data discussed in Strupp *et al*., 1985).

Gossop, M. (1981). *Theories of Neurosis*. New York: Springer.

Grant, D. A. (1964). Classical and operant conditioning. In A. W. Melton (ed.), *Categories of Human Learning*. New York: Academic Press.

Gray, J. A. (1982). *The Neuropsychology of Anxiety: An Enquiry into the Functions of the Septo-Hippocampal System*. New York: Oxford University Press.

Griffiths, E. C., and McDermott, J. R. (1984). Biotransformation of neuropeptides. *Neuroendocrinology*, **39**, 573–81.

Grossen, M., and Kelley, M. J. (1972). Species-specific behavior and acquisition of avoidance behavior in rats. *Journal of Comparative and Physiological Psychology*, **81**, 306–11.

Grossman, A., and Besser, G. M. (1982). Opiates control ACTH through a noradrenergic mechanism. *Clinical Endocrinology*, **17**, 287–90.

Hall, S. M. (1979). The abstinence phobia. In N. A. Krasnegor, *Behavioral Analysis and Treatment of Substance Abuse* (pp. 55–67). NIDA Res. Monograph 25. Rockville, Md.

Hamburger-Bar, R., Ebstein, R. P., and Belmaker, R. H. (1984). Vasopressin effect on learning in 6-hydroxydopamine-pretreated rats: Correlation with caudate vasopressin levels. *Biological Psychiatry*, **19**,735–43.

Hanbauer, I., Kelly, G. D., Saianai, L., and Yang, H. Y. T. (1982). [Met^5]-enkephalin-like peptides of the adrenal medulla: Release by nerve stimulation and functional implications. *Peptides*, **3**, 469–73.

Hanley, M. R., Benton, H. P., Lightman, S. L., Todd, K., Bone, E. A., Fretten, P., Plamer, S., Kirk, C. J., and Michell, R. H. (1984). A vasopressin-like peptide in the mammalian sympathetic nervous system. *Nature*, **309**, 258–61.

Haroutunian, V., and Riccio, D. C. (1977). Effect of arousal conditions during reinstatement treatment upon learned fear in young rats. *Developmental Psychobiology*, **10**, 25–32.

Haroutunian, V., and Riccio, D. C. (1979). Drug-induced 'arousal' and the effectiveness of CS exposure in the reinstatement of memory. *Behavioral and Neural Biology*, **26**, 115–20.

Hoffman, P. L., Walter, R., and Bulat, M. (1977). An enzymatically stable peptide with activity in the central nervous system: Its penetration through the blood–CSF barrier. *Brain Research*, **122**, 87–94.

Holsboer, F., Gerken, A., Bardeleben, U. von, Grimm, W., Stalla, G. K., and Muller, O. A. (1985). Relationship between pituitary responses to human corticotropin-releasing factor and thyrotropin-releasing hormone in depressives and normal control. *European Journal of Pharmacology*, **10**, 153–4.

Iversen, L. L. (1984). Amino acids and peptides: Fast and slow chemical signals in the nervous system? *Proceedings of the Royal Society London*, **221**, 245–60.

Izquierdo, E., Dias, R. D., Perry, M. L., Souze, D. O., Elisabetsky, E., and Carrasco, M. A. (1982). A physiological amnesic mechanism mediated by endogenous opioid peptides, and its possible role in learning. In C. A. Marsan and H. Matthies (eds.), International Brain Research Organisation Monograph Series, vol. 9: *Neuronal Plasticity and Memory Formation* (pp. 89–111). New York: Raven Press.

Izquierdo, E., Perry, M. L., Dias, R. D., Souza, D. O., Elisabetsky, E., Carrasco, M. A., Orsingher, O. A., and Netto, C. A. (1981). Endogenous opioids, memory modulation, and state dependency. In J. L. Martinez, Jr, R. A. Jensen, and R. B. Messing (eds.), *Endogenous Peptides and Learning and Memory Processes* (pp. 269–90). New York: Academic Press.

Johansson, F., Almay, B. G. L., Knorring, L. von, Terenius, L., and Aström, M. (1979). Personality traits in chronic pain patients related to endorphin levels in cerebrospinal fluid. *Psychiatry Research*, **1**, 231–9.

Jones, M. C. (1924). The elimination of children's fears. *Journal of Experimental Psychology*, **7**, 383–90.

Jones, M. T., Gillham, B., Greenstein, B. D., Beckford, U., and Holmes, M. C. (1982). Feedback actions of adrenal steroids. In D. Ganten and D. Pfaff (eds.), *Adrenal Actions on Brain*. New York: Springer-Verlag.

Kalin, H. H., Shelton, S. E., Kraemer, G. W., and McKinney, W. T. (1983b). Corticotropin-releasing factor administered intraventricularly to rhesus monkeys. *Peptides*, **4**, 217–20.

Kalin, N. E., Shelton, S. E., Kraemer, G. W., and McKinney (1983a). Associated endocrine, physiological and behavioral changes in rhesus monkeys after intravenous corticotropin-releasing factor administration. *Peptides*, **4**, 211–15.

Kazdin, A. E., and Wilson, G. T. (1978). *Evaluation of Behavior Therapy*. Cambridge, Mass.: Ballinger.

Kelley, M. J. (submitted, a). The conditioned release of oxytocin in female rats.

Kelley, M. J. (submitted, b). Individual differences in endogenous vasopressin and the psychological consequences of stopping smoking. Presented at the meeting of the International Society for the Study of Individual Differences, Barcelona, Spain, June 1985.

Kelley, M. J. (in press, a). Selective attention and stimulus-reinforcer interactions in the pigeon. *Quarterly Journal of Experimental Psychology*.

Kelley, M. J. (in press, b). Species-specific taxic behavior and event-reinforcer interactions in conditioning. *Learning and Motivation*.

Kelley, M. J. (in press, c). Epinephrine-cue contiguity is required for the modulation of CS excitatory strength. *Physiological Psychology*.

Kelley, M. J. (in preparation). *Neurosis, Neuropeptides and Conditioning: A Primer in Clinical Neuroethology*.

Kimble, G. A. (1961). *Hilgard and Marquis' Conditioning and Learning*. New York: Appleton-Century-Crofts.

Kitchen, I. (1984). The rise and fall of endogenous opioid nomenclature. *Progress in Neurobiology*, **22**, 345–58.

Kleinknecht, R. A. (1982). The origin and remission of fear in a group of tarantula enthusiasts. *Behaviour Research and Therapy*, **20**, 437–43.

Koob, G. F., Dantzer, R., Rodriguez, F., Bloom, F. E., and Le Moal, M. (1985). Osmotic stress mimics effects of vasopressin on learned behaviour. *Nature*, **315**, 750–2.

Kopell, B. S., Willner, W. K., Landi, D., Warrick, G., and Edwards, D. (1970). Cortisol effect on average evoked potential, alpha-rhythm, time estimation and two-flash fusion threshold. *Psychosomatic Medicine*, **32**, 39–49.

Kovács, G. L., Vecsei, L., and Telegdy, G. (1978). Opposite action of oxytocin to vasopressin in passive avoidance behavior in rats. *Physiology and Behavior*, **20**, 801–2.

Kovács, G. L., Versteeg, D. H. G., Kloet, E. R. de, and Bohus, B. (1981). Passive avoidance performance correlates with catecholamine turnover in descrete limbic brain regions. *Life Sciences*, **28**, 1109–16.

Krechevsky, I. (1933). Hereditary nature of 'hypotheses'. *Journal of Comparative Psychology*, **16**, 99–116.

Krejci, I., Kupková, K., Dlabac, A., and Kasafirek, E. (1983). On the effects of neurohypophyseal hormones, analogs and fragments on the extinction of avoidance responding. In E. Endröczi, L. Angelucci, U. Scapagnini, and D. de Wied (eds.), *International Conference on Integrative Neurohumoral Mechanisms: Neuropeptides and Psychosomatic Processes* (pp. 183–94). Budapest, Akadémiae Kiadó.

Krieger, D. T. (1983). Brain peptides: What, where and why? *Science*, **222**, 975–85.

Laczi, F., Gaffori, O., Fekete, M., Kloet, E. R. de, and Wied, D. de (1984). Levels of arginine-vasopressin cerebrospinal fluid during passive avoidance behavior in rats. *Life Sciences*, **34**, 2385–91.

Laczi, F., Gaffori, O., Kloet, R. de, and Wied, D. de (1983a). Arginine-vasopressin content of hippocampus and amygdala during passive avoidance behavior in rats. *Brain Research*, **280**, 309–15.

Laczi, F., Gaffori, O., Kloet, E. R. de, and Wied, D. de (1983b). Differential responses in immunoreactive arginine-vasopressin content of microdissected brain regions during passive avoidance behavior. *Brain Research*, **260**, 342–6.

Laczi, F., Ree, J. M. van, Wagner, A., Valkusz, Z., Járdánházy, T., Kovács, G. L., Telegdy, G., Szilárd, J., Lászlo, F. A., and Wied, D. de (1983c). Effects of desglycinamide-arginine-vasopressin (DG-AVP) on memory processes in diabetes insipidus patients and non-diabetic subjects. *Acta Endocrinologica*, **102**, 205–12.

Lader, M. H. (1980). Psychophysiological studies in anxiety. In G. D. Burrows and B. Davies (eds.), *Handbook of Studies on Anxiety* (pp. 59–88). Netherlands: Elsevier/North Holland Biomedical Press.

Lang, R. E., Heil, J. W. E., Ganten, D., Hermann, K., Unger, T., and Rascher, W. (1983). Oxytocin unlike vasopressin is a stress hormone in the rat. *Neuroendocrinology*, **37**, 314–16.

Lautsch, H. (1971). Dental phobia. *British Journal of Psychiatry*, **119**, 151–8.

Legros, J. J., Chiodera, P., and Demey-Oponsart, E. (1982). Inhibitory influence of exogenous oxytocin on adrenocorticotropin secretion in normal human subjects. *Journal of Clinical Endocrinology and Metabolism*, **55**, 1035–9.

Legros, J. J., Chiodera, P., Geenen, V., Smitz, S., and Frenckell, R. von (1984a). Dose-response relationship between plasma oxytocin and cortisol and adrenocorticotropin concentrations during oxytocin infusions in normal man. *Journal of Clinical Endocrinology and Metabolism*, **58**, 105–9.

Legros, J. J., and Lancranjan, I. (1984b). Vasopressin in neuropsychiatric disorders. In N. S. Shah and A. G. Donald (eds.), *Psychoneuroendocrine Disfunction* (pp. 255–92). London: Plenum.

Le Roith, D., Shiloach, J., and Roth, J. (1982). Is there an earlier phylogenetic precursor that is common to both the nervous and endocrine systems? *Peptides*, **3**, 211–15.

Leshner, A. L., Hofstein, R., Samuel, D., and Wimersma Greidanus, Tj. B. van (1978). Intraventricular injection of antivasopressin serum blocks learned helplessness in rats. *Pharmacology Biochemistry and Behavior*, **9**, 889–92.

Liddell, A., and Lyons, M. (1978). Thunderstorm phobics. *Behaviour Research and Therapy*, **16**, 306–8.

LoLordo, V. M., and Jacobs, W. J. (1983). Constraints on aversive conditioning in the rat: Some theoretical accounts. In M. D. Zeiler and P. Harzem (eds.), *Advances in Analysis of Behavior*, vol. 3 (pp. 325–50). London: Wiley.

McGaugh, J. L. (1983). Hormonal influences on memory. *Annual Review of Psychology*, **34**, 297–323.

Mackintosh, N. J. (1974). *The Psychology of Animal Learning*. London: Academic Press.

Mackintosh, N. J. (1984). *Conditioning and Associative Learning*. Oxford: Clarendon Press.

MacLennan, A. J., Drugan, R. C., Hyson, R. L., Maier, S. F., Madden, J., and Barchas, J. D. (1982). Corticosterone: A critical factor in an opioid form of stress-induced analgesia. *Science*, **215**, 1530–2.

Markely, K. A., and Sze, P. Y. (1984). Influence of ACTH on tyrosine hydroxylase activity in the locus coeruleus of mouse brain. *Neuroendocrinology*, **38**, 269–75.

Matussek, P., and Wiegand, M. (1985). Partnership problems as causes of endogenous and neurotic depressions. *Acta Psychiatrica Scandinavica*, **71**, 95–104.

Meisenberg, G. (1981). Short-term behavioral effects of posterior pituitary peptides in mice. *Peptides*, **2**, 1–8.

Meisenberg, G., and Simmons, W. H. (1982). Behavioral effects of intracerebroventricularly administered neurohypophyseal hormone analogs in mice. *Pharmacology Biochemistry and Behavior*, **16**, 819–25.

Miczek, K. A., and Thompson, M. L. (1984). Analgesia resulting from defeat in a social confrontation: The role of endogenous opioids in brain. In R. Bandler (ed.), *Modulation of Sensorimotor Activity during Alterations in Behavioral States* (pp. 431–56). New York: Alan R. Liss.

Miczek, K. A., Thompson, J. L., and Shuster, L. (1982). Opioid-like analgesia in defeated mice. *Science*, **215**, 1520–2.

Miller, L. H., Fischer, S. C., Groves, G. A., and Rudrauff, M. A. (1977). MSH/ACTH 4-10 influences on the CAR in human subjects: A negative finding. *Pharmacology Biochemistry and Behavior*, **7**, 417–19.

Miller, L. H., Kastin, A. J., Sandman, C. A., Fink, M., and Veen, W. J. van (1974). Polypeptide influences on attention, memory and anxiety in man. *Pharmacology Biochemistry and Behavior*, **2**, 663–8.

Mineka, S., Davidson, M., Cook, M., and Keir, R. (1984). Observational conditioning of snake fear in rhesus monkeys. *Journal of Abnormal Psychology*, **4**, 355–72.

Morley, J. E., and Levine, A. S. (1982). Corticotrophin releasing factor, grooming and ingestive behavior. *Life Sciences*, **31**, 1459–64.

Morley, S. (1977). The incubation of avoidance behaviour: Strain differences in susceptibility. *Behaviour Research and Therapy*, **15**, 365–7.

Munjack, D. J. (1984). The onset of driving phobias. *Journal of Behavior Therapy and Experimental Psychiatry*, **15**, 305–8.

Murray, E. J., and Foote, F. (1979). The origins of fears of snakes. *Behaviour Research and Therapy*, **17**, 489–93.

Napalkov, A. V. (1963). Information process of the brain. In N. Wiener and J. Schade (eds.), *Progress in Brain Research*, vol. 2: *Nerve, Brain and Memory Models*. Amsterdam: Elsevier.

Öhman, A. (1980). Fear relevance, autonomic conditioning and phobias. In D. O. Sjoden and S. Bates (eds.), *Trends in Behavior Therapy*. New York: Academic Press.

Öhman, A., Fredrikson, M., Hugdahl, K., and Riminö, P. (1976). The promise of equipotentiality in human classical conditioning: Conditioned electrodermal responses to potentially phobic stimuli. *Journal of Experimental Psychology: General*, **105**, 313–37.

Ost, L., and Hugdahl, K. (1981). Acquisition of phobias and anxiety responses patterns in clinical patients. *Behaviour Research and Therapy*, **19**, 439–47.

Ost, L., and Hugdahl, K. (1983). Acquisition of agoraphobia mode of onset and anxiety response patterns. *Behaviour Research and Therapy*, **21**, 623–31.

Ost, L., and Hugdahl, K. (1985). Acquisition of blood and dental phobia and anxiety response patterns in clinical patients. *Behaviour Research and Therapy*, **23**, 27–34.

Pagano, R. R., and Lovely, R. H. (1972). Diurnal cycle and ACTH facilitation of shuttlebox avoidance. *Physiology and Behavior*, **8**, 721–3.

Pauls, D. L., Bucher, K. D., Crowe, R. R., and Noyes, R. (1980). A genetic study of panic disorder pedigrees. *American Journal of Human Genetics*, **32**, 639–44.

Pavlov, I. P. (1927). *Conditioned Reflexes*. London: Oxford Press.

Pigache, R. M., and Rigter, H. (1981). Effects of peptides related to ACTH on mood and vigilance in man. In Tj. B. van Wimersma Greidanus and L. H. Rees (eds.), *ACTH and LPH in Health and Disease* (pp. 193–207). Basle: S. Karger.

Plotnikoff, N. P., Kastin, A. J., Coy, D. H., Christensen, C. W., Schally, S. V., and Spirtes, M. A. (1976). Neuropharmacological actions of enkephalin after systemic administration. *Life Sciences*, **19**, 1283–8.

Post, R. M., Pickar, D., Ballenger, J. C., Naber, D., and Rubinow, D. R. (1984). Endogenous opiates in cerebrospinal fluid: Relationship to mood and anxiety. In R. M. Post and J. C. Ballenger (eds.), *Neurobiology of Mood Disorders* (pp. 356–68). London: Williams & Wilkins.

Prioleau, L., Murdock, M., and Brody, N. (1983). An analysis of psychotherapy versus placebo. *Behavior and Brain Science*, **6**, 275–85.

Rachman, S. (1966). Studies in desensitization. II. Flooding. *Behaviour Research and Therapy*, **4**, 1–6.

Rachman, S. (1977). The conditioning theory of fear acquisition: A critical examination. *Behaviour Research and Therapy*, **15**, 375–88.

Rachman, S., and Hodgson, R. J. (1980). *Obsessions and Compulsions*. Englewood Cliffs, N.J.: Prentice-Hall.

Rachman, S., and Wilson, G. T. (1980). *The Effects of Psychological Therapy*. London: Pergamon Press.

Razran, G. (1961). Recent Soviet phyletic comparisons of classical and of operant conditioning. *Journal of Comparative and Physiological Psychology*, **54**, 357–65.

Redmond, D. E., Jr (1981). Clonidine and the primate locus coeruleus: Evidence suggesting anxiolytic and anti-withdrawal effects. In H. Lal and S. Fielding (eds.), *Psychopharmacology of Clonidine* (pp. 147–53). New York: Alan Liss.

Redmond, D. E., Jr, and Huang, Y. H. (1979). II. New evidence for a locus coeruleus-norepinephrine connection with anxiety. *Life Sciences*, **25**, 2149–62.

Redmond, D. E., Jr, and Krystal, J. H. (1984). Multiple mechanisms of withdrawal from opioid drugs. *Annual Review of Neuroscience*, **7**, 443–78.

Reiman, E. M., Raichle, M. E., Butler, F. K., Herscovitch, P., and Robins, E. (1984).

A focal brain abnormality in panic disorder, a severe form of anxiety. *Nature*, **310**, 683–5.

Riad-Fahmy, D., Read, G. F., Walker, R. F., and Griffiths, K. (1982). Steroids in saliva for assessing endocrine function. *Endocrine Reviews*, **3**, 367–96.

Riccio, D. C., and Concannon, J. T. (1981). ACTH and the reminder phenomena. In J. L. Martinez, Jr, R. A. Jensen, and R. B. Messing (eds.), *Endogenous Peptides and Learning and Memory Process* (pp. 117–42). New York: Academic Press.

Rigter, H., Elbertse, R., and Riezen, H. van (1975). Time-dependent anti-amnesic effect of ACTH 4–10 and desglycinamide-lysine vasopressin. *Progress in Brain Research*, **42**, 163–71.

Rimm, D. C., Janda, L. H., Lancaster, D., Nahl, M., and Tittman, K. (1977). An exploratory investigation of the origin and maintenance of phobics. *Behaviour Research and Therapy*, **15**, 231–8.

Ritzmann, R. F., Colbern, D. L., Zimmerman, E. G., and Krivoy, W. (1984). Neurohypophyseal hormones in tolerance and physical dependence. *Pharmacology and Therapy*, **23**, 281–312.

Rivier, C., and Vale, W. (1983). Modulation of stress-induced ACTH release by corticotropin-releasing factor, catecholamines and vasopressin. *Nature*, **305**, 325–7.

Rivier, J., Rivier, C., and Vale, W. (1984). Synthetic competitive antagonists of corticotropin-releasing factor: Effect on ACTH secretion in the rat. *Science*, **224**, 889–91.

Roche, K. E., and Leshner, A. I. (1979). ACTH and vasopressin treatments immediately after a defeat increase future submissiveness in male mice. *Science*, **204**, 1343–4.

Rockstroh, B., Elbert, T., Birbaumer, N., and Lutzenberger, W. (1982). *Slow Brain Potentials and Behavior*. Baltimore, Md.: Urban & Schwarzenberg.

Rockstroh, B., Elbert, T., Lutzenberger, W., Birbaumer, N., Fehm, H. L., and Voigt, K. H. (1981). Effect of an ACTH 4-9 analog on human cortical evoked potentials in a constant foreperiod reaction time paradigm. *Psychoneuroendocrinology*, **6**, 301–10.

Rockstroh, B., Elbert, T., Lutzenberger, W., Birbaumer, N., Voigt, K. H., and Fehm, H. L. (1983). Distractability under the influence of an ACTH 4–9 derivative. *International Journal of Neuroscience*, **22**, 21–36.

Rose, R. J., and Ditto, W. B. (1983). A developmental–genetic analysis of common fears from early adolescent to early childhood. *Child Development*, **54**, 361–8.

Sahgal, A. (1984). A critique of the vasopressin–memory hypothesis. *Psychopharmacology*, **83**, 215–28.

Sapolsky, R. M., Krey, L. C., and McEwen, B. S. (1984). Stress down-regulates corticosterone receptors in a site-specific manner in the brain. *Endocrinology*, **114**, 287–92.

Sartory, G. (1983). Benzodiazepines and behavioural treatment of phobic anxiety. *Behavioural Psychotherapy*, **11**, 204–17.

Sawyer, W. H., and Manning, M. (1984). The development of vasopressin antagonists. *Federation Proceedings*, **43**, 87–90.

Sawyer, W. H., and Manning, M. (1985). The use of antagonists of vasopressin in studies of its physiological functions. *Federation Proceedings*, **44**, 78–80.

Schillar, L. G., and Davison, J. S. (1984). The cholecystokinin antagonist, proglumide, increases food intake in the rat. *Regulatory Peptides*, **8**, 171–6.

Schulz, H., Kovács, G. L., and Telegdy, G. (1974). Effect of physiological doses of vasopressin and oxytocin on avoidance and exploratory behaviour in rats. *Acta Physiologica Academiae Scientiarum Hungaricae*, **45**, 211–15.

Seligman, M. E. P. (1971). Phobias and preparedness. *Behavior Therapy*, **2**, 307–20.
Sherman, J. E., Strub, H., and Lewis, J. W. (1984). Morphine analgesia: Enhancement of shock-associated cues. *Behavioral Neuroscience*, **98**, 293–309.
Smith, G. P. (1984). Gut hormone hypothesis of postprandial satiety. In A. J. Stunkard and E. Stellar (eds.), *Eating and Its Disorders* (pp. 67–75). New York: Raven Press.
Smock, T., and Fields, H. L. (1981). ACTH 1–24 blocks opiate-induced analgesia in the rat. *Brain Research*, **212**, 202–6.
Solomon, R. L., Kamin, L. J., and Wynne, L. C. (1953). Traumatic avoidance learning: The outcomes of several extinction procedures with dogs. *Journal of Abnormal and Social Psychology*, **48**, 291–302.
Solomon, R. L., and Wynne, L. C. (1953). Traumatic avoidance learning: Acquisition in normal dogs. *Psychological Monographs*, **67**, no. 4.
Stacher, G., Bauer, H., and Steinringer, H. (1979). Cholecystokinin decreases appetite and activation evoked by stimuli arising from the preparation of a meal in man. *Physiology and Behavior*, **23**, 325–31.
Strupp, B., Weingartner, H., Goodwin, F. K., and Gold, P. W. (1984). Neurohypophyseal hormones and cognition. *Pharmacology and Therapy*, **23**, 179–91.
Strupp, H. H., Handley, S. W., and Gomes-Schwartz, B. (1977). *Psychotherapy for Better or Worse: The Problem of Negative Effects*. New York: Erosson.
Sutherland, N. S., and Mackintosh, N. J. (1971). *Mechanisms of Animal Discrimination Learning*. New York: Academic Press.
Sutherland, S. (1976). *Breakdown*. London: Weidenfeld.
Tang, J., Chou, J., Tadarola, M., Yang, H. Y. T., and Costa, E. (1984). Proglumide prevents and curtails acute tolerance to morphine in rats. *Neuropharmacology*, **23**, 715–18.
Terman, G. W., Shavit, Y., Lewis, J. W., Cannon, J. T., and Liebeskind, J. C. (1984). Intrinsic mechanisms of pain inhibition: Activation by stress. *Science*, **226**, 1270–7.
Timsit-Berthier, M., Mantanus, H., Devos, J. E., and Spiegel, R. (1982). Action of lysine-vasopressin on human electroencephalographic activity. *Neuropsychobiology*, **8**, 248–58.
Timsit-Berthier, M., Mantanus, H., and Legros, J. J. (1983). EEG—reactivity and event related potential approach to the study of vasopressin. In E. Endröczi, L. Angelucci, U. Scapagnini, and D. de Wied (eds.), *International Conference on Integrative Neurohumoral Mechanisms: Neuropeptides and Psychosomatic Processes* (pp. 63–71). Budapest: Académiae Kiadó.
Torgersen, S. (1979). The nature and origin of common phobic fears. *British Journal of Psychiatry*, **134**, 343–51.
Tricklebank, M. D., and Curzon, G. (eds.) (1984). *Stress-induced Analgesia*. New York: John Wiley & Sons.
Truax, C. (1963). Effective ingredients in psychotherapy. *Journal of Counseling Psychology*, **10**, 256–63.
Truax, C., Frank, I., and Imber, S. (1966). Therapist empathy, genuineness, and warmth and patient outcome. *Journal of Consulting Psychology*, **30**, 395–401.
Urban, I., and Wied, D. de (1978). Neuropeptides: Effects on paradoxical sleep and theta rhythm in rats. *Pharmacology Biochemistry and Behavior*, **8**, 51–9.
Urban, I. J. A. (1984). Electrophysiological effects of peptides derived from proopiomelanocortin. *Pharmacology and Therapeutics*, **24**, 57–90.
Veith, J. L., Sandman, C. A., George, J. M., and Kendall, J. W. (1985). The relationship of endogenous ACTH levels to visual-attentional functioning in

patients with congenital adrenal hyperplasia. *Psychoneuroendocrinology*, **10**, 33–48.

Vito, W. J. de, and Brush, F. R. (1984). Effect of ACTH and vasopressin on extinction: Evidence for opiate mediation. *Behavioral Neuroscience*, **98**, 59–71.

Watkins, L. R., Kinscheck, I. B. and Mayer, D. J. (1984). Potentiation of opiate analgesia and apparent reversal of morphine tolerance by proglumide. *Science*, **224**, 395–6.

Watson, J. B., and Rayner, R. (1920). Conditioned emotional reactions. *Journal of Experimental Psychology*, **3**, 1–14.

Weinberger, N. M., Gold, P. E., and Sternberg, D. B. (1984). Epinephrine enables Pavlovian fear conditioning under anesthesia. *Science*, **223**, 605–7.

Wied, D. de (1984). The importance of vasopressin in memory. *Trends in Neuroscience*, March, 62–4.

Wied, D. de, Gaffori, O., Ree, M. J. van, and Jong, W. de (1984a). Central target for the behavioural effects of vasopressin neuropeptides. *Nature*, **308**, 276–8.

Wied, D. de, Gaffori, O., Ree, M. J. van, and Jong, W. de (1984b). Vasopressin antagonists block peripheral as well as central vasopressin receptors. *Pharmacology Biochemistry and Behavior*, **21**, 393–400.

Wied, D. de, and Jolles, J. (1982). Neuropeptides derived from pro-opiocortin: Behavioral, psychological and neuro-chemical effects. *Physiological Reviews*, **62**, 976–1060.

Williams, T. D. M., Carter, D. A., and Lightman, S. L. (1985). Sexual dimorphism in the posterior pituitary response to stress in the rat. *Endocrinology*, **116**, 738–41.

Wimersa Greidanus, Tj. B. van, Bohus, B., Kovács, G. L., Versteeg, D. H. G., Burbach, J. P. H., and Wied, D. de (1983). Sites of behavioral and neurochemical action of ACTH-like peptides and neurohypophyseal hormones. *Neuroscience and Biobehavioral Reviews*, **7**, 453–63.

Wimersma Greidanus, Tj. B. van, Rees, L. H., Scott, A. D., Lowry, P. J., and Weid, D. de (1977). ACTH release during passive avoidance behavior. *Brain Research Bulletin*, **2**, 101–4.

Wolpe, J. (1958). *Psychotherapy by Reciprocal Inhibitions*. Stanford: Stanford University Press.

Wolpe, J. (1981). The dichotomy between classical conditioned and cognitively learned anxiety. *Journal of Behavior Therapy and Experimental Psychiatry*, **12**, 35–42.

York, C. (1966). *If Hopes were Dupes*. London: Hutchinson.

Zener, K. (1937). The significance of behavior accompanying conditioned salivary secretion for theories of the conditioned response. *American Journal of Psychology*, **50**, 384–403.

Zillmann, D. (1984). *Connections between Sex and Aggression*. London: Lawrence Erlbaum.

Zukin, R. S. (1984). Opiate receptors: Current issues and methodologies. In J. Marangos, I. C. Campbell, and R. M. Cohen (eds.), *Brain Receptor Methodologies*, Part B: *Amino Acids, Peptides, Psychoactive drugs*. London: Academic Press.

Author Index

Subject Index

Stimulus associability, 128
Stimulus intensity, 117
Stimulus selection, 66